Isaac Mayer Wise

History of the Hebrews' Second Commonwealth

With Special Reference to its Literature, Culture and the Origin of Rabbinism and Christianity

Isaac Mayer Wise

History of the Hebrews' Second Commonwealth
With Special Reference to its Literature, Culture and the Origin of Rabbinism and Christianity

ISBN/EAN: 9783337417192

Printed in Europe, USA, Canada, Australia, Japan

Cover: Foto ©ninafisch / pixelio.de

More available books at **www.hansebooks.com**

HISTORY

OF THE

Hebrews' Second Commonwealth

WITH SPECIAL REFERENCE TO ITS

Literature, Culture, and the Origin of Rabbinism and Christianity,

BY

ISAAC M. WISE,
PRESIDENT OF THE HEBREW UNION COLLEGE.

CINCINNATI:
BLOCH & CO., PUBLISHERS AND PRINTERS.
1880.

Entered according to the Act of Congress, in the year 1880, by
ISAAC M. WISE,
In the office of the Librarian of Congress, at Washington, D. C.

Contents.

I. The Medo-Persian Period, — 1
   CHAPTER I.—Restoration of the Temple and Culte-Zerubabel, 1
   CHAPTER II—Restoration of the Law—Ezra, — 9
   CHAPTER III.—Restoration of the State—Nehemiah, — 18
   CHAPTER IV.—Judea under the Government of Highpriests, 28
   CHAPTER V.—Literature and Culture of the Medo-Persian Period, — 35

II. The Grecian Period, — 43
   CHAPTER VI.—Judea under European Rulers—Alexander, — 43
   CHAPTER VII.—Palestine under Egyptian Rulers—The Ptolemys, — 52
   CHAPTER VIII.—Palestine under Syrian Rulers—The Seleucides, — 65
   CHAPTER IX.—Literature and Culture of the Grecian Period, 76

III. The Revolutionary Period, — 92
   CHAPTER X.—Mattathia Starts the Rebellion, — 92
   CHAPTER XI.—Juda Maccabee Saves the Commonwealth, 95
   CHAPTER XII.—Jonathan and Simon Achieve Independence, 107
   CHAPTER XIII.—Literature and Culture at Home and Abroad of the Revolutionary Period, — 119

IV. The Period of Independence, — 135
   CHAPTER XIV.—The Epoch of Popular Government, — 136
   CHAPTER XV.—The Epoch of Royal Usurpation, — 154
   CHAPTER XVI—The Epoch of Pacification, — 167
   CHAPTER XVII.—The Brothers' Feud and Foreign Intervention, — 173

CONTENTS.

V. Palestine under Roman Vassal Kings, - 183
Chapter XVIII.—The Last of the Asmonean Rulers, - 184
Chapter XIX.—Herod and Hillel, - - - 207
Chapter XX.—The Fruits of Despotism, - - - 235

VI The Rule of the Procurators, - - - 244
Chapter XXI.—The Messianic Commotion, - - - 245
Chapter XXII —Agrippa I. and his Time, - - 269
Chapter XXIII.—Military Despotism and its Effects, - 288

VII. The Catastrophe, - - - - - 317
Chapter XXIV.—Preludes to the War, - - - 318
Chapter XXV.—The First Period of the War. - .- 330
Chapter XXVI.—The Destruction of Jerusalem, - - 350
Chapter XXVII.—The Inheritance, - - - 368

Every paragraph being headed conspicuously, the reader can easily find any subject discussed in this volume.

PREFACE.

This volume contains a compact narrative of Hebrew history from 536 before to 70 after the Christian era, divided into Periods and Chapters and subdivided into Paragraphs, in a manner which decidedly assists the memory and makes reading easy and pleasant.

This period of Hebrew history, from Zerubabel to the Fall of Jerusalem, appears to me to be the most interesting and most instructive part of history. It contains not only a political history of an advanced civilization in contact with Persia, Egypt, Syria, Greece, Rome and Parthia, and yet original in itself, but also the combat of Monotheism against Polytheism, and its final results, viz.: Rabbinism and Christianity. Therefore, this volume contains the origin of almost every book of the Bible in its present form, the Apocrypha of the Old Testament, their Greek translations, and the first writings of the New Testament collection, besides the extensive notices of a vast Greco-Hebrew and Aramaic-Hebrew literature; also the origin and work of the Great Synod, the Sanhedrin, civil and criminal law, constitutional provisions, public schools, and other elements of civilization, and the biographical outlines of the principal actors, including John the Baptist, Jesus of Nazareth, and Paul of Tarsus. This volume, I think, in a large measure accounts for the origin of modern civilization and its fundamental ideas.

This part of Hebrew history has been written by Humphrey Prideaux, Morris J. Raphall, Henry Hart Milman (English), I. Salvador (French), I. M. Jost, L. Herzfeld, Heinrich Ewald, H. Graetz and Abraham Geiger (German), all of whom I have carefully consulted and compared without neglecting, however, at any point to consult the original authorities which guided those writers, such as the Bible, with its ancient versions and commentaries, Josephus, Philo, Eusebius, Clemens, of Alexandria, Polyhistor, Herodotus, Xenophon and the Latin historians, and especially the ancient rabbinical literature, the two Talmuds, the

PREFACE.

Midrashim or homiletic collections, and the ancient Hebrew-rabbinical chronicles, histories and historical encyclopedias. I have carefully examined every fact. And yet, I believe I have discovered quite a number of points overlooked by my predecessors, which are of importance to a correct understanding of history.

This book, nevertheless, claims originality in the logical arrangement of the historical material, and the completeness thereof. It is the history of a people, and not of rulers and battles, the history of its life and growth in politics, religion, literature, culture, civilization, commerce, wealth and influence on other nations. The book before you claims to be the first of this kind written from a democratic, free and purely scientific standpoint, without reference to political or religious preferences and considerations, which more or less governed my predecessors; also without any mysticism or supernaturalism to tincture the facts. It is history without miracles, history constructed on the law of causality, where every event appears as the natural consequence of its preceding ones. It claims to be history and the first of its kind in this particular chapter thereof. It is written for students as well as for the general reader.

In 1854 I published my History of the Israelitish Nation, from Abraham to the destruction of Jerusalem by Nebuchadnezzar. The present volume, though a complete book in itself, is a continuation of the former. It begins where the first closes. It is written in the same spirit; history as the record of man's transactions.

THE AUTHOR.

CINCINNATI, February, 1880.

1. The Medo-Persian Period.

From 536 to 332 B. C., Palestine was a province of the Medo-Persian Empire. During that time, the Hebrews' second commonwealth was established, and the principle elements of Judaism were developed, as will be narrated in the following five chapters:

CHAPTER I

Restoration of the Temple and Culte-Zerubabel.

1. THE MEDO-PERSIAN EMPIRE.

Between the fifth and tenth of August, in the year 538 B. C., the city of Babylon was taken by Cyrus, King of Persia, who commanded both the Persian and Median armies (1). The last of the kings of Babylonia, Belshazar or Nabo Nadius, was slain, and the Babylonian Empire was annexed to Media and Persia. These three countries were united in 536 B. C. under Cyrus, after the death of Darius the Mede, and were called the Medo-Persian Empire. It included all Asia Minor, Syria, Palestine, and afterwards also Egypt, all the land from the Caucasian Mountains and the Caspian Sea to the Persian Gulf and the Indus River.

2. THE KINGS OF MEDO-PERSIA.

Fourteen kings reigned successively over this empire, viz.:

1. Darius the Mede	from the year	538	B. C.
2. Cyrus	" " "	536	" "
3. Cambyses	" " "	529	" "
4. Smerdes	" " "	522	" "
5. Darius Hystaspis	" " "	521	" "

---

(1) M. C. Rawlinson's History of Babylon and Assyria.

6. Xerxes   from the year 485 B. C.
7. Artaxerxes Longimanus   "   "   "   465 " "
8. Xerxes II. and   "   "   "   424 " "
9. Sogetianus   "   "   "   424 " "
10. Darius Nothus   "   "   " - 423 " "
11. Artaxerxes Mnemon   "   "   "   404 " "
12. Darius Ochus   "   "   "   359 " "
13. Arses   "   "   "   338 " "
14. Darius Codomanus   "   "   "   336 " "

3. The Dispersed Hebrews.

A few of the Hebrew people had found their way into Egypt and the Ionian Islands, also into Ethiopia, Arabia, India and China. Others may have come with the Phœnicians to the western coasts of Europe and Africa. Still the bulk of Hebrews, of the two former kingdoms of Israel and Judah, inhabited the Medo-Persian Empire. Prophets and bards (2) had kept alive in the breasts of many Hebrew patriots the hope of national restoration to the land of their fathers, the rebuilding of the temple on Mt. Moriah, the reinstitution of their ancient polity, and the reconstruction of the Kingdom of Heaven (מלכות שמים).

4. Deutero-Isaiah.

Most prominent among those eloquent and inspired patriots was the prophet, whose speeches were added to the Book of Isaiah (from chapter xl. to the end), perhaps because his name also was Isaiah. When the armies of Persia and Media, led by Cyrus, overthrew the Babylonian power in Asia Minor and Syria, as older prophets had predicted (3), this second Isaiah, foreseeing the downfall of that empire, recognized in Cyrus the Messiah (4) to redeem Israel. He called upon his people to return to the land of their fathers, and to re-establish the Kingdom of God, in which all the great hopes of Israel should be realized.

5. Mutual Sympathies.

In the combat of the Medo-Persians against Babylonia, the sympathies of the Hebrews must naturally have been with the former. They had nothing to expect of the Assyr-

---

(2) Especially the Prophets, Jeremiah and Ezekiel, the authors of the five chapters of the Book of Lamentations, Daniel and other patriots.
(3) Isaiah xiii.; Jeremiah l. and li.; Ezekiel xxxviii. and **xxxix**.
(4) Isaiah xlv.

ians and Babylonians, who were their enemies and captors, polytheists and idolators, devotees of Zabaism. The Medo-Persians avenged those wrongs, were no idolators, and approached nearest the Monotheism of Israel by the reforms of Zoroaster under Darius and Cyrus (5). Darius reciprocated these sympathies. He appointed Daniel one of his three ministers in the new empire (6), and a Hebrew priest to superintend the tower at Ecbatana, which Daniel had previously built for the king (7).

6. The Edict of Cyrus.

Cyrus having mounted the Medo-Persian throne (536 B. C.) decreed the re-colonization of Judea. He gave the Hebrews permission to return to their country to take possession of their lands, towns and cities, and to rebuild their temple. He appointed Zerubabel, a descendant of the Davidian kings, governor, and Joshua, a scion of Aaron, high priest. He delivered to them the silver and golden vessels (5400) of the temple of Solomon, brought to Babel by Nebuchadnezzar, and furnished them with royal letters to the pashahs, to give them protection and to provide them with animals necessary for sacrifices; as the rebuilding of the temple and the continuation of the sacrificial culte were the main objects of the Hebrews (8).

7. The People and Its Wealth.

The most religious portions of the tribes of Judah, Benjamin and Levy only—"All in whom the Lord had roused his spirit, to go up and to build the house of God, which is in Jerusalem"—followed Zerubabel and Joshua to the land of Judah. The bulk of the people remained in the lands of their captivity. The Zerubabel colony consisted of 42,300 men, hence, about 211,500 souls. There were among them an unknown number of priests (*Kohanim*), 341 Levites, 392 *Nethinim* and Sons of the Servants of Solomon (9), 245

---

(5) Friederich Spiegel's Avesta, etc., *Einleitung*.
(6) Daniel vi. 3.   (7) Josephus' Antiquities x. xi. 7
(8) Ezra i. and vi.
(9) *Nethinim* were descendants of assistant ministers of the temple appointed by King David and the rulers (Ezra viii. 20). The Sons of the Servants of Solomon, counted with the former, must have been descendants of similar assistants appointed by King Solomon. They are supposed (Yebamoth 16 b and Yerushalmi Kiddushin iv.) to have been the scions of Gentiles and Hebrew women, as the Nethinim also were supposed to be.

singers of both sexes, and three prophets (10). They were well provided with servants, horses, mules, asses, camels and treasures, partly the gifts of brethren remaining behind. Having arrived in Jerusalem, a building fund was established, to which the rulers contributed 61,000 gold drachma ($14,-640.00) and 5,000 silver maneh ($151,500.00). They also donated one hundred official robes for the priests (11).

8. The Land Occupied.

The colonists took possession of the land between the Jordan River and the Mediterranean coast (the latter being held by Philistines and Phœnicians), to about twenty miles north and south of Jerusalem. North of them were the Samaritans; south from Hebron to the Dead Sea were the Edomites; east and southeast the Ammonites and Moabites, with some Hebrews among them.

9. Dedication of the Altar.

On the First Day of the Seventh Month, when the first summer's work was done, the colonists assembled in Jerusalem to solemnize this feast (*Leviticus xxiii. 23*), which, according to the Mishah (*Joma 1.*) and Josephus (Antiquities III. 3), always was the civil new year of the Hebrews. On this day and under fear of disturbance by the surrounding Gentiles, the altar was dedicated and the sacrifices made as prescribed in the Law of Moses. The daily sacrifice was not interrupted again up to the time of Antiochus Epiphanes. By order of that assembly contracts were made for building materials, and with the Phœnicians for cedar wood from Lebanon, to rebuild the temple.

10. Building of the Temple Commenced.

In the second month of the second year (535 b. c.) the building of the temple was commenced. With music and song they begun to erect the walls upon the old foundation. The shouts of joy were mighty. Still the old men, who had seen the temple of Solomon, wept.

11. Animosity of the Samaritans.

The Samaritans (*Kuthim*), descendants of Gentile colonists, brought to Samaria by Assyrian kings, had adopted the Law of Moses, and partly amalgamated with Hebrews.

---

(10) Zibachim 62 b.   (11) Ezra ii. and Nehemiah vii. 6 to 69.

They desired to make common cause with the Hebrew colonists, and build the temple with them. Zerubabel and the elders refused this offer, because, as they said, Cyrus had commanded them only to rebuild the temple. Thereupon, the Samaritans, in league with other enemies of the Hebrews, persuaded Cyrus, or his pashahs, to revoke that portion of his edict, and the work on the temple was stopped shortly after the beginning thereof, and remained suspended to the year 521 B. C.

12. Isaiah's Consoling Oracles.

The young colony, surrounded by adversaries, humiliated and scorned by hostile neighbors, and without sufficient protection from the government, was sadly discouraged. Cyrus died, and the people's misery increased under the misrule of his two immediate successors, Cambyses and Smerdes. Palestine was trodden down under the feet of the armies invading Egypt; short crops, famine and diseases followed; the lofty hopes of the Hebrew colony perished under the ridicule of shouting enemies. In that time of tribulation and humiliation, Isaiah's consoling oracles were announced. This prophet predicted a glorious future to the despondent House of Israel. He personified it as "The servant of the Lord," now down-trodden and despised, to rise at last to the pinnacle of glory (12).

13. The Temple Rebuilt.

Times changed. In the year 521 B. C., Darius Hystaspis mounted the Medo-Persian throne, and he introduced beneficial reforms in the empire. The Hebrews, encouraged by two prophets, Zachariah and Haggi, re-assumed work on the temple and its walls, although they had no special permission from the government. Sisinnes, the Governor of Syria and Phœnicia, wrote to Darius that the Hebrews were building a citadel rather than a temple, and awaited instructions. Meanwhile, Zerubabel returned to the Persian court, and found special favor in the eyes of the king (13). Search among the documents of Cyrus, at the tower of Ecbatana, brought to light the original edict of that king concerning the Hebrew colony, and Darius commanded its literal enforcement; granted to all Hebrews the freedom to return to their own country, sent holy vessels to the temple, and supported the rebuilding thereof with ten talents annually, and

---

(12) **Isaiah lii. to liv.**   (13) Apocryphal Ezra iii. and iv.

a salary to officiating priests and Levites, besides subsidies for the altar (14).

14. Dedication of the Temple.

The third day of Adar (March), in the sixth year of Darius (515 B. C.), according to Ezra vi. 15, closing the seventy years of the Babylonian captivity; on the twenty-third day of that month and the ninth year of Darius, according to Josephus, the temple and its inner cloisters were completed. A solemn dedication followed. The Hebrews again had a religious center, to which, for the subsequent six centuries, the looks and hearts of all Israel were directed; where the sublime doctrines of pure Monotheism and its humane ethics were uninterruptedly proclaimed, while the Gentiles were given to Polytheism, idolatry and slavery. The enthusiasm of the Hebrews in and outside of Palestine has found expression in the words of Zachariah, in several Psalms, and especially in the triumphal orations of Isaiah. Gifts were sent to the temple by the Hebrews of Babylonia, of which golden crowns were made for Zerubabel, Joshua and the three messengers from abroad, and deposited in the temple as a memento of glorious days (15). The four fast days of national mourning were abolished (16). It was predicted that the glory of the second temple should excel the palmy days of Solomon's temple; and the time should come when ten men of all nations' tongues would take hold of the skirt of one Jewish man, saying, "Let us go with you, for we heard the Lord is with you" (17). Isaiah also (chapter lvi.) prophesied the influx of the Gentiles to the House of the Lord, which should be called the "house of prayer to all nations." There was general rejoicing, and Israel's ancient hopes for the redemption and unification of the human family under the banner of the One God were uttered in words of divine inspiration (18).

15. Enforcement of the Levitical Laws.

The Levitical Laws, "as written in the Book of Moses," and the ancient official divisions of priests and Levites, were now strictly enforced in and about the temple, among priests and Levites, and also among the laity. The people, together with the lustrated strangers, celebrated the Pass-

---

(14) Josephus' Antiquities xi. iv. 6 and 7; Ezra vi.
(15) Zachariah vi. 9.   (16) Ibid vii. viii. 18.
(17) Ibid viii. 23; Haggi ii. 9.
(18) Isaiah lv. and lvi. 1 to 9.

over according to the law (19). They observed the Sabbath (20), the First Day of the Seventh Month (21), the Day of Atonement (22), ate unleavened bread on Passover (23), and knew that intermarriage with certain nations was prohibited in the law (24). The political laws of Moses were not introduced in the Hebrew colony. Zerubabel had associated with himself the heads of the families (25), and Josephus speaks of "the elders of the Jews and the princes of the Sanhedrin" with Zerubabel, and adds that the government was aristocratical. We know that the land was divided in districts (*Pelech*), that some were governed by one ruler and others by two. Still, it appears nowhere that the political laws of Moses had been introduced. Therefore, it was a religious and no political restoration which was achieved by Zerubabel and Joshua.

16. CHARACTER AND CULTURE.

The Hebrew colonists were intensely religious. In the captivity, many of their idolators amalgamated with the Gentiles, while many more of them repented their sins and acknowledged their errors. Idolatry itself lost its main force by the fall of Babylon and the adoption of the Zoroaster reforms at the Persian court, which contained many an element imposed upon the Gentiles by Hebrew exiles. Besides, only the most religious and patriotic among the Hebrews left their new homes in the East to return to Palestine. They were the poorer class of agriculturists and skilled mechanics, as is evident from the country which they cultivated and the temple they built. They cultivated vocal and instrumental music (Ezra ii. 62; iii. 10), and had among themselves men of the highest literary distinction, like the second Isaiah, Haggai and Zachariah (26), whose productions have lost none of their original force.

17. SUCCESSORS OF ZERUBABEL AND JOSHUA.

It is not known where and when Zerubabel died. *Seder-Olam-Sutta* reports he went back to Persia and died there; others report he went to Arabia and died there. Philo, in his *Breviarium*, gives him fifty-eight years of government,

---

(19) Ezra vi. 19. (20) Isaiah lviii. 13, 14; Nehemiah xiii. 15.
(21) Ezra iii. 1; Nehemiah viii. (22) Isaiah lviii.; Ezkiel xl. 1.
(23) Ezra iv. (24) Ezra ix. (25) Ezra iv. 2.
(26) Zachariah ix. to xiii., was written by a prophet at least one hundred years before Zachariah b. Berechiah b. Iddo; perhaps by Zachariah b. Jebarechjahv, in Isaiah viii. 2.

which is certainly a mistake. His successor in office was his son, Meshullam (27), supported by his brother, Hannaniah, and his sister, Selomith. The successor of Meshullam was Pelatiah (Aramaic Meshezabel), the son of Hannaniah (28). He was succeeded by Meshullam b. Berachiah b. Meshezabel (29), who was superseded by Nehemiah. Joshua, the high priest, according to the Alexandrian Chronicle, lived to the third year of Xerxes (483 B. C.), was succeeded by his son, Jojakim, who (453 B. C.) was succeeded by his son, Eliashib.

18. Under Xerxes.

Xerxes, the enemy of all Heathen temples, having ascended the Medo-Persian throne (485 B. C.), confirmed to the Hebrews of Palestine all the privileges granted them by his father, Darius. When he invaded Greece, it is narrated by his cotemporary, Cherilus (30), a body of Hebrew warriors was in his army. Nothing concerning the Hebrews being on record from 515 to 458 B. C., it is evident that no events transpired during that time to produce any change or disturbance in the new Hebrew state.

---

(27) I. Chronicles iii. 19. Philo *in Breviario* calls him Resa Mysciollam. Resa is the title, Luke iii. 25, 26, copies from Philo.
(28) I. Chronicles iii. 21.
(29) Nehem. iii. 4, 30; vi. 18. See *Geschichte des Volkes Jisrael*, etc., Dr. L. Herzfeld, Vol. 1, p. 378.
(30) Josephus contra Apion i. 22.

CHAPTER II.

Restoration of the Law.—Ezra.

1. ANCIENT SYNAGOGUES.—ACADEMY OF EZRA.

In the seventh year of Artaxerxes Longimanus (558 B. C.) (1), when Jojakim was high priest and Meshullam b. Berachiah chief ruler of the Hebrew colony, Ezra, the Scribe, who was סופר מהיר בתורת משה "An expert scribe in the Law of Moses," appeared on the stage of history as one of its most prominent figures. He was the son of Sheraiah, a lineal descendant of the high priests in Solomon's temple. The ancient tradition (*Meguilla* 29 a, *Rosh Hash-shanah* 24 b, *Nidda* 13 a) reports that a synagogue was built at *Shafjatib*, near the city of Nehardea, by the first exiles to Babylonia; and soon after another was built at Hutzal, one parsang from the former place. Near the latter, there was the academy of Ezra, who "had directed his heart to inquire into the law of God, and to do it, and to teach in Israel statutes and ordinances" (Ezra vii. 10), *i. e.*, political and judiciary law.

2. EZRA'S POWERS.

King Artaxerxes and his seven counselors, appointed Ezra Chief-Justice of the Hebrews west of the Euphrates, with powers to appoint judges and bailiffs, to teach and to enforce the laws, and to punish transgressors with imprisonment, fines, expatriation or death; also to head the colony of all Hebrews who wished to return to Palestine; and to be the special messenger of the king to bring to the temple at Jerusalem his gifts in gold and silver, and also the gifts of other donors.

---

(1) According to Josephus, this occurred in the reign of Xerxes.

3. Arrival of the Ezra Colony.

In Mesopotamia, on the River Ahava or Mygdonius (2) 2,286 men, perhaps 11,430 persons, and among them 42 Levites and 220 *Nethinim*, assembled to follow Ezra to Palestine. After a day of fast and prayer, on the 12th day of the first month (*Nissan*), the colony moved, and reached Jerusalem in the fifth month (*Ab*). After a rest of three days, the gold, silver and vessels in possession of Ezra (3) were delivered to the treasurer of the temple; then the emigrants sacrificed many sacrifices, and the documents brought by Ezra were delivered to the officers of the king.

4. The Samaritan Tradition.

Among the Samaritans a tradition was current, that about the same time 300,000 Hebrews, under Sanbelat, emigrated to the North of Palestine, and the remaining foreigners in Samaria were sent back to their original homes in Persia. Although the Samaritan Joshua (chapter xiv.) is no reliable authority (4), yet it is almost certain that a large number of Hebrews, at an early date, emigrated to Samaria and Galilee, for the latter was, in after times, one of the most populous provinces, and the Hebrew origin of its inhabitants was never doubted. Still, those Hebrews of the northern provinces, as far as the Scriptural records go, had no connection with the Zerubabel or Ezra colony, which assumed the name of Judah, in exclusion of the other tribes of Israel. Therefore, when Josephus (Antiq. x. v. 2) maintains, "There are but two tribes in Asia and Europe subject to the Romans, while the ten tribes are beyond Euphrates till now," he simply recorded a popular myth current in his days (5). This Samaritan tradition, as

---

(2) See Ancient Geography by D'Anville.
(3) The whole sum amounting to about $5,200,000, including vessels of brass, "more precious than gold," supposed to have been *aurichalcum*.
(4) ברכי שומרך by Raphael Kircheim, p. 55.
(5) The myth about the ten lost tribes is also mentioned in the Mishnah (*Sanhedrin* x. 3), which is partly contradicted in the Talmud (*Megillah* 14 b. and *Erechin* 33), where it is maintained the Prophet Jeremiah brought them back to Palestine, and King Joshiah reigned over them. It is evident from many passages of Jeremiah (ix. 22 to x. 18; xxiii. 1 to 8; xxxi. 27 to 37; xxxiii. 24 to 26), that he did attempt the re-union of Israel and Judah, which was done also by the Prophet Ezekiel. It is also evident that not all were driven from the land of Israel (II. Chronicles xxx.), that Joshiah reigned over them (ibid xxxiv. 33 and xxxv. 17; and II. Kings xxiii.), and that some Hebrew inhabitants had been left there after the fall of Jerusalem (Jeremiah xli. 5)

far as Sanbelat is concerned, agrees with the Bible records, but not with those of Josephus (Antiq. xi. vii. 2).

5. Measures to Preserve the Purity of the Race.

Some of the rulers complained to Ezra that many of the Hebrews, priests, Levites and rulers especially, had become heathenized in their manners and appearance, on account of their intermarriages with the Gentiles. Ezra fasted, prayed and preached against this corruption until he had moved many to repentance, and many of the rulers encouraged him to take active measures. Then, in behalf of the rulers, he called a general meeting of the people to Jerusalem, threatening with confiscation of property for non-attendance. On the 20th day of the ninth month the people assembled on the temple mount. Ezra demanded of them to separate themselves from the Gentiles and their own foreign wives, in order to preserve the Hebrew race in its purity. The people consented, but, on account of the rainy season and the magnitude of the work to ascertain who were married to foreign wives, proposed, " Let our rulers remain here for the whole congregation," and let those who have foreign wives come, with the elders and judges of each place, and report themselves. This was done ; the rulers remained in Jerusalem, and in three months (the 10th, 11th and 12th) they ascertained that 17 priests, 110 Levites and 84 Israelites had taken foreign wives, and were willing to separate themselves from them. Among these transgressors there were also four of the sons and brothers of Joshua, the high priest. But these were certainly not all who had foreign wives, and the evil was but partially remedied.

6. The Great Synod.

This, it appears, was the occasion when Ezra constituted the Great Synod (כנסת הגדולה), the people having expressed its will to be represented by the rulers (Ezra x. 14). He could not introduce the political laws of Moses without constituting first a supreme legislature and judiciary, similar to the Council of Seventy Elders. During the Medo-Persian period, the Great Synod was the supreme legislature and judiciary of the Hebrews. It was composed of 120 men, viz.: 44 *Sarim* or *Horim*, " rulers ;" 44 *Seganim*, " proxies," as each ruler had his proxy (6); 22 priests, 8 Levites (Nehe-

---

(6) Nehemiah x. 15 to 28 and xi. 25 to 35, which compare to Ibid ii. 16; iv. 13; v. 7; vii. 5; Nehem. xi. 25 to 35, forty-two districts

miah xii. 1 to 9), the Scribe and the high priest or the governor. All these men were representatives of family groups and districts, as the family groups lived together in their respective districts. It is maintained in the tradition that many prophets were among the men of the Great Synod, which is probable (Nehem. vi. 7, 14 and Haggi).

7. OBJECT OF THE GREAT SYNOD.

The principal activity of this body was as presented in its motto (*Aboth* i. 1): To secure to the Hebrews the judiciary autonomy and a strict administration of justice; to preserve and promulgate the national literature by many disciples; to enforce and to protect the Law of Moses by new barriers (סייגים). These were either prohibitory (גזירות) or commendatory laws (תקנות). Of this latter category, are certainly the ordinances and formulas concerning the courts and administration of justice, the public worship in the temple and synagogue and public instruction, public morals and health and domestic relations; some of which were based upon ancient custom, while others were enacted in connection with Ezra, or also after him, as this body existed to about 292 B. C. These laws were afterward embodied in the Mishnah and other collections of ancient laws and customs.

8. A REPUBLICAN FORM OF GOVERNMENT.

In connection with the Great Synod, over which Ezra presided, he exercised the authority vested in him by the king. So the Hebrew colony received a democratic form of government, independent in the three main elements, viz.: religion, public instruction and the judiciary, and dependent on Persia only by paying a certain tribute, which appears to have been too insignificant to be mentioned in any of the sources.

9. AUTHENTICATION OF THE LAW.

The most necessary work to be done by Ezra and the Great Synod was the authentication of the nation's written law, the Law of Moses, by which it was henceforth to be governed. The law existed before Ezra in the same form as it was presented by him to the Hebrews. It is mentioned expressly as God's law, the Law of Moses, the Book of the

---

are counted, besides Jerusalem (verse 7), which counted for two districts, as is mentioned (*Ibid* iii. 9 to 12), and as is evident from the courts of 23 elders in Jerusalem.

Law, or synonymous to the Word of God, not only by the oldest prophets, who quoted passages from it and imitated others, but also in all ancient historical records (7). These records, fully corroborated in their main statements by the Greek and Latin writers after Alexander the Great and all modern Egyptologists and Assyriologists, admit of no doubt as to their statements of facts (8). Besides, the moral and religious laws of Moses had been introduced and practiced in Palestine before Ezra (see Chapter I.); the Samaritans, who opposed Ezra and his institutions, were in possession of the same Five Books of Moses, with some very slight variations; and only two hundred years after this the Greeks of Egypt accepted the Pentateuch as the Law of Moses, and there was none to doubt its authenticity. It must be borne in mind that Ezra has not proved to be a writer capable of producing anything like Pentateuch passages. He and his cotemporaries, who would not even replace the Urim and Thumim, or the Ark of the Covenant, or any of the lost articles of the temple, would certainly not have attempted to make a new book, or any portion thereof, and call it the Law of Moses. But, aside of all these points, it is authentically recorded (Nehemiah viii. to x.) that the whole people of Israel solemnly confirmed and testified that the book placed before them was the genuine Law of Moses, and this fact, in the uninterrupted tradition of the Hebrews since then, was never doubted. It appears that the Pentateuch existed in numerous fragmentary manuscripts; that many of the copies were defective, burdened with errors by transcribers, glossaries by expounders, amendments by idolatrous kings, especially the political laws of Moses, which had been out of practice since 586 B. C., except in some of the larger colonies in the East; and the ancient copies had been lost in the conflagration of the temple (9). Therefore, the authentication of the nation's law book and the authorization of the revised text, had become imperatively necessary, and was accomplished by Ezra and the Great Synod in thirteen years, as shall be narrated in the next chapter.

(7) Joshua i. 7, 8; viii. 31. 34; xxii. 5; xxiii. 6, 26; II. Kings xiv. 6; xvii. 13; xxi 8; xxiii. 24, 25; Micah iv. 2; Hosea iv. 6; Amos ii. 4; Isaiah i. 10; ii. 3; vii. 16; xlii. 21; Jeremiah ii. 8; ix. 12; xvi. 11; xviii. 18; in many Psalms and elsewhere. See Hengstenberg's Dissertations on the Genuineness of the Pentateuch.

(8) See John Gill's Notices of the Jews; Josephus *contra* Apion.

(9) Corrections made in the text of Sacred Scriptures by the *Sopherim* and the Great Synod, תקון סופרים אנשי כנסת הגדולה, are mentioned in TIIANCHUMA to Exodus xv. 7.

11. The New Alphabet.

After the Law and the other books, to be named below, had been authenticated by Ezra and the Great Synod, it was necessary to mark them most carefully, in order to distinguish them fully from the thousands of unauthenticated copies circulating among the Hebrews in and outside of Palestine. Therefore, Ezra introduced a new sacred alphabet, *i. e.*, to be used for sacred purposes only, called כתב אשורית "Assyrian writing," or also מרובעת, "the square letter," to replace the ancient Hebrew letters called רעץ "common, barbarian, foreign," or also לבונאה, "Libanian," or as inscribed on bricks. These ancient characters preserved on Hebrew coins were henceforth to be used for profane purposes only. This alphabet, now in common use among all the Hebrews, appears to have been invented by Ezra. He improved on the letters in use among Eastern scribes, as is evident from the inscriptions on the ruins of Palmyra, which most resemble Ezra's Hebrew letters, although they are not like them. In these letters the Book of Ezra, preserved in the temple, was written. Then rules were established for transcribers, which afterward became fixed laws, viz.: the sacred book must be written with pen and black ink on parchment (10), in one roll, divided in pages, certain pages must begin with certain words, space must be left between certain passages, certain letters must be written smaller and others larger than the rest, all in the sacred alphabet, in order to distinguish the authenticated copies, and they should only be used, as is done to this day, for public readings in the synagogues and the authentic law book of the nation. The Samaritans did not adopt the Ezra alphabet, nor his revised Pentateuch, nor any of his other books.

12. The Book of Ezra.

The Book of Ezra (ספר עזרא. *Moed Katan* iii. 4), which was preserved in the temple, consisted of seven books (11), viz.: the Five Books of Moses, the Book of the Republic, now Joshua and Judges, and the Book of Kings, as in the Septuagint, now I. and II. Samuel and I. and II. Kings. It was necessary to connect with the law the history of the nation, as the former without the latter is unintelligible.

---

(10) To write with pen and ink on a roll or book was known and practiced before Ezra. See Jeremiah xxxvi. 18.

(11) Sabbath 116 *a* חצבה עמודיה שבעה אלו שבעה ספרי תורה Herzfeld, 22 Excurs., p. 92.

13. THE FORMER PROPHETS.

Ezra was not the author of any of the historical books of the Bible, except, perhaps, of the portion II. Kings from xvii. 6 to the end, as those various books are distinguished by various styles, of centuries apart, and different arrangements of the historical material. Judges and Kings are brevaria, Joshua and Samuel are extensive narratives. Joshua, Judges, and the best part of Samuel, are democratic; while the closing chapters of Judges are royalistic, anti-Saul and anti-Benjamin, and Kings is royalistic, pro-Judaic and anti-Israelitish. In style, Joshua is Pentateuch-like; Judges (except the closing chapters), antique and unfinished; Samuel, independent and accomplished; Kings, from iii. to II. Kings xvii. monotonous and exact. Cotemporary chronography is noticed in Kings and Chronicles, from David to the end of those books, like the lost books of the various prophets, the Chronicles of the kings of Judah and the Chronicles of the kings of Israel. The *Sopher*, or "scribe," and the *Mazkir*, or "Chancellor," were prominent court officers already in the time of David (I. Samuel viii. 17, 18). Before his time, also, sources are noticed, as the books, Milhamoth, Jashar, the Topography of Palestine (Joshua xviii. 6 to 10), and the Genealogy of the Hebrew People (I. Chronicles). These were extensive books, from which extracts were made for popular use. In the Book of Joshua three sources are distinctly mentioned (x. 13; xviii. 1 to 10; xxiv. 26), from which the author drew his information. The book of Judges is a popular democratic text book, and appears to be the work of Samuel (Baba Bathra, 14 *b*), to which, in after times, the pro-Davidian, royalistic, anti-Saul and anti-Benjamin chapters, were added. Samuel to I. Kings iii. 3, is an extensive history of the founder of the Davidian dynasty, and must have been written shortly after David's death, perhaps by the Prophet Nathan (I. Chronicles xxix. 29; II. Chronicles ix. 29); anyhow, by one acquainted with all the details of David's life and reign. The book of Kings, to II. Kings xvii. is a brevarium which points everywhere to its sources, and was written before the destruction of the temple of Solomon, by one of the prophets (12), to which Ezra added the closing chapters. All these books and fragments were compiled by Ezra and the Great Synod in two books, to which they added, occasionally, their own notes, and these misled some critics to place the origin of these books long after they had actually been written.

---

(12) By Jeremiah, according to the Talmud, *Baba Bathra*, 15 a.

15. TALMUDICAL RECORDS OF EZRA ORDINANCES.

The Talmud contains records of Ezra ordinances. Ten are recorded in *Baba Kamma*, 82 *a*. The most important are: (*a*) That Sabbath afternoon, Monday and Thursday morning, a section of the Pentateuch should be read in public. (*b*) That the district courts should be in session on Monday and Thursday; in consequence thereof, these became the market days. To this must be added (from *Numbers Rabba*, 8 and *Jebamoth*, 78 *b*), that he interdicted intermarriage with the *Nethinim* who dwelt in Ophel (Nehemiah xi. 21), consequently, he must have replaced these sub-priests by others, and these are the *Anshai Maamod*, or "Commoners," literally, men attached to standing divisions of priests and Levites. It was believed that the earlier prophets (*Taanith* iv. 2; *Tosephta* iii.), divided priests and Levites in twenty-four divisions, of which each was on duty one week in the temple twice a year, and during the holy days all of them were on duty. To these standing divisions, Ezra added a number of Israelites from various districts; and these were the Commoners, without whose presence the temple service was considered unlawful. Part of them went to Jerusalem with their respective divisions of priests and Levites, and the others on duty congregated that week in their respective district towns, and, excepting some holidays, held divine service at the same time that it took place in the temple, viz.: in the morning, *Shacharith*, in the afternoon, *Minchah*, and in the evening, *Neilah* (*Ibid Mishnah* 4). They read twice, daily, from the first chapter of Genesis, in the morning from the scroll, and in the evening from memory, and fasted four days a week. This was the beginning of the synagogues and public reading of the Law in Palestine.

Ezra took from the Levites their right of receiving the tithes (Deut. xiv. 29) and gave it to the priests (מעשר ראשון), because few of the Levites returned with him to Palestine. Nehemiah, it is maintained, repealed this law in part, so that the tithes could be given to either priest or Levite (13).

The Red Heifer (Numb. xix.), the ashes of which was required for final lustration of him who had touched a dead person, was sacrificed by Ezra. This and other rules concerning lustration ascribed to Ezra, which were in harmony with similar ideas and laws of the Persians, show that the laws of Moses touching Levitical cleanness were re-enforced by Ezra (14).

(13) Maimonides *Hilcheth Maasor* i. 4, and *Keseph Mishnah*.
(14) See *Hachalutz*, by O. H. Schorr, 1869, p. 39.

The District Criminal Courts, afterward called *Sanhedrai Ketannah*, "The Lesser Sanhedrin," two of which were in Jerusalem, consisted of twenty-three persons, who were judges, jurors, advocates and prosecutors in one body. These courts must have been established by Ezra, although the number twenty-three may have been ancient custom (Sanhedrin i. 6).

Free teaching and free trading were also ascribed to an ordinance of Ezra, viz.: that every teacher had the right to open a school anywhere; and that peddlers might hawk their goods also in cities.

Other general customs were also supposed to have originated with Ezra, as, for instance, that Thursday was washday, and Friday the day for baking bread; that the blessings and curses written in the Pentateuch (Leviticus xxvi. and Deuter. xxviii.) should be read in the synagogue on the Sabbaths before the feasts of Pentecost and Booths.

16. The Work Done by Ezra.

Ezra restored the Law and its history to the Hebrews by the fixation of its texts and the protection of these national treasures against interpolation; the establishment of a representative body and courts of justice; the promulgation of the Law by free teachers and the Commoners. But all this was not fully carried into practice before Nehemiah came to Jerusalem. Ezra was a great scribe, as after him all men of learning were called (*Sopherim*), and a patriotic man, who feared the Lord and revered His law; but he, perhaps, was not the energetic man with the executive talent that Nehemiah was, nor was he in possession of the requisite authority to enforce his reforms. He was the man of learning to propose, but not to execute, great reforms. He had conceived the idea that the Law and its expounders must be the governing power in the Kingdom of Heaven, as neither the king nor the high priest could replace the lawful rulers of the theocracy, who, according to the Law, were the prophets (Deut. xviii. 17 to 22) and the council of the elders (Ibid xvii. 8 to 13), and the age of prophecy was closing. But he could not carry it out alone, because he had against him the aristocracy of two dynasties, of David, the King, and Zadok, the high priest of the former commonwealth. To overcome them it took the energy of Nehemiah.

CHAPTER III.

The Restoration of the State.—Nehemiah.

1. NEGLECTED STATE OF PUBLIC AFFAIRS.

Public affairs in the Hebrew colony were unsatisfactory. The governors succeeding Zerubabel extorted high salaries from the colony, as much as forty shekels a day, about $14,500 a year, and permitted their servants to prey upon the people (Nehem. v. 15), but did nothing for the public defense. None of the cities was fortified, the walls and gates of Jerusalem were in ruins, and the inmates exposed to marauders, who pillaged the country, slaughtered and captured many of the Hebrews in Jerusalem also, and scoffed at their weakness (Josephus' Antiq. xi. v. 6). Neither Ezra nor the high priest possessed sufficient power or energy to better the people's condition.

2. NEHEMIAH APPOINTED GOVERNOR.

A young Israelite, Nehemiah, son of Chakaliah, who was the king's cupbearer, in Susa, having been informed of this deplorable state of affairs, resolved to succor his people. After devout prayer, he approached the King, Artaxerxes Longimanus (1), with the petition to be sent to Jerusalem, where the graves of his ancestors were, that he might rebuild the city. The king granted him a furlough, appointed him Governor of the Hebrew colony, gave him letters to the pashas west of the Euphrates to give him safe conduct; also to Asaph, the overseer of the royal forests, to furnish him the wood necessary for the rebuilding of the walls and gates of Jerusalem, and to build himself a house;

---

(1) Xerxes, according to Josephus' Antiq. xi. vi. 7.

and to Adeus, the Pasha of Syria, Phœnicia and Samaria, to assist and pay due honor to Nehemiah.

3. Nehemiah's Journey and Arrival.

In the first month of the 20th year of Artaxerxes (445 b. c.), Nehemiah left Susa. Many Hebrews from Babylonia followed him voluntarily. The pashas gave him a military escort, so that his arrival in Jerusalem created a sensation among the rulers of the surrounding nations, and was not entirely welcome to the aristocracy among the Hebrews.

4. Preparations for the Rebuilding of the Wall.

Speed and secrecy were characteristics of Nehemiah. When he had rested three days in Jerusalem, he secretly, at night, inspected the walls to estimate the amount of work required. Next day he assembled the rulers in the temple, informed them of the privileges granted him, and demanded speedy action before their enemies could interfere. The walls were measured and the work was divided proportionately among the rulers, who brought in the people from the various districts to do the required work. Sanbelat, the Horonite, Governor of Samaria; Tobias, the Ammonite, and Geshem, the Arabian, most likely governors also, being present in Jerusalem when these preparations were made, scoffed at and ridiculed them; but Nehemiah drove them out of the city, and the work was speedily begun.

5. Beginning of the Work.

The Hebrews went energetically to work on the fortifications. Eliashib, the high priest, with the other priests, were first at the work. Meshullam ben Berechiah, who had been superseded by Nehemiah, also assisted in the great popular enterprise. Rulers, people, and women also (Nehem. iii. 12), worked with enthusiasm. The materials, wood excepted, were at hand from the overthrown walls and towers; the old foundation and the principal parts of the old wall had not been destroyed, and so the work progressed rapidly.

6. The Obstacles.

Sanbelat, Tobias and Geshem, not believing the Hebrews capable of erecting fortifications, first ridiculed them among the surrounding hostile nations. But when they heard of the progress made, they conspired against the Hebrews, and found support among the aristocracy and pseudo-prophets of Jerusalem. Nehemiah, to prevent a surprise by the enemy, placed outposts around the city. This alarmed the builders; but Nehemiah organized them in squads, armed them and prepared them for an attack. Henceforth, the workmen were not permitted to leave the city at night; half of them did military duty, while the other half worked on the wall, as did also the men of Nehemiah's body-guard. But now the poor among the people cried for relief. They said they were impoverished, indebted, with their estates mortgaged and their children sold into servitude. Nehemiah assembled the rulers and wealthy men, and they relinquished all the debts and returned all mortgaged estates and hired persons. Now Sanbelat came again, and, in connection with the other conspirators, tried to entice Nehemiah out of the city in order to assassinate him; this failing, he threatened to expose him to the king as one who intended exciting a rebellion, to have himself proclaimed king; but Nehemiah was too prudent to be entrapped and too firm to be terrified. Prophets rose in Jerusalem and opposed Nehemiah; the aristocrats corresponded with Tobias and betrayed Nehemiah's designs and intentions: one wanted to hide him in the temple, pretending that they wanted to assassinate him that night, in order to make him ridiculous among the people, and to expose him to the displeasure of the priests. All these obstacles did not discourage Nehemiah, nor did they retard his work. He proved too much of a man and patriot for the aristocrats and pseudo-prophets of Jerusalem, with all their allies among the surrounding nations.

7. The Work Finished.

On the 25th day of the sixth month (*Ellul*), in fifty-two days (2), the walls and the gates were completely restored, as they had been 121 years ago, before Nebuzradon had destroyed them. This changed the status of the Hebrew colony, which had now a solid center for self-protection, and was no longer exposed to the incursions of its barbarous neighbors.

8. The Location and Fortifications of Jerusalem.

Jerusalem is situated in 31° 46′ 43″ North Latitude and 35° 13′ East Longitude, 2,000 feet above the level of the Mediterranean, and 29 miles east of it in an air line. It rests

---

(2) In two years and four months, according to Josephus, and so long it took, perhaps, to finish the towers.

on four hills, Zion, Moriah, Bezetha and Acra, which were connected by bridges and fills. But in the time of Nehemiah, Mount Zion only, with the Temple Mount east and Ophel south thereof, was the city which was fortified. In the west of Zion is the valley and brook of Gihon, which, almost at a right angle, turns east, then south, and forms the valley of Hinnom. East of the city and temple is the valley of Jehoshaphat and the brook Cedron, uniting with Gihon in the north-east of Hinnom. From the lower side the city was considered impregnable. The wall of Nehemiah inclosed Zion, Ophel and the temple, and was thickest at the north, parallel with the valley of Tyropæon, where it was called the broad wall (Nehemiah iii. 8; xii. 38), although it was thick enough everywhere for a procession to march upon. The city had ten gates, viz.: the gates of PINNAH and EPHRAIM on the north; the gates of JESHENAH, DAGIM, HATZON, HASSUSIM and HAM-MAIM on the east; and the gates of GAI, ASHPOTH and AYIN on the west. In the south and southeast the hills were so steep that no gates were placed there. There was a watch tower over each gate, and two other towers were between each gate east and west, four between the two northern gates, one at each corner north-east and north-west, and one south-east, where the eastern wall of Zion and the western wall of Ophel met in a sharp angle; so that the walls had nineteen towers, connected by parapets and embrasures. A stone bridge connected Zion with the temple, and bridges led west over the Gihon and east over the Cedron to Mount Olive.

9. THE PROTECTION OF THE CITY.

After the fortifications had been completed and the gates placed, Nehemiah still apprehended a surprise from the hostile neighbors in connection with the aristocracy in Jerusalem. Therefore, he appointed two new rulers over the city, his brother, Hanani, and one Hananiah, and organized the militia to watch at day time upon the walls and at the gates, which were not opened before sunrise. With this protection, he was prepared to carry into effect the proposed reforms of Ezra and his own.

10. DEDICATION OF THE WALLS AND THE CENSUS.

The people were summoned to Jerusalem to witness the dedication of the wall and to establish the genealogy of every family, which was the Hebrew form of taking the census. The multitude came to the capital and witnessed the solemn dedication of its walls (Nehemiah xii. 27), on the 25th day of the sixth month, closing with a great feast in the temple. Then the census was taken. The genealogies handed down from the time of Zerubabel were corrected by numbers and facts presenting themselves at the time. So the foundation was laid to regular government, as Moses had done in his time (Numbers i.), and David in his (II. Samuel xxiv).

11. Solemn Acceptance of the Law.

On the First Day of the Seventh Month, the Law, as authenticated by Ezra and the Great Synod, was laid before the assembled people, "men and women, and all intelligent enough to understand" (Nehem. viii. 2). In the southern part of Ophel, before the Water Gate or Eastern Gate, there was a large free space where a platform was constructed, upon which Ezra stood with fourteen chosen men, supported by fourteen Levites, the latter stationed at various points among the crowd to interpret to those who did not understand at once. Now Ezra pronounced the ineffable name over the assembly, and all fell upon their knees and worshiped, and with uplifted hands responded a solemn Amen! Then he showed them the new style of writing, and began to read the authenticated Law, which was received with great enthusiasm, and also with tears of sorrow, on account of the disobedience of the fathers which had brought so much calamity on Israel. At noon, the assembly was dismissed to celebrate the feast in gladness. The next day the elders assembled and made proclamation to the people to build booths for the approaching feast, as prescribed in the Law, which was cheerfully done, so that all the roofs of Jerusalem, the outer courts of the temple, and the open spaces were covered with booths, and the Feast of Booths was celebrated with great rejoicing. During the seven days of the feast, and the eighth day being the Feast of Conclusion, the Law was read daily before the people. The 24th day, being the day after the feast, another solemn convocation took place. The reading of the Law was closed; then followed the confession of sins and solemn worship, and, at last, an instrument was written and signed by the representatives of the people, testifying that on that day all Israel had sworn a solemn oath that this was "the Law of the Lord which He had given by Moses, the servant of the Lord;" and that they would forever observe all this Law, its commandments, statutes and ordinances. Thus the written Law, as authenticated by Ezra, was solemnly accepted as the law book of Israel and the second commonwealth of the Hebrews; the new State was constituted.

12. New Enactments.

All persons born of Gentile women were (politically) separated from the congregation, and intermarriage with Gentiles was interdicted. Buying and selling on Sabbaths and holidays was forbidden. The Sabbath year was again introduced, but not the Jubilee year. A tax of one-third shekel, instead of one-half, per annum for each man was imposed to sustain the public sacrifices in the temple. Lots were drawn to establish the privilege as to which of the families should bring the wood to the temple, and nine families received that privilege (Mishnah, *Taanith* iv. 5). The gifts due to priests and Levites were to be brought to the temple, and there one-tenth of the tithe should remain for the support of the priests while in actual service, and the balance to be divided among all priests and Levites who did their share of duty in the temple service; so that none of them, withdrawing himself from duty, could receive any support from the public taxes. So the right of citizenship was settled, the Sabbath and Sabbath year enforced, and provisions made for the maintenance of the temple worship and its servants.

13. The Population of Jerusalem Augmented.

The next reform of Nehemiah was the augmenting of the population of Jerusalem. One-tenth of the population of the whole State was required to reside permanently in the capital. Many families did so voluntarily, and the others were drawn by lot. This made Jerusalem a large city, so that Herodotus (3), who shortly after traveled in Syria, reports that Jerusalem was then as important a city as Sardis, the metropolis of Asia Minor. Having a perfect military organization, Jerusalem was not only fully competent for self-defense, but it was also in a position to afford protection to the inhabitants of the whole country, which put an end to the incursions of hostile neighbors, and counterpoised the authority of the aristocratic families in Jerusalem.

---

(3) Herodotus Thalia v.; Prideaux, in the years 610 and 444. Herodotus called Jerusalem Cadytis, as the Syrians called it *Kadusha*, and the Arabs call it *Al-kuds*, all derived from *Kedosha*, the holy one, the holy city.

14. Permanence of the Great Synod.

The permanence of the Great Synod was also established by Nehemiah, he enacted that the 44 *Seganim* must remain permanently in Jerusalem and have their regular meetings in the temple (Nehem. v. 17; xiii. 11), while the 44 *Chorim* or *Sarim* doing the executive business in their respective districts, met in the Great Synod at stated times only. It appears that the twenty-four rulers of the *Mishmaroth*, in which priests and Levites were divided, as well as the high priest and the scribe, were also among the permanent members of the Great Synod, so that the body consisted of seventy permanent members as the Sanhedrin in aftertimes always did.

15. The Military Organization.

The military organization in the city consisted of 468 men of Judah and 928 men of Benjamin, under the command of Joel ben Zichri, and his lieutenant, Judah b. Hassenuah. The inner temple was guarded by 120 priests, under Zabdiel b. Haggedolim. The outer courts of the temple were guarded by 172 Levites; so that the city had a garrison of 1688 warriors (Nehem. xi. 6, 8, 9, 14, 19), besides the *Nethinim*, in Ophel, who had an organization of their own, under (Ziha and Gishpa.)

16. Nehemiah Returns to Susa.

In twelve years, from the 20th to the 32d, of Artaxerxes Longimanus, Nehemiah organized the Hebrew State in Palestine, in all its departments; in the temple and its service, with its priesthood, the fortification and defense of Jerusalem and the country, the permanence of its legislative and judiciary departments, the regulation of taxes and public duties, and all that on the Law and the democratic basis as proposed by Ezra. He took no salary as governor, and kept a princely household for his people and foreigners, who came to Jerusalem. Before he left, Petahiah b. Meshezabel was appointed governor (and he was not of the house of David); Sheriah b. Hilkiah was appointed chief priest in the temple (and he was not of the high priests' family); so he had overcome the aristocracy in Jerusalem, as he had discomfited the enemies of his people among the adjacent nationalities. In 433 b. c., when Pericles governed Athens, and Hippocrates lived in Cos; when Socrates taught the Athenians his new philosophy, and Meton discovered the nineteen years' cycle of the lunar years, Nehemiah had completely restored the Hebrew State and returned to Persia, to King Artaxerxes.

17. THE SUCCESSOR OF EZRA.

It is not known where or when Ezra died. He disappears from the records of history before Nehemiah, and his successor is mentioned, Zadok, the Scribe (Nehemiah xiii. 13). The traditions maintain that both Ezra and Nehemiah died on the ninth day of the tenth month (*Halachoth Guedoloth*, 39 b), without telling where; and then it is maintained that Ezra was the Prophet Malachi (*Meguillah* 15). If so, he must have lived for several years after 433 B. C., for this prophet flourished several years after that time.

18. SKEPTICISM AND CORRUPTION.

Within nine years after Nehemiah had left, an alarming skepticism took hold on the minds of priest and people. The leading idea upon which the Laws of Moses had been re-accepted and re-enforced and the State re-constituted was, that Israel had been punished and exiled on account of his disobedience to the Laws of Moses; therefore, renewed and faithful obedience to that code would secure to Israel God's special favor and protection, and the complete restoration of the Kingdom of Heaven. But now (431 B. C.) a grievous pestilence, coming from Ethiopia, Lybia and Egypt, invaded also the land of the Hebrews, and cut off many of them (4); droughts and locusts destroyed the crops (Malachi iii. 11); now many despaired and yielded to a discouraging skepticism (5). Priests left the altar and derided it (Malachi i. 7, 12). The people treated the sanctuary with criminal indifference; brought no longer the tithe to the temple, as Nehemiah had ordained, so that its ministers had to leave it (Ibid iii. 10; Nehemiah xiii. 10); married foreign women again (Malachi ii. 2; Nehem. xiii.), violated the Sabbath, the legislators left the temple, and the state of morals was very low (Malachi iii. 5; ii. 10). In all this skepticism and subsequent corruption, the priests had taken the lead (*Ibid* ii. 8), so that Eliashib, the high priest, had given a cloister in the temple to Tobias, the enemy of Israel, and his grandson had married the daughter of Sanbelat. Under these circumstances, the Prophet Malachi uttered his chastising speech and threatening oracle, with special severity against the priests. The corruptionists

---
(4) See Plutarch in Pericles, Thucydides lib. 2; Hippocrates lib. 3.
(5) See Malachi ii. 17; iii. 13 to 15.

asked: "Where is the God of justice?" and the prophet replied with the prediction that the lord, the angel of the covenant (Nehemiah), would suddenly appear in the temple and purify it again, and purify them also. And so it came to pass that Nehemiah unexpectedly returned to Jerusalem, 424 B. C., invited, perhaps, by Malachi and the law-abiding citizens.

19. Nehemiah Again in Jerusalem.

Nehemiah having again taken into his hands the reins of the government, acted this time not only with energy, but with severity. Having again, on the First Day of the Seventh Month, read the law for them, he forced them to send away their foreign wives and to swear an oath that they would never again violate this law. Those who resisted, he smote and plucked out their hair; and the son of Joiada, and grandson of the high priest, who had married a daughter of Sanbelat, was driven out of Jerusalem and the country. Having purified the priests and people, he brought back the *Seganim*, the permanent portion of the Great Synod, to their seats in the temple. He drove Tobias from his cloister in the temple, and again enforced the regular delivery of the tithe and other taxes, and the offerings of wood to the temple, and appointed new officers to conduct this matter. Then he called to account the *Horim*, the executive rulers, for their neglect of duty, especially in permitting violations of the Sabbath; he stopped this, and would not even permit the merchants, on the Sabbath day, to stay near the walls of Jerusalem outside of the city. So, by the exercise of severe authority, he enforced obedience to the Law, and reformed the State and temple permanently.

20. The End of Nehemiah.

It is not known how long Nehemiah lived after his second coming to Jerusalem, where or when he died. In the Talmud (*Sabbath* 103 *b*) it is maintained that some of Nehemiah's severe Sabbath laws were modified in aftertimes. In *Sanhedrin* 93 b, he is also credited with the authorship of the largest portion of the books of Ezra and Nehemiah, which could be understood only as referring to the notes from which those books were afterward composed. So the three pioneers of the second commonwealth of the Hebrews passed away unnoticed in the historical sources. Each of them left his imperishable monument. Zerubabel established the temple, Ezra the Law and the foundations to literature and a democratic government, and Nehemiah the State, with its governing institutions. Gradually it assumed the name of Judah or Judea (Nehem. v. 17; vi. 6, 7; xiii. 24). Its population, in the time of Nehemiah, extended south to Be'er Sheba, including Hebron, which was afterward lost again, down to Kabze'el (Joshua xv.), on the ancient borders of Edom, and up north to Gebia, the ancient border of Judea (II. Kings xxvii.), a tract of land of about sixty miles in length and breadth (Nehem. xi. 25).,

As men and patriots, these three pioneers were immaculate, and as founders of the new form of the theocracy they are remarkable for the total absence of all miracles and supernatural pretensions in their work. They appear as natural, earnest and hard-working men, who had nothing to do with evil spirits or angels, or any supernatural support besides God's aid to good and honest work.

CHAPTER IV.

Judea under the Government of High Priests.

1. JOIADA, HIGH PRIEST AND CHIEF RULER.

After the death of Nehemiah and the high priest, Eliashib (413 B. C.), the Persian Court did not appoint governors of Judea. Samaria was the seat of the Persian Satrap for Syria, Phœnicia and Palestine. The sons of David had lost prestige under Nehemiah. (Psalm lxxxix.) The ruler acknowledged by the Law, the prophet (Deuter. xviii. 15), was no more; the last prophets under Nehemiah, with the exception of Malachi, had proved unworthy of their illustrious predecessors. Therefore, the high priest was now the first man in the theocracy, and, contrary to the Laws of Moses (Leviticus x. 3), he was acknowledged the chief ruler of the nation, although he was no longer the bearer of the Urim and Thumim (Ezra ii. 63). He presided over the Great Synod, was the representative of the people before the king and his satrap, and gradually he established himself in the highest dignity of the nation.

2. THE TEMPLE ON MOUNT GERIZZIM BUILT.

Menasseh, the son of the high priest, Joiada (1), having married Nicaso, the daughter of Sanbelat, we have stated before, was driven out of Jerusalem. Other priests guilty of the same offense left with him, and sought refuge in Samaria. His attempt to regain his sacerdotal position after the death of Nehemiah, was foiled by the indignation of the people and the high priest. Unwilling to relinquish his title, he proposed to desert his wife. His father-in-law promised him a temple on Mount Gerizzim similar to

---

(1) Not the brother of Jaddua, as Josephus has it: Antiq. ix. viii. 2.

that of Jerusalem, in which he should be the high priest.
Sanbelat obtained a grant to this effect from Darius Nothus,
who was then involved in a war with Egypt (2), and the
temple was built, and the same culte introduced as in
Jerusalem. Menasseh was its first high priest, and other
expatriated priests were his subordinates. All the reforms
of Ezra and Nehemiah were rejected, and the Pentateuch,
in its more ancient form and letters only, was retained, in
which some changes were made. Deuter. xi. 29 to 32 was
placed after the Decalogue in Exodus, to prove that God had
sanctified Mount Gerizzim as the place for Israel's sanctuary. The Samaritans tried to prove that they were descendants of Joseph, and the claims of Sichem as the holy
city were older than those of Jerusalem. It does not appear that the Hebrews of Judea were much opposed to the
new temple, which was strictly monotheistic and Mosaic in
its culte, especially as they had repeatedly rejected the
Samaritans; although there is a tradition on record (3) that
the priests and elders of Jerusalem pronounced the great
ban over the Samaritan temple and its priests. Those who
were dissatisfied with the Ezra and Nehemiah reforms,
sought refuge in Samaria and found protection, so that the
new temple contributed indirectly to the maintenance of
the peace in Judea, and extended the power of the high
priest's family.

3. A High Priest Slays his Brother in the Temple.

Joiada died 373 B. C., after an official career of thirty-two
years, and was succeeded by his oldest son, Johanan.
Joshua, or Jesus, his younger brother, was the favorite of
Bagases, the Persian Satrap of Syria, under Artaxerxes II.,
and he promised the high priesthood to Jesus. Accordingly,
he appeared in Jerusalem as the high priest appointed by
the king's satrap, and Johanan held the office by right of
primogeniture. The quarrel lasted several years, and neither was willing to resign. The Hebrews could certainly not submit to the innovation of having their high priest
appointed by the king or his satrap. In the year 366 B. C.,
Jesus one day entered the inner court of the temple and attempted, by force, to discharge the high priest's functions.
This led to a personal encounter, in which Johanan killed
his brother Jesus. This fratricide brought Bagases to
Jerusalem. Nothwithstanding the protestations of the

(2) Not Darius Codomanus, as Josephus has it.
(3) Pirkai R. Eliezer xxxviii. end.

priests, he entered the inner court of the temple to inspect the place where the assassination had taken place; and then imposed a fine upon the people, to pay to the king fifty shekels for every lamb sacrificed on the altar. As there were eleven hundred and one lambs sacrificed a year for the congregation, the fine amounted to 55,050 shekels per annum. The amount of the fine was small, but the principle that the king should exercise the right of interfering with their divine services was mortifying to the Hebrews, and they looked upon it as a punishment inflicted upon them by Providence for the crime committed in the temple. Still, they paid that fine seven years (to 359 b. c.), when Artaxerxes II. died, and a revolution at the Persian court relieved them of this burden.

4. The Esther and Mordecai Story, 346 b. c.

The events which transpired during the reign of the third Artaxerxes, as he called himself, although he was called Darius Ochus (son of Artaxerxes II.), are narrated in the Book of Esther and in Josephus (4). That the Ahasveros of the Bible was one of the Medo-Persian kings, and not the father of Darius, the Mede (Daniel ix. 1), or Cambyses (Ezra iv. 6), one whose name was Artaxerxes, is evident from the concurrence of the Septuagint, the apocryphal Esther and Josephus; all of them call him Artaxerxes. In the Syriac version, Peshito, he is plainly called Achshirash, son of Achshirash, which is Artaxerxes, the son of Artaxerxes, which could refer to Darius Ochus only. It is evident that the Esther and Mordecai story can not be connected with any one of the kings of Medo-Persia preceding Artaxerxes III., and that his character, as described by Diodorus Siculus and Quintius Curtius, corresponds exactly to the Ahasveros of the Bible. The man who killed eighty of his brothers and filled the land with human gore, looks more like the Ahasveros of Scriptures with his bloody edicts than does any of his predecessors. Besides, he was an enemy of the Hebrews, who, it appears, gave support to the Phœnicians who revolted against Persia. In the eighth year of his reign, when he had taken Zidon, he besieged and took Jericho, took many captives of the Hebrews, led part of them with him into Egypt and sent others to Hyrcania, on the Caspian Sea, to settle parts of that country (5). Therefore, the Hebrews were disliked at the king's court, and Esther's parentage was not made known, and Mordecai,

---
(4) Antiq. xi. vi.
(5) Josephus contra Apion, etc., H. Prideaux, 351 b. c.

although he had saved the king's life, was in disfavor at court. The dates given in the Book of Esther fit exactly in the life of Ochus. He gave his great banquet in the third year of his reign, when he had been firmly settled on his throne. He married Esther in the seventh year of his reign, before he took the field against Phœnicia and Egypt. The bloody edict against the Hebrews was issued in the twelfth year of his reign, after his victories over Egypt, when he, according to Diodorus Siculus (Lib. xvi.), yielded himself entirely to a life of laziness and pleasure, and left the administration of government entirely to his favorite ministers. After this king had disposed of his wife, VASHTI, he married Esther, "the star," who was also called HADASSAH, "the myrtle." She was a niece of Mordecai, of the tribe of Benjamin, which the king knew not. The king's favor was bestowed entirely upon a haughty and revengeful Amalakite, whose name was Haman. This bloody despot, in the absence of the king, exacted divine honors of the courtiers also. Mordecai, a man of strictly monotheistic principles, refused to bend his knee before the mighty minister, which kindled his wrath against the proud Hebrew, and he determined upon taking revenge on the whole race. He persuaded the king, by false representations and heavy bribes, to issue a decree against all the Hebrews in the empire, outlawing them and their property, and giving permission to slay all of them on the thirteenth day of Adar, and to take their property. The decree, however, had been issued a year previous to its execution, so that it appears it was intended more against the property than the lives of the Hebrews, who might have left the country meanwhile. By the influence of Mordecai upon his niece, Queen Esther, and her influence upon the king, the mighty minister was overthrown, and ended, with ten of his sons, upon the gallows. The royal decree could not be revoked according to the laws of the empire; therefore, the Hebrews were given ample means of self-defense, and on that fatal thirteenth day of Adar, when they were attacked by avaricious and blood-thirsty enemies, they successfully defended themselves and did terrible execution. In memory of that event, the fourteenth day of Adar was made a half holiday, called PURIM, on account of the lots cast by Haman, and also the fifteenth day, called *Shushan Purim*, because the Hebrews of Susa had made a special day of festivities. Esther was the favorite queen, and Mordecai, after that event, occupied the highest position at the king's court. The Hebrews of Susa and the immediate vicinity, it appears, were the victims singled out by Haman, while those at a distance from the

Persian capital were not molested by the edict, and were not attacked; consequently, needed not defend themselves. This was certainly the case with the Hebrews of Palestine. Therefore, the *Purim* feast was established by Mordecai and Esther, and not by any lawful authority in Jerusalem, and was most likely observed a long time in the East before it was introduced in Palestine.

5. THE LAST HIGH PRIEST OF THIS PERIOD.

Johanan remained in office up to the year 341 B. C., when he died and was succeeded by his son, Jaddua, who was the last of the six high priests of this period, named in Nehemiah xii. 10, 11, in the Alexandrian Chronicle and in Josephus. According to the Talmud, there were two more, Onias I. and Simon the Just, who is said to have held this dignity forty years, and was high priest when Alexander arrived before Jerusalem.

6. THE GREAT SYNOD AND ITS WORK.

Nothing is said in Jewish sources about the high priests after Nehemiah's time, because no political disturbances or changes took place in Judea, and the internal development of that period was credited to the Men of the Great Synod, over whom the high priest presided, and without whose consent nothing could be done. The Great Synod carried the Ezra and Nehemiah reforms into general practice. The observation of the Sabbath became so general that warriors would not fight on Sabbath. Intermarriage with foreign women, and with it also bigamy, had become almost extinct, so that for centuries no case of either was reported. The abomination of idolatry had been extended so far that Hebrew soldiers, under Alexander, would rather stand any punishment than assist in rebuilding a Heathen temple. Therefore, most of the post-biblical laws of the Hebrews and the ancient customs, also those called הלכה למשה מסיני, "Rule by Moses from Sinai," in reference to the Sabbath, marriages, idolatry, temple service, taxes, Levitical cleanness, including those concerning forbidden food, the judiciary and procedure, had their origin with the Men of the Great Synod. They expounded the Laws of Moses and extended provisions in the sense of the Ezra and Nehemiah reform. In the same sense, the *Sopherim* taught the people. Therefore, the general statement (6): "The Men of

---

(6) Jerushalmi, Shekalim v.: אנשי כנסת הגדולה תקנו מדרש הלכות ואגדות

the Great Synod established exigese (to expound the laws), rules (statutes), and sermons."

In civil and criminal law there are also certain principles and post-biblical statutes which were never disputed by the Sadducees, and must, consequently, have originated with the Great Synod. This body, therefore, laid the foundation to the post-biblical or rabbinical code of the Hebrews, although it is not ascertained in each case which particular law, principle or custom can claim this antiquity.

7. THE SOPHERIM AND THEIR WORK.

The learned men after Ezra were called *Sopherim* (singular *Sopher*), "Scribes;" because to be a skilled writer was the first criterion of a man of learning. To transcribe the authenticated Law as deposited in the temple was one of the Scribe's occupations. His next occupations were to read, expound and teach it. The text was without vowel points, without divisions of words, verses and chapters; hence it was nearly hieroglyphic, so that the correct reading thereof was traditional, and had to be communicated from master to disciple. As the Great Synod legislated by expounding and extending the Law, these additions also had to be taught orally. The teachers, to be trusted in all these points, had to be distinguished for learning and piety, and to keep themselves posted in all the enactments of the Great Synod.

8. THE SYNAGOGUE AND THE SOPHER.

One hundred years after Ezra, there was a synagogue in every important town in Judea, which was the court-house and the place for public worship and instruction, as was also the case in the temple synagogue (7). By the *Anshe Ma'amod*, or "Commoners," the temple service, with the exception of the sacrifices, was imitated in their respective places in the country. The Great Synod legislated for the temple, and the synagogical service was arranged accordingly. In the temple, certain Psalms were sung by the Levites; the *Shema* and the Decalogue were read twice every day, with certain brief benedictions before and after; and this was done also in the synagogues until it was considered a duty that every person should pray those very prayers twice a day. When the Great Synod added seven benedic-

---

(7) It appears, however, that in the temple the *Lishchath Hag gazith* was two stories high; the lower hall was the synagogue, and the upper one was the hall of the Sanhedrin.

tions to the daily exercises (8), this was also done in the synagogues, and at last by the individuals. In the temple, certain portions of the Law were read on Sabbath, holidays and new moons, which was also done in the synagogues, with the Ezra addition of such readings on Monday, Thursday and Sabbath afternoon. These readings of the Law required a skilled and informed reader, a *Sopher;* hence, there had to be a Sopher in every synagogue to read and to expound the Law. Some of the *Sopherim* were, at the same time, teachers, and others judges, while a number of them were members of the Great Synod. So a new power rose up gradually in the land, which took the place of the prophets of old; a power independent of the accident of birth, because any gifted man could become a *Sopher.* It was the power of intelligence, which vied with priest and prophet for the first rank and authority (9).

---

(8) The eighteen benedictions שמונה עשרה are of a later origin. The ancient sources have but seven; three in praise of God, אבות גבורות קדישת השם, and three of thanksgiving and blessing in conclusion רצה' הודיה, ברכת כהנים between which a seventh was inserted, except on New Year, when three were inserted, and the Day of Atonement, when various others were added. *Mishah, Yoma,* vii. 1; *Rash Hashonah,* iv. 5.

(9) The Great Synod is also credited with having authenticated or even written some of the Biblical books [*Baba Bathra,* 15 a]. This point will be discussed in another chapter.

CHAPTER V.

Literature and Culture of the Medo-Persian Period.

1. THE CANON.

The seven books of the Canon established by Ezra and the Great Synod, are now before us as תורה, the Thorah, Law, Pentateuch or Five Books of Moses, and נביאים ראשנים; the Former Prophets, comprising the Books of Joshua, Judges, I. and II. Samuel, I. and II. Kings. This division was made at a later period (*Baba Bathra*, 14 *b*), and was not adopted by the Greek translators.

2. THE POPULAR LITERATURE.

Besides the Canon, there was considerable literature in the possession of the Hebrews, which was afterward added to the Canon, and is now before us as the Books of Isaiah, Jeremiah, Ezekiel, eleven minor prophets, Psalms, Lamentations and Proverbs, besides the various books of prophets and chronographers to which the author of Chronicles refers. All these books, perhaps, in a fragmentary condition, must have existed at that period. Some of the Psalms, besides the oldest ones, were used by the Levites; such as Psalms lxvii., xcii., xciii., xcv. to c., cxi. to cxiii., cxxxv. and cxxxvi., cxliv. cxlv., and others (1). Others were used in private devotion, such as Psalms x., lxxi. lxxvii. and cii. Psalms cxxxv. and cxxxvi. were most likely the *Hallel*, or festive hymn, sung by the Levites at the *Mussaph*, or additional sacrifice of the new moons and three feasts.

3. THE LITERATURE PRODUCED DURING THIS PERIOD.

The Medo-Persian Period was eminently productive in Hebrew literature. We possess from that period—

---

(1) See Mishnah *Tamid*, vii. 4.

(*a*) Prophetical books, viz.: the second Isaiah (Isaiah xl. to lxvi.), Haggai, Zachariah (except ix. to xii.), Malachi and Jonah.

(*b*) Historical books, viz.: Ruth, Chronicles, Ezra and Nehemiah.

(*c*) Various Psalms.

(*d*) The Book of Job.

4. The Book of Ruth.

It is evident from Ruth iv. 7, and the fact that none of the earlier historiographers mention the names of Boaz, Ruth, Elimelech or Naomi, and the linguistic peculiarities of that beautiful idyl, that it was written from a tradition which, perhaps, was preserved in the Davidian family long after the event which it describes transpired. It appears to have been written early in the Medo-Persian Period (2) and in defense of Gentile mothers in Israel, against whom the Ezra and Nehemiah reforms were so severe. The little book places before the reader, to the very best advantage, a daughter of Moab, who is rich in all virtues and becomes the mother of the royal house of David. The objects of the author are plain. He wants to show that not all Gentile women are objectionable, as some of them might be like Ruth; that the ways and means of Providence are obscure, and must be submitted to with faith and fortitude, which was a special theme of that period, as shall be shown below; and that the heathens will be converted, as the second Isaiah had predicted with so much force. Perhaps the wife of the high priest of the Gerizzim temple was the immediate cause that this idyl was written. Its tendency is evident and the time of its origin can not be doubtful, although the author's name has not been preserved.

5. The Book of Jonah.

That the Book of Jonah was not written after this period is evident from the fact of its having been accepted in the prophetical canon, established soon after this. That it was not written before is evident from the following points: (*a*) Its lyric portion (chapter ii.) is an imitation of older Psalms. (*b*) It is based on a fable, a method adopted by none of the other prophets. (*c*) It is cosmopolitan; speaking of and to Heathens in a spirit of catholicity, without reference to or preference for Israel, which distinctly marks its origin in a time after the exile, when the Hebrews had come in close

---

(2) See Dr. Abraham Geiger's *Urschrift*, etc., p. 49, etc.

contact with many nations between the Caspian Sea, the Indus and the Nile. (*d*) It speaks favorably of the Assyrians, the arch-enemies of Israel, which points to an age when that empire was no more. (*e*) It discusses the problem of Providence, showing why and when God punishes not the wicked, a question matured in the minds at the time of Malachi, and no prophet or philosopher discusses a theme before its existence in the public mind. (*f*) It demonstrates the point that the Pagans can and will be converted, as predicted by the second Isaiah.

6. THE PSALMS OF THIS PERIOD.

For similar reasons as in Section 5, we conclude that Psalm civ. is from this period; it is a hymn on the cosmos and a defense of Providence; it has for its foundation the first chapter of Genesis, and its author rises to a height in cosmology unknown then among Gentiles. Psalm ciii. is an amplification of Exodus xxxiv. 6, 7, and David did not imitate. Psalm cxix. with eight verses to each letter of the alphabet, in fervent praise of the Law with all its ordinances and statutes, is certainly from this period, and shows by its mnemotechnic construction that it was the text book in the lower schools conducted by *Sopherim*, as expressed in verses 7, 9, 25, 33, 34, etc., which also imbued the pupils with a desire after loftier interpretations of the Law, as in verses 10, 14, 18, etc. Psalm xix. is certainly of this period, as its cosmic start and its praise of the Law prove. The WHOLE LAW, as proposed by Ezra and Nehemiah, with all its ancient statutes and ordinances, was not equally welcome to all, and all Psalms in praise of the WHOLE LAW, its profound signification and hidden meanings, as well as most of the didactic and the alphabetical Psalms are products of this period. Psalms cxxvii. and cxxxvii., of course, are of this period.

7. THE BOOK OF JOB.

The oldest notice concerning the origin of the Book of Job is in the Talmud (*Baba Bathra*, 15), where, it appears, two opinions stand uncontradicted: (1) The story of Job is fictitious; and (2) Job was one of those who returned from the Babylonian exile. There was a pious man in the land of Uz, who passed through a series of visitations (Ezekiel xiv. 14, 20), came out consistently and triumphantly, returned to Palestine (Job xlii. 10), and, after his death, was made the hero of this wonderful book on Providence. The Book of Job could not have been written in the prophetical age: because (*a*) it is, in form and style, entirely different from all prophetical writings. It is not imperative, like Moses; not historical, like the former Prophets; not predictive, like the latter Prophets; not psalmodic, like David, and not gnomic, like Solomon: it is purely lyric-didactic in the dialogue form, like Plato and portions of the Avesta. (*b*) It philosophizes and is full of skepticisms, and a prophetical age doubts not and reasons not discursively. The prophet utters intuitive knowledge, and Job is discursive. No fruit ripens before its season or out of its climate. (*c*) It opens with an allegory (3) in heaven, which is not an imitation of Isaiah vi. or Ezekiel i., but of a Persian court, and has as a prominent figure among the heavenly satraps, Satan, unknown in Hebrew literature before Zechariah, a poetical fiction, which points directly to the Ahriman of the Persians accommodated to the allegory. (*d*) Like Jonah and Psalm civ., it is cosmic and cosmopolitan in its conceptions. (*e*) Throughout the arguments of Job and his four friends, the name of Jehovah is mentioned but once (xii. 9), and there in a quotation. This points directly to a time when the Hebrews would not use the tetragrammaton, which was certainly not in the time of the prophets. (*f*) It contains quotations and imitations of Psalms and Proverbs, and is held in the meter and parallelism of the latter. Still, the Book of Job could not have been written long after the prophetical period, for at the beginning and the end, God, as Jehovah, is introduced, speaking to Satan, to Job and also to Eliphaz, not with דבר, "to speak," but ענה, "to impose" knowledge, which is not exactly the prophetical form. None of the writers of the next period, not even the author of Daniel, had the boldness to let God speak to them. Therefore, the origin of the Book of Job must be placed near the end of the prophetical period; hence, near Malachi, with whom the prophetical period closes. This prophet affords us the key to Job's philosophy. The prevalent skepticism which Malachi attacks (i. 2, 8, 12; ii. 17; iii. 14, 15), concerns Providence especially in these two points: (1) Why should we Hebrews observe God's laws when we are treated no better than the Heathens? To this, the authors of Ruth and Jonah reply, because you are no better than the Heathens, who are also God's children, to trust in Him with faith and fortitude or to repent their sins on hearing God's threatening oracles. Do the same and God will be gracious to you, as he was to Ruth and the people of Nineveh. (2) Why are those who do fear the Lord

---

(3) All names and numbers in the book are plainly allegoric.

nevertheless subject to severe affliction? To this, the Book of Job responds with different reasons (4), and one is, God, who has given. may take away, and He who takes away gives back seven-fold. The afflictions of the righteous are visitations of grace (5), intended to purify and to elevate him in the scale of human perfection. Malachi said (i. 11), "For from the rising of the sun to his setting, my name is great among the Gentiles; and at every place sacrifice is made to my name, and pure meal offering; for my name is great among the nations, saith Jehovah Zebaoth." This is also a leading idea with Jonah, Psalm civ. and with Job, whose four friends are supposed to be foreigners, who know nothing of Jehovah. Therefore, there can be no doubt that Job was written shortly after Malachi, hence near to 400 B. C., while Ruth and Jonah may have been written some decades before. The prevailing skepticism, it appears, also gave rise to Psalm l. and the re-introduction among the temple songs of Psalm liii. (Psalm xv.), with the new conclusion. The author of Job exhausts the various philosophisms on Providence which reason advanced in his days, and shows that Job and his friends, Elihu included, fail to account for Job's afflictions, the real cause of which is stated in the very beginning of the book; hence, their reason fails in solving the mysteries of Providence. Therefore, God himself appears, at last, to solve the problem, or rather to inform Job that man can not solve it, that he must believe, confide and hope. So the book proves the necessity of revelation and faith and the insufficiency of reason. Therefore, it was supposed Moses must have written it.

8. I. AND II. CHRONICLES, EZRA AND NEHEMIAH.

That the author of I. and II. Chronicles was also the compiler of Ezra and Nehemiah, which were but one book, has been established by Dr. L. Zunz (6). Ezra and Nehemiah consist of original notes by those men, written in the first person, and portions written by the compiler, which are in style like the Chronicles; and the beginning of Ezra is taken from the close of Chronicles. Therefore, we know that these books were written after the Nehemiah census

---

(4) See MOREH NEBUCHIM, III. Volume, chap. xvii., and SEPHER IKKARIM, iv. *Maamar*, chapt. vii.

(5) יסורים של אהבה *Berachoth*, 5.

(6) GOTTESDIENSTLICHE VORTRAEGE. The chapter on the *Chronist* was translated in English by myself, and published in the *Asmonean* in the year 1852.

had been taken (compare Nehem. xi. and I. Chron. ix.), and shortly before the advent of Alexander the Great (about 350 B. C.), as the high priest Jaddua is mentioned in Nehemiah (xii. 11). This author ignores the ancient Hebrew Republic, the reign of Saul, and barely refers to the kingdom of Israel. The main portion of his book (from I. Chron. x. to II. Chron. ix., 29 chapters), is devoted to David and Solomon, whom he glorifies, omitting the most grievous sins of both. So he neglects the prophets and glorifies the priests. The main center of his thoughts was the temple and the priesthood. He wrote at a time when the house of David appeared only as a reminiscence of past glory, chiefly as the builders of the temple; the prophets were no longer a living power among the Hebrew people: the temple was the main center, and the high priest the chief ruler.

9. The Language Spoken.

The Hebrews of Judea, during this period and long after it, spoke Hebrew, and called the language יהודית, *Jehudith* or Jewish (Nehem. xiii. 24). The glowing patriotism of the Hebrews in exile, with orators like Ezekiel and the second Isaiah, and a literature as described above, rendered it impossible to forget the language of their country in fifty years; especially, as many of their leaders outlived the captivity and returned to their home which they had left as young men (Ezra iii. 12). But if they had forgotten their national language, the patriotism of Nehemiah and the enthusiasm of Ezra would certainly have restored it with the Law, as the best medium of preserving both the Law and the nationality. Nehemiah complains about the offspring of those who had foreign wives, that they could not speak any language correctly; but those were few only, and because he complains about the jargon of the few, the correct *Jehudith* must have been the language in general use. This is evident from the addresses and notes of the prophets, Ezra and Nehemiah, which must have been Aramaic or Syriac, if such had been the language of the country, or written in strict imitation of the more ancient classical Hebrew, like the Book of Job, which was no popular address. But those speeches and notes, as well as the original passages in Chronicles, show new and advanced forms of a spoken Hebrew, tinctured with Aramaisms, adopted by contact. Therefore, it is unhistorical to speak of any *Targum*, " Aramaic version," or any *Meturgamon*, " Translator," of Scriptures introduced by Ezra.

10. The Religious Idea.

A nation's literature is the barometer of its cultural atmosphere: the age which produced the Books of Ruth, Jonah and Job, and Psalm civ., must have been enlightened, tolerant and humane. With the second Isaiah, Malachi and Jonah, there is an end to all one-sided and narrow-minded particularism. Jehovah is the author and governor of the universe, the Father of the human family, and Israel is "His servant," charged with the mission of redeeming and uniting the human family in the universal Kingdom of Heaven, under the banner of truth, freedom and justice. Therefore, Israel must preserve His integrity among the nations and be holier than others, which can be done only by obedience to the whole Law. If those writers did not reflect the spirit of their age, they must certainly have made it. With this religious idea at the base, the second commonwealth of the Hebrews was started, and the Democratic form of government was made an indispensable necessity. Whether a lay governor or the high priest collected the foreign king's taxes, was indifferent; the nation, with all its institutions, temple, synagogue, schools and courts of justice, was governed by the Law, its expounders, and the people's representatives in the Great Synod. No Messiah was expected; no prince of the house of David was wanted; no miracles were wrought; no fantastic speculations or transcendental hopes indulged in; the people and its leaders were sober and practical. Their inclination to skepticism demonstrates a new era of intelligence.

11. Art and Science.

The Hebrews were agriculturists. No traces of commerce, except domestic trade, are found in this period. In the sciences, the advanced knowledge of that period is demonstrated by the temple on Mount Moriah and the walls of Jerusalem, which embodied leading principles in mathematics and physics and sublime ideals of beauty in architecture. Cosmology, far in advance of all cotemporary nations, is expressed in the second Isaiah, Job and Psalm civ. The author of the Book of Job speaks astronomical figures of speech as though that science had been popular among his cotemporaries, and philosophizes on the highest problems with an ease and grace which betoken his own intimacy with metaphysics, and his supposition that many would understand him well. It is not formal philosophy formally expressed; it is its substance in the graceful garb of beauty, and this pre-supposes both depth of thought and an ennobled taste. It would be highly interesting and instructive to discover the actual state of that period's civilization in its literature, but our method of brevity would not allow this research. We can only refer to general characteristics. We have before us a small nation far advanced in the religious and ethical idea, the arts of civilization and the main sciences; a nation without sculptors and painters, but with musicians, singers, orators, poets, philosophers and writers admired to this day as intellects of the highest order, and we have the right to judge the age by its exponents.

II. The Grecian Period.

This period, extending from 332 to 167 B. C., from the coming of Alexander the Great to Jerusalem to the insurrection of the Hebrews under Mattathia, the Asmonean, will be narrated in the next four chapters, being the sixth, seventh, eighth and ninth, of this book. It is usually called the Macedonian Period, because the Macedons were the main supporters of Alexander, and many of the Greek settlers in Asia and Egypt were called so. It is more correct, however, to call it the Grecian Period, because the Grecizing aptitude of the Hebrews is characteristic of this period of history; its aggressions and the defense made against it are the underlying principles which led at last to the Maccabean insurrection and the civil war. The most important events of this period are: the growth of the Hebrew commonwealth, the origin of the Sanhedrin, the Greek translation of the Law, the mutual influence of the Greek and Hebrew mind, and the consequent literature.

CHAPTER VI.

Judea under European Rulers.

1. Two New Kings.

The year 335 B. C., gave to the then civilized world two new kings of historical fame; Codomanus, called Darius III., was made King of Persia, and Alexander, King of Macedon and commander-in-chief of all Greece, after he had destroyed the city of Thebes, slain 90,000 of her inhabitants, and sold 30,000 surviving captives into slavery. The last of the Medo-Persian kings, Darius III., was a brave though unfortunate monarch. Alexander, born at Pella, in 356 B. C., was then not quite 22 years of age. He was an atrocious barbarian, although Aristotle was his tutor, Socrates and Plato had humanized the Greeks, and Demosthenes had but lately delivered his Philippics and Olynthiacs. Alexander inherited his father's (Philip of Macedon) unbridled ambition and warlike spirit, and was a native martial genius, as great and successful as he was rash, passionate and wicked. He conquered Asia, from the Black and Caspian Seas to the Indian Ocean, from the Hellespont to beyond the Indus River, Egypt and Eastern Europe to the Adriatic Sea and the Danube River; and yet he was a base drunkard and assassin, guilty of the most atrocious crimes committed by man. He was the greatest warrior of his age.

2. Asia Minor and Syria Conquered.

In the year 334 B. C., with an army of 34,000 men, and seventy talents (about $72,000) in his treasury, Alexander crossed the Hellespont at Sestus, into Asia Minor. A few days later, at the river Granicus, he encountered the Persian army, outnumbering his five to one, and routed it in open battle. This victory brought into his possession the royal treasury at the city of Sardis and all the provinces of Asia Minor, which had many and dominant Greek cities. Securing the fruits of this victory, he marched eastward into Cilicia, and secured to himself the straits between this province and Syria. The battle of Issus was fought there (333 B. C.). The vast army of Darius was routed; his camp, baggage, mother, wife and children were captured, and Syria was open to the invader. Having sent Parmenis, one of his lieutenants, to take Damascus and Cœlosyria, Alexander, with his main army, marched into Phœnicia, and met with no resistance anywhere until he reached the city of Tyre, which he was forced to besiege fifteen months, and then to take it by storm.

3. Jerusalem Submits to Alexander.

The protracted siege of Tyre could not have been undertaken without receiving provisions for the army. The next agricultural countries were Judea and Samaria. Therefore, Alexander sent embassadors to Samaria and Jerusalem, demanding submission and provisions. The Samaritans sent supplies and a corps of eight thousand men to Alexander's army. The Hebrews refused, because, as they said, their oath of allegiance to the king of Persia was sacred and inviolable. This provoked the ire of the great warrior, and, after he had taken Tyre, he marched to Jerusalem. Judea had no army and could offer no resistance. The Persians were far away beyond the Euphrates. The alternative was either submission to Alexander or a siege of Jerusalem, with the fate of Tyre before it. The high priest, Jaddua (1), in order to pacify the conscience of his people concerning the oath of allegiance, had recourse to a divine dream, in which, as he said, God had commanded him to submit to Alexander, and to meet him in a certain solemn manner. This was satisfactory. The city was decorated, the high priest and priests (2) in their sacerdotal robes, the rulers and citizens in white garments, forming a stately procession, went forth to receive Alexander, at Zophim, "Prospect," a hill west of Jerusalem, from which the temple and city could be overlooked. Nothing could be more welcome to him than the submission of a strong city and a rich country; and nothing could be more flattering to his vanity than this demonstration of friendship and submission. Therefore, Alexander, approached by the high priest, bowed to him reverently and treated him kindly. In explanation of his conduct, he, like Jaddua, also referred to a dream which he had before crossing the Hellespont (3). He was led in triumph through the decorated city to the temple, where he made sacrifices to the God of Israel, received the oath of allegiance, secured to Judea all the privileges enjoyed under the Medo-Persian monarchs, and exemption from tribute every Sabbath-year. The people had no cause to regret the change of rulers, and the priests called every boy born that year Alexander. No changes in the internal government of Judea were made.

4. Samaria Annexed to Judea.

The Samaritans were not as fortunate as the Hebrews. They invited Alexander to visit their capital and temple, and he did not do it; they also begged exemption from tribute every Sabbath-year, and it was not granted, although they had assisted him before Tyre with men and provisions. They were dissatisfied, and soon after avenged themselves. For Alexander, going into Egypt, appointed one of his fa-

---

(1) According to the Talmud, Simon the Just, the grandson of Jaddua, then high priest, was in office forty years, 368 to 292 b. c. He was vice-high priest *Segan*, for he prepared a red heifer, and may have been the governor *de facto* already in the time of Jaddua.

(2) There were then, in all Judea, about 1,500 priests, says Hecateus.

(3) Josephus' Antiquities xi. viii. 5.

vorites, Andromachus, Governor of Syria and Palestine. This governor coming to the city of Samaria, the people rose against him, set fire to the house in which he was, and he perished in the flames. Alexander, on returning from Egypt, caused all to be slain who had taken any part in this outrage, drove the rest of the inhabitants out of the city of Samaria, colonized it with Macedonians, annexed the whole territory of Samaria to Judea free of extra tribute (331 B. C.) (4), and left to the exiles the city of Schechem, near their temple of Mount Gerizzim, which ever after remained the capital of that sect. The eight thousand Samaritan soldiers in Alexander's army were sent to Thebes, in Egypt, and settled there. The Hebrews of Judea were brought in close contact with Galilee, which, it appears, was included in Samaria.

5. A Crime of Alexander.

Alexander marched from Judea into Egypt. He was detained two months before the city of Gaza, which he finally took by storm. Here Alexander committed another of his atrocious crimes. The Persian commander, Betis, of this city, was taken alive. Holes were cut behind the sinews of his heels; the valiant man was tied to a chariot, and, as Achilles had dragged the dead body of Hector on the walls, dragged through the streets of Gaza till he was dead.

6. The Site of Alexandria Selected.

In a very short time Alexander subjected all Egypt to his sway. In the winter of 332 B. C. he journeyed from Memphis to the temple of Jupiter Ammon, in the desert of Libya, where he had himself declared by the priests a son of that god. On his way thither he discovered a site in the Delta of the Nile opposite the Island of Pharus, which, in opposition to Tyre, he selected for a new commercial city, to be called Alexandria. It was laid out at once and building commenced. On returning from Libya to the site of Alexandria, he invited colonists to this new city, and among them also the Hebrews, to whom he granted equal rights with the Macedonians as a reward of their fidelity and assistance (5).

7. End of the Medo-Persian Empire.

In the year 331 B. C., which Ptolemy, the astronomer, counts the first of Alexander's reign over the East, Alexan-

---
(4) Josephus contra Apion ii. 4.
(5) Josephus' Wars ii. xviii. 7 and Contra Apion ii.

der marched across the Euphrates and Tigris Rivers in pursuit of Darius and his army. The two armies met in October above Ninevah, near a place called Aribela, and Darius was defeated. He fled into Media, was captured by two of his own lieutenants and after some time slain by them. Alexander, a short time thereafter, was in undisputed possession of the whole Medo-Persian Empire, and invaded India beyond the Indus River, not, however, before he had burned down the ancient city of Persepolis and had committed all the outrages of a drunken villain.

8. THE HEBREWS REFUSE TO REBUILD A HEATHEN TEMPLE.

Up to the year 324 B. C., Alexander was incessantly engaged in conquests, the organization of government and the practice of vices. In this year he came back to the city of Babylon, which he intended to make his capital, and to beautify to its utmost capacity. He, carrying Greek idolatry into the East, also undertook to rebuild the temple of Bel destroyed by Xerxes. The soldiers were ordered to remove the debris. When the turn of the Hebrew soldiers came in this work, they absolutely refused to do it. Severe punishments were inflicted in vain; they insisted upon the prohibition of their religion to assist in any way in the building of a Heathen temple. So the Laws of Moses were then understood. The soldiers were at last dismissed from service and sent to their respective homes.

9. THE DEATH OF ALEXANDER.

Alexander died suddenly in the spring of the year 323 B. C., thirty-two years old. Some maintained he had been poisoned, and others naturally believed that he wasted away by excesses, polygamy, concubinage, sodomy and orgies of the worst kind; he died the death of a vile drunkard. His companion, Hephestion, had died the same death.

10. THE FAMILY OF ALEXANDER EXTINGUISHED BY ASSASSINATION.

After the death of the great conqueror, his generals settled the royal succession upon Aridaeus, calling him Philip, who was the idiotic and bastard brother of Alexander, and his son by Roxana, born after his death, called Alexander Aegus. Perdiccas was declared regent, or governor of the kings. The vast empire was divided into provinces, each of which was placed under a governor selected from Alexander's principal men. Their duty was to preserve the empire for the kings; but their object was to become independent kings themselves, which initiated a period of treachery and perpetual warfare, lasting up to the year 301 B. C. Perdiccas, the governor of the kings, was slain by his own men in Egypt (321 B. C.). His successor, Antipater, died (319 B. C.), and Polysperchon took his place. In 317 B. C., Olympias, the mother of Alexander, seized the government and slew King Philip, his wife and their friends, and was herself slain the next year. Now, Alexander Aegus was nominally the king. But in the year 310 B. C., the same year when Epicur, being thirty-two years of age, began to teach his philosophy at Mytilene, Cassander slew both Alexander Aegus and his mother, Roxana, and proclaimed himself king of Macedon. The same year the son of Alexander, Hercules, was put to death, and shortly after (308) Cleopatra, the sister of Alexander, was also killed; so that **the whole family, except one of Alexander's sisters, was exterminated.**

11. The Governors of the Empire.

Among the governors appointed after the death of Alexander, the following only interest us here: (1) LAOMEDON, the Mytelenian, governor of Syria and Palestine, to 320 B. C. (2) PTOLEMY LAGI, governor and afterward king of Egypt, founder of the Ptolemy dynasty. (3) SELEUCUS, appointed governor of Babylon in 321 B. C., afterward king of Syria and Asia to the Indus River, the founder of the Seleucidan dynasty. (4) ANTIGONUS, originally governor of Pamphilia and other provinces, proclaimed himself and his son Demetrius, in 306, kings of Asia, and fell in battle in 301 B. C., and his son was slain by Seleucus in 282 B. C. (5) EUMENES, the greatest and most faithful man among the surviving warriors of Alexander, was betrayed by his army and slain by Antigonus (315 B. C.). The wars, confederations, treacheries and depredations of the governors after the death of Alexander, shook all foundations and undermined the faith of the then civilized world in Asia, Europe and Africa. The nations, their will, liberty and rights, had come down to zero. Military chieftains, supported by mercenary troops, trampled under foot cities and nations, changing masters after every battle, and those masters betrayed one another as often as they had made covenants.

12. Fate of Palestine and the Capture of Jerusalem.

During the reign of Alexander, and under Laomedon, as governor of Syria, it appears Palestine enjoyed peace and a rising prosperity; for no complaints of any kind have been chronicled, and the name of Laomedon is not even mentioned in the Hebrew sources. In 321 B. C., Perdiccas, marching a large army through Palestine into Egypt, the country may have been benefited by it, because the Hebrews were as faithful to the heirs of Alexander as they had been to him. Perdiccas having been slain in Egypt, Ptolemy invaded Syria by his general, Nicanor, who defeated and slew Laomedon, while Ptolemy himself invaded the maritime country of Palestine and Phœnicia. The Hebrews offered stout resistance, and Ptolemy would have been obliged to besiege Jerusalem much longer than he had time to spare, had he not taken it by treachery (6). He came as a friend on the Sabbath day to offer sacrifices, but craftily managed to possess himself of the city, before its inhabitants discovered his real designs. He took a large number of Hebrew captives with him into Egypt, many of whom were made slaves, while others were given lands to settle on. So Palestine and the neighboring countries were annexed to Ptolemy's province.

13. Palestine Changing Masters.

In the year 315 B. C., after the death of Eumenes, Antigonus became master of Asia. Seleucus fled into Egypt, and Ptolemy, in 314, was obliged to retire from Palestine, and leave it to Antigonus. He retook it in 312, but had to restore it the same year to Antigonus, in whose power it remained up to 301 B. C. It appears that Jerusalem, like several maritime cities, was dismantled by Ptolemy before his retreat, and remained in a defenseless state until it walls were rebuilt by Simon the Just (7). No trace is left in Hebrew sources of the government of Antigonus except his name, which, like Alexander's, had been adopted by the Hebrews; and shortly after his death, one of the most prominent Hebrews was Antigonus of Sochu.

14. Emigration to Egypt.

Between 320 and 314, and then again in 312 B. C., many Hebrews emigrated to Egypt, settling in Alexandria, while some of them were intrusted with military posts to guard

---

(6) Josephus' Antiquities xii. 1.
(7) Ben Sirach, chapter 50, 4.

various cities on account of their acknowledged fidelity. Among the soldiers with Ptolemy, there was also Meshullam, an expert archer and horseman, of whom Hecateus (8) narrates that he guided a party through the wilderness. An augur accosted them, pointed to a bird, and maintained that if that bird stopped the party should, but if the bird went onward, the party should proceed also. Meshullam shot at the bird and killed it, maintaining that the bird, knowing nothing concerning its own fate, could not possibly predict that of others. This brief anecdote is characteristic of the Hebrew's aversion to superstition. Hecateus (9) also narrates that among the Hebrew emigrants there was one chief-priest, Hezekiah, who was learned, eloquent, and conversant with the Greek. He had with him the Hebrew Scriptures and expounded them to the Greeks There can be no doubt that, in the long intercourse in war and peace with Persians and Greeks, and especially from and after the time of Alexander, the Hebrews, or rather the learned among them, became well acquainted with the Greek language, so that Aristotle could also converse with a Hebrew, and confess that he and other philosophers had learned much of him. Therefore, Hebrews could easily emigrate to Egypt and fraternize with the Macedonians.

15. FINAL PARTITION OF THE EMPIRE.

In the year 302 B. C., four of the new kings, viz.: Seleucus, Ptolemy, Cassander and Lysimachus, conspired against Antigonus and his son, Demetrius, and succeeded the next year in overthrowing and slaying the aged Antigonus. Now the empire of Alexander was finally divided, so that Cassander and Lysimachus divided among themselves the European portion of the empire, Seleucus received Asia to the Indus River, and Ptolemy Egypt, Lybia, Arabia, Cœlosyria and Palestine. This last partition brought Palestine permanently under the power of Egyptian rulers.

16. THE SELEUCIDAN ERA.

Seleucus had been appointed governor of Babylon in 321, fled before Antigonus into Egypt in 315, and returned in 312 B. C. This year was made the beginning of the Seleucidan Era, except with the Babylonians, who commenced it

---

(8) Josephus' Contra Apion i. 22. Hecateus of Abdera was a philosopher and statesman in the time of Alexander and Ptolemy Lagi.
(9) Josephus' *Ibid.*

311 B. C. It was in general use both in Asia and Europe to the eleventh century, A. C.

17. STATE OF THE HEBREWS, 300 B. C.

The State of the Hebrews at the close of this turbulent third of a century was decidedly improved. The temple service was not interrupted for a day by the inroads of Greek idolatry in Asia. The succession of high priests was legitimate, from father to son. Jaddua died 321 B. C. and was succeeded by his son, Onias (*Elhanan*), who remained in office to the year 300 B. C., when he died and was succeeded by his aged son, Simon, surnamed the Just, who appears to have been the chief of the nation during the whole of this turbulent time. The city of Jerusalem counted 120,000 inhabitants, and had a circumference of fifty furlongs or 35,000 feet, says Hecateus, which appears to have included the various suburbs. The territory of Palestine, as established by Alexander, extended north to beyond 33° North Latitude and south to nearly 31° North Latitude, with the Idumeans in the south-eastern corner, and a Hebrew population of perhaps two millions, protected by several fortified cities, and in possession of one city on the Mediterranean Sea, Joppe. The two great powers now existing, Egypt and Syria, were both very friendly to the Hebrews. Ptolemy also treated them well in Egypt. Seleucus treated them no less generously. In the many cities which he built, and also in Antioch, on the Orontes River, which he built on the spot of the ancient Riblah (10) and made his capital, and of which Daphne was a suburb, he planted Hebrews from the East, and gave them equal rights with the Macedonians. This brought the Hebrews from the distant East again, and in large numbers, to Syria and Asia Minor, and in direct contact with the Greeks. The Samaritans and Idumeans could no longer molest the Hebrews. The former had been disarmed by Alexander, and now emigrated to Egypt in large numbers; and the latter had been enfeebled by Antigonus. No change in the internal government of the Hebrews had taken place. They maintained their freedom in the exercise of their religion, the administration of justice and public instruction, paid tribute to Ptolemy as they did to Persia, and left to the king the military power and the protection of the country.

(10) Sanhedrin 96 *b*.

CHAPTER VII.

Palestine Under Egyptian Kings.

1. KINGS OF EGYPT.

All kings of Egypt after Ptolemy, the son of Lagus, whom the Rhodians surnamed Soter the Savior, up to its annexation to Rome, were called Ptolemy. The Ptolemys of this period were:

1. Ptolemy Soter, - - to 284 B. C.
2. Ptolemy Philadelphus, - " 246 " "
3. Ptolemy Euergetes, - " 221 " "
4. Ptolemy Philopator, - - " 204 " "
5. Ptolemy Epiphanes, - " 180 " "
6. Ptolemy Philometor, - " 145 " "

Their capital was Alexandria. They were unlimited monarchs and gods. Besides Philopator, all of them were favorably inclined to the Hebrews, whose rights and privileges they respected, and interfered not with their internal development in religion, public instruction and the administration of justice, either in Palestine or outside thereof. The Hebrews were a State in the State of the Ptolemys, to which they were bound by the tribute they paid, and the military service which they rendered. These kings Grecized Egypt in religion, art, science and social forms, and gave the impulse to a new state of science, especially in mathematics, mechanics, astronomy, cosmology, geography, criticism, grammar and eclectic philosophy, as also in botany and zoology. Euclid was born in Alexandria (about 300 B. C.), and taught mathematics in its famous school. At the same time Archimedes (born 287 B. C.) lived and taught at Syracuse. Great expeditions by land and sea were undertaken in the interest of science. The great canal, connecting the Nile with the Red Sea, was rebuilt, and one for large ships added. Observatories and colossal lighthouses were erected like that of Pharus. Alexandria was the center of commerce and science. There were the Serapeum, the Museum and the Great Library at Bruchium and Serapeum, which Ptolemy Soter started. In the museum a number of learned men were supported by the king to discuss the sciences and to advance them. So while philosophy, poetry, the fine arts, virtue, honesty, purity, freedom and religion were rapidly declining, commerce, wealth, science and the mechanical arts just as rapidly advanced and shed their luster over all empires of antiquity, so that we still largely subsist on the sciences built up in Alexandria.

2. SIMON THE JUST.

The Hebrews of Palestine intimately connected with Egypt and in constant communication with their brethren in Syria and Asia Minor, soon felt the Greeizing influence and the approach of the prevailing corruption. Simon the Just, who was a great priest and a wise governor, had made it his motto: "The world stands upon three things: the Law, worship and charity" (*Aboth* i. 2); the Law to govern the land in justice and equity; the worship to connect it with God and virtue; and charity to unite the human family. He repaired the temple, now over 200 years old, added to its fortifications and enlarged its reservoir. He repaired the walls of Jerusalem and re-fortified it, and was considered the last of the great and saintly high priests (1), as he was the last president of the Great Synod. He enforced the laws of Levitical cleanness as Ezra did, and, like him, made the sacrifice of the Red Heifer (or two, *Parah* iii. 5), to obtain its ashes of purification; still he opposed the ascetic practices of the Nazarites (2), and but once ate of a Nazarite sacrifice (3). In after times this Simon became almost mythical (4), and the myths concerning him show that he was considered the last high priest in whom learning, piety,

---

(1) Ben Sira 1.; Josephus' Antiquities xii. ii. 5 and iv. 1; and Aboth i. 2.
(2) Numbers vi.
(3) *Tosephta* in *Nazir* iv. and *Yerushalmi ibid* i. 6.
(4) *Yerushalmi in Yoma* v. 3 (and Tosephta ii.); vi. 3; *Ibid in Sotah* ix. 14; and *Tosephta Ibid* xiii. In Yoma vi. 3, a quarrel between Simon and his brother, Onias, is noticed, which occasioned the latter to retire into Egypt, and to build an altar there.

patriotism and statesmanship were united. After him the decline of this period begins.

3. CLOSE OF THE PROPHETICAL CANON.

In the time of Simon the Just, the Great Synod established the Prophetical Canon by taking the Post-Mosaic history from the Book of Ezra, and by authenticating and transcribing in the square Hebrew letters the ancient prophetical orations of Isaiah, Jeremiah, Ezekiel and the Twelve Minor Prophets. This was done to give authority to those books, to introduce them for public readings in the synagogues, and to give them authority and circulation among the people. In all public readings, however, the Law had the precedence, a section from the Prophets closed the exercise, and was, therefore, called *Haphtorah*, the closing exercise (5). The order of the prophetical books was Joshua, Judges, Samuel, Kings, Jeremiah, Hezekiah, Isaiah and the Twelve Minor Prophets, beginning with Hosea and closing with Malachi (6). The Macedonian invasion and wars carried into Asia with the Greek culture and idolatry, a moral corruption, against which the powerful words of the ancient prophets must have been considered most effective. Therefore, the fourteenth chapter was added to the Book of Zachariah. This chapter was the speech of one of the last prophets who had seen the wars of Alexander and his successors, and the migration of the Hebrews to Egypt. In that tumultuous time, he predicts the final triumph of Monotheism and threatens all transgressors with the divine vengeance, also those of Egypt, who would not come at least once a year to Jerusalem to worship the Lord of Hosts in his holy temple. Those men of the Great Synod closed the Prophetical Canon with the impressive admonition: " Remember the Law of Moses, my servant, which I have commanded him at Horeb for all Israel (also those in foreign lands), ordinances and statutes. Behold, I send you Elijah, the Prophet (men zealous, bold, patriotic and godly like him), before the coming of the great and tremendous day of Jehovah (to crush wickedness, corruption and idolatry): and he shall bring back the heart of the fathers to their children, and the heart of the children to their fathers, that I smite not the land with destruction " (the rising generation having already been infatuated with Grecian frivolity and laxity of morals).

(5) See Rapaport's *Erech Milin*, Art. i. אפטרא.
(6) *Baba Bathra* 13 b and 14 a.

4. THE ORIGIN OF THE SEPTUAGINT.

Simon the Just was dead (292 B. C.), his son, Onias, was a minor, and so Eleazar, the brother of Simon, ascended to the high priesthood. Two great events in the history of the Hebrews took place under this man's administration: the establishment of the Sanhedrin and the Greek translation of the Pentateuch. All ancient testimony concerning a Greek translation of the Pentateuch (7) agrees to establish the fact that Ptolemy Philadelphus, advised by his learned librarian, Demetrius Phalerus, desired a Greek translation of the Laws of Moses for the great library. Aside from all religious and literary standpoints, an intelligent king must have felt the necessity of possessing, in his own language, the laws which governed so large and influential a portion of the population under his scepter. Therefore, he obtained authorized translators from Palestine, appointed by the high priest Eleazar. It having been maintained that there were seventy-two of those translators, the translation was called the Septuagint, to which, in aftertimes, translations of the Prophets, Hagiography and the Apocrypha were added, and the whole collection retained the name of Septuagint. The copy of the Laws of Moses as translated for Ptolemy has been lost, and the Septuagint extant shows in some passages translations from manuscripts or traditional readings, varying from the authenticated copy of Ezra and the Great Synod (8). The Hebrews of Egypt, at the time of Philadelphus, had no need yet of a translated Pentateuch, nor did Aristobul, in the time of Philometor, use it; therefore, the Septuagint was not protected against interpolations with the same religious zeal as was the copy of Ezra in the hand of the priests, Levites and Scribes, which was read publicly in the temple, synagogues and schools, where every change, however slight, would have been noticed. When the Egyptian Hebrews began to use the Septuagint in place of the original, it had already assumed its extant form.

5. THE PHILOSOPHY OF PALESTINE CARRIED INTO EGYPT.

Every religious reformation in history begins with a new translation of the Bible. This was also the case with the

---

(7) Aristeas, in his letter; Aristobul, the founder of the Alexandrian philosophy of religion in the time of Ptolemy Philometor, Philo, Josephus, Eusebius, Clemens, Hyronimus and the Talmud.

(8) See August Ferdinand Daehne's Geschichtliche Darstellung der juedish-alexandrinischen Religions-Philosophie; Dr. Z. Frankel's Vorstudien zu der Septuagint; Dr. Abraham Geiger's Uhrschrift und Uebersetzungen der Bibel; Zunz, Herzfeld, Graetz, Jost and Raphael.

Septuagint, which carried the elements of the Palestinean philosophy into Egypt and disclosed it to the Greeks. That the Hebrews had a philosophy of their own, admits of no doubt. That they, from and after Ezra, philosophized, is evident from the Hebrew literature of the Medo-Persian Period, which contains all the elements of philosophy traceable in the Septuagint. The translators made some intentional changes (9), mostly directed against Polytheism, and could not avoid carrying into their work the philosophical views of their age and country, as most all translators invariably do. The development of this new philosophy is to be noticed hereafter.

6. Ptolemy's Gifts to the High Priest.

Aristeas and Josephus describe royal gifts sent by Ptolemy to the high priest, and the epistles of both on this occasion. Remarkable among those gifts was a golden table of excellent workmanship, and two cisterns of gold, both of which are so minutely described by Josephus that he must have seen them (10), and this is no mean evidence in establishing the fact that the Greek version of the Pentateuch was made by order of the king.

7. Hebrews Freed from Slavery.

Ptolemy Philadelphus emancipated all Hebrew slaves, and paid for them a ransom of 460 talents; and he, as well as his son and successor, always remained a patron and friend of the Hebrews. The generosity of this Ptolemy has been lauded by his biographers, and his wealth was prodigious. He is reported to have left in the treasury after his death, seven hundred and forty thousand Egyptian talents. The Egyptian talent being $3,852, one-fifth more than the Attic, the whole of his cash wealth would have amounted to $2,840,480,000. Jewish history gratefully mentions Philadelphus among the Heathen benefactors of Israel. He, in connection with Demetrius Phalerus, by the Greek version of the Laws of Moses, opened a new phase of culture; the Heathens of the Greek tongue became acquainted with the Hebrew's Bible, and this was the beginning to the end of Heathenism in those countries.

---

(9) Meguillah ix., fifteen such changes are noticed. Yerushalmi ibid notices thirteen; so also in *Mechilta*. Characteristic is the change of ארנבת, "the hare," among the unclean animals, which they replaced by other words on account of LAGUS, "hare," the grandfather of Philadelphus.

(10) Josephus' Antiquities xii. ii. 9 and 10.

8. The Cities Built.

Philadelphus built many cities and temples, and was as active in advancing the interests of commerce as that of literature and science. He turned the course of trade from Tyre to Alexandria by two new cities on the Red Sea, Berenise and Myon Hormus, connected by a highway through the wilderness, with Coptus on the Nile. In Palestine also, he built a port near the ancient Acco, on the Mediterranean Sea, above Mt. Carmel, which was called Ptolemais. West of the Jordan he rebuilt the ancient Rabbah of Ammon, and called it Philadelphia.

9. Origin of the Sanhedrin.

The origin of the Synedrion, Synhedrion, or Sanhedrin, consisting of seventy or seventy-two members, replacing the Great Synod, of one hundred and twenty members, occurred soon after the year 292 B. C., under the administration of the high priest Eleazar. In support of this fact, the following points must be taken into consideration:

The Great Synod closed its existence, with Simon the Just, before 292 B. C. (*Aboth* i. 2). Josephus, the Mishna and all other sources agree that Simon I. was the high priest who was called the Just.

The Laws of Moses, together with the enactments and institutions of Ezra and Nehemiah, were the inviolable laws of the land; these laws, however, could not be enforced without a supreme and sovereign council at the head of the commonwealth (11).

In the rabbinical sources, the perpetual existence of this sovereign council is everywhere taken for granted; in Josephus and the Books of the Maccabees, it is mentioned wherever occasion offers, previous to and during the Asmonean revolution (12).

An interregnum between the Great Synod and the Sanhedrin could have been brought about only by a violent political eruption, or by a despotic act of one of the kings of Egypt; neither of which did take place from 300 to 200 B. C., while Antiochus the Great, in 203 B. C., already grants privileges to the Senate of the Hebrews (Josephus' Ant. xii. iii. 3).

It is evident that the body highest in authority among

---

(11) Exodus iii. 16; iv. 29; xxiv. 1, 9; Numbers xi. 16; Deuter. xvii. 8.
(12) Josephus' Antiquit. xii. iii. 3; and xii. iv. 11, II. Maccabees iv. 44; Ibid xiv. 37; III. Maccabees i. 8.

the Hebrews, at the time of the high priest Eleazar, consisted of seventy-two men, as Aristeas, Philo and Josephus agree that seventy-two translators, "six of every tribe," were sent to Philadelphus by Eleazar. Had the body holding the highest authority been composed of a larger number of men, Eleazar would certainly have sent a corresponding number of translators. If the Aristeas letter be considered spurious, it could not be supposed that Josephus would have adopted the phrase, "six of every tribe," if he had not known that in the time of Eleazar the geographical tribe division and the supreme body of seventy-two members existed.

In the Mishna, the simultaneous existence of the Sanhedrin and the twelve tribes division is always presupposed (13), although this distinction was soon forgotten in foreign lands, except in Mesopotamia (14). Perea and Galilee, the most populous provinces of Palestine, were certainly inhabited by people of the ten tribes, who never left their original homes, and those who came back from the exile to claim their properties. Their only title was vested in their genealogies; hence every land holder anyhow was obliged to uphold his genealogy, and this preserved the geographical tribe divisions (15).

When Alexander added Samaria, and with it Perea and Galilee, to Judea, the twelve tribes of Israel were re-united again, and the Great Synod could exist no longer, because it consisted exclusively of the aristocracy of Juda, Benjamin and Levi. It had to be replaced by the old Council of Elders, "six of each tribe," which was done in the time of the high priest Eleazar; and this Council of Elders received the Greek name of Synedrion or Sanhedrin.

In memory of this re-enfranchisement of all Hebrews in the land and their perfect equalization, the Feast of Xylophory, on the Fifteenth day of Ab, was introduced and kept to the last days of this commonwealth (Wars II., xvii. 6) as the principal feast of that kind. The institution was established by Nehemiah (Nehem. x. 35), and the privilege of bringing the wood for the altar was claimed by certain families of Juda, Benjamin and Levi (Mishna *Taanith* iv. 5); except the Fifteenth Day of Ab, which was Xylophory

---

(13) Sanhedrin i. 5; Horioth i. 5.

(14) *Berachoth*, 16 a: "We know not whether we descend from Reuben or from Simeon."

(15) I. Chronicles ix. 1; Ezra ii. and Nehemiah vii.; Mishnah *Kiddushin* iv. 1. According to R. Juda (*Yerushalmi Ibid*), those remaining between the Euphrates and Tigris also kept intact their genealogy.

(*Korban Ezim*) for all, especially for those families who brought wood to Jerusalem, when Ptolemy Soter's invading army (or the Antigonus invasion in 296 B. C.) prevented the pilgrims from doing so. That feast was of special importance, "Because on that day the Tribes were permitted to come one into the other" (16). This certainly refers to the emancipation of Perea and Galilee, in consequence of which the Sanhedrin was established.

10. ORGANIZATION OF THE SANHEDRIN.

The Sanhedrin, after it had been convoked by the chief-magistrate of the land, met daily (Sabbaths and holidays excepted) in the temple, in the hall called *Lishchath Haygazith*. Twenty-three members made a quorum. The Senators (*Zekenim*) sat in a hollow semi-circle, with the presiding officer in the center, and three rows of assessors before them. The President was called NASSI, "prince," afterward HEBER; the AB-BETH-DIN, "Chief-Justice," was next to him in rank. Two scribes, the Hazan, "Sergeant-at-Arms," the *Shamesh*, "Warden," and the *Methurgamon*, "Orator," were the other officers of that body. The Hazan opened, and the Methurgamon closed, the sessions. During this entire period, the high priests presided over the Sanhedrin, and it was, therefore, called בית דין של כהנים גדולים "The High Court of the High Priests." The high priest, Eleazar, was its first President, and Antigonus of Sochu, was, perhaps, its first chief-justice. This high priest, in after times, was famous for fabulous wealth, humility and learning, and was called Eleazar Harsi; and this chief-justice became the founder of a new school. The manner of electing or appointing senators is unknown; in after times, they were appointed by ordination and promotion. The senators filled vacancies by electing candidates who had received the ordination and had been promoted from court to court. The Sanhedrin was the highest judiciary and legislative authority in the Hebrew commonwealth, and claimed also the right of appointing the high priest, declaring war, deciding the controversies of tribes, instituting criminal courts for districts or cities, called Minor Sanhedrin of Twenty-Three, and establishing the limits of the city of Jerusalem.

---

(16) See *Meguillath Taanith* v., which explains itself by the above paragraph; also the two Talmuds, *Taanith* 28 and *Yerushalmi Ibid* ix. 7.

11. THE SCHOOL OF ANTIGONUS.

The traditional material, resulting from the enactments and decisions of the Great Synod from 455 to 292 B. C., must have increased considerably in bulk and importance. It was part of the law of the land, the jurisprudence and theology of the age. The highest authority for the knowledge of the traditions, the laws and customs of the nation, was the Sanhedrin, and in that body the NASSI and AB-BETH-DIN. But after Simon the Just, none of the high priests or any other person of political authority was distinguished for that species of learning; so that it is maintained in the history of the traditions that the prophets delivered it to the Great Synod, this Synod to Simon the Just, he to Antigonus, of Sochu, and both to Jose b. Joezer, who lived to 162 B. C., and Antigonus died 263 B. C. It is evident, therefore, that the traditions were transmitted in the school of which Antigonus was the founder. The scribes looked not to the Sanhedrin for the highest authority in the traditions; the school of Antigonus assumed that authority (17). In this school, John, and his son, Mattathia, the Asmoneans, Jose b. Joezer and Jose b. John (perhaps a brother of Mattathia), were the most prominent bearers of the traditions (18). Therefore, when the rebellion broke out and the party of the traditions rose against the Grecizing government party, Jose b. Joezer and his colleague appear as the exponents of the traditions and the heads *de jure* of the Sanhedrin, although they had no political authority and were called SCHOLASTS in the history of the traditions.

12. THE RISE OF HASSIDIM AND GRECIANS.

In the school of Antigonus, another tradition maintains, a party rose that denied future reward and punishment; and there can be no doubt that the parties that afterward fought out the civil war had their origin in the prevailing circumstances and the school of Antigonus, the center of

---

(17) This is stated plainly in *Yerushalmi* SOTAH ix. 10, viz: That all heads of the Sanhedrin after Jose b. Joezer down to R. Akiba were no scholasts (אישכולה) because they were also recognized as the political heads of the nation (פרנסית ישמשי). But Jose b. Joezer, and his predecessors up to Simon the Just and R. Akiba and his successors, who possessed no political authority, were scholasts (אשכלות), the heads of schools. This includes, also, Antigonus, of Sochu, as the head of a school, noticed, also, elsewhere in the Traditions. THEMURAH 15 b.

(18) Yuchasin, Shalsheleth Hackabala and Seder Haddoroth I., Art. Jochanan, father of Mattathia, Antigonus and Jose b. Joezer.

the traditions. That teacher is reported to have said: "Be ye not like servants who attend to the master for the sake of receiving a reward; but be ye like servants who attend to the master, not for the sake of receiving any reward, and let the fear of heaven be upon you." This was understood by one portion of his disciples to be a denial of future reward and punishment. This, however, was only a link in the chain of a new creed which gradually formed in the minds of Grecizing Hebrews, and led on the one side to apostacy and on the other to the rebellion of the Asmoneans. Jerusalem and its temple had become the center for millions of Hebrews in the Egyptian and Syrian empires, and in consequence thereof the wealth of nations was poured into the Hebrew capital, and commerce with foreign countries increased rapidly. Merchants coming in contact with Alexandria and Antioch, and going with Greeks and Macedonians to the distant East and West, were, perhaps, the first to Grecize at home. The men in power by royal appointments, in contact with courts and courtiers, were naturally Grecized, and exercised that influence on their fellow-citizens. The spirit of the age was Grecian, and so was the aristocracy in general. Gradually those Hebrews yielded to the foreign influences and attempted to combine the Hebrew and Greek standpoints, revelation and philosophy, absolutism centering in the king-god and freedom centering in the Law of Moses, the sensual culte of the beautiful and the traditional worship of the One God, frivolity and earnestness, laxity and austerity of morals. The progress of the Grecian party pressed the national Hebrews to extreme orthodoxy, firm adherence to the laws and traditions, and the exclusion of the Greek elements, until finally, two distinct parties, with well-defined principles, existed among the Hebrews, viz.: the HASSIDIM, " the law-abiding men," also called יראי יהוה " the worshipers of Jehovah;" and the GRECIANS, or Hellenists. The former were the conservatives and had with themselves the scribes and the school of Antigonus; and the latter were the progressionists, backed by wealth, State power and the spirit of the age. Up to the year 175 B. C., the high priest and Sanhedrin stood between those two parties to maintain the peace; but after that time the high priest also embraced the cause of the Grecians, which brought on the revolution.

13. THE PRINCIPLES OF THE PARTIES.

The principles of the two parties, as developed to the end of this period, were the following:

HASSIDIM.	GRECIANS.
1. Sinai, Revelation, the THORAH is the supreme guide of man and society.	1. Wisdom or philosophy is the supreme guide of man and society.
2. The laws and customs of Israel, as expounded by the proper authorities, prescribe the duties of the Israelite; the taxes and the military service belong to the king.	2. The king's laws and decrees prescribe the duties of the Israelite, outside of his religious belief.
3. The study and practice of the Law is the highest virtue.	3. The cultivation of wisdom is the highest virtue.
4. Virtue or righteousness is its own object, independent of any happiness it may or may not bring.	4. The object of virtue or righteousness is pleasure and happiness.
5. There is a just reward or punishment in life eternal.	5. There is no reward and no punishment in life eternal.

In Palestine the parties pressed each other to the extremes of the Asmonean revolution. In Egypt, many of the Hebrews deserted the ranks of Israel and identified themselves with the Macedonians (19).

14. THE DAVIDIAN ARISTOCRACY REVIVED.

In the year 277 B. C., the high priest Eleazar died. He was succeeded by his uncle, Menasseh, who kept this holy office to the year 250 B. C., and yet nothing is known about him. He was succeeded by Onias II., the son of Simon the Just, who remained in office from 250 to 218 B. C., and history has nothing to record of him, except that he loved money, and in his old age was indolent and careless. He neglected to pay the annual tax of twenty talents of silver to the king. Ptolemy Euergetes sent an ambassador to Jerusalem with a threatening message. Onias did not care for the office, and adopted no measures to adjust the matter. He had a nephew, Joseph, whose mother was the sister of Onias (20), and whose father, Tobiah, or Tobias, was of the House of David (21). He, a man of prudence and courage, offered to go to Alexandria and settle the matter with the king. He obtained the consent of the people and high

---

(19) I. Maccabees i. 11, 43; III. Maccabees i. 3; vii. 10.
(20) Josephus' Antiq. xii. iv. 2.
(21) Luke iii. 24, 25; Philo's Brevarium; Herzfeld's *Geschichte*, d. J., Vol. I.

priest, and went to Alexandria. By gifts and shrewdness, he succeeded, over many competitors, in being appointed collector of taxes in Phœnicia, Cœlosyria and Palestine, and went back to Asia with two thousand soldiers to collect the king's taxes. He was a merciless publican to many a city, especially to Askelon and Scythopolis, but remained in his office for twenty-two years (225 to 203), till Antiochus the Great conquered Palestine, and became very rich. This, for some time, revived the power of the Davidians in Jerusalem, which had been overcome by Nehemiah. There were now two political powers in Jerusalem, the high priest and the tax collector, whose conflict will be noticed below.

15. Antiochus the Great Seizes Palestine and Loses it Again.

The following kings reigned in Syria before this time:

1. Seleucus Nicator - - to 280 B. C.
2. Antiochus Soter - - - " 261 " "
3. Antiochus Theus - - " 246 " "
4. Seleucus Callinicus - - " 226 " "
5. Seleucus Ceraunus - - " 223 " "

The brother of this last Seleucus, and sixth king of Syria, was Antiochus the Great, who was particularly a friend and benefactor of the Hebrews. In 219 and 218 B. C., Antiochus took from Ptolemy Philopator Cœlosyria, Phœnicia, Galilee, Samaria and the land west of the Jordan. The Hebrews had suffered much during the two years' war. The next year Antiochus had advanced as far as Raphia, where Philopator defeated him and retook his lost provinces in Asia. In Raphia, a heathenized Hebrew, Dositheus, had saved Philopator's life; besides, after his victory, an embassy from the Sanhedrin came to him with congratulations and gifts. Therefore, he went to Jerusalem and sacrificed to the God of Israel in the temple when Simon II. was high priest (22) the first year, as his sires had done before him.

16. Philopator Discomfited in the Temple.

The king, having for the first time seen this temple, insisted upon entering its *sanctum sanctorum*. All representations and supplications were in vain; he insisted upon satisfying his curiosity. Neither the entreaty of the priests and elders nor the lamentations and prayers of the multi-

---

(22) III. Maccabees i.

tude, changed his resolution. Philopator entered the temple, surrounded by his friends and guards; but no sooner had he stepped over its threshold than he fell helpless to the ground, and his attendants were obliged to carry him out of the sanctuary; and thus discomfited, he left the city with threats of vengeance on his lips.

17. Persecution of the Egyptian Hebrews.

Philopator having returned home, resolved upon taking vengeance on the Egyptian Hebrews, all of whom he had brought to Alexandria, and commanded them all to be killed by enraged elephants. They were saved, however, by a miracle, says our Egyptian narrator in the third book of the Maccabees, and Philopator became a friend and patron of the Hebrews after that, although they did not love him nor his successor, and soon embraced the opportunity to demonstrate their displeasure.

18. Antiochus the Great Seizes Palestine the Second Time.

In the year 204 B. C., having lived thirty-seven years of intemperance and debauchery, Philopator died, and left his crown to his son, Ptolemy Epiphanes, then five years old. Antiochus the Great, in league with the king of Macedon, made war upon Egypt with the intention of dividing the kingdom of the Ptolemys between himself and the king of Macedon. He marched into Cœlosyria and Palestine and occupied them in 203 and 202 B. C. After he had beaten the Egyptian General, Scopas, in the north, 200 B. C., the Hebrews invited him to Jerusalem, and submitted the kingdom to him, after it had been one hundred and one years an Egyptian province. It was in the time when Scipio had defeated Hannibal in Africa, and thus closed the second Punic war. Hannibal came as a fugitive to Antiochus, in whose service he closed his eventful life. This final victory of Antiochus over Egypt was also a victory of the Hassidim over the Grecians in Palestine; for the concessions made by him to the Hebrews were very much in favor of the Hassidim, as shall be narrated in the next chapter.

CHAPTER VIII.

Palestine Under Syrian Rulers.

1. ANTIOCHUS MAGNUS, A BENEFACTOR OF THE HEBREWS.

Antiochus favored the Hebrews because they had embraced his cause against the Egyptians, received and treated him well in Jerusalem, and assisted him in expelling the Egyptian garrison. He admired them " on account of their piety toward God." This admiration was made traditional at the Persian court, by Cyrus, and among the Macedonian rulers of Egypt and Syria, by Alexander. Palestine had suffered terribly by the Egypto-Syrian wars, and lately, by Philopator's cruelties and the villainies of his rapacious general, Scopas. Therefore, Antiochus settled a large income on the temple, granted special privileges to the priests, scribes and the senators, and provided for the repair of the temple and its cloisters. He freed the city of Jerusalem for three successive years from taxes, reduced the tribute of the land by one-third, set all captive Hebrews free, restored to them all confiscated property, and re-confirmed their rights and privileges to live according to their own laws. When, afterward, Ptolemy Epiphanes was given half of the income from Palestine, Antiochus wrote him an epistle, informing him of these privileges granted to the Hebrews and requiring him to respect them (1). He also commanded all his subjects that none should go in the temple beyond the boundary line established by the laws of the Hebrews (referring to Philopator's sacrilege); that no carcass or hide of any unclean animal should be brought to the city of Jerusalem, and no such animal be bred up there, all under the penalty of three thousand drachmas of silver (2). He placed no

---

(1) Antiq. xii. iii. 3.
(2) It was also prohibited, afterward, to keep a dog in the city of Jerusalem.

less confidence in the Hebrews outside of Palestine. When a rebellion broke out in Lydia and Phrygia, he commanded two thousand Hebrew families from Mesopotamia and Babylon to be placed in those countries, promising them the right to live according to their own laws, land for their husbandry and the culture of wine, material support to start, and the freedom from taxation for ten years; because, he said in his epistle, " they will be well-disposed guardians of our possessions because of their piety toward God, and because I know that my predecessors have borne witness to them, that they are faithful, and with alacrity do what they are desired to do" (3).

2. A Royal Marriage.

In the year 193 b. c., Antiochus gave in marriage his daughter, Cleopatra, to Ptolemy Epiphanes, then seventeen years old, and settled upon her as a dowry, half of the income derived from the provinces of Cœlosyria and Palestine, which, nevertheless, remained *de facto* Syrian provinces.

3. Conflict with the Romans.

The Roman power, after the second Punic war, made itself felt in Greece and Asia Minor. Therefore, already in the year 202 b. c., the Egyptian rulers had invoked the protection of Rome for their infant king, and promised them the guardianship and the regency during the king's minority. The Romans accepting this offer, sent ambassadors to Philip, king of Macedon, and to Antiochus the Great, to inform them of this fact. This was the beginning of the conflict which lasted to the year 190 b. c., when, under the two brothers, Lucius Scipio and Scipio Africanus, the Romans overthrew the army of Antiochus in the battle of Magnesia, and forced him to accept disgraceful terms of peace, with the loss of all Asia Minor up to Mt. Taurus, and the payment of 500 talents now, 2,500 more on the ratification of the peace by the senate, and then one thousand tallents every year for the next twelve years. The treaty was ratified in the year 189 b. c. Antiochus outlived this catastrophe to 187 b. c., when he was slain in the province of Elymais in the act of plundering a Bel temple. His oldest son, Seleucus, succeeded him as king of Syria, and was called Seleucus Philopator.

---

(3) Josephus' Antiq. xii. iii. 4.

4. Hyrcan, the Son of the Tax Collector.

Simon II. died 195 B. C. and was succeeded by his son, Onias III., as high priest. Both these high priests are lauded as men of piety and patriotism in comparison with their successors. But the aristocracy of Jerusalem began to be ill-behaved; many of them were selfish, faithless and, at last, treacherous. The demoralization began in the House of David, and poisoned also the family of Aaron. The tax collector, Joseph, son of Tobias, who was of the House of David, reached the zenith of power in Jerusalem by birth, wealth, position and the indolence of the high priests. He had seven sons by one wife, and an eighth, Hyrcan, begotten in incest with his niece. He grasped the momentous opportunity when Antiochus was dead, and the queen of Egypt the same year gave birth to her first son (afterward called Philometor), to secure again the collectorship of Palestine. He was too old to go, like other courtiers, to Alexandria to congratulate the king and queen. His seven sons refused to go on that mission; Hyrcan only would undertake the enterprise. He was young, shrewd, intriguing and bold, and succeeded in ingratiating himself with the queen and the king. Instead of advancing the cause of his father, he obtained for himself the lucrative appointment over a number of competitors, and squandered one thousand talents of his father's money. His brothers were enraged at his conduct and success. On his return to Jerusalem, they met him at a distance outside the city and a fight ensued. Hyrcan slew two of his brothers and several of their attendants, and went on to Jerusalem. Seeing himself confronted by his angry father and surviving brothers, who had the support of the Sanhedrin, Hyrcan retired with his men to the southern frontiers beyond Jordan, in the vicinity of Heshbon, and there built a castle between rocks, well fortified, and laid out magnificent gardens in the valley. He called this place Tyre, and was there outside of the jurisdiction of the Sanhedrin, a terror to the Arabs up to 175 B. C., when he, out of fear of the power of Antiochus Epiphanes, committed suicide, leaving his paternal heritage in the temple treasury at Jerusalem (4).

5. The Sons of Tobias.

Onias III. regained some of the political power lost by his immediate predecessors. When, after the death of Jo-

---

(4) Josephus' Antiq. xii. iv.; II. Maccabees iii. 11.

seph, the tax collector, his sons, called the Sons of Tobias, disputed the high priest's authority, Onias, supported by the Sanhedrin, subdued them by force of arms, and at last ejected them from the city. They were the first to turn traitors against their country and their religion, and encouraged Antiochus Epiphanes to invade Palestine and to apostatize its people (5). This was certainly one of the causes that the House of David, with its dynastical claims, disappeared so entirely from the records of the Hebrews, that up to the fall of Jerusalem no mention is made of them in Palestine.

6. The Spartans and the Hebrews.

The fame of the Hebrews, by the channels of commerce, literature and migration, had reached into Greece, and the king *de facto*, Aretus or Darius, of Lacedemonia, sent an ambassador, Demotoles, and an epistle to Onias III., in which it was set forth how the discovery had been made by that people that they were descendants of Abraham, and therefore, an alliance between the two nations was proposed.

7. Heliodorus Discomfited in the Temple.

King Seleucus was well-disposed toward the Hebrews. The aristocracy of Jerusalem, however, continued to harass Onias in the discharge of his duties. There was one, Simon, a Benjaminite, who was one of the officers in the temple. He wanted of Onias the office of market master, which was not given to him, and Simon turned traitor. He went to Appollonius, the governor of Cœlosyria and Phœnicia, and informed him that the treasury of the temple in Jerusalem contained an enormous sum of money. Appollonius reported it to the king, who sent his treasurer, Heliodorus, to investigate the matter. He came stealthily to Jerusalem and was kindly received by the high priest. On communicating to him the object of his visit, he was told that the treasury contained no more than 400 talents of silver and 200 talents of gold, which was there mostly for safe keeping for widows and orphans, and some of which belonged to Hyrcan and to others. Heliodorus insisted upon going into the temple and inspecting its treasury. All protestations and prayers were fruitless. When Heliodorus, followed by some of his soldiers, entered the temple treasury, he was met by three gigantic men; one on horseback, in golden ornaments. The horse reared, came down on

---

(5) Josephus' Antiq. xii. iv. 11, and v. 1; Wars 1. i. 1.

Heliodorus, threw him to the ground, and the two men chastised him severely. Heliodorus was carried away speechless, and his men were stunned. He left Jerusalem without having seen the temple treasury. Simon maintained there was nothing supernatural in all that; it was all the contrivance of Onias, who was a traitor to the king. So Onias had two sets of enemies at Antioch, Simon and the Sons of Tobias. They had their followers in Jerusalem, who would continually raise disturbances, and it came to assassinations. Onias, dreading the probable interference of Appollonius, and ignorant of the fact that his worst enemies and traitors were his own brothers, went to Antioch to the king with the prayer to restore peace in Jerusalem (6).

8. Antiochus Epiphanes, King, and Jason, High Priest.

Meanwhile, the political situation in Antioch changed. Heliodorus raised a successful sedition against Seleucus, who was slain and the regicide usurped the crown of Syria. However, the king's brother, Antiochus, speedily returned from Rome and slew Heliodorus. This prince had been a hostage in Rome for thirteen years. Seleucus had lately sent his son Demetrius there in exchange for Antiochus, who returned in time to avenge his brother's death and to receive the crown of Syria. Having been in Rome so many years, he lost sight of the traditions of his family, and became a terror to the Hebrews. It was before that new king that Onias had to encounter his enemies. His brother, Jason (Jesus, or Joshua), underhandedly, applied to the king to make him high priest, offering him a bribe of 440 talents, for which he asked the privileges of Grecizing the Hebrews and making the citizens of Jerusalem also citizens of Antioch. Jason prevailed. Onias, whose presence in Jerusalem was justly dreaded on account of his popularity, was removed from office and commanded to stay at Antioch. Jason was sent to Jerusalem as high priest, 175 b. c.

9. Jason's Administration.

This first triumph of the Jerusalem aristocracy was not entirely welcome to all of them: for the sons of Tobias did not like Jason, who was not radical enough for them. As a stroke of policy, it must certainly have pleased those who wanted to be like the Greeks, with whom a huge idolatry, frivolity, laxity of morals, Epicurism and skepticism in the

(6) II. Maccabees iii. iv.

beguiling forms of art and under the mask of the beautiful, made up the spirit of the age. The stern Laws of Moses, the institutions of Ezra and Nehemiah, the binding customs and the code of ethics reared on that basis, were in their way, and some of them wanted to see them annulled at once. But this was not in the power of Jason; it was not in the power of any mortal being. Therefore, he, with the same object in view, went to work cautiously and with serpent-like prudence, which the impetuous radicals disliked. He built a *gymnasium* and made it fashionable for the aristocratic youth to attend in the ephebeum, to imitate the Greeks in games and nude exercises, which made it necessary to hide the sign of the Abrahamic covenant by surgical operations (מושך ערלה), and had the effect of withdrawing the young priests from the temple, it appearing despicable to them. Next year he went a step farther. The quinquennial games, in honor of Hercules, being celebrated at Tyre, and the king being present, Jason, attended by his partisans, went there as a spectator, of course, and offered to that deity 3300 drachmas, which the Tyrians were ashamed to accept, and the money was applied to ship building. Notwithstanding all these innovations, the people kept the peace.

10. JOSE BEN JOEZER AND JOSE BEN JOHN.

All of them made two mistakes, viz.: Jerusalem was not Palestine, and the aristocracy was not the Hebrew people. Under such circumstances, Jason certainly could not preside over the Sanhedrin, which was a conservative body, representing all parts of the country. The disciples of Antigonus turned up as heads of the Sanhedrin, viz.: Jose b. Joezer, of Zeredah, in Ephraim (I. Kings x. 13) as the presiding officer, and second to him, Jose ben John of Jerusalem. The former certainly was a son of Aaron and one of the *Hassidim* (חסיד שבכהונה): and the latter appears to have been a brother of Mattathia, the Asmonean, hence, also a priest. They were the bearers and exponents of the traditions received from the school of Antigonus of Sochu. The motto of this Jose b. Joezer was: "Let thy house be the meeting place for the wise, cover thyself with the dust of their feet, and drink with thirst their words" *i. e.*, he advised many private meetings to discuss the public affairs, and urged wise counsel to prevail. He wanted the wise men to lead and the common men to obey in that threatening crisis. His colleague's motto was: "Let thy house be widely open (form no secret societies), let the poor be members of thy household (the rich were corrupted to the core), and converse not too much with the woman" (7). Both mottoes point to revolutionary preparations and the formation of secret societies, although, apparently, the first urges the study of the Law and the second the practice of charity. An ordinance of those heads of the Sanhedrin, preserved in the Talmud (*Sabbath* 14 b), also points to revolutionary preparations. They declared Levitically unclean the land of the Gentiles and all glassware; so that none should leave the country; that the Hebrews in foreign countries should come to Palestine, and none should use glassware, either because it was imported from Syria or in order that none should drink with the Syrians and the Hebrew aristocracy, who used glassware (8).

11. The Appointment of Menelaus.

The differences of the two parties, Hassidim and Grecians, had now taken a definite shape by their representatives, the high priest at the head of the aristocracy and the Jose b. Joezer Sanhedrin at the head of the democracy. The former, however, were not yet united on account of the Sons of Tobias, who disliked Jason. However, this also had to be overcome. Antiochus, who had called himself Epiphanes and wanted to be a god, made preparations to invade Egypt in favor of his young nephew, Ptolemy Philometor, whose mother, Cleopatra, had died (172 B. C.), hoping to get the king and the land in his power. Inspecting the sea coast fortifications, the king came to Joppe and also to Jerusalem, where he had a brilliant reception by Jason and his compatriots. Still, next year (171 B. C.), Jason sent his brother, Menelaus (Elhanan or Onias), to the king to pay the tribute. Menelaus, by flattery and the offer of 300 tal-

---

(7) Aboth i. 4, 5, האשה, "the woman." This is taken from Ben Sira, ix., and refers, most likely, to Cleopatra, the sister of Antiochus Epiphanes, then queen of Egypt, who was friendly to the Hebrews, many of whom may have expected friendly offices of her; but Jose had more confidence in the poor of his own people than in that royal woman.

(8) The ordinances of Jose ben Joezer preserved in the *Mishnah* (Jedaim viii. 4) are three, viz.: that a certain class of locusts (איל קמצא) was lawful food; that the blood and water issuing from the slaughterhouse does not make unclean; and that only he who touches one who is surely dead, is unclean. These must have been made in war time to increase the articles of food, to protect the warriors against the existing laws of Levitical cleanness by touching blood or a slain and dying person or animal, which this ordinance declared as not certainly dead; hence not making one unclean. See *Siphri* in *Chukkath*, 25, אשר ימות, and Jacob Bruell's *Mebo Hammishnah*, p. 25.

ents more per annum than his brother paid, but chiefly by
the influence of the Sons of Tobias and their party, caused
the king to remove Jason from his office and to appoint
Menelaus high priest. Jason, after some resistance, fled
into the land of Ammon, and Menelaus, backed by the
Syrian garrison and the Grecian party, who had promised
to heathenize Jerusalem, was now in power. It was the
policy of Antiochus Epiphanes to Grecize and to unify the
remainder of the Syrian empire, which consisted of a con-
glomeration of nationalities, tongues, traditions and religions. He was misled by the Jerusalem aristocracy into
the belief that this could be done in Palestine also. But
neither he nor they had a correct knowledge of the character of the Hebrews. No actual resistance was offered to
Menelaus and his apostatizing schemes, because the people
outside of Jerusalem had not yet felt the influence of that
new policy.

12. ASSASSINATION OF ONIAS AND THE FIRST MUTINY.

Menelaus had promised more than he could raise. The
captain of the garrison pressed him to pay, which he could
not do; so both of them were summoned to appear before
the king. He went to Cilicia to quell a revolt, and they had
to appear before Andronicus, the temporary regent. Menelaus, by the agency of his brother, Lysimachus, left in his
place in Jerusalem, stole valuable vessels from the temple,
sold them at Tyre and elsewhere, to pay his debt and to
bribe Andronicus, in order to dispose of Onias III., the
leader of the HASSIDIM. Andronicus treacherously slew
Onias, which roused the indignation of Jews and Gentiles
at Antioch against the traitor and assassin, and led to a
mutiny in Jerusalem. The embittered patriots rose against
the sacrilegious thief, Lysimachus, who sent 3,000 men under Tyrannis, to quell the rebellion; but they were overpowered by the people, and Lysimachus was slain beside
the treasury within the temple.

13. MORE OPPRESSION—SENATORS SLAIN.

Antiochus avenged the death of Onias on Andronicus,
who was slain on the spot where he had assassinated the
ex-high priest; but changed not his policy in Jerusalem.
The king soon after came to Tyre (171 B. C.). Here, an embassy of the Sanhedrin, consisting of three senators, appeared before him. They accused Menelaus of being responsible for the mutiny in Jerusalem. Menelaus bribed

Ptolemy Macron, who persuaded the king to absolve Menelaus and to slay the three delegates of the Sanhedrin. The Tyrians, feeling the outrageous injustice done by the king, made a demonstration by giving an honorable burial to the murdered senators. The excitement in Jerusalem was feverish. Sights were seen, predictions made, rebellion was ripe; still Menelaus, protected by the Syrian garrison, was master of the situation.

14. Jason's Return.

The same year Antiochus invaded Egypt. A false rumor of his death was spread in Palestine, over which the Hassidim doubtlessly rejoiced. Jason, seizing upon this opportunity, came with a thousand men to Jerusalem, took it, drove Menelaus into the castle of the Syrian garrison for protection, slew many of his brother's partisans and assumed again the high priesthood.

15. First Slaughter in Jerusalem.

This alarmed Antiochus; he thought the whole province was in rebellion against him. He marched with his whole army to Jerusalem, took it, ransacked it, slew many thousands of its inhabitants and captured many more who were sold as slaves. Jason fled from land to land, and died a despised man among the Lacedemonians. Terror reigned in Jerusalem, now fully in the hands of the aristocracy, marshaled by Menelaus. Many of the Hassidim left the city, and among them was also the hoary Mattathia, the Asmonean, with his family, who fled to Modain.

16. Second Slaughter and Partial Destruction of the City.

The Hebrews bore all these outrages without active resistance, because, divided among themselves as they were, resistance to the military power of Antiochus must have appeared sheer madness to the patriots, who were without organization and arms. In the year 169 B. C., Antiochus again invaded Egypt, and his arms were victorious; when unexpectedly, a Roman embassador appeared and, in behalf of Rome, haughtily commanded him to desist and to leave the country. This sudden check changed the king to a madman. There was good ground of fear that the Hebrews might revolt and declare in favor of Egypt. Therefore, Antiochus sent to Jerusalem an army of twenty-two thousand men under the command of Appollonius to enforce his edict, that there should be but one religion and one law for all subjects of Antiochus Epiphanes. Appollonius was cheerfully received by the king's creatures at Jerusalem. But no sooner was he in full possession of the city than he began to plunder and to destroy it, to slaughter indiscriminately friend and foe, without regard to age or sex, and that on a Sabbath day when none expected an attack. The number of the slain was believed to have been 80,000, and 10,000 captives were led away and sold as slaves. The finest buildings of the lower city were burnt down, the upper city walls were demolished and all the materials were used to build the citadel on the highest point of Acra, opposite the temple, which it overlooked and domineered. The city being ransacked, the temple was entered and plundered of all its valuables. Now the apostatizing edicts of the king were proclaimed over the ruins of the city and the dumb corpses of its slain inhabitants to the aristocrats and the lackeys, who were now the lords of Jerusalem under the guardianship of the king's soldiers and Philip, the governor of the devoted country.

17. The Temple Paganized and the People Apostatized.

Jerusalem was not Palestine. The people adhered to their faith and worshipers visited the temple, although the daily sacrifices had ceased. Therefore, when the citadel of Acra was completed and the Temple Mount could be conveniently governed, which took one year's time, the temple was paganized. On the 25th day of the month of *Kislev*, 167 B. C., being a Heathen feast-day, the idol erected upon the altar and other idols placed on the Temple Mount and in the city, were dedicated and the Heathen worship permanently introduced. Meanwhile (168 and 167 B. C.) the work of apostatizing the Hebrews was rigorously prosecuted by special commissioners all over Palestine and all over Syria. The Hebrew books were burnt or used to paint idols in the scrolls of the law. The observation of any and every Hebrew law was prohibited under the penalty of death. Heathen altars were erected in the towns and cities, swine and other unclean animals were sacrificed upon them, and the Hebrews commanded to eat of the sacrifices. All this was rigorously enforced, and every resistance was punished with death, whether in Palestine or outside thereof. Two women in Jerusalem, who had the courage to circumcise their children, were dragged through the city with their babes hung on their necks, and hurled down from the city walls. Seven sons of one mother, whose name was Hannah, were slain in her presence, one after the other, because each of them steadfastly refused to obey the king's mandate by doing anything contrary to the laws of Israel. A hoary and highly esteemed priest, Eleazar, into whose mouth they forced a piece of the swine sacrificed to the idol, was slain on the spot by the king's hirelings because he refused to yield. All that cruelty could invent and the heartless slaves of a savage despot could enforce, was done to apostatize the Hebrews, to annihilate their republic, law, religion, literature and civilization, to replace the ancient faith of Israel by the Greco-Syrian paganism.

18. The Samaritans and Others Yielded.

Antiochus Epiphanes, having on his side the Hebrew aristocracy led by Menelaus and the Sons of Tobias, most likely believed that people could be apostatized in a very short time and fully naturalized among the Syrians. He was encouraged in this belief also by the Samaritans, who yielded at once, denied their being Hebrews, gave up the Law, and dedicated their temple to Jupiter Hellenius. They called Antiochus Epiphanes a god, as he wished to be called, and escaped unhurt. Many of the Hebrews, to save life and property, submitted to the king's command and bent their knees to his idols. He had them completely under his control, a helpless people, and was accustomed to believe there was not much difference in the various gods, as all Heathens thought, especially at that time of frivolity and corruption. And yet he was grievously mistaken. Truth is indestructible; her apostles are invincible, her God is long-suffering, but he visits the iniquities of the fathers upon the children and children's children to the third and fourth generations of them who hate him.

CHAPTER IX.

Literature and Culture in the Grecian Period.

1. HEBREWS AND GREEKS.

The Caucasian race, at an early stage of its history, separated into two families, the Aryan and the Semitic. Numerous words in the languages of these two families, also traditions and myths, point to their common origin. With the Aryans, intelligence and civilization culminated in the Greeks; with the Semites, in the Hebrews. These were the two most advanced nations of antiquity. There was a radical difference between them. The Greeks were Polytheists, idolators, materialists, worshipers of nature in its manifestations. The Hebrews were Monotheists, spiritists, worshipers of nature's internal and eternal cause, JEHOVAH. In consequence of these fundamental principles, the attention of the Greeks was mainly directed to the exteriority of nature and its objects, phenomenon and form; and the Hebrews' attention was directed mainly to the interiority of nature and its objects. Therefore, the plastic arts and beauty in language, art and philosophy, culminated in Greece; and the purely intellectual elements of civilization, religion, theology, ethics and the code of human rights, were developed in Palestine. Beauty is Greek and truth is Hebrew. In philosophy, too, the form is Greek and the substance Hebrew. The Greeks were cheerful and gay priests of beauty and aesthetics; and the Hebrews serious and stern apostles of truth and law. So the Hebrews became prophets and the Greeks artists.

2. HEBREWS AND GREEKS MEET.

The Hebrews, like the Greeks, had come in contact with all the ancient civilizations of Asia and Africa and learned much, while they lost much of their one-sidedness. They had been acquainted with the Greeks (*Javan*) and the inhabitants of the Ionian Islands (*Joshebai, Ha-iyim, Harechokim*) as early as the seventh century B. C. The relations between Persia and Greece also must have brought the Hebrews in contact with Greeks. Aristobul, the Alexandrian philosopher, maintained that the Greeks were acquainted with the Pentateuch long before the time of Ptolemy Philadelphus, and ancient Christian writers, on the statements of Greek authors, advanced that Pythagoras, Plato and Aristotle, no less than Solon and Lycurgus, had learned much of the ancient Hebrews, whom they sometimes called Phœnicians, and at other times, Syrians, because externally and in language they did not differ materially, and the Greeks were more familiar with the maritime countries (1). From and after Alexander the Great, however, the contact of the Hebrews and Greeks was constant in Egypt, Syria and Greece. The classical writers begin to mention the Hebrews as a distinct people, with traditions, laws, religion and customs of their own (2).

3. Heathen Writers on the Hebrews.

The Heathen writers of this period who make mention of the Hebrews, or treat of their history and laws, are the following:

1. BEROSUS, the Babylonian astronomer, a priest of Bel, born 330 B. C. He moved to Cos, the birth-place of Hippocrates, and then to Athens. He wrote, in three books, a history of the Chaldeans, fragments of which were preserved by Josephus, Syncellus and Eusebius. He confirms the history of the Hebrews from Noah to Cyrus, and adds to it valuable information.

2. HECATÆUS OF ABDERA, a philosopher and statesman in the time of Alexander the Great, a favorite of Ptolemy Lagi. Among the various books written by this author, there were also a history of the Hebrews (Joseph. contra Apion i. 2), and a book on Abraham (Antiq. i. vii. 2). He was so friendly to the Jews that some doubted the authenticity of those books, and others advanced that Hecatæus had embraced Judaism.

3. ARISTEAS, the author of the epistle to Philocrates, on

---

(1) Original passages see in Josephus' contra Apion, also in Clemens of Alexandria, Origines, and Eusebius.
(2) See C. Mueller's *Fragmenta Historicorum Graecorum;* John Gill's "Notices of the Jews," etc.

the origin of the Septuagint, under Ptolemy Philadelphus. The author presents himself as a heathen at the Court of Ptolemy. He and Andreas were sent to Jerusalem to the high priest to obtain a copy of the Law and authorized translators thereof. He evinces particular admiration for the laws and philosophy of the Hebrews. In the seventeenth century A. c. the epistle of Aristeas was declared a forgery; its author was supposed to have been an Egyptian Israelite of the second or first century B. C. Scaliger, Voss and Hody were of this opinion. In defense of this epistle, its English translator, Lewis, Wil. Whiston and Charles Hays, wrote in the eighteenth century. The indorsement of Philo, Josephus and the ancient Christian writers, are in its favor. The arguments of August Ferdinand Daehne against the authenticity of this epistle, although it has been repeated by most all modern writers, is nevertheless worthless on account of the following mistakes: (*a*) He advances that the Hebrews did not philosophize, and the Books of Job, Ecclesiastes, Wisdom of Solomon and several Psalms, prove that they did. (*b*) He advances that the Hebrews were narrowed down to a literal observation of the laws, and we have proved in the former period their catholicity and the universality of their speculations. (*c*) He advances that the spirituality in Hebrew theology is of Alexandrian origin, for which there is no cause whatsoever, as the *Jehovah* theology is in itself the loftiest spiritual speculation, which was only too lofty for the Alexandrians, who made for themselves a manifested God, an accommodated God, formally distinguished from God himself. Aristeas may have been a heathen who, like others, admired the sublimity and simplicity of Hebrew theology and law. He learned the philosophical views of the Hebrews in Alexandria and Jerusalem, and made them his own, although they lacked the formality of the Greeks. The high priest, Eleazar, in that epistle, expounds a law allegorically, as many other laws were expounded in Jerusalem outside of the courts of law, by preachers and teachers of religion (3). There was no Alexandrian Jewish philosophy before Aristobul, and no such theosophy before Philo, who belongs to the Josephus period, and the Aristeas letter may be authentic.

4. Other Heathen writers about the Hebrews in this

---

(3) It is a mistake to maintain that the allegorical exegese originated in Alexandria, when the Bible contains numerous allegories and also their explanations, and the various forms of the *mashal*, fable, legend, parable and allegory reappears in every Jewish production of Palestine.

period were DEMETRIUS PHALEREUS, the first librarian of the
Alexandrian library (4), and HERMIPPUS, of Smyrna (5),
who advanced the intelligence that Pythagoras imported
Hebrew and Thracian opinions in his system; CLEARCHUS,
a disciple of Aristotle; ARTAPANOS, who makes of Moses
the teacher of Orpheus, and of Joseph the inventor of philosophy; and the Egyptian priest, MANETHO (6), whose villainous
charges against the ancestors of the Hebrews have been
discussed by so many authors.

4. HEBREW BOOKS OF THE GRECIAN PERIOD.

In order to determine intelligently which books belong
to this period, the following points must be borne in mind:
(*a*) As by contact, the Gentiles learned from the Hebrews,
so the latter must have learned of the former. The close
of the Grecian period proves that the Hebrews had learned
too much of the Greeks. Therefore, analogies in any book
to a system of Greek philosophy do not prove that such
book was written outside of Palestine or after this period.
(*b*) Not all ideas uttered by any Greek philosopher must
necessarily have come from Greece to Palestine, as reason-
ers far apart may simultaneously utter the same ideas, and
many of them have come to Greece from Palestine. (*c*)
Philosophy invents not; it classifies discoveries and estab-
lishes the laws thereof. Every philosophical system was
preceded by its substantial ideas and truisms. Mankind
knows more than science grasps, and thinks more than
philosophy utilizes. Least of all, the Alexandrian philosophers were original, who, at their zenith of glory, were
eclectics. (*d*) The substantial elements of the Alexandrian Jewish philosophy and theosophy are laid down in
the Greek version of the Bible and the Hebrew books written during this period, consequently they were carried from
Palestine to Egypt, and not *vice versa*, which the Septuagint proves beyond a doubt. The particular method of harmonization of Bible and philosophy, by allegorizing most
liberally Scriptural parts, laws and sentences, is Alexandrian. But this by no means says that Palestinean preachers did not allegorize at all. They did, as is evident from
very ancient rabbinical passages (7). (*e*) The issues of the

---

(4) Josephus' contra Apion i. 23; Euseb. Prae. Evang. ix. 21.
(5) Origenes contra Celsus i. 15 (about 200 B. C.).
(6) Suidas *voce* Manetho; Josephus' *contra* Apion i.; Boekh, *Manetho*; John Gill's Notices, etc., p. 3, 110.
(7) See, for instance, Mishnah, *Rosh Hashanah* iii. 8; *Meguillah* iv.
9, בעריות. המכנה. In aftertimes, it was prohibited as being מגלה פנים
בתורה שלא כהלכה *Aboth* iii. 11.

period which, at last, drove one party to extreme orthodoxy and stern righteousness, and the other to extreme Grecism and apostasy, were these: (1) Concerning man's highest authority, whether it was the THORAH, Sinai, Revelation or WISDOM; (2) Concerning ethics, whether orthodoxy and righteousness were inseparable or separable; whether righteousness in the name of God leads to wisdom or *vice versa;* whether righteousness contains its own reward or it must lead to pleasure and happiness; (3) Concerning eschatology, whether there is reward and punishment in life eternal, which involved the question of immortality and the form thereof, or righteousness must be rewarded in this life, as it appears from one set of arguments in the Book of Job; and (4) Concerning politics, whether, in consequence of the above issues, the *Thorah* is the supreme law of the land, or whether the king and his will are. These issues of the period determine its literature, as authors in all ages write on the issues before them. The Hebrew books of the Grecian period which have reached us are Ecclesiastes (*Koheleth*), the Song of Songs (*Shir Hash-shirim*), Esther (*Meguillath Esther*), Daniel, the Wisdom of Joshua, son of Sirach, and the Wisdom of Solomon.

5. THE SONG OF SOLOMON.

Considering what has been written on the Song of Solomon or the Song of Songs (*Shir Hash-shirim*), it is hardly necessary to say again that King Solomon was not the author of this most beautiful of all poems; because (*a*) the Solomon of this song is conquered and ironically dismissed by the simple shepherdess, Sulamith, of Galilee; his wealth, power and wisdom are derided by a peasant girl's invincible affection for her friend. King Solomon could not have made himself the subject of a satire. (*b*) It contains Grecisms and Aramisms which point to a time when the Syriac and Greek languages had already left their imprints on the Hebrews. (*c*) There is no God and no name of God in the whole song; it could not have been written in the prophetical time, when the name of God was first and last on the lips of the inspired speakers. (*d*) It is in form Grecian, and not Hebrew; it is a drama with two choruses and a coryphaeus to each. The ancient rabbis (MISHNAH, *Yedaim* iii. 5) differed in opinion as to whether the Song of Solomon and Ecclesiastes were to be classed with Sacred Scriptures of the third class (Hagiography), although R. Akiba maintained that the Song of Solomon was most holy. Take, on the other hand, the time of Ptolemy III., when the Grecizing Hebrews

were enthusiastic for the king and wisdom, as the highest
authority and ideal. Solomon was, in the Hebrew traditions, of all kings the greatest and wisest, the ideal of
royal power and wisdom. An excellent poet, whose name
has not reached posterity, personifies the congregation of
Israel with its simple, sublime belief in revelation and its
unshaken faith in God, and calls that allegorical figure Sulamith, whose simplicity is as touching as her affections
and fidelity are admirable and sublime. Her friend, to
whom all her devotion belongs, never appears on the stage;
because he represents the God of Israel, whom the poet
would not personify. He places the simple shepherdess,
Sulamith, in juxtaposition to the wisest, mightiest and
most pompous king, Solomon, surrounded by all the
magnificence, splendor and beguiling pomp of his court.
He represents most happily the spirit of that age and
the ideals of the Grecian Hebrews. The king loves Sulamith; it was no age of persecution; he loves her as a
king with a thousand wives loves a maiden, and she loves
him in moments of weakness. But her faith, her fidelity,
her watchful conscience, triumph over all allurements; she
rejects the conquered king and returns to her friend on the
mountains, like invincible virtue. The daughter of Israel
has never been glorified more successfully than in this song,
and yet it is an allegory, written in behalf of the *Hassidim*
and against the Grecian Hebrews, written in a most amia-
ble spirit, inoffensive, yet forcibly argumentative, pleasing
to the senses, yet suasive in the main point; so that R.
Akiba could say of it "all songs are holy, but this song of
songs is most holy."

6. THE BOOK OF ESTHER.

The Book of Esther is an imitation of the Song of Solomon, only that it is a drama and the former a historical
romance, written in the time of Seleucus. Like the Song
of Solomon, it has no God and no name of God, and is full
of Aramisms. It is written so that each chapter is intended
to surprise the reader, exactly in the style of the romance;
and there are different versions of the story in Hebrew,
Greek and Syriac, which, however, agree in the main facts,
so that there can be no doubt that each writer had an object
in view, according to which he shaped and presented the
historical facts. Like the Song of Solomon, the Book of
Esther was also written for profane reading, and handles
the same questions. Sulamith becomes Esther; the daughter of Israel is placed in the position where the poet of

Solomon's Song could not have placed her; she is a queen. She is not as noble and generous as Sulamith, the congregation of Israel is not as faithful as it was, and Mordecai, the vigorous and ever-watchful *Hassidism*, must somewhat harshly remind her to bestir herself in behalf of her devoted people; but then she rises nobly, piously, prudently and successfully. The king is represented as an imbecile and fool, which was well directed against the royal idealism of the Grecian Hebrews. The author personified Seleucus in Ahasveros, Heliodorus in Haman, Onias in Mordecai, the congregation of the faithful in Esther. Both the historical facts and the allegory are well presented, and in the very sense of the poet of the Song of Solomon. Judith and Susanna, written in other periods, are imitations of the two books just discussed, personifying the congregation of Israel by a noble daughter of Israel, as Tobit is an imitation of Job.

7. THE BOOK OF ECCLESIASTES.

All the arguments advanced in regard to the Books of Job and the Song of Solomon apply with equal force to the Book of Ecclesiastes, to establish the fact that it was not written prior to this period; nor could it have been written later, as shortly after this period the third part of the Canon, the Hagiography, in which this book was placed immediately after the Proverbs of Solomon, was closed (Baba Bathra 19 b). Ecclesiastes iv. 13 to 17, and x. 17, appear to point to Antiochus the Great and the child Ptolemy Epiphanes; and verse 20, to the tax collector, Joseph and his sons, the espionage in Jerusalem during the wars of Antiochus the Great with Egypt. Ibid ix. 13 apparently points to the fate of Hannibal. It is, therefore, safe to place the origin of this book in the early days of the reign of Epiphanes, before 200 B. C. The author's name was not ascertained, for it is fictitious. He calls himself *Koheleth*, a son of David, king in Jerusalem (Ecclesiastes i. 1), and says (Ibid i. 12) that he was king over Israel in Jerusalem, hence he was king no more when he wrote that book. The editors of this book call him *Hak-koheleth* (Ibid xii. 8), showing that it is not a proper noun; it is *the koheleth*. There is no reason whatsoever to believe that King Solomon wrote this book under a fictitious name (8). And yet the

---

(8) See Nachman Krochmal's *Moreh Nebuchei Haz-zeman, Shaar* xi., *Simmon* viii.; and in *Kerem Chemed* of the year 1841, p. 79. Krochmal thinks Ecclesiastes was written toward the end of the Medo-Persian Period, which is a mistake, because the Greek Skepti-

ancient expounders and translators ascribed this book to
Solomon. They wanted to exclude it from the Canon because it contradicts the words of David and contains contradictory statements (9) which incline to unbelief (10);
still they sustained it because its beginning and close are
"words of the law" (11). This assumption is not based
upon the "Ben David," for any other son of David, in any
century, might have so called himself. The words "king at
Jerusalem" (i. 1) may refer to David and not to *Koheleth*,
and in verse 12 he simply maintains that the *Koheleth* was
once king of Israel in Jerusalem, but was so no more. *Koheleth* is an allegoric name. It signifies "congregation" in
the abstract. The author, who was a Davidian of Jerusalem, assumes the title *Koheleth*, "THE congregation," which
in better times reigned over Israel in Jerusalem, but was
now deposed by the incursions of Grecian philosophy and
customs, the progress of commerce and materialism. He
had learned of the *Shir Hash-shirim* poet to personify
the congregation of Israel, in behalf of which the great and
wise king argues against the Grecians of his age; and this
great king, without mentioning his name, speaks of himself
as if he were Solomon. It is, in this particular point, the
counterpart of Solomon's Song. There the poet represents
in Solomon the royal master with all his claims, as the
Grecians presented the king, succumbing at last to the
majesty of the congregation of Israel personified in Sulamith. Here the philosopher represents a philosophical and
apologetic Solomon in defense of the congregation of Israel.
He calmly reviews all the claims of the Grecians, with all
the philosophisms and sophisms of the age, the fatalism
and astrology of the orientals, the Skepticism and Epicurism of the Greeks, with their Eudemonism and pleasure-
seeking virtues. He hints at the Stoics (vii. 15) and chastises the self-complacent rationalism of his age, which
sought the supreme good in "Wisdom," and relied upon its
ability to explain all enigmas of existence. He chastises
no less the supposed importance of the king, power, wealth
and satiating enjoyment. He has thought of all and tried
all which his generation knew and had; he has denied with
them the consolation of immortality and the happiness of
virtue. Like them he has thrown aside all traditions of the

---

cism and Epicurism, against which the book evidently argues, did not
exist at that time.
(9) Talmud Sabbath, 30 *a* and *b*.
(10) *Midrash Koheleth Rabbah*.
(11) Talmud ibid.

fathers and all doctrines of revelation. But at the end of each experiment he finds "Vanity of vanities, saith Koheleth, it is all vanity and windy imagination." Your philosophisms and sophisms can only lead me to despair, to end in suicide, he told his cotemporaries, for they explain nothing and render life intolerable: "For in much wisdom is much tribulation; the increase of knowledge is the increase of affliction." The cup of joy emptied to its very bottom brings bitterness and disgust. The kings reign and oppression prevails. The rich and the poor, the sage and the fool, must die, and none of them finds happiness in life or acknowledgement after it. With all your wisdom, power, wealth and splendor, you are miserable after all, he tells his readers; therefore, there can be no truth in your philosophy and sophistry. Therefore, he concludes (chap. xii. 1 to 7), "Remember thy Creator in the days of thy youth," etc. "And the dust returns to the earth as it was, and the spirit returns to God who has given it." The only consolation left to man is in God, revelation and immortality. *Koheleth* took to task all the questions of his age, and seeks to prove that salvation and true wisdom are only in the congregation of Israel, with her God, revelation and immortality doctrines. Greek philosophy and the Grecian claims for the sovereignty of wisdom and the king, have found no more successful skeptic and critic than *Koheleth*. Therefore this book was accepted afterward in the Canon.

8. THE PSALMS OF THIS PERIOD.

An age of extensive commerce and domineering materialism, as the Grecian period was, is favorable to the progress of the practical sciences and arts, and hostile to religion, philosophy, poetry and the fine arts. Therefore, the sacred lyre was also silenced in Israel. Yet Psalms xlix. and lxxiii. were evidently written shortly after KOHELETH and discuss the same themes. Psalm fifty can hardly be misunderstood; it was directly against Menelaus and his brother, when the holy vessels had been stolen from the temple. Psalms xlii. to xliv., as also Psalms lxxiv. to lxxix., can be understood only in connection with the bloody decrees of Antiochus Epiphanes, the subsequent massacres and the desolation of the temple. Concerning Psalm lxxiv., it is maintained in the Talmud (*Sanhedrin* 96 *b*) that it refers to the destruction of the first temple; but this opinion is controverted in verse 9 of that Psalm. With the suffering of the faithful, the sacred lyre resounded again, and this time with tearful strains. Psalm lxxi. appears to be the prayer of Mattathia at the outbreak of the rebellion, which opens the next period.

9. THE BOOK OF DANIEL.

Daniel was no prophet, it is maintained in the Talmud (Sanhedrin 94 b), and the book which bears his name was not accepted in the Prophetical Canon; still the book stood in very high esteem in the days of Josephus. Its Aramaic chapters (ii.-vii.) were certainly not written in Palestine, because they are classical, and the Hebrews at the end of this period were better acquainted with the Greek than the Aramaic. Therefore, it must be admitted that the Aramaic portion of the Book of Daniel was written in Babylon and by Daniel himself, or one who had access to his notes and dates. Josephus (Antiquities xi. viii. 5) states that the Book of Daniel was shown in Jerusalem to Alexander the Great, "wherein Daniel declared that one of the Greeks should destroy the empire of the Persians," and Alexander supposed that he himself was the person intended. Yet it is evident (12) that the Hebrew portion was written after 170 B. C., by a patriot secreted somewhere in the country, to rouse the Hassidim to the terrible combat against Antiochus Epiphanes, and to inspire them with the certainty of victory. Its mystic, apocalyptic style, its hypostasis of angels called by mysterious names, its vivid, lucid and exact description of historical events in the dim twilight of prophecy, and its powerful appeal to the national feelings and consciousness that the Kingdom of Heaven must outlive all potentates and empires, betray the object and time of its origin in the time of persecution, to pour inspiration into the hearts of the patriots. Therefore, the origin of this book is easily accounted for. The originally Aramaic chapters contain no prophecy reaching beyond the fall of Babylon. They refer to the four last kings of the empire, in which Daniel himself was a prominent sage and statesman. The style of the book, however, is so mysterious that it admits of various interpretations. In Palestine, especially, where the Aramaic was but partially understood at that time, it was no difficult task to expound some of its passages to the satisfaction of Alexander, or to discover in others different prophecies. A patriotic man, when the persecutions by Antiochus Epiphanes had become intolerable, seized upon that book and added to it, prophecies in the name of Daniel,

---

(12) H. Ewald's Geschichte Ezra's, etc., p. 342-348; Dr. L. Philipson's Bible, *Einleitung zum Buche Daniel.*

which predicted the whole history to the downfall of that king and the triumph of the Kingdom of Heaven. Its expounders did the same thing by imposing on the book any subsequent facts of history as predictions made in the misunderstood and misconstrued book, so that the rabbis were obliged to declare that Daniel was no prophet. The eminent services which it had rendered in the war of independence, the original Daniel chapters which it contains, and its Gnost-kabbalistic elements, secured it a place in the third division of the Canon.

10. THE WISDOM OF JESUS, SON OF SIRACH.

Two books of the Pseudo-Solomonic literature are among the Apocrypha of the Old Testament; the one of Jesus, son of Sirach or Sira, which, in the main, is an imitation of Solomon's Proverbs; and the other called the Wisdom of Solomon, or also the Book of Wisdom or Ecclesiasticus, is original and Pseudo-Solomonic. Ben Sirach appears to be older than *Koheleth*. The Hebrew originals of those two books have been lost (13). Both of them are gnomical like Solomon's Proverbs, and in the same form of paralellism; so that the Hebrew original is distinctly marked in the Greek translations. Ben Sirach's Hebrew original was known to and extensively quoted and imitated by the rabbis (14); and Hieronymus reports to have seen it. The Greek translation was written by the author's grandson in Egypt, the Syriac, Aramaic and Arabic translations were written later. It is called in the Talmud "Ben Sira," and is mentioned among other apocrypha, although the expounders of the Mishnah again speak of it as being worthy of a place in the Hagiography. The author calls himself (1. 27) Joshua (Jesus), Son of Sirach, from Jerusalem, and his grandson informs us, in his introduction to the Greek translation, that he came to Egypt in the thirty-eighth year of the government of Ptolemy Euergetes, but that monarch reigned only twenty-five years (247 to 222 B. C.). It must refer to Physcon, who called himself Euergetes II., whose reign actually commenced 170 B. C., and, with several intermissions, lasted to 117 B. C.; hence the translator came to Alexandria 132 B. C. Therefore, it is within the bounds of possibility

---

(13) Ben Sirach has been translated into Hebrew from the Syriac of the London Polyglot, by Juda Loeb Ben Seb, end of the eighteenth century. Wisdom of Solomon has been translated by Naphtali Hartwig Wessely, Berlin, 1778.

(14) Forty-two Hebrew verses are extant, and others in the Aramaic translation scattered over the Talmud.

that the author, in the early days of his life, had seen Simon the Just, who died 292 b. c., whom he describes (chap. l.). But he must not necessarily have seen him in order to describe him, as he describes many others whom he had not seen. This Simon the Just appears to him as the last saintly high priest. It will be safe to place the author, 255 b. c., before the author of *Koheleth*. Jesus b. Sirach was a man of practical wisdom, sound morals and profound religiousness, who had learned and traveled much and had searched much more in the Law of God (Ben Sirach li. 13, etc.; xxxi. 11; xxxix. 4). Although he had gathered a treasure of experience in his travels, yet he found Wisdom to have her seat upon Zion, her power and resting-place in Jerusalem, and her roots in the people of Israel (Ibid xxiv. 10-12) (15). He was an orthodox writer, who believed that research in the Law of God was equivalent to searching after all the wisdom of all ages and nations (*Ibid* xxiv. 25, xxxix. 1, e. s.), and that the highest wisdom could be reached only by those who kept God's commandments (Ibid I. xix. 23). He recommends to fear God and to honor His priests (Ibid vii. 28), to pay due regard to the sages and traditions of the nation (Ibid viii. 9). He believed in Providence and man's moral freedom (Ibid xi. 17), in revelation and the election of Israel (Ibid xvii.), in mercy and forgiveness of sin (Ibid xxviii). In principles, lofty and humane, and in religion faithful and enlightened, Sirach's son taught his people whatever wisdom, honor, virtue and righteousness command, and his beautiful sentences were adopted and imitated both by the ancient rabbis and the various authors of the New Testament. It is a good text-book of the Hebrew's religion and ethics. Still it was not accepted in the Canon (*Tosefta Yedaim* II.), and was reckoned among Apocrypha. The causes are these:

1. Ben Sirach's book is not original in its ideas. The author knew Solomon's Proverbs (Ibid xlvii. 12, e. s.), and imitated them, without reaching the poetical beauty, brevity and force of the original.

2. He is uncertain and wavering in respect to future reward and punishment, which was then an established belief and a test of orthodoxy, as is evident from Koheleth, Daniel and various Psalms.

3. His expressions and figures of speech concerning wisdom are contradictory and, in some instances, heretical. He hypostasizes wisdom (Ibid xxiv. and elsewhere), al-

---

(15) This is the first time we meet the Shekinah idea in Hebrew literature.

though he otherwise speaks of it as the Pharisees of later days did of the Shekinah. He localizes and materializes it, which was Grecian and in itself sufficient to exclude his book from the Canon.

4. He speaks in many instances like a fatalist, to an extent which was not palatable to the last compilers of the Canon (16).

5. He says of himself that he was not inspired (In Ben Seeb xliv. 39, 40). He ascribes all his learning and wisdom to his own love of wisdom and his exertion to find it (li. 13 e. s.) and speaks of prophecy as something of past days (In Ben Seeb xxxvi. 13, e. s.), so that it even appears that he opposed the prophetical pretenses of his age.

11. THE WISDOM OF SOLOMON OR ECCLESIASTICUS.

This Pseudo-Solomonic book of nineteen chapters is an epistle of King Solomon to the princes and rulers of nations, in which they are admonished how to reign in justice and wisdom, according to the will of God. It is a direct polemic against the prevalent Heathen and Grecian doctrine of the sovereignty, irresponsibility and godship of the king. It is a successful apologetic attempt in favor of the Hebrew theocratic principle, the belief in immortality, future reward and punishment, the supremacy of divine justice and Providence, and the system of ethics resulting from these principles. He advances nothing that was then new in Jerusalem, although he seems to incline sometimes to Pythagoras or Plato. His God is the same spiritual, invisible and infinite Maker, Preserver and Governor of the Universe, which He contains and which contains Him not, as taught by Moses and the Prophets. His immortality doctrine is a commentary on Solomon's צדקה תציל ממות "Righteousness delivereth from death," as most all his doctrines are. He is, in style, perfectly biblical, and so he is in all his ideas, except concerning Satan (ii. 24) and in regard to wisdom, which appeared to him also in the hypostesized form of Shekinah (not as an intermediate being between God and man); although it is difficult to expound his poetical figures of speech with certainty (17). There is no cause what-

(16) See Dr. A. Geiger's *Urschrift*, etc., p. 201; Ben Seeb's and M. L. Gutmann's Introductions to Ben Sirach; Leopold Duke's *Blumenlese*, etc., p. 23; A. F. Daehne's *Geschichtliche Darstellung*, etc., *Zweite Abtheil.*, p. 126, e. s., and their sources as quoted; Franz Delitzsch's *Zur Geschichte der Jued. Poesie*, Sec. 26.

(17) Naphtali Hartwig Wessely in his *Ruach Chen* has supplied most of the Biblical passages on which the phraseology in the Wisdom of Solomon is based.

ever to suppose that this book was not written in Hebrew or not in Palestine. It is not as popular a book as Ben Sirach's, hence it was not as popularly known; still many of its passages passed into the literatures of the rabbis and the New Testament without credit given to the author. It was not accepted in the Canon for reasons given, Section 10, hence the Hebrew original was not preserved. The book is beautiful in style and sublime in its contents, but it contains no original truth. It is, in form, an introduction to the Laws of Moses. The first ten chapters are a general introduction, enlarging on the spirit and essence of the laws. The other nine chapters are commentaries on the miracles connected with Israel's departure from Egypt, with polemics against idolatry. Here the author stops abruptly at the account of Israel's passage through the Red Sea. The conclusion of this book has evidently been lost. Neither Solomon, nor Zerubabel, nor Philo, as was variously supposed, could have been the author of this book, which, in form and contents, in style and doctrine, belongs to Aristobul, the founder of the Alexandrian Jewish Philosophy, of whom we treat in Chapter xiii. (18).

12. THE CULTURE OF THIS PERIOD.

The literature of this period is a monument of a high state of culture. The spoken language still was the Hebrew, although the Syriac and Greek had made deep inroads upon its terminology and grammatical forms. This is evident especially from KOHELETH, the Hebrew chapters of Daniel and the Book of Sirach's Son, which were written for the people, and must have been written in the popular dialect. Again, the Song of Solomon, Wisdom of Solomon, and the Psalms, are works of art, and prove how far the Hebrews had advanced in the beauty of form. The Pseudo-Solomonic literature, which has its echoes in the rabbinical legends of later dates, is distinguished by its high-toned ethics and catholicity, so that it gave rise, in later days, to the superstition that the evil spirits dread the name of Solomon, and at the mentioning of it, submit to

---

(18) Whether Aristobul is the BEN LAANAH of the Talmud Yerushalmi or the BEN THGLAH of the *Midrash Kohelath*, whose book is placed in connection with that of Sirach's son, can no more be ascertained, as, besides the names, nothing is known either about these authors or their books. The same is the case with the MEGUILLATH HASSIDIM (Yerushalmi Berachoth end), of which one verse is quoted: יום תעזבני יומים אעזבך, "If thou forsakest me (the Law) one day, I forsake thee two."

the will of the exorcist (Josephus' Antiquities viii. ii. 5). The religious idea appears in those writings with a force and clearness, especially in the doctrines of God, providence, immortality and righteousness, as found nowhere outside of Palestine. The only new idea in this connection is the Shekinah of Ben Sirach and Wisdom of Solomon, and the angels as messengers of God in the Book of Daniel; and this is the source of Jewish Gnosticism and the *Kabbalah*. Gnosticism is the first instance in the belief that metaphysical knowledge is wisdom and the supreme good of man; and secondly, that this wisdom can be obtained in a direct way of Sophia or wisdom hypostatized (of which Shekinah is the Judaized idea), or of angels, as in Daniel (viii. 16, ix. 21, etc.), or of the BATH-KOL, a voice heard which echoes its meaning in the individual's intelligence (Ibid viii. 13), or by intense prayer (Ibid ix.). This Gnosticism was chiefly directed to the MERKABAH, the throne of God and the angels about it, to which Isaiah vi. and Ezekiel i. afforded a Biblical starting point; the MA'ASEH BERESHITH, the mysteries of the Creation according to Genesis i.; and the AROYOTH, the mysteries of human physiology, to which Leviticus xviii. and xx. afforded the Biblical starting point. These theosophical, cosmological and physiological speculations being communicated orally, hence, received of a master, were afterward called KABBALAH, while the juridical and ethical material transmitted in the same manner, was called THORAH SHE'BE'AL PEHI, the oral law, or also MASSORAH, the tradition. No idea of a Shekinah, angelology, kabbalah, or any kind of Jewish gnosticism could be discovered prior to the close of the Grecian period, and also, there is no idea of demonology discernible. The two forces of Grecism and Hebraism acting upon the mind, produced this deviating line without being marked out in either.

The attention paid to transcendental and political subjects did not disturb the people in the progress of agriculture, industry and commerce, of which the books of this period give lively descriptions, in the wealth of numerous individuals and the refined luxury of the rich, against which the moralists raise their voices. Among the luxuries of the rich there were, besides costly garments, precious jewels, elegant houses and furniture, carriages and sedans, servants, choice asses and horses, costly articles of food, imported or home productions, also vocal and instrumental music at banquets and every other joyous occasion, public orators and jesters; all of which is expressed in the books of this period, and points to a high state of agriculture, industry and commerce (19). The wealth in the temple treasury was not very large at the end of this period, which proves that the gifts sent to the temple from abroad increased largely after this period. The fact that teachers and physicians had already formed separate and more respected classes of society, and that the apothecary was distinguished from the physician (20), points to a division of the scientific vocations and a considerable progress of society; as the extensive travels and lofty speculations of the few afford an insight into the advanced spirit of that age.

---

(19) See Dr. L. Herzfeld's *Handelsgeschichte der Juden*, etc., Secs. 23 and 28.
(20) Ben Sirach xxxviii. and xil.

III. The Revolutionary Period.

From 167 to 142 B. C., the Hebrew people, under the successive leadership of Mattathia, the Asmonean, and his sons, Juda, Jonathan and Simon, went through that revolution, which is called the Maccabean war, because Juda as well as his warriors was called Maccabee, which ended with the independence of Judea. The word Maccabee is said to be made of the initial letters of the Bible phrase: מי כמוכה באלים יהוה, "Who among the mighty is like thee, O God," supposed to have been the motto inscribed on Juda's banner. The kings of Syria during this period were:
1. Antiochus Epiphanes,
2. Antiochus, son of the former, - 162 B. C.
3. Demetrius I., - - - - 161 B. C.
4. Alexander, - - - 152 B. C.
5. Demetrius II., - - - 146 B. C.
6. Antiochus, son of Alexander, - 144 B. C.
7. Tryphon, - - - -

CHAPTER I.

Mattathia Starts the Rebellion.

1. THE ASMONEAN FAMILY.

Among the resident priests of Jerusalem (1) there was the House of Joarib or Jehojarib, that was not of the high priest's family. One branch of the family of Joarib was called HASHMONAI or ASMONEAN, and one member of it was the

(1) I. Chronicles ix. 10; Nehemiah xi. 10.

chief priest, John, son of Simeon, whose son was Mattathia He had fled with his family from Jerusalem to Modin, a town north-east of Jerusalem, about fifteen miles from the Mediterranean, in the province of Dan. He had five sons, John Gaddis, Simon Thassi, Juda Maccabee, Eleasar Auran and Jonathan Apphus (2).

2. Outbreak of the Rebellion.

One of the king's commissioners, Apelles, who went about the country to apostatize the Hebrews, came also to Modin, erected a pagan altar, and invited the people to sacrifice to the gods, especially the swine of Ceres, and eat from the sacrifices. Only one old man indicated obedience to the king's mandate; Matthathia slew him, together with Apelles and his men. So the signal was given for active resistance. Hitherto the Hebrews had offered passive resistance only. Bound by the oath of allegiance, and intensely religious as the patriots were, they would not have recourse to arms. Many thousands had fled to the mountains and to the wilderness. Some, about a thousand of the latter, were brutally slaughtered in the caves of the southern desert, on a Sabbath day, when they would not fight. The surviving patriots being thus driven to the alternative of apostacy or death, Mattathia raised the banner of active resistance, and declared that they would also fight on the Sabbath day, if necessary. Many patriots came forth from the caves and augmented the ranks of Mattathia, who led them to the mountain fastnesses, where the king's soldiers could not easily attack them, and initiated the bloody work of self-defense.

3. The Work Done by Mattathia.

From his mountain fastnesses, Mattathia, with his ill-armed and poverty-stricken band of patriots, made incursions into the villages and towns. The heathens and apostates were slain or expelled, the pagan temples and altars destroyed, the children circumcised, the law of the land enforced, and as many copies of the Hebrew manuscripts as could be found were saved. This encouraged and sustained the faithful, chastised and cowed the renegades, and harassed the king's troops. They could not possibly withstand the attacks at all points by those desperate men, whose number was augmented after every successful attack, and whose

---

(2) I. Maccabees ii. 2.

courage grew with every victory. It was not in Mattathia's power to do more than this. He succeeded in uniting a body of men to set bounds to the king's apostatizing policy. He was old and unable to fight a Syrian army. He left the whole work, so courageously begun, to be accomplished by his sons. His hour of death approaching, he appointed Simon, the most prudent of his sons, governor, and Juda Maccabee, the most valiant among them, general in the army, admonished and encouraged them all, and died after one year's work in the service of his people (166 B. C).

CHAPTER XI.

Juda Maccabee Saves the Commonwealth.

1. Juda Defeats and Slays Apollonius and Seron.

The insurrectionary patriots now had a government of their own under Simon, and the nucleus of an army under Juda Maccabee, supported by his brothers and other chiefs, as they had a Sanhedrin *de facto* under Jose b. Joezer. The policy of Mattathia was upheld. Juda surprised villages and towns, mostly at night time, expelled the Syrian officers, garrisons and partisans, restored the law of the land, and left the places in possession of his compatriots, until the Syrian governor at Jerusalem, Philip, found himself unable to quell the growing power of the rebellion in the northern country. The southern cities up to Hebron had been seized by loyal Idumeans, and the maritime cities by Macedonians, Greeks, Syrians and renegade fugitives from the interior. Juda being looked upon as the chief of lawless hordes, Apollonius, now governor of Samaria, took the few troops he had and the bands of volunteers he could raise, and marched into Judea (166 B. C.) to put and end to the rebellion. He was met by Juda somewhere north of Jerusalem, who defeated the invading army with great slaughter, and slew also, Apollonius, the heartless enemy of Jerusalem, whose sword Juda wore ever after that. This gave to the patriots new courage, plenty of arms and provisions, and exposed the whole of Samaria to their incursions. Seron, the governor of Cœlosyria, seeing the rebellion now right at the borders of his province, marched southward with his troops and as many volunteers as he could raise. He occupied the strong position of Bethhoron, where Joshua had fought a great battle. There Juda with his men, by forced marches, surprised and confronted the enemy. The Hebrews were fatigued, hungry and alarmed by the superior numbers of the enemy. Juda, who was as fiery an orator as he was a valiant man, inspired them with confidence and courage. They fell on the enemy, slew eight hundred of them, slew Seron, and drove the shattered army to the maritime cities. This brought into the power of Juda the whole northern country up to the Lebanon, and gave to his army the proud consciousness of victory. They were now morally certain that God's anger was no longer upon Israel, and that His warriors stood again under His special protection. Juda's fame spread, his army grew in number and spirit, prophets predicted the glory returning to Zion, inspired bards sang the praise of Jehovah and His warriors, visions were seen, dreams were dreamed, and the whole religious enthusiasm was aroused in the souls of the Hebrews. Even the king was now roused from his lethargy and sensuality to behold the fruits of his perverse and cruel policy, but now it was too late. Three causes co-operated in favor of the rebellion: the martial genius of Juda Maccabee, which was the greatest after Alexander; the enthusiasm and superior intelligence of the Hebrews; the decline and corruption of the Syrian Empire. The first might have been suppressed and the latter overawed in time; but it was too late now.

2. THE KING'S DESIGNS CONCERNING THE HEBREWS.

The death of two governors and the defeat of their armies alarmed the king. Although deeply engaged in the public games at Daphne, and in debaucheries of all kinds, he roused himself to an appreciation of the crisis. His treasury had been much exhausted by his extravagance; he was indebted to the Romans 2,000 talents, and no taxes were paid by the Hebrews, Persians and Medians. He collected a large army and divided it with Lysias, whom he appointed regent of Syria and tutor of his son, Antiochus. With the other half of the army he crossed the Euphrates to subject the Persians and Medians, and to collect the taxes. His command to Lysias was, to send an army into Judea, to destroy Jerusalem utterly, to slay or sell into slavery all the Hebrews, to divide their land by lot among strangers, and to extinguish the entire nation. The king, with his army, left for the east in the spring of 165 B. C.

3. THE NICANOR AND GORGIAS INVASION.

Lysias appointed Ptolemy, the son of Dorymenes, governor of Cœlosyria, who sent Nicanor and Gorgias, two expe-

rienced generals, at the head of a regular army of 20,000
men (1) to Palestine to carry out the king's command.
There came to Nicanor a large number of volunteers from
the petty nations about Palestine and renegade Hebrews,
so that the invading army numbered about 40,000 infantry
and 7,000 cavalry. Nicanor invited slave dealers from the
maritime cities to come and buy Hebrew slaves, 90 for a
talent. His intention was to sell 180,000, in order to raise
2,000 talents with which to pay the Romans. A large number of slave dealers came with plenty of money and shackles
to Nicanor's camp, expecting a flourishing business.

4. Preparations in Palestine.

The patriots of Palestine also made their preparations
during the winter. In the spring of the year (165 B. C.)
they met at Mizpah. A day of public humiliation and
worship was celebrated in an extraordinary manner, in
sackcloth and ashes, and under the thundering noise of the
priests' trumpets. The tithe was brought thither and Nazarites appeared with their sacrifices to make the multitude feel
keenly the absence of the temple and altar; and the multitude lamented and wept. Juda, in his language of liquid fire,
encouraged the despondent people to go and fight for their
religion, law, sanctuary, homes, life and liberty, and acquainted them with the fact that they had already been
sold or devoted to the sword. The army was then organized
according to the Laws of Moses. When all who were faint-
hearted were gone, a host of 6,000 men was left, which was
divided into four corps, commanded by the four brothers of
Juda, he being then their commander-in-chief. So prepared,
the heroic band went forth, for the first time to meet in
battle a regular army, drilled in the tactics of Alexander,
and commanded by renowned generals.

5. Defeat of Nicanor and Gorgias.

The Syrians had come down through Phœnicia and were
encamped near Emmaus, on the plain of Philistia, at the
foot of the mountains of Judah. Juda marched from Mizpah to meet the enemy there. His approach becoming
known to Nicanor, he sent Gorgias, with 5,000 men, to surprise Juda's camp in the mountains. On being informed
thereof, Juda at once hurried to the enemy's camp, took

---

(1) According to Josephus and I. Maccabees iii. 9, Nicanor's army
consisted of 40,000 infantry and 7,000 cavalry, and according to II.
Maccabees viii. 9, 20,000 men, which entitles to the above statement.

Nicanor by surprise, routed him, burnt his camp, and drove his shattered army to the plains of Edom and the cities of Jamnia and Ashdod, before the return of Gorgias. When he returned and saw the disaster, he fled with his troops into Idumea. The victory was great, and no less great was the thanksgiving and psalmody of the victors. A large quantity of gold, silver, purple and arms had fallen into their hands, and they had won the conviction that they could rout a well-disciplined army commanded by reputed generals. Nicanor passed through the country disguised, and arrived, perfectly humiliated, at Antioch. It appears he was dismissed from the Syrian service by Lysias, and went to Rome to Demetrius, the nephew of the king, with whom he returned to Syria in 161 B. C.

6. The Defeat of Lysias at Beth Zur.

The victory at Emmaus was not decisive. In the spring of the year 164 B. C., Lysias came with another army to Idumea, collected the scattered forces of Nicanor and Gorgias, and mustered, as was supposed, sixty thousand men, besides five thousand horsemen. He marched northward as far as Beth Zur, and encamped in that arena of rocks and narrow passes. Juda, and this time with ten thousand men, defeated also proud Lysias, who left 5,000 dead behind, and retreated back to Antioch with the conviction that the Hebrews were prepared to die rather than lose their liberty, and that they had a desperate manner of fighting.

7. Re-Dedication of the Temple.

Juda was now absolutely master of the interior country from Dan to Hebron, with the exception of the fortified places, and among them, Acra, in Jerusalem. It was in his power to take Jerusalem, and he did occupy it without resistance. The host that had followed him to the holy city, finding the temple deserted and desecrated by idols, its gates burnt, and weeds growing in its courts, lamented painfully and rent their garments. Juda besieged the citadel of Acra, and meanwhile a large party of working men repaired the temple, tore down the polluted altar, and built a new one according to the Law, made the most necessary sacred vessels and priestly garments, destroyed all idols and emblems of idolatry in the city and on the Temple Mount, and began to repair its fortifications. In the fall of the year 164 B. C. (I. Maccabees iv. 32), after three years of desolation and profanation, again, on the 25th day of *Kis-*

lev, the temple was solemnly re-dedicated, and the ancient culte re-introduced according to Israel's laws and customs. It was a day of joy to all patriotic hearts. Seven days of public worship and rejoicing were added, and those eight days of dedication were afterward made the Feast of Light, called *Hannukah*, for all Israel, to be celebrated annually in memory of the re-dedication of the temple. At the same time, Beth Zur was fortified to protect the country against invasions from the south, and the siege of Acra was continued. There can be no doubt that Juda was the acting high priest, although this is not stated in our sources.

8. Successful Exploits in Idumea and Ammon.

The Haman-like edicts of Antiochus Epiphanes to apostatize or to exterminate the Hebrews, had the good effect of arousing the patriots to heroic deeds, and of bringing thousands from Syria and Mesopotamia to Palestine. They had the evil effect of arousing the petty nations around Palestine to deadly hatred against the Hebrews, whose utter destruction was looked upon as a loyal duty, to execute the mandates of the god-king. Therefore, while Lysias was unable to invade Palestine again, the petty nations surrounding it continued the hostilities in a most barbarous manner, a war of extermination against the Hebrews. South and south-east were the Idumeans, commanded by Gorgias, and the Ammonites, by Thimotheus. In the spring, 163 B. C., Juda invaded the eastern part of Idumea and the land of Ammon, and conquered it as far south as Acrabatene and the southern point of the Salt Sea, and east thereof up to Jazer, also called Gaser or Geser (2), at the foot of the mountains of Gilead, and returned then to Jerusalem.

9. Successful Exploits in Gilead and Galilee.

After a few weeks of rest, Juda was informed of the distress of the Hebrews in Gilead by Timotheus, and of northwestern Galilee by the inhabitants of Ptolemais, Tyre and Sidon. His protection was urgently necessary, as the Hebrews of Gilead had fled to the fortified places, in which they were not prepared to hold out long, and many of Gilead and Galilee had been slain or captured. Besides, there was danger of an invasion from the south by the Idumeans, under Gorgias. After consultation with the peo-

---

(2) Josephus' Antiq. xii. viii. 1; I. Maccabees iv. 15; v. 8.

ple, Simon was sent, with 3,000 men, to Galilee. Two captains, Asariah and Joseph, were left in Judea with a sufficient force for defense and with the special order not to take the offensive. Juda and Jonathan, with the main army, crossed the Jordan into Gilead. The two expeditions were eminently successful. Juda twice defeated and captured Timotheus, and released him on parol; all important cities of Gilead were taken, and all Gilead, together with Western Ammon and Eastern Idumea, became again a Hebrew province, called afterward Perea. Simon was no less successful. He drove all enemies out of Galilee, pursued them to the gates of Ptolemais, and brought back to Jerusalem all who wanted to leave Upper Galilee. Asariah and Joseph, however, acting in violation of orders, attacked Jamnia, where Gorgias commanded. They were repulsed with a loss of about 2,000 men. Juda and Simon returning to Judea, the army was concentrated again, and an attack in force was made on the Idumeans. Hebron was recaptured and destroyed, and the Idumeans driven southward. Next Juda subjected to his sway a part of Samaria, and the martial spirit had risen so high in Israel that officiating priests also fought in the ranks, but they were not good warriors (3).

10. Joppe, Jamnia and the Arabs Chastised.

The inhabitants of Joppe had invited two hundred of their Hebrew townspeople to their booths to a friendly entertainment, and then threw them into the sea. A similar plot was ripe in Jamnia against the Hebrews. A horde of five thousand Arabs had been engaged by those maritime cities for their protection. Juda was not prepared to take those cities, but he chastised them severely; he burnt their harbors and shipping, and defeated the five thousand Arabs, with whom he made a treaty of friendship, and permitted them to return to their homes and tents (II. Maccabees xii.). These exploits and victories impressed the Hebrews with self-confidence and the conviction that they were amply prepared for self-defense.

11. Death of Antiochus Epiphanes.

While Juda and his compatriots were engaged in reaping the fruits of their victories, the career of Antiochus Epiphanes was ended by his unexpected death (163 B. C.). He had been victorious in Media, but had sustained a disastrous defeat in Persia, while attempting to ransack a

---

(3) I. Maccabees v. 67.

Heathen temple of its valuable treasures (4). He retreated to Ecbatana and there heard the news of Juda's successes over Nicanor and Gorgias. In his mortification and rage he hastened back to Syria, with the most horrid threats of vengeance on his lips. On the road he met other messengers, who informed him of the defeat of Lysias and the re-dedication of the temple in Jerusalem, and his rage became furious. His chariot upset, and his body sustained a severe shock. He rode on, however, and when he could no longer endure the motion, he had himself carried on a litter till he was worn out and had to stop at Tabae, on the line between Persia and Babylonia, where, after weeks of horrible suffering in body and mind, he died of a most horrid disease, a miserable and disappointed man (5). Before his death, he appointed Philip as regent and tutor of his son, and delivered to him the insignia of royalty.

12. LYSIAS' SECOND INVASION OF PALESTINE AND A TREATY OF PEACE.

Lysias being informed of the king's unexpected death and the appointment of Philip, proclaimed the king's son his successor, called him Antiochus Eupator, and retained for himself the high position of regent and the king's tutor. Juda, meanwhile, made preparations to take Acra and drive the Syrian garrison and the renegades from that stronghold, which commanded the northern accesses to the temple. He pressed them hard with a zealous and valiant army by bulwarks and engines of war. The renegades succeeded in persuading Lysias to give them his support. At the head of a large army, supposed to have counted 120,000 men and thirty-two elephants, Lysias and the infant king invaded Palestine (162 B. C.) by way of Idumea, concentrating at Beth Zur, which he besieged. Juda was obliged to raise the siege of Acra and to meet the enemy. He marched to Bethzacharia, about ten miles from Beth Zur, and made ready for an attack. Lysias attacked him, and a hard-fought battle ensued. Juda was compelled to fall back, and retreated to Jerusalem, although the losses of Lysias that day had been very severe. In that battle, Eleazar Auran, the brother of

---

(4) The temple of Diana in the city of Elymais, according to I. Maccabees vi. 1; Joseph. Antiq xii. ix. 1; or a temple at Persepolis (Venus?) according to II. Maccabees ix.

(5) He confessed the wrongs he had done to the Hebrews, and saw, in his sudden death, God's justice, according to the above sources.

Juda, died a hero's death. He saw one of the elephants in the enemy's ranks armed with royal breast-plates, and, supposing the king to be on that animal, fought his way through the enemy's ranks, slipped under the elephant and killed him. The animal fell on him and ended the life of a hero. Lysias, however, took Beth Zur, sent its inhabitants naked out of that city, garrisoned it, and then besieged Jerusalem and the temple. The Hebrews inside defended the place heroically. It was the Sabbath year and provisions became scarce in the city. They could not have held out much longer, when, unexpectedly, peace was offered them by Lysias. He had been informed that Philip, with the king's army, had returned from the East and claimed his position. An honorable peace was obtained. The king restored to the Hebrews all the rights and privileges which they had enjoyed before the war. Menelaus was deposed and condemned to death in the tower of ashes at Berea in Syria, and the terms of peace were guaranteed by an oath of the king and the captains with him. The Roman embassadors, Quintius Memmius and Titus Manlius, also supported this treaty with the consent of the Roman people, and asked the Hebrews to send messengers to them to Antioch (6). The king did not keep his oath entirely; for on being received in the city as a friend, he saw the strength of its walls, and commanded portions thereof to be leveled. Nor did he fulfill all the other stipulations of the treaty; for, instead of appointing as high priest, Onias, the son of the last legitimate high priest, he appointed Alcymos, a man of obscure extraction, who was a Helenist, and stood in bad reputation among the patriots (7). The mission of Juda would have been fulfilled had Lysias not violated the stipulations of the treaty.

13. Demetrius, King of Syria, and the First Bacchides Invasion.

Although Lysias and the king returned in time to Antioch, routed and slew Philip, and Lysias maintained himself in his high position, it did not last long. In the year 161 B. C., Demetrius, son of Seleucus, who had been in Rome as a hostage for twelve years, escaped, came to Syria and claimed the crown. Lysias and the infant king had no friends. They were slain, and Demetrius was proclaimed king contrary to the will of Rome. Alcymos, who was unable to

---

(6) II, Maccabees xi. 34.
(7) Ibid xiv. 3.

maintain himself in Jerusalem, appeared, in company with other Grecian Hebrews, before the new king, and they succeeded in persuading him to send an army to Palestine in order to establish his and Alcymos' authority. Bacchides was charged with the execution of this order. He came with Alcymos and an army to Jerusalem, and promised peace to the people, now tired of war and poorly provided with the necessaries of life. Having promised, under oath, protection to all who might come to him, many prominent scribes and leaders of the *Hassidim* party came to him to sue for peace. But Bacchides treacherously seized and slew sixty of them, among whom, it appears, was also Jose b. Joezer. Then he marched to Beseth, seized and slaughtered many of the *Hassidim* leaders and the peaceable citizens. Having thus struck terror into the hearts of the surviving patriots, he left an army with Alcymos and returned to Antioch.

14. Juda Rises Again.

After the conclusion of peace with Lysias, Juda retired from the contest, as, by the stipulations of the treaty, all had been granted for which he had been fighting. However, the treacherous conduct of Bacchides and the Hellenistic inclinations of Alcymos, again roused Juda and his compatriots to active hostilities, and the horrors of the civil war were renewed. Juda and his men again went about the country and slew the Hellenists, while Alcymos maltreated and slaughtered the *Hassidim*. Gradually, Juda succeeded again in collecting so strong a body of men around him that Alcymos could no longer maintain himself in Jerusalem. He and the leaders of his party again went to Antioch and prevailed on the king to invade Palestine. This time Nicanor was sent to bring Juda and his patriots, living or dead, to Antioch.

15. Nicanor's Invasion and Death.

Nicanor, the same year, came to Jerusalem at the head of a large army, and, like Bacchides, he heralded peace. He invited Juda to a conference, and he came. Terms of peace were arranged; Juda and Nicanor communicated in a friendly way till the jealousy of Alcymos was aroused. He complained, and the king renewed his orders to Nicanor, who was unwilling to renew the combat. He attempted to capture Juda treacherously and to send him to the king; but the Maccabee was cautious enough to thwart this scheme, and the war began anew. Juda marched at the head of a heroic band toward Jerusalem and Nicanor went out to meet him; a battle was fought near Caphersalma, Nicanor was defeated, lost nearly 5,000 men, and retreated to Jerusalem. Going up Mt. Zion to the temple, trembling priests came out and showed the pieces of the sacrifice they had made for the king. Nicanor, in his rage, cursed them, blasphemed God, and swore a terrible oath, that he would level the temple to the earth if Juda and his men were not delivered up to him (8). The priests went back to the temple and cried to God for help, and the army of Juda was augmented and roused to a desperate struggle. On the thirteenth day of Adar, 161 B. C. (9), Nicanor went forth to capture Juda. Not far from the city he was furiously attacked by Juda's little army. Nicanor fell, his army was routed and scattered in all directions. The alarm was sounded throughout the land; from all towns and villages armed multitudes issued forth, and the invading army was entirely annihilated. Nicanor's head and right arm were brought to Jerusalem, and the thirteenth day of Adar was made a national holiday, called Nicanor's Day. So the Hebrews proved again that they could stand patiently any aggression except interference with their religion and their temple.

16. Embassadors to Rome.

The victory secured to the Hebrews a brief period of peace. Alcymos fled to Antioch, and, for a short time, Juda was governor and high priest *de facto*. He gained time enough to send an embassy to Rome to cultivate the friendship of the Senate and the people (10). As Demetrius

(8) The year 160 B. C. began next month, the first day of Nissan.

(9) It is narrated, II. Maccabees xiv. 37, that Nicanor sent five hundred men to capture a certain senator whose name was Razis. This man was called father of his people, and was distinguished for patriotism and benevolence. Nicanor, it appears, wanted to have that man in his power in order to mortify his numerous friends by maltreating him. The senator, it appears, occupied a strong castle, which was taken by the soldiers, and he being in danger of being captured, committed suicide in a most heroic manner, in preference to falling into the hands of Nicanor.

(10) I. Maccabees viii.; Josephus' Antiq. xiii. x. 6. Dr. Graetz doubts the authenticity of this embassy, on the ground of names inserted by Josephus which could not be historical. But the account of I. Maccabees affords no ground for any reasonable doubt, as the writer thereof must have seen the tablets which he describes, and Josephus, in the same paragraph, has also the second error of reporting the death of Alcymos before the second invasion of Bacchides.

was not acknowledged by the Romans as king of Syria, an embassy of the warlike and victorious Hebrews must have been welcome in Rome. The embassy was eminently successful. The Roman senate acknowledged the Hebrews' independence, and received them as friends and allies. Demetrius was informed of this fact and commanded not to make war upon the Hebrew nation. The decree of the Roman senate was engraved upon brazen tablets and sent to Jerusalem, where they were exhibited in the temple. Still, this could not have benefited Juda and his compatriots personally, who were declared the heads of a rebellion against the king, the peace and prosperity of the Hebrew people. It was a faction, in the judgment of Demetrius, which had to be subdued for the benefit of the country and lawful government; nor could the embassy have come back from Rome in time to prevent the next invasion and the calamities which it produced.

17. BACCHIDES' SECOND INVASION—DEATH OF JUDA.

Early in the year (160 B. C.), shortly after the death of Nicanor, Demetrius sent to Palestine with Alcymos, the right wing of his army, under command of Bacchides. Galilee was invaded first, Maisaloth and Arbela (11) were besieged and taken, and many of the inhabitants, besides those who had sought refuge in the caves, were put to the sword. Without further resistance the army reached Jerusalem in *Nissan* (first month), and Alcymos was high priest once more. Bacchides, who had come again as a herald of peace to the loyal people, attempted no desecration of the temple while at Jerusalem, and Alcymos conducted the service in a lawful manner. The people, in this year of famine, seeing itself re-assured in its rights and privileges by the conduct of Bacchides, settled down to a peaceful life, and Juda saw himself deserted. Three thousand men had remained for a long time faithful to their heroic chief. Gradually they also disbanded, most likely for want of provisions, and he was left at Bera (12), with 800 men. Bac-

---

(11) Maisaloth and Arbela, it appears, were one city in the time of Josephus. Compare I Maccabees x. 2 to Josephus' Antiq. xiii. xi. 1. Arbela must have been loyal to the patriots; the second highest officer of the next Sanhedrin, Natai, was from that city; therefore, it was so severely visited by Bacchides.

(12) Not Bezetha, as Josephus has it, unless Bera was afterward called Bezetha. Bera or Beroth was in Benjamin (Joshua xviii. 25), near the Jordan (Ibid ix. 17), the place to which Jotham, Gideon's son, fled before Abimelech (Judges ix. 17).

chides detailed 22,000 men to capture him. Juda's men advised him to retreat and to wait. He, however, considered it a disgrace, and insisted on accepting the challenge. Once more he wielded his irresistible sword, and, with his small band, inflicted a serious blow upon the enemy. But his number was too small. Although the right wing, commanded by Bacchides in person, had been defeated, and retreated before Juda, the enemy's left wing and the cavalry rallied, came up in his rear, and, with sword in hand, he fell on the battle-field, and with him two hundred of his companions. The benefactor of his people and savior of Israel's religion, temple, nationality, law and honor, lay slain among his enemies, and all good men in the land mourned.

CHAPTER XII.

Jonathan and Simon Achieve Independence.

1. JONATHAN AND THE SIX HUNDRED HEROES.

It is not certain that John and his two brothers were present at the battle of Bera, for Bacchides gave them permission to carry the remains of Juda to Modain, and to bury them in the sepulcher of Father Mattathia, which they did. It was a few weeks thereafter that Jonathan and his brothers joined the six hundred comrades of Juda who had escaped out of that battle. They were encamped on the eastern bank of the Jordan and near its mouth, protected on the north and west by a swamp, on the east by the Jordan and on the south by the Dead Sea. Jonathan was chosen captain of that small band of heroic patriots to replace the slain chieftain, the hero of so many battles, whose brave comrades were now fugitives and outlaws. Recognizing his precarious state, Jonathan sent all his superfluous baggage to the Nabbateans, a friendly tribe of Arabs. John, with some men, formed an escort. The hostile tribe of Amri, from Medaba, fell on John, killed him and his men, and captured the baggage. Jonathan, after some time, slew most of the Amrites, assembled at a large wedding; but that could have afforded him little consolation for the great loss in so critical a situation, the loss of his brother and his valuable companions, and a large portion of the means at his command. Bacchides soon discovered Jonathan's camp and went to capture it. He attacked the Hebrews on the Sabbath day, expecting to meet with but little or no resistance. Nevertheless, Jonathan gave him a warm reception, fought him all day, and when night had set in, the whole band swam across the Jordan. In the morning, detachments of the enemy pursued them, but were slain before they could rally on the eastern shore. Bacchides pursued them no further and returned to Jerusalem. Jonathan and his men fortified themselves in the oasis of Bethagla, and remained there two years.

2. Pacification of the People.

Bacchides put Alcymos and the Hellenists in power, and took the sons of the most prominent patriots as hostages, to be kept at Acra. He fortified a number of cities on the frontier and in the heart of the country, and strengthened old fortifications at Acra, Beth Zur and Gaza. The fortified places were provisioned, and garrisoned by Syrians and Hellenists, most of whom made their permanent homes there; so that all apostates and renegades again lifted up their heads proudly, and the patriots were suppressed and ill-treated. The taxes imposed on the country were very oppressive (I. Maccabees x. 25, etc.; Antiquities xiii. ii. 3), and the famine lasted nearly two years. The party now in power would not venture any aggression against the Hebrews' religion, Law or the temple, on account of the Lysias treaty, the Roman warning, and especially, perhaps, in memory of the chastisement given to Nicanor and his army. It was overbearing, oppressive and revengeful, so that the pacification was insincere. Still there was peace, and the nation recruited its strength.

3. Death of Alcymos.

Alcymos was struck down by the hand of Providence early in the year 159 B. C. He died after a brief illness. In the outermost court of the temple was a trellis, beyond which Gentiles, and also Hebrews, who had not passed through the Levitical lustration, were not permitted to go. Alcymos had that trellis removed, and opened the whole of that court to all classes of people. It was an arbitrary deed committed in the temple, and that sufficed to excite the ire of the jealous multitude. The trellis, it was maintained, had been there since the days of the prophets. Alcymos broke it down, therefore, he died so suddenly. After the death of Alcymos, Bacchides returned to Antioch. No high priest was appointed, and no account has reached us as to how the internal government or the temple service was carried on.

4. Third Bacchides' Invasion and Peace with Jonathan.

During the two years of peace, Jonathan also recruited his strength. His numbers were gradually augmented by dissatisfied patriots and idle adventurers. He grew up to be a dreaded chieftain, as David did in the time of Saul. He was not only the terror of the nomadic tribes, but also of the Hellenists. As they persecuted the patriots, he took vengeance on their chief men. After the death of Alcymus, that party being without a leader, this state of affairs grew worse, and the Hellenists persuaded the king once more to send Bacchides with an army in order to capture Jonathan and his men, and restore peace. They promised to capture Jonathan by strategy, but this failed and cost them fifty of their chief men. Bacchides marched with an army to Bethagla, and besieged it. Jonathan and Simon were prepared to meet him. At the head of half their men, Jonathan marched out of the fortifications, and by a circuitous route, came up in the rear of Bacchides and opened an attack on him. At a given signal, Simon sallied out of the fortifications with his men, destroyed the siege engines, and Bacchides, pressed between the two corps, lost a large number of his men. He felt that he was not prepared to overthrow Jonathan, and was very angry at the Hellenists, who had misled him to believe that it was an easy task. Jonathan being informed of Bacchides' state of mind, sent peace commissioners to him, and peace was concluded. Jonathan was permitted to recross the Jordan with his men, and live there in peace. Bacchides was to send back all Hebrew captives held abroad, and swear never to return as an enemy to this country. Thereupon, Bacchides, with his men, returned to Antioch, and Jonathan recrossed the Jordan with his. He took up his residence at Michmash, and was tacitly acknowledged the head of the Hebrew people; and the Hellenists were obliged to keep the peace. Five years of pacification and profound peace followed. The excitement abated, and a change of political opinions ensued. The Hellenists, as a party, almost disappeared; so, also, did the *Hassidim*. The former had lost all and the latter had gained all for which the fighting was done, viz.: civil and religious liberty, the laws and institutions of the fathers. However, new parties soon grew out of this new political situation.

5. Jonathan, High Priest.

Demetrius had a castle built, in which he kept aloof from the people, and lived in indolence and sensual gratification. The Syrians hated him, as did the Hebrews. Alexander Balas, his cousin, the son of Antiochus Epiphanes, or, according to Diodor of Sicily, and others, an impostor resembling that prince, succeeded in collecting an army and ships and effecting a landing at Ptolemais, where he was received and proclaimed king of Syria (152 B. C.). This event roused Demetrius from his lethargy. He made preparations to fight his antagonist. Jonathan was the only man in Palestine who could organize a military force of Hebrews, and they were reputed soldiers. Alexander being at Ptolemais, they could easily give him their support. Therefore, Demetrius sent a flattering letter to Jonathan, giving him permission to raise and equip an army, to fortify Jerusalem, and ordered that all hostages in Acra be delivered up to Jonathan. This struck terror to the Syrian garrisons of the various fortified cities, and, except those in Acra and Beth Zur, they left the country. The hostages delivered up to Jonathan were sent to their respective homes, arms were forged, Jonathan organized an army and began to fortify Jerusalem with square stones. Alexander, who could ill afford to lose so valuable an ally, sent a letter to Jonathan, together with the purple robe and the diadem, appointing him high priest (and chief ruler) of the Hebrews, with the title of "friend of the king." Jonathan accepted this offer, and the first day of the Feast of Booths (152 B. C.) he appeared in the temple in the sacerdotal robes as high priest, and was enthusiastically received by the assembled multitude. Demetrius, on hearing this, wrote a second letter to Jonathan, promising him and his people much more than Alexander had done. But his offers were refused and no response made. The man who, eight years previous, had swam the Jordan under the cover of darkness, a hunted and condemned rebel, now stood at the head of his people, the high priest and commander-in-chief, almost an independent prince, by the will of his countrymen and with the consent of the king. That memorable Feast of Booths gave rise to Psalm cxviii., in which the history of those eight years and the enthusiasm of the multitude are reflected in inspiring strains.

6. Jonathan Honored by Two Kings.

Alexander defeated Demetrius, who was slain. The new king married Cleopatra, the daughter of Ptolemy Philometor. The wedding was celebrated at Ptolemais. Jonathan repaired thither and presented himself, in person, to the new sovereign. His enemies had also come to be heard. Jonathan and his rich gifts so pleased the king that the highest honors were bestowed on the Hebrew high priest, who sat in the purple robe with the king on his throne, and at the wedding, had his seat between the two sovereigns of Syria and Egypt. Confirmed in all his titles and appointed governor of Judea, Jonathan returned to Jerusalem, and his enemies were silenced.

7. Re-organization of the Sanhedrin.

No Sanhedrin is mentioned during the eight years' interregnum. It appears again with the supremacy of Jonathan (1). The last chief of the provisionary Sanhedrin, Jose b. Joezer, was slain by Alcymos or Bacchides. The colleague of the former, Jose b. John, of Jerusalem, may have continued to preside over that body, but this is uncertain. With the supremacy of Jonathan, the re-organization of the commonwealth, on strictly national principles, must have taken place, which includes the functions of the Sanhedrin. Jonathan, and after him his brother, Simon, with the title of Heber, חבר, or "Unificator," as found on the coins of Simon and his successors, must have presided over the Sanhedrin, which, on that account, was called בית דין של חשמנאים "The High Court of the Asmoneans." So the Kingdom of Heaven was completely restored, as the *Hassidim* wished. The Law of Moses was lawfully enforced by the proper authorities, a pious and patriotic high priest watched over the divine worship in the temple, and the dispensation of justice, peace and righteousness prevailed; the Thorah was read and taught again all over the land by pious scribes, the glory of the Lord was revealed again upon Mount Moriah and His grace over Israel, and no foreign power or potentate interfered with Israel's domestic affairs. National independence was certainly not on their programme; and so they had all they wished. Therefore, the old party divisions were obliterated, and those Hebrews who were with the Syrian garrisons in Acra and Beth Zur were known only as renegades and apostates. There can be no doubt, however, that many of the Hellenists left the country and settled down in Egypt and Asia Minor.

8. Jonathan Defeats Apollonius Daus (148 b. c.).

There was peace and prosperity among the Hebrews when Demetrius, the son of King Demetrius, returned from Crete to Syria. Alexander, who had been feasting and debauching in Phœnicia ever since his wedding, was roused to action. He went to Antioch to make his preparations. His

---

(1) I. Maccabees xi. 23.

governor of Cœlosyria, Apollonius, the son of the Apollonius slain by Juda, revolted and followed the fortunes of Demetrius II. This Apollonius, a wicked braggart like his father, came through Phœnicia to Jamnia with an army, and sent an insulting challenge to Jonathan, who came at once with a well-equipped army of ten thousand men, including Simon's corps, and took the city of Joppe. On the plain, the two armies met, and a battle was fought, in which both sides showed great bravery and strategy; still Apollonius was routed and many of his army fled to Ashdod, hotly pursued by the Hebrews. The Hebrews took Ashdod also, and the enemy having sought refuge in the temple of Dagon, that temple was burned down. Next Jonathan marched to Askalon, and was kindly received in that city. So the whole maritime coast was again under his control, and he returned to Jerusalem. King Alexander, whose enemies Jonathan had fought, conferred honors on Jonathan and sent him the golden buckle, which was a mark of distinction for the king's kinsmen only.

9. DEMETRIUS II.

Alexander not being able to overthrow Demetrius, asked assistance of his father-in-law. Ptolemy Philometor came with a large army and navy to the assistance of his son-in-law. Passing through Ashdod, its Gentile inhabitants showed him the ruins of the Dagon temple and the suburbs, also the bones of the slain, in order to incense him against Jonathan. But it was of no avail. When Jonathan met the Egyptian king at Joppe, he was well received, and went with Philometor as far as the river Eleutheros. By the treachery of Alexander, however, events took a peculiar turn; Philometor took his daughter from Alexander and gave her to Demetrius. Alexander fled to Arabia and was assassinated, and Demetrius II. was king of Syria (146 B. C.).

10. DEMETRIUS II. SELLS HIS CLAIMS ON JUDEA FOR THREE HUNDRED TALENTS.

While the two kings of Syria made war upon one another, Jonathan besieged Acra once more. The war closing before Acra had been taken, the renegades in that castle sent deputations to the new king and asked his assistance. Demetrius came angrily to Ptolemais and summoned Jonathan thither. He appeared in company with some distinguished senators and priests, and with rich gifts, and made a favorable impression on the king, whose anger changed to the highest grace. He confirmed Jonathan in all his high offices, and conferred on him the title of "the first friend of the king." Jonathan, taking advantage of the king's favor and his momentary poverty, offered him three hundred talents for all taxes and tributes hitherto paid to Syria, of Judea and its Samaritan districts of Lydda, Apheremon and Ramathen, formerly paid to Syria. The king accepted the offer, received the money, signed and sealed the documents, and Judea, with its three Samaritan districts, was released from all foreign tribute.

11. The Hebrews Defend the King at Antioch.

Demetrius II. was of a peaceful disposition. He dismissed a large portion of his army. Still the people of Antioch hated him. Jonathan sent an embassy to him, requesting him to recall the garrison of Acra, which was a point of their treaty. The king replied that he would do that and even more whenever it would be in his power. But at present he was hard pressed by rebellious Antiochians, and demanded of Jonathan three thousand men to subdue the rebellion. Times had changed. Three thousand Hebrew soldiers were sent to Antioch to protect the king, and they did protect him. The rebellion was overcome. The citizens of Antioch sued for peace after many of them had been slain. Peace was restored and the Hebrew soldiers returned to their country; but Demetrius kept none of his promises, and was desirous of annulling the treaty made at Ptolemais. Still Jonathan managed to keep the peace.

12. Antiochus Theos, King of Syria.

Demetrius II. had no time to carry out his treacherous designs against the Hebrews. For Diodotus Tryphon, who had been governor of Antioch under Alexander and Demetrius II., conceived a plot to place himself on the throne of Syria. Demetrius had dismissed many of his soldiers and, contrary to custom, paid them no wages in time of peace. They augmented the number of his enemies. Tryphon, observing this state of affairs, went to Arabia, persuaded Zabdiel, who was the guardian of Alexander's son, the boy Antiochus, to intrust the young prince to his care, as he would place him on the throne of his country. Zabdiel consented; Tryphon took the prince and brought him into Syria. The dissatisfied soldiers and citizens supported him, an army was organized, a battle was fought, the forces of Demetrius were routed, his elephants fell into the hands of Tryphon, who took Antioch; Demetrius fled to Seleucia, and the boy Antiochus, surnamed Theos, was placed on the throne of Syria (144 B. C.).

13. JONATHAN AND SIMON IN FAVOR OF ANTIOCHUS.

The power of Demetrius was not crushed yet, and it was necessary to the plans of Tryphon to secure the support of the Hebrews. Therefore, a royal decree was sent to Jonathan, confirming him in his dignities of high priest and governor of Judea, and in the possession of the three Samaritan districts, to which a fourth (Jamnia?) was added. He was permitted to wear the purple and the golden buckle, with the title of "the king's first friend;" to use the golden vessels at his table, and to keep a princely household. Jonathan accepting these offers and declaring in favor of Antiochus, was commissioned to raise an army of Hebrews and Gentiles to subject the country to the new king; and Simon was appointed the king's general for the East, from the ladder of Tyre to Egypt. It was a peculiar change of events. The rebel chiefs were now the king's right-hand power. It was a serious mistake on the part of Jonathan, but he could place no confidence in Demetrius, who had deceived him, and could only embrace the cause of Antiochus Theos.

14. SUCCESSES OF JONATHAN AND SIMON.

It was not difficult for these two renowned warriors to raise and discipline a large army. Jonathan soon marched at the head of an army toward the sea coast, and met with no resistance till he came to Gaza. He found this city with its gates closed, and besieged it. The damage to the district and suburbs of Gaza by sword and fire was so heavy that its garrison capitulated, and Gaza declared in favor of Antiochus. The most prominent citizens gave their sons as hostages, and Jonathan took them with him to Jerusalem. Next he marched across the Jordan and then as far north as Damascus, to enforce submission to the new king, and he was successful everywhere. Meanwhile, the forces of Demetrius re-organized and invaded Galilee in order to bring Jonathan out of Syria. The enemy was encamped at Kedesh, on the northern borders of Galilee. Leaving Simon behind to protect Judea, Jonathan led his forces to the northern shore of Lake Genesareth. A battle was fought on the plain; Jonathan having been outmaneuvered, part of his army fled, panic stricken.

However, Jonathan and his most valiant captains attacked the enemy with success; his troops rallied and the enemy was defeated with a loss of three thousand men. Meanwhile, Simon had laid siege to Beth Zur, held by a force of Demetrius. The garrison capitulated and were permitted to join the shattered forces of their master. The success was complete. The two brothers had carried out their mission in behalf of their king, and the Hebrews of the four provinces, viz.: Judea, Samaria, Galilee and Perea beyond Jordan up to Damascus and down to Gaza, were once more, as in the time of David and Solomon, masters of their country.

15. An Embassy to Rome and Sparta.

Being absolutely in possession of all Palestine, with a military force superior to any of the two kings of Syria, Jonathan could only think of preparing for independence at the next turn of political affairs. To this end, the favor of the Romans was indispensable, for their authority in Syria and Egypt was well established. Therefore, Jonathan sent embassadors to Rome to renew the existing treaties, which might have been affected by Jonathan's embracing the cause of Antiochus Theos. The embassy was eminently successful in Rome in securing the friendship of the senate for the Hebrew people. According to instructions, the embassadors also went to Sparta to renew the league of friendship with the Lacedæmonians and other nations. They were also successful in this mission. This was the prelude to the independence of Palestine.

16. Other Successes.

Meanwhile, the army of Demetrius had been re-organized and reinforced, and made another attempt at overthrowing Jonathan. They had come to the borders of Palestine and fortified a camp at Amathis. Jonathan, with his forces, was not far from them. Having learned the enemy's intention to surprise and attack his camp, he was prepared for them, and they met with an unexpected repulse. Finding the Hebrews so well prepared, the Syrians fled hurriedly during the night, so that they could not be overtaken next day. Jonathan, by a detour, also conquered an Arabian tribe in the north-east, and then returned to Jerusalem. The sea coast cities taking advantage of the re-appearance of the forces of Demetrius, revolted again. But before Jonathan's return, Simon overwhelmed them, and placed a garrison at Joppe.

17. Other Preparations for Independence.

The two brothers having returned to Jerusalem, the Sanhedrin was convoked and the necessary laws were enacted to strengthen its fortifications and other cities, also to fortify cities hitherto unprovided with works of defense. A wall or ditch between the city and Acra was to be constructed in order to cut off its garrison and the renegades from all communication with the city. The work was begun at once. Jonathan superintended it in Jerusalem and Simon in the country. Before, however, the embassy could have returned from Rome, or the fortifications could have been constructed, a catastrophe changed the situation.

18. Jonathan Captured.

Tryphon was ready to dispose of the young king and to mount the Syrian throne. Jonathan was in his way, and he was to be put out of the way by vile treachery. Tryphon came with an army to Bethshan, and Jonathan was ready with 40,000 men to meet him. Tryphon dreaded a battle, and sent presents and hypocritical declarations of friendship to Jonathan, and succeeded in entrapping him. He went to Ptolemais with a thousand men by invitation, to have a friendly interview with Tryphon. On his arrival there the gates were closed, Jonathan's men were massacred, and he was captured (143 B. C.). Tryphon despatched a strong force to overwhelm the Hebrews in the field, who were now without a commander-in-chief; but they retreated in time and reached Jerusalem.

19. Simon Dictator—Death of Jonathan.

The people of Jerusalem, at these tidings, yielded to fear and sadness. They knew the hostile nations around them would rise up against them, and the treacherous Tryphon, with a strong army, was at the door. Simon did not lose his courage. He convoked the people to the Temple Mount, and offered them his services. He said he was no better than his father and his four brothers, and like them he was ready to die for his people. He was enthusiastically received and proclaimed chief ruler of the nation, or rather a dictator for the time being. The fighting men rallied about him, and he went to work with Asmonean energy. He sent one captain, Jonathan, son of Absalom, to Joppe, to secure the sea coast cities against Tryphon, while he continued the fortification of Jerusalem and making ready for active service. Tryphon, Jonathan in bonds with him, moved his army into Judea. Simon met him at Adida, which he had fortified. Tryphon seeing his schemes crossed by the unexpected energy of the Hebrews, once more resorted to hypocrisy and treachery. He sent word to Simon that he would release Jonathan in consideration of one hundred talents paid down, and two of Jonathan's sons sent him as hostages. Simon suspected the sincerity of his enemy in this offer also. He called a council of war, and laid Tryphon's propositions before it. They were accepted. The money and the hostages were sent, and Tryphon did not keep his promise. He went with his army southward to Idumea to invade Judea from that side, followed closely by Simon. The garrison of Acra having sent word to Tryphon that in order to rescue them he must hasten to Jerusalem, he made ready to proceed there at once. That night, however, a heavy snow fell, which made it impossible to reach Jerusalem. Tryphon retreated through Gilead into Cœlosyria, marking his path by smoking ruins and massacred men. In Gilead, he also slew Jonathan and had him buried at Bascama. Then he returned to Antioch, afterward slew the young king, and placed upon his own head the crown of Syria.

20. SIMON SUCCEEDS JONATHAN.

All Israel was in deep mourning. The man who had built up the independence of his people had been treacherously slain. Simon, who had successfully crossed the schemes of Tryphon, was now the most honored and most powerful man in the land. Syria had, in fact, no king. Tryphon was a crown-robber, and Demetrius II. was powerless. The time was favorable to gain the independence of Palestine. Simon, therefore, while he continued energetically to fortify the cities, sent to Bascama to bring the remains of Jonathan to Modain, and buried them in the Asmonean sepulcher, over which he afterward erected the wonderful mausoleum of white marble, with its seven massive columns, and which was considered a wonder of architecture by Josephus and Eusebius. Tryphon having sent an embassy to Rome with costly presents, and the embassadors of Jonathan not yet having returned, Simon also sent embassadors to Rome and Sparta, with the same instructions which had been given by Jonathan. In Rome, the embassadors of Tryphon were dismissed with a dubious reply, and those of Simon received the highest honors and were dismissed with a treaty highly encouraging to Simon and his people. Once knowing the feeling in Rome, Simon sent another embassy to Demetrius acknowledging his title to the Syrian crown, and offered him his assistance against Tryphon on condition that he acknowledge the independence of Judea. Demetrius accepted the proposition, and sent to Simon the royal decree, with general amnesty for all past offenses, declaring the independence of Judea, dated 170 s. e. (142 b. c.).

21. Judea Independent—Simon, Prince and High Priest.

Simon captured and fortified Gazara, Beth Zur and Joppe. He built a house for himself at Gazara, made of Beth Zur an armory, and improved the harbor of Joppe. Returning from this expedition, he was received in Jerusalem with unbounded enthusiasm. The independence of Judea was acknowledged by the legitimate king of Syria and the Romans, and Simon was its prince and high priest, after thirty-five of the most eventful years in the history of the Hebrews. Now the Seleucidan era was replaced by the era of the Hebrew prince, and all public documents were dated in the first, second, etc., year of Simon or other princes after him. Mattathia had aroused the patriots to active resistance. Juda made a nation of warriors out of patient and religious agriculturists and merchants, and re-conquered his people's rights, sanctuary and nationality. Jonathan cultivated the feeling of independence stirred up by the war, in defense of the sanctuary, educated the people up to this new state of affairs, and organized an army out of the irregular fighting men. Simon at once realized the hopes of Jonathan and accomplished the task without much resistance. Juda was an enthusiastic lion, Jonathan the organizing politician, and Simon the prudent statesman.

CHAPTER XIII.

Literature and Culture, at Home and Abroad, of the Revolutionary Period.

1. THE POLITICAL PARTIES OR SECTS.

Political parties and religious sects were identical in the Kingdom of Heaven among the ancient Hebrews; because the God whom they worshiped was also the king, legislator and judge of the nation and every individual thereof, by whatever persons He was visibly represented in either of these various functions, and His kingdom is in time and eternity. Revolutions decide old issues and produce new ones, which are the causes of new parties. "At this time," says Josephus, viz.: toward the end of Jonathan's administration (about 145 B. C.), "there were three sects among the Jews: Pharisees, Sadducees and Essenes." He intends to say that before this particular time, these sects were not known. They originated at that particular time, and then they differed only in regard to fate (1). There is no mention made, in any record, of these names of parties or sects prior to the notice of Josephus, and they can not be antedated. Parties so strongly marked could have gone forth from the revolution only. Their names are significant of their particular principles.

2. THE PHARISEES.

PHARISEES, Hebrew (פרשים), "the Separated," signifies men who separated themselves from all that is Levitically unclean; hence, from contact with Gentiles, Hebrews who adhered not to those observances, unclean animals and the

---
(1) Antiquities xiii. v. 9.

hides thereof, diseased animals and men, or skeletons thereof. This party, according to its religious ideas, was numerous in Jerusalem at the time of Antiochus the Great (2), and must have increased during the revolution, when the strictest observance of the national laws and customs was the watchword of the patriots. The origin of these views is in Ezra's "Commoners" (אנשי מעמד), who being demi-priests, at least one week annually, learned and practiced the laws of Levitical cleanness, and with the form of the temple worship, carried them among the people; only that those men were no party or sect before this period. The scribes in and outside of the Sanhedrin expounded the Law, multiplied its provisions in accordance with the public requirements and feelings, and were especially rigorous on the point of Levitical cleanness. With these Hassidim, of course, the knowledge, expounding and practicing of the Law, religious observances and deeds of charity, were the main objects of man's existence; the scribes, custodians and expounders of the Law must have been their highest authorities; and Israel's national existence must have appeared to them to have this one purpose only, viz.: to preserve and promulgate the Law. The principal functions of the government could only have been, in their opinion, the enforcement of the Law, the upholding of the culte, and the protection of the nation in the free exercise of its religion. The religious idea predominating among them, they were naturally impractical politicians. As long as the sanctuary and the Law were in danger, they fought bravely, as men and patriots. When the Lysias-Juda treaty had been made, they laid down their arms and made friendly overtures also to Bacchides. They rose up again when Nicanor threatened the destruction of the sanctuary, and having destroyed him and his army, they again laid down their arms. Four centuries of dependence on different foreign potentates had produced the conviction that it mattered little who did the profane business of the State, collected the taxes and fought the battles, so long as the sanctuary, the Law, and the religious exercises were secured. Therefore, after the fall of Nicanor, they did not support either Juda or Jonathan, although they did not oppose them. But when Jonathan and Simon became chief generals of Antiochus and commanded Gentile troops, they certainly could no longer rely upon the support of those Hassidim and scribes. This must have been the time when the Pharisees were distinguished as a party or sect. In all matters

(2) Antiquities xii. iii. 4.

of profane government, they were fatalists, viz.: they maintained that if God wants Israel independent, He has decreed it so, and it must come to pass with or without their exertion; but they would not deny the freedom of will in matters of religion and morals. This was their standpoint at that time. In all matters of religion and ethics, of course, they were rigidly orthodox.

THE SADDUCEES.

SADDUCEES, Hebrew צדוקים (3), rulers, governors and victors, the party of rulers and victors. Josephus gives no religious characteristic of the Sadducees at that time, and it appears they had none to distinguish them as a sect. The Hellenists were extinguished. The Sadducees, in after times, the same causes producing the same effects, adopted their doctrines in regard to future reward and punishment, and the validity of the traditions; but at the time of Jonathan such was not yet the case. Their origin was political. By the influence of Jonathan, Simon and their compatriots, the idea of national independence gained ground among a class of Hebrews, most likely the young, less rigorous and ritualistic than others, and from that class the warriors were drawn who supported Jonathan and Simon. After every successful revolution anywhere, the warriors claimed the executive offices, the right and power to govern, and to lay the foundation to a new aristocracy. This was also the case in Jonathan's time. His warriors made the same claims, and met with no opposition, as the Pharisees only claimed the right to have the judiciary and the schools under their control, and looked upon the executive function as a profane business. That those victors who achieved national independence and held the executive offices called themselves the *Tsaddikim*, and as a party, *Tsaddukim*, was quite natural, after they had rendered that great service to the nation: In their estimation, political independence was as essential as religious liberty, and

---

(3) *Tsaddukim* is the correct reading, by comparison of the Hebrew and Greek, and not *Tsedokim*, as derived from the family name of the priests of the house of Tsadok. The word *Tsaddik* may have been changed into *Tsadduk*, to make it consonant with *Parush*, "Pharisee," and to distinguish it from the common application of the word *Tsaddik*, "the righteous." That the term צדיק *Tsaddik*, also signifies rulers, governors and victors, implying both strength and justice, and also wisdom, is well established. Gesenius, in צדיק, 3, Albert Schu ten's rendition, and Fuerst, in צדק, where he compares it with the Aram. זדק "to be firm, strong, hard, faithful, true, tried."

the former was necessary for the security of the latter. They did not believe in the decrees of fate in relation to profane government. They held that it must be established upon the independence of the nation, and that this must be won by the warrior's strong arm. To them the scribe was not the highest authority; the military and political chief was. While, therefore, the Pharisees honored in Jonathan, and afterward in Simon, the lawful and law-abiding high priest, the son of Mattathia and brother of Juda, the Sadducees saw in those illustrious persons the highest ideals personified, the God-sent redeemers of Israel. This was the party in which the political and martial ideas predominated.

4. THE ESSENES.

ESSENES, supposed to be identical with אסא "physicians," וחיקין "ascetics," or also men of distinguishing morals and manners, and OSIOTIS חסידים "the very pious," all of which is based upon conjecture, was the name of the third party (4). A secret order, established in the days of persecution, whose members called themselves the strong and mighty men, to preserve the Law and the traditions, came out of the revolutionary time as a body of some importance. Its members were, in practice, most rigorous Pharisees, in eating their food in Levitical cleanness. Up to the time of Herod, they had nothing to do with public affairs, and left them to fate, recognizing their object of existence in religious practices and the contemplative life only. What the Essenes became afterward is reported in Philo and Josephus (Antiq. xviii. i. 5 and Wars ii. viii.). Besides their communism and celibacy, their main characteristics, appear to be given in the Book of Daniel. They became interpreters of dreams, predicted future events by researches made in Holy Scriptures, and claimed to be in communication with the angels, exactly like Daniel; so that it appears that this secret order was started by the person or persons who, about 170 B. C., brought out, in its present form, the Book of Daniel, and was based on principles contained therein.

5. THE PSALMS OF THIS PERIOD.

In times of war, the pen is at rest; the poet only draws inspiration from the exciting events. Therefore, in Pales-

---

(4) The Aramaic חסנא "strength, power," as used in Daniel ii. 37 and iv. 27, with the signification of hiding and storing away, which it has in the Arabic, and in the Hebrew חסה, fully accounts for the word Essenes. Later in history, they received different names, perhaps on account of various sects among them.

tine, during the excitement of the revolutionary war, no prose writers flourished, and the poet's lyre only re-echoes the strains of that age. It was an era of deep and rousing religious excitement. Priests became warriors, prophets rose, and divine bards sang new songs to the glory of God, the sufferings and victories of Israel. The patriotic religious inspiration which, at home, transformed peaceable peasants into heroes, and pious Levites into sublime poets, aroused abroad also, especially among the Grecian Hebrews, the spirit of prophesy and religious enthusiasm which adopted the Pagan style of the Sibylline form. In Palestine, however, some Psalms only bear characteristics of the Maccabean age. Thus, Psalm lxxi., as stated before, appears to belong to Mattathia. Psalm cxliv. appears to be the battle song of the Maccabees. Psalms xlvi., xlvii., xlviii., lxvi. and lxvii. are evidently monuments of Maccabean victories; and Psalm cvi. can not well be placed in any other time. The *Hallel* Psalms, cxiii. to cxviii., the *Hallelujah* Psalms, cxlvi. to cl., and, perhaps also, the anonymous Psalms, xcv. to xcix., are certainly from this period of lofty inspiration. There may be other Maccabean Psalms in our collection, but there are none of a later date. The Psalm collection in the Bible must have been made shortly after this period.

6. CLOSE OF THE HAGIOGRAPHIC CANON.

The third part of the Bible Canon is called כתובים "Hagiography," and consists of the Books of Ruth, Psalms, Job, Proverbs, Ecclesiastes, Song of Solomon. Lamentations, Daniel, Esther, Ezra (and Nehemiah) and Chronicles (*Baba Bathra*, 14 *b*). This order of the books was changed afterward. These books were collected, authenticated, transcribed in the sacred characters, and added to the Biblical Canon in the time of Simon. The whole Canon, as it is now before us in its three divisions, was known to the grandson of Joshua b. Sirach and had been translated into Greek in his time, as he repeatedly states in his introduction to the Greek translation of his grandfather's book. There is no book and no portion of one in the Canon which did not exist in the time of Simon, although phrases may have been changed afterward by transcribers, expounders or translators (5).

---

(5) This work may have been accomplished in the beginning of the next period, between 140 to 134 B. C., but certainly no later.

7. THE HEBREWS IN PARTHIA AND THEIR CONNECTION WITH PALESTINE.

The Parthians, supposed to be Scythians, of the Indo-Germanic family, inhabited a territory south-east of the Caspian Sea, from which they were separated by the narrow strip of country called Hyrcania. Their country was mountainous, and the people were distinguished for bravery, predatory expeditions, and voluptuous pleasures, without possessing agricultural or other arts of peace and civilization. When the Medo-Persian Empire had been overthrown by Alexander the Great, and the seat of government removed from Persia, under Seleucus Nicator, to the distant Antioch, the Parthians became bold and troublesome to their neighbors. In 256 B. C., Arsaces I. roused the Parthians to rebellion against this Syrian ruler, and achieved the independence of Parthia and Hyrcania. Between this and 150 B. C., the Parthians, governed by the Arsaces dynasty, subjected to their sway nearly all of the Medo-Persian Empire, as far east as to the borders of India and Chinese Tartary, and as far west as the Euphrates, so that the same country was called either Parthia or Persia. In the time of Simon, Arsaces VI. or Mithridates I. was king of Parthia. He added Bactria and a part of India to Parthia, and in 138 B. C., captured Demetrius II., king of Syria. The largest number of the Hebrews, who had remained in the East, were now Parthians; a few of them had gone to China and India, and some to Arabia. The Parthian Hebrews, usually called Babylonian or Persian, were descendants of all the tribes of Israel (6). As the history of that empire up to 200 A. C. was entirely neglected by Eastern chronographers (7), so, also, was the history of the Hebrews in the East. It is only by the facts of a later period and the notices in the Talmud, that we know anything at all about them. According to these meager notices, it appears that the Hebrews there always formed a State within the State, governed by their own laws and customs, and by a prince of the House of David, as they, in aftertimes, maintained in their traditions, whose title was "Head of the Captivity" (ריש גלותא). An imperfect list of those princes, from the last king of Juda, has been preserved (8). Schools of law and theology flourished among them, it is claimed, even superior to those of Palestine. Although de-

---

(6) *Berachoth*, 16 b, דלא ידעינן אי מראובן קא אתינן או משמעון קא אתינן.
(7) Sir John Malcolm's History of Persia, end of IV. Chapter.
(8) *Seder Olam Zutta*; see also Dr. Julius Fuerst's *Kultur und Literaturgeschichte der Juden in Asien*, Chapter I.

pendent on Jerusalem in the proclamation of the new moon and the consequent establishment of the festivals, and looking toward that city and temple as the religious and holy center of Israel, an independent method of expounding the Law developed among them, which influenced the doctors of Palestine no less than they influenced the Babylonians. The pilgrimages to Jerusalem and the similarity of the political situation before Simon, held together the Hebrews of the East and of Palestine, who always considered themselves one people. Doctors from the East settled frequently in Palestine, and taught in its academies, as doctors of Palestine did in the East. Pious men in the East, however, were not buried there; their corpses were sent to Palestine for interment. Nor could one be an authorized judge or teacher there unless ordained by the heads of the Sanhedrin in Palestine. The Hebrews of the East were even more purely Jewish than those of Judea, because less exposed to persecutions, wars and Grecian influence. They did not temporize. During the revolutionary war, and shortly after, large numbers of them must have emigrated into Palestine, especially east of the Jordan and Galilee, where, in the next periods, we find large numbers of Hebrews, which was not the case in the time of Juda Maccabee. With these immigrations, the Aramaic language was carried into Palestine, although the Syriac was certainly used before in Galilee, and the difference between the Syriac and West Aramaic is very little.

8. THE LITERATURE OF THE PARTHIAN HEBREWS.

The literature of the Parthian Hebrews appears to have been extensive, although mere fragments thereof have been preserved in the Greek, Aramaic and Syriac. These fragments are the Books of Tobit, Baruch, Judith, Susanna and other fragments from an older Book of Daniel, all of which were originally Aramaic and were written in the East before or during this period.

1. SUSANNA is one of the Daniel fragments which were not accepted in the Canon (9). It consists of sixty-four verses (Greek) and reports a story from the youth of Daniel. Susanna is the wife of a celebrated elder of the Israelites in Babylonia, in the time of King Nebuchadnezzar. Many distinguished persons, and among them, two elders

---

(9) Other fragments of this kind are the Prayer of Asariah, Psalm of the Three Men in the Fiery Furnace, Bel and the Dragon, which are without originality. The latter is imitated in the Talmud *Berachoth* 6 a.

and judges, meet in Joakim's house, and these latter fall in love with his beautiful wife, attempt to debauch her, and failing therein, accuse her of adultery, in consequence of which she is condemned to death. Led to the scaffold, God raises the holy spirit of Daniel; he cries out against the injustice to be committed; Susanna and the elders are led back to the seat of judgment; Daniel conducts a second trial, proves the innocence of Susanna and the guilt of the elders. The latter are put to death, and Daniel's fame is great in the land. The whole narrative is Babylonian. The criminal procedure described therein is similar to the Palestinian, and yet differing from it sufficiently to point distinctly to a time and place distant from Jerusalem and prior to the criminal law established in the next period of this history. Its language was undoubtedly Aramaic, the time of its origin pre-Maccabean (10).

2. THE BOOK OF TOBI, Tobit or Tobias, consists of sixteen chapters (Greek) and reports the story of Tobi and his son Tobiah, residents of Nineveh, in the time of Salmenasar, Sanherib and Esarhaddon, kings of Assyria. Several versions and translations of this book exist (11). Tobit is a pious Hebrew of the tribe of Naphtali, led into captivity by Salmenasar. In Nineveh, he became the king's purveyor, and amassed wealth, part of which he deposited with his friend Gabael, who resided in a city afterward called Rages (built by Seleucus Nicator). In his captivity, Tobit is as pious and charitable as he was in his own country, and adds to his works of benevolence particular care for burying the dead, which was prohibited among the followers of Zoroaster (12). In consequence of this he is persecuted by the king, leaves the capital of Assyria, returns after the death of Sanherib, continues his works of charity, becomes blind and poor, is maltreated by his wife, who supports him by her labor, and, like Job, he wishes to die. He remembers the treasures he had deposited with his friend, and asks his son, Tobiah, to go to the distant city and obtain them of his friend Gabael. The son seeks a trust-

---

(10) The rabbis had no better opinion of the Babylonian elders than the author of Susanna had. (*Sanhedrin*, 93 a).

(11) See the Book of Tobit, etc., by Ad. Neubauer, Oxford, 1877.

(12) See Johann Friederich Kleuker's Zend-Avesta; the passages noticed in his *Verzeichniss der Sachen*, etc., under the term Tod. This circumstance proves that the Book of Tobit was written after the reign of Darius and Cyrus. None of these books were written near the fall of Jerusalem, as they are not noticed by the *Tena'im*, and several passages from them occur in the New Testament, also in Paul's Epistles.

worthy companion and finds the angel Raphael, who, in the form of a young man called Asaria, goes with him. On the way, they bathe in the Tigris River; a huge fish (like that of Jonah), threatens to swallow Tobiah. Encouraged by the angel, he catches and kills the fish, and takes its liver and gall. Reaching Ecbatana, they go to the house of Raguel, a friend of Tobit, where they are hospitably entertained. He has an only daughter, whose name is Sarah, who had been married seven times, but her husbands were killed in the bridal chamber by the demon Asmodi. Tobiah desires to marry Sarah; her father informs him of the fate of her seven husbands, but Tobiah marries her nevertheless. By advice of the angel, he burns the liver of the fish in the bridal chamber, and prays with his wife. This banishes Asmodi far away into Upper Egypt, and both Tobiah and Sarah are saved. The angel goes to Rages, receives the treasures, and then they return to Tobit with great wealth. When the blind man approached his son to embrace him, he anointed his father's eyes with the gall of the fish, and Tobit instantly recovered his sight. He was again happy and rich, gave praise to God, and the angel returned to heaven. The whole story, in its moral lesson, is an imitation of Job, and like it, is based on a popular legend. The numerous quotations from the Bible and frequent imitations of Bible passages, prove that the book was written long after Ezra, after Job and Jonah, perhaps in the Grecian period. The angel in the form of man, the demon Asmodi, known only in the Babylonian Talmud (13), the golden rule advanced by Tobit (iv. 15) and brought to Palestine by Hillel, the Babylonian, and the whole tone of the book, like the miraculous properties of the liver and gall of the fish, point to the East at a considerable distance from Palestine. It is the didactic production of a Babylonian sage in imitation of Job, in vindication of Providence, and in laudation of humanitarian piety. It bears distinctly the eastern colophon, and points to the origin of the Babylonian Hagadah.

3. THE BOOK OF JUDITH is a book of sixteen chapters. It was originally Aramaic. A general of Nebuchadnezzar, whose name was Holofernes, in the eighteenth year of that king's reign, overran a part of Palestine and besieged Bethuel, a town of the tribe of Simeon (Joshua xix. 4; I. Chronicles iv. 30). The inhabitants of Bethuel were in great distress. A heroic and very ascetic widow, Judith, the daughter of Meraris, the scion of sixteen sires, a woman of great

---

(13) GUITIN 65; see S. L. Rapaport's *Erech Millin*, Art. Ashmodai, the demon of sensual love, who also dethroned King Solomon.

beauty and piety, resolves to risk her life in order to save her city and its inhabitants. She goes to the camp of Holofernes, wins his affections, is alone with him in his tent, he falls asleep, and she slays him with his own sword, as Jael did Sisera. She escapes from the camp, the defenders of the city sally forth, rout the besieging army and drive it hence. The honors showered upon Judith, her hymn of praise, and the story of her old age, close the book. The names and dates in this book are unhistorical, its moral principle, eulogizing an assassin, is low and points to a time of hostility and fanaticism. The patriotic idea predominates in the whole book to such an extent and with so much fanaticism and asceticism, that the time of its origin can not be doubtful. It is certainly an allegory based on some ancient tradition, written in the East after the flight and death of Antiochus Epiphanes, sent to the Hebrews of Palestine to encourage and to rouse them to the heroic struggle. This is also partly the idea of De Wette and Grotius. The apostatizing edict of Antiochus Epiphanes was directed against all the Hebrews of the Syrian Empire, and caution was necessary in writing a patriotic book. Therefore, this form was chosen. This guides us also in ascertaining the time when the Book of Baruch was written.

4. THE BOOK OF BARUCH consists of five chapters and an appendix of one chapter. The book opens with an introduction of nine verses, in which Baruch b. Neriah, the scribe of the Prophet Jeremiah, is mentioned as the author of those speeches which were read in Babel before the captives and King Jechonia, in the fifth year of the captivity, when money was collected and, together with some of the temple vessels, sent to Jerusalem, accompanied by an epistle admonishing those who remained in Jerusalem to pray for King Nebuchadnezzar, to adhere steadfastly to the Law, and be mindful of the fact that God punished Israel on account of his disobedience; and that He will again be gracious to him as he returns to the Law and its precepts. True wisdom is in the revealed Law, and the hope of Jerusalem is in submission to its commandments. The sixth chapter is an epistle of Jeremiah in reply to the former, and a polemic against idolatry and its practices. The book was originally Aramaic. The seventh generation after Jeremiah (Baruch vi. 3) mentioned as the time of Israel's redemption, is given in *Seder Olam Sutta* as the time of Nicanor; so that it can hardly be doubtful that the death of Nicanor was the immediate incentive for writing this book, as a congratulation and encouragement to those in Palestine who fought against idolatry and oppression. It contains numer-

ous quotations from Ezra, Nehemiah, Job and late Psalms. As in Judith, the same unhistorical highpriest, Joiakim, is mentioned, and, like the former, it is full of ascetic hints. Nebuchadnezzar and all the dates are equally unhistorical in both books; so that their simultaneous origin can hardly be doubted. Judith appears to favor the complete independence of Palestine, and Baruch, civil and religious liberty under the kings of Syria, as the two parties at home proposed. The Baruch story appears to be true; the letters and prayers, however, were written in the East after the death of Nicanor.

9. The Hebrews in Egypt.

The Hebrew population of Egypt had largely increased in the Grecian period, and was considerably augmented in the revolutionary time. Besides, numerous Grecian Hebrews, who must have sought refuge in Egypt, the men of learning and letters, and many other non-combatants, like Onias and Aristobul, went to Egypt, and especially to Alexandria, to the Island of Cyprus and to Cyrene, where some of them had lived since the time of the first Ptolemy (Joseph. contra Apion ii. 4), and afterward became very wealthy and prominent (Ant. xiv. 7, 2). With the Macedonians and Greeks, they belonged, in all those countries, to the favored class of citizens in commerce, industry and politics, while the native Egyptians were treated as a conquered race, of inferior intelligence. The principal homes of the Hebrews in Egypt were in Alexandria, Memphis, Cairo and the commercial cities on the Red Sea. In Alexandria they were renowned artisans, merchants and ship-owners. Alexandria having become the metropolis of the world's commerce, the Hebrews, undoubtedly, from that starting-point, penetrated into Europe, and were engaged in the trade at the various ports of the Mediterranean, Adriatic, North and Baltic Seas and the Atlantic Ocean; although they were known there only as Greeks or Phœnicians. In Egypt and the other countries, they lived according to their own laws and were governed by one elected head, with the title Ethnarch or Alabarch, who resided in Alexandria and presided over the Alexandrian Sanhedrin of seventy or seventy-one. This officer and this body governed the Egyptian Hebrews in their religious and social affairs. With the exception of a short period under the reign of Philopator, they always lived in peace, in excellent harmony with the Macedonians and Greeks, and were, like them, hated by the Egyptians. Therefore, and especially when, during the revolution, many of the Grecizing Hebrews immigrated into Egypt, they adopted the Greek language, not only in their families, but also in the synagogues, read the Bible in the Greek translation, and their doctors were largely influenced by the philosophy and poetry of Greece and the learning of Alexandria. The pilgrimages to Jerusalem still united them with the mother country and language; but this was also disturbed by the Onias Temple.

10. THE ONIAS TEMPLE.

In the year 163 B. C., Onias, son of Onias III., the last legitimate highpriest, came to Alexandria, and in a short time, he and another Hebrew, Dositheus, were appointed chief commanders of the royal army. The Hebrews had already distinguished themselves under Philopator, in an insurrection of the native Egyptians against that king. With a loss on the part of the Hebrews of 40,000 or, as some report, of 60,000 men, they put down the rebellion. In 162 B. C., they rendered the same service to Philometor, and this time more by prudence than valor. This, perhaps, was the cause of the appointment of Onias and Dositheus to the highest military position, although Philometor and his mother were special friends of the Hebrews and their religion. Again in 156 B. C., the Alexandrians rose against Philometor, and again Onias pacified them. Onias, considering himself the legitimate highpriest, now made use of the favor of the king and queen to claim, in Egypt, the rights of which he was deprived in Jerusalem. He obtained the privilege from the king of rebuilding an ancient temple in the district of Heliopolis, north-east of Memphis, which appears to have been anciently a Hebrew temple (Isaiah xix. 18 to 21). He intended that this renowned temple should have the same culte as that of Jerusalem, and Onias to be its highpriest. The temple was built (150 B. C.), an altar erected before it, all according to the Laws of Moses; priests were appointed from among the sons of Aaron, and the entire culte of Jerusalem was imitated. Some of the Greco-Hebrews, especially of Alexandria, continued their pilgrimages to Jerusalem, but the masses of the people all over the country sacrificed in the Onias temple at Heliopolis, and so, gradually, most of the Egyptian Hebrews were Grecized.

11. THE HEBREWS PROTECT CLEOPATRA.

Once more Onias and Dositheus appeared on the stage of Egyptian history. It was in 145 B. C., when Philometor was dead, and Cleopatra, in behalf of her only son, had assumed the reins of government. A party of Egyptians, however, declared in favor of Physcon, the brother of Philometor and king of Cyrene, and sent embassadors to him. Cleopatra prepared for self-defense, and her two chief captains, Onias and Dositheus, stood by her with an army of Hebrews. The Roman embassador, Thermus, however, settled the difficulties and prevented a civil war. Cleopatra married Physcon, who was to govern Egypt till the young prince became of age. But Physcon, on the wedding day, slew his nephew in the arms of his mother and assumed the sole power over Egypt and Cyrene. So Egypt was placed under the iron rule of one of the most brutal and inexorable despots, who, with the exception of three years of banishment (130 to 127 B. C.), maintained himself on the throne of Egypt to his death in 117 B. C. This murderous and incestuous glutton called himself Euergetes II., but his name was Physcon.

12. ARISTOBUL AND THE LITERARY ACTIVITY IN EGYPT.

The Asmonean revolution and the subsequent victory of the Palestinean orthodoxy drove, with the Grecizing Hebrews, also a number of philosophers and writers to foreign countries, and especially to Egypt; so that from and after this period, Hebrew philosophy had its main seat in Alexandria. Among those who came to Alexandria was Aristobul, of Paneas, in Upper Galilee, a man of priestly extraction, who became tutor of the king and chief of the Hebrews of Alexandria. He was still alive in the year 124 B. C. (II. Maccabees i. 10); yet his main activity belongs to this period. The Alexandrian Jewish philosophy begins with him. He was as eminent a Greek writer as he was a profound reasoner and enthusiastic believer in Judaism. All that is true and good in the ancient Grecian poets and philosophers appeared to him taken from the shrine of the Hebrews. Not only Pythagoras, Plato and Aristotle, but also Orpheus, Aratos, Linos, Homer and Hesiod, according to Aristobul, adopted and advanced Hebrew precepts and admired the mighty sires of this nation's superior mind. The main portions of the Pentateuch, he maintained, had been known to the Greeks long before the book was translated, under Ptolemy Philadelphus. In his time, as the translator of Ben Sirach's book states in his introduction, the whole Hebrew Bible had been translated into Greek, and the activity of Greco-Hebrew scribes must have been very extensive, although, besides the Bible and some Apocrypha, only fragments of that period are extant, and quotations by later authors. The works of Aristobul have also been lost (14); and of his principal work, "Commentaries on the Pentateuch," dedicated to the king of Egypt, Eusebius (15). and others, fragments only have been saved. In them there are quotations from Greek poets, supposed to have been interpolated by Aristobul to prove his hypothesis concerning the ancient Greek writers and their knowledge and appreciation of the Hebrew Scriptures. It appears beyond doubt, from those fragments, that Aristobul was the first who wrote a commentary on the Pentateuch. If not the first author, he certainly was the first writer of the philosophical *Derasha*. He began his work in Palestine with the book called "The Wisdom of Solomon," which contains the general introduction to the "Commentary," and then a commentary or *Derashah* on the Exode, and the miracles connected with it. In Egypt, perhaps, he commenced with a Grecian translation of this book, which he continued with a commentary on the laws.

13. THE PRECEPTS OF ARISTOBUL.

The Book of Wisdom and the fragments of Aristobul's Commentaries, contain the following doctrines:

God Himself is inscrutable to human reason; He has partially manifested Himself in the creation, and in revelation to men who can and do rise above the sensual to the source of all intellectual and physical being (16).

God is perfect in wisdom, goodness, power and holiness; all anthropomorphisms and anthropopathisms in Scriptures are allegorical. So the hand of God signifies his power, the word and speech of God signifies creative deeds in nature or the human mind, etc.; wisdom or Shekinah is the manifestation of God's inspiration at a certain place or to a certain person or persons.

---

(14) De Rossa, in his *Meor Enayim*, and others, report that a manuscript of Aristobul was extant and kept in a convent at Mantua, but it has not yet been found.

(15) *Præparatio Evangelica* (divided into fifteen books) vii. 14; viii. 10; ix. 6; xiii. 12.

(16) The formula which in aftertimes gave rise to the dualism of (ישתי רשיות) father and son, God and Demiurgos, or God and Logos, belonged to Aristobul, who attempted to make Heathens understand the God of Israel. The precept itself was certainly commonly known and understood among the Hebrews as the *Jehorah Elohim* theology. It is found again in the Talmud הוא מקומו של עולם ואין העולם מקומו, "He is the world's place, but the world is not His place. He is the immanent in nature, but not absorbed therein; and in Paul's Epistle to the Romans i. 19, 20; Acts xvii. 22, e. s.

The world is governed by God's eternal wisdom, goodness and providence; no evil comes from Him; every man receives his due on this earth or in eternal life.

Man's duty on earth is to advance steadily in wisdom and goodness, to come so much nearer the Deity by love and cogitation, which is the supreme good here and hereafter.

The ancient Grecian savans also have taught this creed, in philosophical formulas or myths, all of which, however, is contained in Hebrew Scriptures, expressly or allegorically.

Kings, no less than those over whom they rule, are subject to God's laws and responsible to Him for their doings and omissions.

With the translation of the entire Scriptures and the commentaries of Aristobul into the Greek language and conceptions, the combat of Grecism and Judaism was carried among the most intelligent Heathens, and became an active principle of history, which is still at work in our days.

14. OTHER WRITERS OF THE GRECO-HEBREWS.

Commentaries on the Pentateuch after Aristobul became the fashion among the Greco-Hebrew writers. Such books, of which fragments have been preserved by Alexander Polyhistor, Eusebius and others (17), are EUPOLEMOS, one of Juda's embassadors to Rome (Euseb. Praep. Evang. ix.), who wrote historical commentaries in two books; ARTAPANUS (See p. 79), who appears to have been a Heathen of an older date; DEMETRIUS, ARISTEAS, and CLEODEMOS, whose age and faith is not ascertained. The fragments of their writings show that, instigated by the success of Aristobul, many Greco-Hebrews and Heathens wrote commentaries on the Hebrew Scriptures, and popularized them among the Greeks. The history of the Hebrews from 176 to 161 B. C., an abstract of which is in II. Maccabees, was written by YASON OF CYRENE. He wrote the history of Mattathia and Juda Maccabee from verbal reports as they had reached him, and was inclined to the marvellous and supernatural. His book has been lost. MELON wrote a book against the Hebrews, of which a small and insignificant fragment is extant (18). The Greco-Hebrew poets also arose

---

(17) See Dr. L. Herzfeld's *Geschichte des Volkes Jisrael*, II. Band, p. 458 e. s., and *Excurs*. 30. Alexander Cornelius Polyhistor wrote about 80 to 90 B. C., and was the main compiler of Greco-Hebrew fragments, from whom the Christian historians chiefly copied.

(18) See Polyhistor, chapters xvii., xviii., xix., xxxvi., xxxvii.; C. Mueller's *Fragmenta Historicorum Graecorum;* John Gill, Herzfeld and Eusebius, as quoted above.

in this period of enthusiasm, patriotism and pre-eminent expectations of the return of glory to Zion. They adopted the popular Heathen form of Sibylline prophecies to laud the greatness and hopes of Israel; and those poems have become portions of the existing Sibylline books, *Oracula Sibyllina*, edited by Gallæus at Amsterdam, 1689. The original Sibylline books were burnt in Rome, with the temple of Jupiter, in the year 84 B. C. Again, Augustus confiscated and burnt about two thousand of them. In consequence of the Maccabean revolution and brilliant successes, the spirit of the age among the Hebrews everywhere was patriotic, enthusiastic and profoundly religious. Israel's faith, law and history were lauded and expounded to the Heathens. Started by the Book of Daniel, a superabundance of glory was predicted to Zion by the excited phantasy of poets and enthusiasts. The hopes were too lofty to be fulfilled; a large number of prophecies remained unrealized, and fancy forged of it Messianic hopes, as they appear in some of the Sibylline songs of this and coming periods.

IV. The Period of Independence.

Sixty-nine years of independence (142 to 63 B. C.) followed the revolutionary war. During this time, the Hebrews grew up to a first-class commonwealth in internal organization, laws and institutions, military capacity, moral, intellectual and religious character, into a state of prosperity and wealth, interrupted only for a short time by the feuds of the Sadducees and Pharisees. Although hemmed in by the powers of Egypt, Syria and Parthia, the Hebrew government was strong enough to maintain its independence and to check the violence of the petty nations round about. The rulers of this period were:

1. Simon, prince and highpriest, - - 142 B. C.
2. John Hyrcan, prince and highpriest, with Joshua b. Perachia and Nitai, of Arbela, at the head of the Sanhedrin, - 134 B. C.
3. Juda Aristobul, king and highpriest, - 107 B. C.
4. Alexander Jannai, king and highpriest, with Simon b. Shetach part of the time at the head of the Sanhedrin, - - 105 B. C.
5. Salome Alexandra, queen, and her son, Hyrcan, highpriest, with Juda b. Tabbai and Simon b. Shetach at the head of the Sanhedrin, - - - - - - 78 B. C.
6. Hyrcan and then Aristobul, king and high priest, with Shemaiah and Abtalion at the head of the Sanhedrin, - - 69 to 63 B. C.

CHAPTER XIV.

The Epoch of Popular Government.

1. THE DEMOLITION OF ACRA.

The Hebrew people looked upon the year 142 B. C. as the beginning of the new era of independence. Simon, although exercising the functions of an independent prince, was, nevertheless, cautious enough not to assume sovereignty opposite foreign powers, as long as a turn of events in Syria could overthrow the new State. By his energetic course of action he realized the projects of Jonathan in driving the foreign garrisons and the Syrian sympathizers out of the country, fortifying the cities and placing them under the control of loyal men, and completing the fortifications of Jerusalem. The garrison and inhabitants of Acra, cut off from the city by a wall, could hold out no longer. In the year 141 B. C. they capitulated and left the country. Enthusiastic demonstrations on the part of the people marked the event, the last vestige of foreign supremacy had disappeared; therefore, the 23d day of the second month was appointed a national holiday (1). In order, however, that the citadel and hill of Acra, which was higher than the Temple Mount, should never again command the temple, the citadel was demolished and the hill, in the course of three years, was dug down to a level with Zion. This left the Temple Mount the highest point in the city. The walls of the temple were strengthened by Simon and the foundation laid to Castle Baris, afterward Fort Antonio, at the north-western corner of the temple square, which was finished and named by Simon's son and successor. The residence of Simon, afterward called the palace of the

---

(1) I. Maccabees xiii. 51; Meguillath Taanith II.

Asmoneans, on the western slope of the Temple Mount, was also built by him, although his successors enlarged and beautified it.

2. THE ASMONEAN DYNASTY ESTABLISHED.

A grateful people, however patriotic it may be, is no less liable to fatal errors than traitors are. The services rendered to the Hebrews by the sons of Mattathia, and personally by Simon, were certainly eminent. Those heroes and statesmen won the independence of Israel. Therefore, the people committed the fatal error of conferring upon Simon and his descendants forever the hereditary rights of its prince, highpriest and commander-in-chief, to stand at the head of the Kingdom of Heaven, under the Laws of Moses. This was done in the year 140 B. C., the 28th day of Ellul, when priests and people, together with the Sanhedrin and rulers, were convoked to a great and solemn meeting in the upper court of the temple (2). Then and there the hereditary titles and prerogatives of prince, highpriest and commander-in-chief were conferred on Simon, which placed him and his heirs at the head of the Hebrew people forever. Unlike Gideon of old, he accepted all those dignities, and they were secured to him in a solemn covenant made in the temple. This became the source of many miseries to Israel. Yet it appears that at the time, it was the unanimous will and wish of the Hebrew people. The decree of the nation was engraved on brazen tablets and placed before the community on the walls of the temple and other public places; copies thereof were deposited in the temple treasury. So the Asmonean dynasty was established, and the old dynasties of David and Zadok were declared superseded forever, since their last representatives, Jason and Menelaus, on the part of the Zadok family, the sons of Tobias, on the part of the Davidian family, had betrayed the cause of Israel in his last struggle.

---

(2) I. Maccabees xiv. This place of meeting is called SARAMEL, which ought to read SAMAREL, the divine court or guarding place of the temple. This was the Upper Court, also called the Inner Court, which then comprised both the Courts of Israel and priests, separated only by steps (DUCHAN). In this court were the altar and the royal throne. The trophies were kept there It was 128 cubits long from east to west, and 135 cubits wide from north to south, surrounded by colonnades and porches of three rows of marble pillars projecting from the cloisters which inclosed it.

3. Demetrius II. and Antiochus Sidetes.

In the year 142 b. c., Demetrius, misled by the Greeks and Macedonians of Parthia, invaded that country, where he lost his army and his liberty. The general of King Arsaces captured him. Demetrius was treated well; King Arsaces gave him his daughter, and the captive king abandoned his wife, Cleopatra, who was at Seleucia. He being a captive, his brother, Antiochus Sidetes, came to Syria with an army to overthrow Tryphon. Cleopatra had succeeded in collecting a considerable army at Seleucia to enforce her claims. She now sent to Antiochus and offered him her hand and her influence. The marriage was consummated. Cleopatra married the third king of Syria, and Antiochus Sidetes took the field against Tryphon, whom he defeated and drove behind the walls of Dora. Tryphon fled from Dora to Apamia, where he was captured and slain. This settled the crown of Syria upon Antiochus Sidetes and Cleopatra. There were then two queens, Cleopatra, the one in Syria, and her mother in Egypt, now the wife of Physcon.

4. Simon and Antiochus Sidetes.

Previous to his landing in Syria, 140 b. c., Antiochus Sidetes had sent letters to Simon in which, although the independence of Judea was not clearly acknowledged, still all other rights and privileges of the Hebrews and of Simon, personally, and the perfect independence of Jerusalem and the temple were fully guaranteed, and the sovereign right of coinage added (3). This last point proves that the independence of Judea was not fully acknowledged by this prince. Simon accepted the privileges, and sent a second embassy to Rome, this time with a golden shield of great value as a gift to the people, to make sure of independence. While Antiochus besieged Dora for the first time, Simon's embassadors returned and read to Antiochus a copy of the treaty with the Romans, renewed and strengthened with Simon, other copies of which had been sent to Demetrius and to various nations in league with Rome. This was doubly obnoxious to Antiochus. The independence of Judea and the Roman acknowledgment of Demetrius and not of himself, were the objectionable points. Simon was now willing to support Antiochus with men, money and provisions, as an ally, not as a vassal; but the king refused all offers and overthrew Tryphon without Simon's aid. After the death of Tryphon, tranquility being restored in

---

(3) I. Maccabees xv. 2.

Syria, Antiochus claimed one thousand talents especially for Joppe, Gazara (4) and Acra, for damages done and taxes collected. Simon, on his part, maintained that it was the land and property of their fathers which the Hebrews had recaptured, and consented to pay one hundred talents for the citadels and fortifications of Joppe and Gazara. The opulence of Jerusalem and Simon's household being reported to the king, together with the counter-propositions of Simon, an invasion of Judea was resolved upon and Cendebeus was sent to carry it on.

5. Simon and his Sons Defeat Cendebeus.

Simon's oldest sons, Juda and John (afterward Hyrcan), were his military lieutenants. John resided at Gazara and guarded the sea coast. Cendebeus invaded Judea from the sea side in the neighborhood of Jamnia and Joppe, and fortified there a place called Kedron, a short distance from Gazara. John came to Jerusalem for advice and assistance. Simon, though advanced in age, accepted the challenge. He had now ready an army of 20,000 infantry and an adequate number of cavalry. Giving to his two sons the command of the main army, he brought up the rear and directed the strategical movements of the whole. After leaving Jerusalem, Juda and John tarried all night at Modain, near the graves of their heroic grandfather and uncles. Next day they proceeded to meet the enemy. A battle was fought and Cendebeus was defeated with a loss of two thousand men; the survivors fled to Azotus and Kedron. Juda was wounded in the battle, but John pursued the enemy to Azotus, took it and burnt it. The victory was important, because it demonstrated the power of Judea to maintain its independence.

6. The First Hebrew Coins.

Simon coined no money till the year 138 B. C., when, by the defeat of Cendebeus, he felt convinced that the independence of Judea was firmly established. Now the ancient silver Shekel, half and quarter Shekel, were re-introduced, called (שקל ישראל) "Shekels of Israel," dated from the first, second year, etc. of (לגאלת ציון) "the Redemption of Zion" or ירושלם קדשה "Jerusalem the Holy." The inscriptions were in the ancient (Hebrew) letters, and the

---

(4) Gazara is not identical with Gaza. Gazara was an important strategic point west of Jerusalem. See Dr. Stark's Gaza, etc., p. 495, e. s.

effigies were the palm tree, with the priestly chalice on the reverse. The half shekel had under the palm tree, two baskets filled with dates, and on the reverse, two palm branches and a citron between. There are extant, of Simon's coins, the shekel, half-shekel and quarter-shekel (5).

7. The Death of Simon.

Four years of peace and prosperity followed in Palestine, under the administration of Simon, who was as diligent a student of the Law as he was an energetic governor, pious highpriest and popular prince. There was none to disturb or molest him; he was the favorite of his people and the terror of his enemies. In his own family, however, he had nourished a poisonous serpent, his own son-in-law, Ptolemy, son of Habub, governor of Jericho. He invited Simon and his wife, with their two sons, Juda and Mattathia, to his castle at Dock, near Jericho. The guests arrived and partook freely of the royal banquet, also of the wine. When they were under its influence, armed servants of Ptolemy rushed into the hall and slew the hoary prince. His wife and sons were captured and imprisoned in the castle, men were despatched to slay John Hyrcan, to take possession of the city of Jerusalem, and to notify Antiochus Sidetes of the foul assassination. Ptolemy expected that Antiochus Sidetes would come at once and put the assassin at the head of the Hebrews. It was in the month of Shebat, 134 B. C., when Simon, 73 years old, fell by the hand of the assassin hired by Antiochus Sidetes.

8. John Hyrcan Succeeds Simon.

John Hyrcan, residing at Gazara, was informed of the assassination of Simon in time to foil the other schemes of Ptolemy. When his emissaries arrived at Gazara, they were captured and slain. John arrived in Jerusalem before Ptolemy's men, and had taken the reins of the government into his hands before his enemy had done anything. Being the legitimate heir of Simon, he was at once proclaimed prince and highpriest. John was before Dock before Ptolemy could prepare for the emergency. He threatened to whip John's mother in case her son should assault the castle, and did so at the first attempt. Although the mother repeatedly encouraged her son not to heed her pains, but to take the castle and punish the assassin, still John could

---

(5) See *Geschichte der Jued. Munzen*, Dr. M. A. Levy, p. 40, etc.

not overcome his filial compassion, and accepted the proposition of Ptolemy to let him go unharmed and to leave the country. Ptolemy acted upon the terms of the amnesty, but before doing so, he first slew John's mother and his two brothers, and then fled to Philadelphia, in Ammon, a disgraced assassin.

9. Palestine Invaded by Sidetes.

Antiochus Sidetes came with a large army to Palestine before John was prepared to meet him. Before John could raise an adequate force, the enemy encamped before Jerusalem, which was besieged during the whole summer. It was the Sabbath year, 134 to 133 B. C., and provisions were scarce. Want of water in the city increased the sufferings. Still the defenders would not yield, and the walls of Jerusalem appeared impregnable. They sent the non-combatants out of the city, but Antiochus would not let them pass through his lines, and after much suffering they had to be taken back into the city. The Feast of Booths approached and the rainy season came near. John asked of Sidetes seven day's armistice during the feast, and animals to make the prescribed sacrifices. It was granted. During the feast peace was negotiated and concluded. Antiochus was satisfied with 500 talents of silver and hostages, to secure the fulfillment of the main stipulations, viz., that John Hyrcan would support the Syrian king in his contemplated invasion of Parthia. Antiochus destroyed some of the fortifications of Jerusalem and left the country, keeping only Joppe and Gazara under his sway; he claimed them as Syrian cities. But where did John Hyrcan find the money? He paid 300 talents at once. It was most likely taken from the temple treasury, and the unsuspecting people were told that he had opened the sepulcher of David and found 2,500 talents therein.

10. The Zuggoth—A Concession Made by John Hyrcan.

In the Hebrew records, the two heads of the Sanhedrin are called *Zuggoth* "the pair," of which Jose b. Joezer and Jose b. John would have been the first, if they had been *de jure* the heads of the Sanhedrin; but they were not; they were scholasts (אשכלות), representative men of the Antigonus school. Therefore, Joshua b. Perachia was the first Nassi, prince president, and Nitai, of Arbela, in Galilee, the first Ab-Beth-Din, chief-justice, of the Sanhedrin; the first Zuggoth, who were no priests, and the heads of the Sanhedrin *de jure* and *de facto* (שישמשו פרנסות) (6). They were appointed by John Hyrcan (7), and this closed the "High Court of the Asmoneans," to be succeeded by the Sanhedrin, organized as a body of laymen, although the priests were not excluded, presided over by the principal scribes, the bearers of the traditions, independent of their birth (8). This was a memorable concession to the Pharisees, who, as the sequel will show, were opposed to the concentration of power in one individual, and, like the prophets of old, did not favor the monopoly of spiritual and scholastic functions by the tribe of Levy. They placed the scribe higher than the priest and the sage above the prophet (9). This concession, it is maintained in the Mishnah, so pleased and pacified the multitude that the hammer, announcing by its noise in Jerusalem the time to pay the taxes, was abolished, as no person in the land was suspected of negligence in the payment thereof; all the agitators and ruffians were overcome, peace, satisfaction and good government were completely restored (10). John Hyrcan, perhaps, was not the man to preside over the Sanhedrin to the satisfaction of the Pharisees. His father was an acknowledged student of the Law (I. Maccabees xiv. 14), and had been appointed by Mattathia as the chief counselor of the nation (*Ibid* II. 65); while Hyrcan was not distinguished for learning, and could inherit only the titles expressly con-

---

(6) The priest of the same name, Joshua b. Perachia, in the time of Hillel, of course, was another man. See Jacob Brill's *Mebo Hamishnah*, p. 20, and *Jalkut Simoni*, Sec. 761. This, perhaps, was the man who is mentioned in the Talmudical legends as the teacher of Jesus of Nazareth.

(7) This is stated twice in YERUSHALMI, *Maaser Sheni* v. 8 and *Sotah* ix. 11, העמיד וגות; only that those expounders who misunderstood the passage *ibid*, at the beginning of *Halachah* x., in regard to the Ascheoloth, imposed strange ideas on that plain statement.

(8) It is not proved from Josephus xx. ix. 1, that the highpriest was the president of the Sanhedrin, because the body mentioned there was not the Great Sanhedrin, its convocation was not lawful, and it is not said that the highpriest presided. Nor does Antiq. xiv. ix. 4 and 5 prove it, because Hyrcan was an exception to the rule. He, personally, was appointed by Julius Caesar as the highest authority of the Hebrews in all questions about Jewish customs (Antiquities xiv. x. 2), and this particular privilege was not made hereditary.

(9) MISHNAH *Horioth* III., 8, YERUSHALMI Sanhedrin xi. 6. נביא וזקן לביה הן דומין וגו׳

(10) MISHNAH *Maaser Sheni* v. 15; *Sotah* ix. 10. The commentaries do not admit this exposition of the above Mishnah; still I can find no other sense in the terms. The *Meorerin* are agitators and the *Nokefit* "ruffians," or those who strike. The hammer can only refer to the taxes, as the two sentences are closely connected.

ferred on his father, of highpriest, prince and commander-in-chief. Like his people, he was intensely religious, patriotic and zealously attached to the ritual Laws of Moses; he may, therefore, have made this concession from religious scruples and patriotic motives; although, it appears, that circumstances forced him to it. Succeeding his father under distressing circumstances, and having partially lost his independence and treasures in his defense against Antiochus Sidetes, he depended too much on public favor to rule without the popular consent; and the Pharisees, or more particularly the scribes, governed public opinion. Anyhow, it proved a wise and pacifying concession.

11. Joshua B. Perachia and Nitai of Arbela.

Little is known about the Sanhedrin over which the first Zuggoth presided. It could only have been with its consent that John abolished the Confession at the bringing of the tithe, although it is literally prescribed in the Law (Deuter. xxvi. 12 to 15); because it is stated therein, "And I have also given it to the Levite," while this was not done any longer. One-third of the tithe was brought to Jerusalem for the priests and Levites in active service, as Nehemiah had ordained. The other third was given to either the priests or Levites. The last third was given to the poor, etc., and to the pious students of Jerusalem (11). This shows that the Pharisees were no literalists, and made considerable changes in the Laws of Moses. We also know that the Nassi, or president of the Sanhedrin, could not make a law; for Joshua b. Perachia prohibited the use of wheat imported from Egypt, on account of its being Levitically unclean, and the prohibition was not accepted; "Then that wheat is unclean to Joshua b. Perachia, and clean for everybody else," was the conclusion (12); although the laws concerning Levitical cleanness had become so popular that John, during his official term, sacrificed two red heifers, which had not been done since the time of Simon the Just (13). There can hardly be any doubt that this Sanhedrin established the law that no war upon any foreign nation could be commenced without the consent of the Sanhedrin (14), as it was called upon to regulate its relations to the executive power, and to enact the main political laws which

---

(11) Yerushalmi, *Maaser Sheni*, end בראישנה ונ׳
(12) See Zachariah Frankel's *Darkei Ham-mishnah* p. 34.
(13) Mishnah, *Parah* III. 5.
(14) *Ibid Sanhedrin* I. 5.

the new and independent state required. We know, furthermore, of the two heads of this Sanhedrin, that they, as their predecessors and successors did, disagreed on the point of *Semicha*, the ordination of the scribes (15); and that they left on record the following characteristic mottoes (16): Joshua b. Perachia said, "Procure thee a teacher, purchase thee an associate, and judge every man charitably." Nitai, of Arbela, said, "Keep far away from a bad neighbor, associate not with the wicked, and think not that punishment would not come." Nitai's motto may be political and refer to the treaty with Antiochus Sidetes, as also with some petty nations around Palestine, whom John and his sons afterward conquered and who became merged in the Hebrews. The motto of Joshua affords an insight into the spirit of that age, when the study of the Law to unravel its profound teachings was considered the most meritorious exercise of the Hebrew mind. Joshua demanded regular education by a competent master, with classmates, and led by the principle of charity and benevolence. He evidently opposed that solitary eremitism to penetrate into the mysteries of the creation, the cosmos and human physiology (MISHNAH *Hayigah* II. 1), which then, with the rise of the Essenes, had its beginning. Therefore, it is most likely that the next following Mishnah, in which the difference of opinion about *Semichah* is recorded, refers to the preceding one, and not to sacrifices. Those who are engaged in those mystical researches should not be ordained as judges, teachers and senators, according to Joshua and others, and may be ordained according to Nitai and others. Both adages may also refer to this point. According to Joshua, none must study alone, and the mysteries of human physiology (עריות) must be expounded before no more than two at a time, the mysteries of the creation (מעשה בראשית) before no more than one at a time, and the mysteries of the cosmos (מרכבה) before one only, who is himself a sage and competent of independent and intelligent judgment. It is also against this ordinance that Nitai says, "to keep away from a bad neighbor," etc. There can be no doubt that the contemplative life and mystical speculations had their start then with the Essenes.

12. THE INVASION OF PARTHIA.

Under the pretext of releasing his brother, Demetrius, from captivity, in reality, however, to re-establish the former

---

(15) *Ibid Hagigah* II. 2.
(16) *Ibid Aboth* I. 6, 7.

THE EPOCH OF POPULAR GOVERNMENT. 145

boundaries of the Syrian kingdom in the East, Antiochus Sidetes, in 131 B. C., invaded Parthia with an army of above 80,000 men and a larger number of camp followers. John Hyrcan, with his army, went with the king on this expedition. It was successful in the first attempt. Babylonia and Media were conquered, and the eastern borders of Syria re-established as in the time of Antiochus the Great. The Hebrew soldiers in the field never forgot their religious obligations. The Feast of Pentecost happening on a Sunday, Antiochus was obliged to suspend operations for two successive days (17). Their part in the successful campaign became obvious in the next. For with the beginning of the winter, John Hyrcan returned to Jerusalem with his army, either because Antiochus believed he needed their assistance no longer, or because they had performed their task according to the treaty. In the next campaign, the army of Antiochus was overthrown and he was slain by the Parthians. Demetrius II., previously released from captivity, had returned to Syria and ascended again its undermined throne.

13. JOHN HYRCAN'S FIRST CONQUESTS.

John Hyrcan, after his return from the East, had a well-organized army of disciplined soldiers. The death of Antiochus and the loss of his army, paralyzed Syria momentarily; the returning Demetrius could not enter the field, and when he had partially recovered his strength, Syria was threatened by other invaders, who claimed its crown. Hyrcan seized upon the opportunity and made the attempt to take from Syria such cities and districts as were claimed to be integral portions of the Hebrew land. He went across the Jordan, and, after a siege of six months, took Medaba at the south-eastern frontier (Isaiah xv. 2), the district and city of Samega on the eastern line, re-crossed the Jordan, took Shechem and Gerizzim from the Samaritans or Cuthim, and destroyed their deserted temple, which, it appears, was still a Heathen place of worship, as it had been made in the year 167 B. C. This appears to have been accomplished in one campaign (130 B. C.), carried on simultaneously in Samaria and beyond Jordan (18). Hyrcan had inherited an aversion against the sectarian Samaritans who deserted Israel

---

(17) Josephus' Antiquities xiii. viii. 4.
(18) It is certainly doubtful whether John Hyrcan had taken Aleppo or Halab, on his return from Parthia, it not being afterward mentioned anywhere that he possessed it. See Graetz, Vol. III., 7th Note, p. 448.

in the time of need and stood aloof during all the years of national struggle, were opponents of the Hebrews at home and in Alexandria, and a hostile organization in the heart of Palestine. This conquest made an end to their political organization without, however, changing their sectarian belief.

14. John Hyrcan's Second Conquests.

Having thus rounded the eastern boundaries, the southern line had to be rectified. The Idumeans had always been engaged on the side of Israel's enemies, especially so in the late struggles for independence. They occupied part of the Hebrew territory, and claimed to be children of Abraham. Their enmity to the Hebrew people could rise only from religious prejudices. Therefore, John Hyrcan (in 129 B. C.), invaded Idumea. Having driven the Idumeans out of Dora (19), which they had held, and out of Marissa (20), he overran their entire country and subjected it completely. In order to prevent any recurrence of hostilities on their part, the alternative was proposed to them, either to become completely naturalized citizens in the Hebrew commonwealth, by circumcision and submission to the laws, or to leave the country. They preferred the former, and were merged in the Hebrews. The same year, Mithridates mounted the throne of Parthia, and Cleopatra, Physcon being exiled, governed Egypt.

15. John Hyrcan's Embassy to Rome.

These successes in the field encouraged Hyrcan to free himself from the alliance and obligations into which he had been forced by Antiochus Sidetes. He sent an embassy to Rome to procure its consent in annulling the treaty made in distress, with a king not acknowledged by the Romans. The mission was successful, the propositions of John Hyrcan were fully entertained, and the resolves of the senate made known to the rulers of the nations leagued with Rome. Next year, Hyrcan sent a golden cup and shield to Rome, which were well received, and another decree was issued in confirmation of the independence of the Hebrews and their alliance with the Roman people.

---

(19) Dora was on the sea shore, where Turtura now is, and was most likely still garrisoned by Idumeans.

(20) Marissa, anciently, must have been a city of the Israelites near the sea shore; therefore, the northern city of the same name, near Hazai, was called Marissa, of the Gentiles.

16. Another Alliance with Syria — Changes in Syria and Egypt.

When Demetrius had returned from Parthia, after the death of his brother, Antiochus Sidetes, he made peace with his first wife, Cleopatra, who had taken up her residence at Ptolemais. He went (127 B. C.) with an army to Egypt to assist his mother-in-law, Cleopatra, against Physcon. Meanwhile, several Syrian cities rose in a formidable rebellion against him, and he was obliged to abandon the contest and to flee to her daughter at Ptolemais. Physcon, to avenge himself on Demetrius, set up an impostor, whose name was Alexander Zebina, as a son of Alexander Balas. He gave him an army, and Alexander invaded Syria to take possession of its crown. Many dissatisfied Syrians supported him. In the year 126 B. C., the contestants fought a battle near Damascus, in which Demetrius was defeated. He fled to his wife at Ptolemais, but the revengeful woman had the gates of the city closed against him. He fled to Tyre, and was there captured and slain. Now his wife claimed the Syrian throne and held a portion of Syria, and Alexander Zebina was king over the other portion. John Hyrcan entered into an alliance with this Alexander, from which he derived no benefit, and the league was of short duration, for in the year 124 B. C., Seleucus, the son of Demetrius and Cleopatra, claiming his hereditary right, was proclaimed king of Syria, and after a year's reign, he was assassinated by his own mother. She gave the crown to her second son, Antiochus Grypus (also called Philometor, and on his coins, Epiphanes). He married the daughter of Physcon, who furnished him with an army to overcome his opponent, which was done in 122 B. C., and Alexander Zebina was slain. Antiochus Grypus was naturally an enemy of the Hebrews on account of their alliance with Alexander. He would certainly have invaded Judea if the two kingdoms of Syria and Egypt had not been disabled by internal dissensions. Cleopatra attempting to poison her son, Grypus, he slew her as she had slain his brother. Next year Physcon died and was succeeded by his second wife and sister, also called Cleopatra, with her son, Lathyrus, who called himself Soter. In 114 B. C., Antiochus Cyzicenus, a half brother of Grypus, son of Antiochus Sidetes and Cleopatra, claimed the Syrian crown. He had married another daughter of Physcon, also called Cleopatra, who had brought him a considerable army; and these two half brothers, married to two sisters, carried on a bloody war in Syria.

17. JOHN HYRCAN'S THIRD CONQUESTS.

These political commotions in Syria and Egypt protected John Hyrcan against the evil consequences of his imprudent alliance with an impostor, and afforded him the opportunity of maintaining profound peace in Judea up to the year 110 B. C. In this year, the Syrian Empire was divided between the two brothers; Cyzicenus reigned at Damascus over Coelosyria and Phœnicia, and Grypus at Antioch over the rest of Syria. The Hebrews had become strong enough not to fear either of the two kings. Therefore, John Hyrcan sent an army, under his two sons, Aristobulus and Antigonus, to take the city of Samaria, which, since the days of Alexander the Great, had been inhabited by Pagans, who of late had done great wrongs to the Hebrew colony at Marissa. They besieged that city, and its inhabitants, hard pressed, sent to Antiochus Cyzicenus for help. An army was sent from Damascus to assist them. The two Hebrew princes, however, without raising the siege of Samaria, advanced with part of their army, met and defeated the enemy, and drove them behind the walls of Scythopolis, and then continued the siege of Samaria. Antiochus was reinforced with 6,000 men sent by Lathyrus from Egypt, contrary to the will of his mother. The enemy ravaged the country, as they could not venture a pitched battle. This army was also met by the Hebrews and forced to retire to Tripoli, where it was left under command of two generals, one of whom, Callimander, was slain in battle; and the other, Epicrates, who was bribed by the Hebrews, delivered to them Scythopolis and the adjacent cities, and did them no more harm. In the year 109 B. C., Samaria was taken and razed to the ground. Ditches were dug and the water let in upon the spot where the city had stood, so that it was called *Ir Nebrechta*, "city of ditches," and the day of its capture, the 25th of Marcheshvon, was made a national holiday, because it was the last Pagan stronghold in the country.

18. THE HEBREWS IN EGYPT.

The Hebrews of Egypt, Cyrene and Cyprus, under the reign of Cleopatra, were very prosperous. She felt an aversion against her son Lathyrus, and would not intrust him with the command of her army. The two sons of the priest Onias, Chelkias and Ananias, enjoyed her confidence and commanded her armies. Therefore, hers was called the Onias party, and all her soldiers were called Hebrews, although they were mercenary troops of various nationalities.

However, this state of affairs in Egypt contributed largely to John Hyrcan's successes, and afterward saved his son from utter destruction.

19. The Spirit of the Age.

The spirit of the age in Palestine was intensely religious, patriotic and exclusive. It was by religious enthusiasm that the battles had been fought and independence gained. A very pious priestly family stood at the head of the nation, and the enemies fought and overcome were heathens, apostates and renegades, of sensual proclivities and lax morals. All around Palestine there were heathen temples, pagan myths, debasing cultes, slavery and degradation; while down from Mount Moriah, and from a thousand synagogues and academies, there were daily proclaimed and expounded those sublime doctrines and principles of monotheism, freedom and ethics, which prompted the Hebrew to become wiser and holier than his neighbor. In their religious zeal, the Hebrews could not help being exclusive, although they never underrated human nature and God's paternal goodness to all men; never ceased to hope for the redemption of all the human family, and to pray for it. The seventy bullocks sacrificed upon the altar on the Feast of Booths, they believed were offered up annually in behalf of the seventy nations, supposed to compose the human family, to make atonement for them, that they be not extinguished (21). They were not exclusive against men, for they accepted the Idumeans, or any other Gentile, among themselves to equal rights and religious hopes. They were exclusive against Paganism and the corruption of its votaries. Their country and their religion were so closely united by the Mosaic laws, the institutions of Ezra, the reminiscences of fourteen centuries of history, and they had just made such great sacrifices for both, that they were as zealously patriotic as they were religious. However, piety with them was not based upon metaphysical speculations and abstractions. They justly pointed to their Grecized neighbors, who, with the philosophy and poetry of Greece, had run into all kinds of absurdities and degradations. They abandoned Greek philosophy, and although it was not expressly prohibited to learn Greek and study philosophy, yet it was under the ban of public opinion.

---

(21) Compare *Succah* 55 b, and Pesikta of R. Kahana 193 c and the *Midrashim* quoted in Solomon Buber's note to this passage.

Philosophical studies had been exiled from Palestine to find a home among the Hebrews of Egypt and Asia Minor. Piety with them signified the conscientious practice of the Laws of Moses, as understood and expounded by their own legitimate authorities, the Sanhedrin, scribes and priests; and this was also their practical patriotism. The fundamental principle was sound, although it naturally led many over-conscientious men into literalism and formalism. In their anxiety to do exactly as the Law commands, every letter thereof became very important to them, and every word suggested new restrictions and observances. While the Sanhedrin was engaged in expounding the Law, to establish derivative laws, as the new state of affairs and daily emergencies required, especially in establishing an independent government, the Sopherim in synagogues and academies imitated the method, and surrounded private life with derivative laws, restrictions and observances, which were eagerly embraced and conscientiously practiced by the religious and patriotic multitude. The majority of Sopherim and members of the Sanhedrin were Pharisees, and so the majority of the people became Pharisaical in spirit and belief, if not strictly in practice. This made them temperate, frugal, anxiously moral and zealously religious; although it led many into the practices of dire ascetics, and an undue separation from Gentiles and non-Pharisees, on account of the laws of Levitical cleanness.

20. THE POLITICAL PARTIES.

The spirit of the age manifested itself in the three parties in correspondence with their respective fundamental principles. The Essenes standing aloof from the political idea were forced into the contemplative life, the rigid practice of Levitical cleanness, and, not counterpoised by either philosophical thought or political ideals, descended into the depth of mysticism, with a peculiar angelology and fantastic cosmology, a mystic-allegoric method of expounding Scriptures, claims of superior holiness, the gifts of prophecy, oneirocritics and therapeutics; but exercised no visible influence on the government and legislation of the nation. Among the Sadducees, with whom the political idea predominated, the establishment of a strong independent government, with a rigid penal code to support it, was the main object. They opposed the progressive legislation of the Pharisees, and maintained the Law of Moses and the customs of the fathers rigidly enforced to the very

literal sense of "Eye for eye," etc. (22), were sufficient to
govern the nation, and to place its prince in an independent
position. The Pharisees, with whom the religious idea
predominated, did not wish a strong government and any
concentration of power in one person. They started from the
fundamental laws and principles of Moses and the fathers,
repealed or amended existing laws, changed the penal laws
of Moses to suit a more advanced civilization, and strictly
adhered to the principle, that in the Kingdom of Heaven all
men are equal, all amenable to the same law, with equal
duties, rights and responsibilities. This was averse in
principle and practice to the theory of a strong government
with an idolized prince at its head, and was the main point
of difference between Sadducees and Pharisees, although
many other points and observances on which they differed
evolved in course of time. At this period this point of
difference came to the surface.

21. Hyrcan Turns Sadducee.

All sources agree that John Hyrcan was an eminent
man and a worthy heir of his ancestors' glory and dignity
(23). Like his people, he was intensely pious and patriotic,
so that posterity ascribed to him the gift of prophecy
by the medium of the Bath-Kol (24). He governed, with
the Sanhedrin, a democratic people, in strict obedience to
the laws and customs of the nation. Having governed a
long time in domestic tranquility, and with so many brilliant
successes in the field, he, like many other successful
rulers, felt the desire of extending his power and elevating
his personal dignity. He had assumed the title of Highpriest
of the Most High God (25) to distinguish him from
the rulers of various petty nations who bore the title of
highpriests. But this added neither to his power nor to his
dignity at home. He had the fighting men on his side,
supported a corps of mercenary troops, and could rely upon
the Sadducees, who, like the aristocracy everywhere, would
support him in any attempt of personal aggrandizement.
Therefore, an incident, apparently insignificant, sufficed to
change his domestic policy. After his victory in Samaria

---

(22) Meguillath Ta'anith iv.; Joseph. Antiq. xiii., xi., 6 and
paral. passages in the two Talmuds.
(23) I. Maccab. xvi. 23; Joseph. Antiq. xiii., xi. 7; *Berachoth* 29 a,
and paral. passages.
(24) Josephus, ibid.; Yerushalmi, *Sotah* xi. 14. *Bath-Kol*
"daughter-voice," is an inner voice in the intelligence, produced like
an echo by an outer voice or noise, interpreted by the recipient.
(25) *Rosh Hashanah*, 18 b.

and a successful campaign against the black inhabitants of the wilderness (26), Hyrcan invited his admirers to a grand banquet. Having entertained them munificently, and being in a good humor, he asked them to tell him frankly whether he had done any wrong. The Pharisees attested unanimously to his righteousness and piety. One of his guests, however, whose name was Eleazar b. Poira (or Jehuda b. Gedidia), a man of evil intentions, embraced this opportunity to rouse his ire against the Pharisees, and he said that it was reported that his mother had once been a captive among Gentiles, in consequence of which he was not lawfully entitled to the high priesthood, and he should, therefore, resign this office and be satisfied with his secular power and dignity. The story was false, says Josephus; Hyrcan was provoked against Eleazar, and the indignation of all the Pharisees against him was very great. The falsity of the slander being exposed, the question was: What punishment should be inflicted on the slanderer? A Sadducean friend of Hyrcan, whose name was Jonathan (27), embraced this opportunity to convince him how inadequate the penal laws of the Pharisees were, and how their peculiar legislation placed him on a level with any other man in Israel. Hyrcan asked the prominent Pharisees why Eleazar should not be punished with death; and they replied: "He deserved stripes and bonds, but it did not seem right to punish reproaches with death." This was strictly according to Pharisaical principle. They would not admit that capital punishment could be inflicted in any case except where the Laws of Moses expressly command it. This limitation of power and the accusation made by Jonathan that this was the opinion of all Parisees, and that all of them wished to see him resign the high priesthood, changed the mind and policy of Hyrcan. He abandoned the Pharisees and embraced the political principles of the Sadducees. This put an end, for the time being, to popular government. The Pharisees were driven from the offices and out of the Sanhedrin, and Sadducees appointed in their place. Whether any of the Pharisees were slain and Joshua b. Perachia, with his disciple, Juda b. Tabbai, fled to Egypt with other prominent Pharisees, as is maintained in the Talmud, can not be established as an unquestionable fact, as the Talmud confounds Hyrcan and Alexander Jannai. It appears, however, from Josephus (28) that there was an

---

(26) *Kiddushin*, 66 a.
(27) The Talmud calls him Eleazar, and the first man Juda b. Gedida. (28) Antiq. xiii., xi. 7.

insurrection which had to be quelled, hence it must have cost lives. It is certain that this incident, with its sequences, made an end of popular government and elevated to power the Sadducees, their policy, and their method of literalism and rigor, especially in the penal laws. When Hyrcan asked, What will become of the THORAH if the Pharisees are put down? his friend replied: "Let it be rolled up and placed in a corner, and whoever wishes to learn let him come and learn," *i. e.*, we need no more laws; let everybody understand them to suit himself, so also the prince and the rulers to suit themselves.

CHAPTER XV.

The Epoch of Royal Usurpation (108 to 78 B. C.).

1. THE LAST YEARS OF JOHN HYRCAN.

Both Josephus and the Talmud agree that John Hyrcan, toward the end of his administration, abandoned the Pharisees and embraced the policy of the Sadducees (1). Comparing the beginning of the fifth with the close of the third paragraphs in Josephus, it appears that this change was made shortly after the victory over Antiochus Cyzicenus, hence in the winter of 109 to 108 B. C. Whenever it was made, it was a step toward oligarchy in the government of the Hebrews. The will and claims of the majority were subjected to the interests of the minority, which for years to come was a source of calamity to the Hebrews. A military force was necessary now to support the government, and Hyrcan maintained foreign troops as all kings did after the example of Alexander the Great (2). He introduced the pernicious policy of relying upon his wealth, army, dependent officers and a subservient Sanhedrin, instead of the will of his people. "The Jews envied Hyrcan," says Josephus, "and the Pharisees were the worst disposed toward him;" simply because they were theocratic democrats.

2. THE END OF JOHN HYRCAN.

Hyrcan had five sons, Aristobul, Antigonus, Alexander, Absalom, and one whose name is unknown. He hated Alexander and had him educated in Galilee, while the warlike Aristobul and Antigonus were his favorites. Before his

---

(1) Berachoth 29 a.
(2) Joseph. Antiq. xiii., viii. 4.

death, it appears, he repented his misstep in preferring the Sadducees to the Pharisees, and made the attempt to divide the highest power. He appointed his wife his successor as prince of the nation and his son, Juda Aristobul, as highpriest. After he had made this last will, John Hyrcan died, in the autumn of the year 107 B. C., leaving behind him the name of a great ruler, highpriest and prophet.

3. THE FIRST ASMONEAN KING.

The widow of John Hyrcan did not succeed in assuming the reins of government. Her oldest son and highpriest, Juda Aristobul, overpowered her, perhaps before his father's will was made known, threw her and three of her sons into prison, and had himself proclaimed king of Judea, although one of his coins still extant bears the plain inscription, "Juda, the high priest and unificator of the Jews;" the others bear also the Greek inscription of "Basileus" (3). It was reported that he starved his mother to death in her prison, but this appears to be an invention. If this had been true, why should he not have disposed in a similar manner of his brothers. The ancient Hebrews were enemies of the royal title and prerogatives, and had much to say against the first usurper, Abimelech, son of Gideon (Judges ix.). They most likely did the same to Juda Aristobul. He kept with himself his brother Antigonus only, who had been his companion in arms. He called himself *Phil-helen*, "friend of the Greeks," and they lauded him particularly as a man of candor and modesty.

4. JUDA ARISTOBUL'S REIGN.

The reign of the first Asmonean monarch was brief (106 to 104 B. C.), and the Hebrew sources, except Josephus, have preserved no notice of it. From the policy of John Hyrcan to his son's usurpation, there was but one light step. He continued his father's domestic policy and did the same in the field. Carrying on a war with the Itureans (afterward Trochonites) in the Northeast, he partly subjected them to his sway. Because they were descendants of Abraham (by Ishmael) he compelled them either to be circumcised or to leave the country; and they preferred the former. He was a sickly man, and being obliged to return to Jerusalem before the work was completed, he left the army in charge of his brother Antigonus.

---

(3) M. A. Levy, Juedische Muenzen p. 55; Josephus' Antiq. xiii., xii. 1.

5. The End of Juda Aristobul.

Antigonus, successful in the conquest of Iturea, had his enemies at the royal court, and perhaps also in the secret conclaves of the Essenes, as one of them, whose name was Juda, prophesied that prince's assassination at Strato's Tower. That city and Dora having revolted and established a government of their own, under Zoilus, it appears that the intention was that Antigonus should go there to overthrow it, instead of which he came to Jerusalem to celebrate the Feast of Tabernacles, by the command of his jealous brother. Having appeared in the full splendor of his armament in the temple, the young warrior proceeded to present himself before the king. The subterranean passage between the temple and the Asmonean palace was also called Strato's Tower. There Antigonus was assassinated by the king's guard. Aristobul outlived his brother only a few days. The death of these two brothers is shrouded in mystery. The tale found credence among the people that the king ordered the assassination of his brother in case he should attempt to appear before him armed. His messengers to Antigonus, summoning him to his presence, maliciously told him the contrary. Therefore he was assassinated. When the king heard it, he repented, and his sickness became alarming. He vomited blood. A servant, carrying it away, stumbled where Antigonus had been slain and the spots of his blood still remained. The king's blood was spilt on those very spots, a cry of horror alarmed the palace, reached the ears of the king, and he was so shocked that remorse and agony seized him violently and ended his life. This appears to have been an invention of the popular resentment against the usurper.

6. Alexander Jannai Succeeds his Brother.

After the death of Aristobul, his childless widow, Salome, opened the prison gates of the captive princes and married the oldest of the surviving sons of John Hyrcan, as the Laws of Moses ordain (4). His name was Jonathan Alexander, the first of which was mispronounced Janneus, and then Jannai. He assumed the reins of government with the title of king, and then also of high priest (5). On

---

(4) Deut. xxv. 5.
(5) Leviticus xxi. 14. As highpriest he could not marry a widow. Having betrothed her and then being made highpriest, the marriage is legitimate. Mishnah, Jebamoth vi. 4. The laws of the *Mishnah* concerning the king certainly had no existence then, as there was none before Aristobul, and laws are made when needed.

his first coins he was still called " Jonathan, the highpriest and unificator of the Jews." But on his later coins he is called " Jonathan, the king " (BASILEUS) (6). The first was a concession to the anti-royalistic Hebrews, which was dropped as he sat more firmly on his throne.

7. OPENING OF THE FOUR YEARS' WAR.

What Antigonus, perhaps, was destined to do, had he not been assassinated, to reduce to obedience the revolting seaports, Alexander Jannai undertook at once. He sent part of his army to Ptolemais, and another against the cities of Dora, Strato's Tower and Gaza. He defeated the army of Ptolemais and besieged it. Syria, still divided, could not assist Ptolemais, and Egypt, under Cleopatra, was friendly to the Hebrews. Cleopatra had driven away her son, Ptolemy Lathyrus, and associated with herself her son Alexander. Lathyrus was king of Cyprus. The Ptolemaisians applied to him for assistance, and he came to Phœnicia with a large army. The Ptolemaisians fearing Lathyrus worse than the martial Hebrews, on account of his hostile mother, did not receive him in the city and refused his support. However, Zoilus and the people of Gaza invited him and he landed his army there. This necessitated Alexander Jannai to raise the siege of Ptolemais, and to operate with his whole army against Lathyrus. Unable to overcome him, Alexander played a double game of politics. He treated with Cleopatra to secure her support against Lathyrus, and promised him four hundred talents for the person of Zoilus and the cities under his government. Lathyrus was ready to do this, when he learned the double dealings of the Hebrew king, and broke off all friendship and alliance with him.

8. DISASTROUS DEFEAT OF THE HEBREWS.

Next year (104 (or 3) B. C.), Lathyrus opened a vigorous campaign. One part of his army undertook the siege of Ptolemais, and he, with the main army, invaded the interior of Palestine. He took Asochis and Sepphoris, in Galilee, and marched across the country to the banks of the Jordan. Meanwhile Alexander had raised an army of 50,000 men, with which he confronted the enemy. A battle ensued, and Alexander was defeated with a loss of 30,000 of his men. This disaster exposed Palestine to the mercy of Lathyrus, who ransacked it and massacred the inhabitants

---

(6) Levy, Juedische Muenzen *ibid.*

most barbarously. The fortified cities alone saved it from utter ruin after that battle. The next spring, Cleopatra landed an army in Phœnicia under the command of her two Hebrew generals, Chelkias and Ananias. Lathyrus quit the siege of Ptolemais, which was continued by Ananias, with a portion of Cleopatra's army, and the other, under Chelkias, marched after Lathyrus to Coelosyria. Chelkias lost his life on the march. Lathyrus took advantage of this incident and marched with his entire army to Egypt to overthrow his mother, and Alexander gained time to re-organize an army, in which he was very slow. Next year, Lathyrus was defeated in Egypt, and retreated back to Gaza.

9. A Narrow Escape.

While the war was carried on in Egypt, Ananias took Ptolemais, and Palestine was now exposed to the mercy of Cleopatra as it had been to that of Lathyrus. She came to Ptolemais. Alexander went to see her and brought her rich presents. He gained her favor. But her counselors advised her to kill him, to seize Palestine, and annex it to Egypt again. There was, however, another power behind the throne, and that was Ananias and the Egyptian Hebrews, with whose loyalty, influence and power she could not dispense. Ananias admonished the queen that such treachery committed on a confiding friend would alienate from her cause all the Hebrews in the world, and bring upon her the condemnation of all honest men. He plead vehemently the cause of his kinsmen, and succeeded. Alexander returned in peace to Jerusalem. The same year Lathyrus went back to Cyprus and Cleopatra to Egypt, and Alexander Jannai was king once more.

10. Conquests of Gaza, Raphia and Anthedon.

After a siege of ten months Alexander took Gadara, and shortly thereafter, also the strongly-fortified Amathus, which protected the frontiers of Coelosyria. In the latter place he captured the treasures of Theodorus, prince of Philadelphia. He, however, surprised Alexander and his army, killed ten thousand of them, retook his treasures, captured all of Alexander's baggage, and sent him back to Jerusalem in disgrace. Still the disaster did not discourage him. Lathyrus having returned to Cyprus, Alexander went with his army to repossess himself of the sea coast. He opened this campaign by taking Raphia and Anthedon, southeast of Gaza, which he then besieged for two successive years, and after he had sustained great losses, he finally took it (97 B. C.). His conduct toward this city and its heroic defenders was barbarous. He took bloody revenge on them who had called in Lathyrus and had cost his army so many lives. He left the city in ruins when he returned to Jerusalem. Still he was again master of the whole sea coast, and the revenues derived from an extensive traffic. In all these wars the people did not engage as they did under the predecessors of this king. He fought his battles mainly with mercenary troops, many of whom were foreign adventurers, officered by Sadducees. His soldiers lacked the valor and zeal of the Maccabees, and he the skill and talent of the Asmoneans, both in the field and in the cabinet. However, notwithstanding all the disasters, he was fortunate and successful in the main, and might have gained the affections of his people if he had not wantonly misused his opportunities.

11. Riot and Revenge.

As long as the king and highpriest refrained from interference with the religious prejudices of the Pharisees, they did not interfere with his affairs, although the government was not conducted, and the laws were not administered, to their satisfaction. They could stand a Sadducean government, while they would not tolerate a Sadducean highpriest in the temple. There were in the temple established customs which were looked upon as inviolable and holy, and some of them as the criteria of Pharisean orthodoxy. Among the latter, there was the libation of water and wine upon the altar during the Feast of Tabernacles, which was a ceremony of particular solemnity (7). The Feast of Tabernacles is the time, they maintained, when the Almighty decrees rain and dew for the coming year, to be plentiful and seasonable or otherwise (8). This belief was old, it being referred to by an ancient prophet (9). This libation, at least on the first day of the feast, was made by the highpriest and under the eyes of the assembled multitute of the pilgrims. It was during this feast in the year 95 B. C., when Alexander Jannai appeared in the temple in the sacerdotal robes. At the solemn moment when he had received the bowl of water to be poured upon the altar, he poured it out at his feet. This was sacrilege,

---

(7) Mishnah, *Succah* iv. 9.
(8) Mishnah, *Rosh Hashanah* i. 2.
(9) Zachariah xiv. 16 to 19.

it was an affront to the Pharisees, and the indignation of the multitude was enkindled. They pelted him with the citrons (*Ethrogim*) which they had in their hands (10), reviled and exasperated him. His body-guard of mercenaries came to his rescue, and slaughtered in and about the temple no less than six thousand men. Ever after that melancholy event, he was surrounded by a foreign body-guard, and a partition wall of wood was made across the inner court of the temple, behind which only the priests were permitted to go; so that the people should never again come near the highpriest (11). This massacre made Alexander Jannai the most hated and most miserable man of his people. He was now entirely in the hands of the Sadducees, and his body-guard bore the deadly hate of the masses, and he was without a friend. It appears that his own family was against him, for his wife, his oldest son and his brother-in-law, Simon ben Shetach, were uncompromising Pharisees.

12. Conquest and Disaster Beyond Jordan.

Confusion and civil war rendered Syria impotent. Antiochus Gryphus being assassinated, his son, Seleucus, succeeded him, and having defeated and slain his uncle, Antiochus Cyzicenus, reigned over all Syria until the son of Cyzicenus, Antiochus Pius, or Eusebus, defeated him and drove him out of Syria. After his death his two brothers, Antiochus and Philip, made war upon Antiochus Pius. The first was slain. Philip prevailed, and reigned over a part of Syria, while another of his brothers, Demetrius Eucerus, by the aid of Ptolemy Lathyrus, meanwhile reigned at Damascus. Both maintained themselves in power after the death of Antiochus Pius, which took place shortly afterward. Alexander Jannai had nothing to fear from either Syria or Egypt, and therefore could think of new conquests. Having terrified his people at home, he again crossed the Jordan to make war upon the Arabs. The first year's campaign (94 B. C.) was eminently successful. Moab and part of Gilead were made tributary to Palestine. The second year's campaign completed the subjection of Gilead and ended with the capture of Amathus, taken and lost eight years before. The third year's campaign, however, proved disastrous to the Hebrew king. He had invaded Gaulonites, east of the lake of Tiberias, where King

---

(10) Leviticus xxiii. 10.
(11) Josephus' Antiquities xiii., xiv. 5; Succah 48 *b*.

Obedas reigned, and, after losing the greater part of his army, he fled back to Jerusalem in disgrace.

13. Six Years of Civil War.

The defeated king having lost also the victor's prestige, his enemies among his own people rose against him in a fearful rebellion, which lasted six years. From the year 92 to 89 B. C., the two parties fought without any decisive result on either side. Thousands of human lives were sacrificed by the embittered combatants. In the year 89 B. C., Alexander Jannai earnestly appealed to his people for peace, and offered them any terms they could reasonably demand. They placed no confidence in the king's promises, and sent him word that peace would be restored whenever he committed suicide. In order to overcome him and his party, the infuriated Pharisees summoned to their aid Demetrius Eucerus, king of Damascus, who came with 40,000 infantry and 3,000 cavalry. Alexander met him in the vicinity of Shechem with 6,000 mercenary troops and 20,000 of his own people, and was routed in a pitched battle. He lost all his mercenary troops and about 10,000 more of his men, and fled with the rest to the mountains. Now his victorious enemies either pitied him or feared the victorious king of Damascus, and 6,000 of them joined Alexander's army in the mountains. This frightened Demetrius and he retreated back to his own country. Still Alexander Jannai, fearing a revolt in the East also, was obliged to give back Gilead and Moab to the king of Arabia. Next year (88 B. C.), Alexander Jannai continued the civil war with more success, although his enemies were not discouraged by defeat and losses. The year after (87 B. C.) he forced them to a pitched battle and defeated them. The survivors sought refuge in the fortified city of Bethoma, which the king closely besieged nearly one year, and having taken it, he brought eight hundred of its defenders to Jerusalem. Eight thousand of the rebels escaped, and sought refuge abroad. A catastrophe, bloody and monstrous, closed the civil war (86 B. C.). Alexander gave a hilarious feast to his concubines and courtiers at a spot outside of the city, where those eight hundred captive Pharisees were crucified, and while they were lingering between life and death on the crosses, their wives and children were slaughtered before their eyes; the king and his riotous company ate, drank and were merry. This outrageous barbarity brought Alexander Jannai the name of Thracidas, the Thracians being then considered the most infamous people. It was in the same year, when Sylla, with a Roman army, defeated Mithridates in Greece, and next year the civil war commenced in Rome. In the same year the works of Aristotle were found and seized by Sylla at Athens, carried to Rome, copied there by Tyrannion, and then published for the first time by Andronicus Rhodius.

14. CONQUESTS IN THE NORTHEAST.

No sooner had the civil war been brought to a close than Alexander Jannai planned new conquests. He could not prevent Antiochus Dionysius, the king of Damascus, successor to Demetrius, from marching with his army through Palestine, in making war upon Aretas, king of Arabia. When soon after Aretas was made king of Coelosyria and invaded Palestine, Alexander lost the battle of Addida; but a treaty of peace was made, and Aretas withdrew. And now (84 B. C.) many cities in the East having revolted during the civil war, Alexander again crossed the Jordan to enforce his authority; in this he was successful. He then pressed onward into the Valley of Antioch, and within three years (from 84 to 81 B. C.) he took the cities of Pella, Dio, and Gerasa, with the treasures of Theodorus, Golan and Seleucia, and at last also the fortress of Gamala and several other cities. He destroyed Pella because its inhabitants refused to embrace Judaism. All the other cities and districts, it appears, were Judaized, and many cities like Macherus (Wars vii., vi. 3) were fortified (12). Palestine now embraced the land from the border of Egypt up to Ptolemais, where Queen Selen now governed; beyond Jordan from the boundaries of Moab to the Syrian Desert up to the Valley of Antioch, with an open caravan route to the Euphrates; southward, including Idumea, to the end of the Sinai Desert; and to the north beyond the ancient Dan, including Gaulonites and Trachonites, to the north-

---

(12) The fortifications and citadels built by Jonathan, Simon, Hyrcan and Jannai are mentioned occasionally in subsequent history without any records of their builders. Many of these fortifications were on *Tur Malka* "King's Mountain," called so because the royal family and also the governing family preceding it had their plantation there (*Berachoth* 44 a; YERUSHALMI, *Taanith* iv. 8.), a district of a thousand towns. It was near the Mediterranean Sea (*Berachoth, ibid.*) in the neighborhood of Caesaria (YERUSHALMI, *Demai* II. i.), including Antipatris (TOSEPHTA *Ibid.* I.); hence *Tur Malka* is not Mount Ephraim as Graetz maintains; it is that chain of mountains which runs from the vicinity of Samaria northeast to Caesaria and ends in Mount Carmel, including the maritime district between Joppa and Caesaria.

east. The land was nearly as large now as it had been in the palmy days of David and Solomon. During the king's absence from Jerusalem, the home government, conducted most likely by the queen and her brother, Simon b. Shetach, was administered with moderation and prudence, so that the king returning to the capital (81 B. C.) was well received by the people.

15. SIMON B. SHETACH AND ALEXANDER JANNAI.

As heartless a warrior as Alexander Jannai was in time of war, in time of peace he led a riotous life, spending his time in debauchery and excesses. At the age of forty-seven his health was undermined. He suffered of quartan ague, and found no relief through his medical advisers. Therefore, the home government was not disturbed by him, and Simon b. Shetach succeeded by sagacious arguments in the Sanhedrin in exposing the ignorance and inconsistency of some of the Sadducean senators, who, one after the other, were thus compelled to resign, and to see their places filled by Pharisees, until at last the majority of that body was again Pharisean (13). Although Simon b. Shetach was obliged once to leave Alexander Jannai's court (14), perhaps in the time of the civil war; still the sources mention no political difficulties as the cause thereof, and his return to court was brought about without any change of policy. Alexander Jannai certainly was the president of the Sanhedrin, represented in this office by Simon b. Shetach, who was distinguished for strict and impartial justice no less than for superior wisdom and learning (15). He yielded to the severity of the Sadducees in imposing capital punishment, and ordered the execution of eighty women in one day in the city of Askalon for witchcraft or, perhaps, idolatry (16), although the Pharisean laws would not permit more than one execution on the same day and place, or the hanging of a woman (17); and refused to save his own son, condemned on the testimony of false witnesses, because it had been done according to the letter of the

(13) MEGILLATH TAANITH X.
(14) BERACHOTH 48 a and *Yerushalmi ibid.* vii. 2, translated in the *American Israelite*, October 26, 1877.
(15) He was considered a second Ezra, והחזיר התורה לישנה. "He restored the traditional law" (*Kiddushin* 66 a). The Karaites, therefore, maintain that Simon b. Shetach was a base impostor. (See ORACH ZADDIKIM by Simchah Isaac b. Moses, edit. Vienna 1830, 18a.)
(16) MISHNAH in *Sanhedrin* vi. 4.
(17) *Ibid.* in the Mishnah.

law (18). He succeeded, however, in modifying the Sadducean penal code by abolishing the convicting force of circumstantial evidence, in cases of capital crime, without the direct testimony of at least two witnesses who had seen the commission of the crime (19). To this, in all cases except murder, there was added afterward the necessity of "forewarning" the criminal before the commission of the crime, by informing him of its magnitude and the punishment threatened by the law, so that it be certain that the crime was committed with malice and forethought (20). This Simon b. Shetach is credited with two important reforms. He made a change in the marriage contract by securing the wife's dowry as a first lien upon her husband's property; while in former days it was merely promised and not secured; now it was deposited with the bride's father; then it was deposited with the bridegroom's father. But all these customs proving barriers to marriages, or causes of frivolous divorces, this reform was introduced (21). He made attendance in the public schools compulsory (22), and was the first man recorded in history as making such a law. All these reforms must have been carried through the Sanhedrin during the last six years of Alexander Jannai's government; because they bear the name of Simon b. Shetach, who could not have been NASSI after Alexander's death, with his own sister as queen. Nor could they have been adopted during the civil war on account of their Pharisean tendency. Nor is it likely that Simon b. Shetach, before that period, could, on account of his youth, have been acknowledged as an authority either in the Sanhedrin or among the people. It is evident, therefore, that the policy of conciliation was introduced immediately after the civil war.

16. ANECDOTES OF SIMON B. SHETACH.

The maxim of this chief scribe preserved in the *Mishnah* (23) bears evidence that he was engaged chiefly in matters of public law. He said: "Examine the witnesses

---

(18) YERUSHALMI *Sanhedrin* vi. 5.
(19) *Sanhedrin* 37 a; *Ibid.* Mishna iv. 1, 5.
(20) התראה MISHNAH *Sanhedrin* v. 1., appears to be of a later origin. In regard to the witnesses he succeeded in having established the law, that in penal cases no witness having given his testimony once be permitted to testify again in the same case and court against the culprit.
(21) YERUSHALMI, *Kethuboth* viii. 10, and BABLI, *ibid.* 82 b.
(22) YERUSHALMI, *ibid.* ושהיו התינוקות הולכין לבית הספר,
(23) ABOTH i. 9.

thoroughly, and be cautious with thy words, not to suggest falsehoods to them." Therefore, he could maintain himself at his post in the Sanhedrin, although a Pharisee, during the reign of Alexander Jannai. One of his cotemporaries and colleagues was Onias (חוני מעגל), a man of miracles, known to his cotemporaries as a special favorite of the Almighty. When he prayed for rain, it did rain, although he prayed in an uncouth manner, which appeared blasphemous to the polite and refined courtier. Simon b. Shetach sent him word: "If thou were not Onias we would decree excommunication upon thee. But what can be done with thee who conducted thyself before God like a spoiled son before his father, who after all does his will?" (24) He was no less outspoken and bold against the king who being called as a witness before the Sanhedrin, because one of his servants had killed a man, Simon demanded of the king to stand while testifying. He objected, "Not as thou sayest, but as these say." But none of the Sanhedrin had the courage to support Simon, and he severely rebuked their cowardice in violating the law out of fear (25). We have before us the representative of the Pharisean principle: "Whatever the political state may be, uphold the law and it will uphold society." Nevertheless he opposed asceticism. Persecution intensifies the religious sentiment and produces ascetics. In the Syrian persecution the Nazarites increased (26), and that was the original form of Hebrew asceticism. The Pharisees being persecuted in the days of Alexander Jannai, the number of Nazarites increased. Three hundred of them came at one time to Jerusalem to fulfill their vows. Simon was enabled so to construe the law that it was unnecessary for one-half of them to make the prescribed sacrifices, and that the king donated to them the three hundred animals needed (27). Most likely it was he who advanced the idea that the sacrifice of the Nazir was a trespass offering, on account of his sin in abstaining so long from wine and other gifts of God. He said that he only once ate of a Nazir's sacrifice, which was that brought by a beautiful youth, who in sincere devoutness had cut off his opulent tresses to escape worldly allurements (28). He appears

(24) *Taanith* iii. 8.
(25) *Sanhedrin* 19 b.
(26) I. Maccabees iii. 49.
(27) YERUSHALMI, *Berachoth* vii. 2, *Genesis Rabbah* 51, and *Ecclesiastes Rabbah* 3.
(28) SIPHRI *Nasa* 22, which was also said of Simon the Just.

like a lone star at the court of Alexander Jannai. In regard to the property of heathens, it was reported of him that he had bought an ass of one, and found a costly gem hidden in the hair of the animal. He returned it at once, and the heathen receiving it said: " Praised be the God of the Jews " (29). He had thus declared that the heathen's right to property was no less inviolable than the Hebrews'; and that there was a better method of converting heathens than the one adopted by Hyrcan, Aristobul and Jannai. Posterity said of him that in his and Queen Alexandra's time, it rained every Sabbath night; every grain of wheat was as large as a sheep's kidney (30); so much was God pleased with them.

17. THE END OF ALEXANDER JANNAI.

In his sickness also, Jannai preserved his martial spirit. In the hope of overcoming his disease by exertion and exercise, he marched with his army across the Jordan, and conducted the siege of Ragaba. His wife followed him and was with him when his sickness became critical and he felt his end approaching. The queen wept at the dying man's couch, and bewailed the lot of her children, who would have no protector and be among those who hated their father. The king's admonition was: " Be not afraid of the Pharisees, be not afraid of the Sadducees, be afraid only of the painted ones, who do the deed of Simri and claim the reward of Phineas (*Sotah* 22 b);" referring to hypocrites and time-serving politicians. Then he advised her to conceal his death from the soldiers till Ragaba was taken, after which she should return in triumph to Jerusalem, and place the Pharisees in power. " Expose to them my body," said he, " and give them permission to dishonor it or even refuse it a burial, and they will inter it with the highest honors, and thou wilt reign in safety." He appointed her queen of the realm, and died in peace, before Ragaba, in the year 79 B. C., fifty years old, after a reign of twenty-seven years. His last will was the same as his father had made twenty-nine years before. Had it been carried into effect, it would have saved to the country a hundred thousand lives and avoided the calamities of a protracted civil war. It took twenty-nine years to discover the fatal mistake of changing the republic into a kingdom and replacing the democracy by an oligarchy.

(29) *Deuter. Rabbah* 3; YERUSHALMI, *Baba Mezia* ii. 5.
(30) *Leviticus Rabbah* 35; also in Saphra and Talmud.

CHAPTER XVI.

The Epoch of Pacification.

1. QUEEN SALOME ALEXANDRA.

The reign of a queen over the Hebrews was a new feature in their history. Although woman's position in the ancient Hebrew State was fully equal to that of the man (1), still no woman had reigned or occupied a very prominent position in the Hebrews' Second Commonwealth. There loomed up from gray antiquity the classical figures of Miriam and Deborah, counterpoised, however, by the records of Bath Sheba, Athalia and Jezebel. Jephtah's daughter, Ruth, Hannah and Abigail, who, like the poet's Sulamith, are lovely personifications of sublime virtues without direct influence on the nation's political affairs. A queen upon the Asmonean throne was a novelty. Queen Salome (שלמצא) was nearly sixty-four years old at her husband's death, when she assumed the name of Alexandra. Only two of her sons are known, Hyrcan and Aristobul. Her genealogy is unknown, and besides her brother Simon b. Shetach, none of her relatives are mentioned.

---

(1) She was dispensed from complying with such commandatory laws of the Bible, which depend on a fixed time; from appearing as a witness before any criminal court, and as long as married, from paying any damages, if she wounded a man or destroyed any property. She could hold property in her own name, and dispose of it without her husband's consent, if she acquired it after her marriage by inheritance or otherwise; while her dowry and the husband's additions made thereto, remained a first lien upon his property. She was not expressly enfranchised, but there existed no law to debar her from holding public offices, although the customs of the country and the prevailing conceptions of chastity would not permit it.

2. Hyrcan II. Highpriest.

Alexandra did exactly as her deceased husband had ordered. Ragaba was taken, and the soldiers returned in triumph to Jerusalem without any knowledge of the king's death. She assembled the heads of the Pharisees, put in their charge the government and her husband's dead body. This had the predicted effect. Those leaders persuaded the people that the deceased monarch was a righteous man, and all his wickedness was forgiven and forgotten. "So he had a funeral more splendid than any of the kings before him" (Josephus), and Alexandra was safely enthroned in Jerusalem. She appointed her oldest son, Hyrcan II., highpriest, and it was an excellent choice, because he was a man of peace, less passionate, ambitious and warlike than his Asmonean ancestors; and this was the Pharisean ideal of a highpriest (Aboth i. 12).

3. The New Sanhedrin.

The political prisoners were released and the fugitives returned from foreign lands. Among the latter was also Juda b. Tabbai, the disciple of Joshua b. Perachia, who, it is reported, had gone with his teacher to Alexandria. The Pharisean heads assembled in Jerusalem, appointed him Nassi, and sent him a written summons to Alexandria, upon which he returned to Jerusalem and accepted the presidency of the Sanhedrin, with Simon b. Shetach as chief-justice and vice-president (2). All this, of course, was done with the sanction of the queen.

4. The Work Done by this Sanhedrin.

The first work done by this Sanhedrin was the repeal of the penal code and all laws of the Sadducees based upon literalism. They had established a code of capital punishments, which they could not support by biblical arguments. They enforced literally, eye for eye, tooth for tooth, etc., all of which were repealed, and the day when this was accomplished, the 14th day of Tamuz, was made a national holiday (3). The entire penal law, as preserved in the Mishnah and elsewhere, in undisputed paragraphs, was either re-introduced from former traditions or enacted by this Sanhedrin, with the proviso that the laws should not be

---

(2) Mishnah, *Aboth* i. 8, 9, and *Chagigah* ii. 2; Yerushalmi *Chagigah* ii. 2.
(3) Megillath Taanith iv.

written in books, in order not to assume equal importance with the Laws of Moses. The written law being taught and read in the synagogues and schools by the Scribes from manuscripts, was called מקרא or קרא, "The Reading;" and the traditional law being taught orally and repeated by the students, was called מתניתא or משנה, "The Repeated Matter." In regard to capital punishment, the main principles were:

1. The penalty of death can not be imposed except in cases expressly stated in the Laws of Moses, to be punished with death (4).

2. This highest penalty could not be imposed except by order of a regular court of twenty-three, called "The Lesser Sanhedrin"—with the exception of a few cases reserved for "The Great Sanhedrin"—established and acknowledged as such by the latter body, and only after the regular procedure prescribed by law (5).

3. The *modus* of the procedure to be direct and verbal accusation before that court, and not by inquisition, except in case of manslaughter (6).

4. The evidence must be based on direct testimony and supported by circumstantial evidence, and, except in the case of manslaughter, the commission of the criminal deed must have been preceded by a "forewarning" (7).

5. The penalty to be imposed on false witnesses to be the same as their testimony, if true, would have brought on the culprit.

6. The pleading for the defense may be done by any of the members of the Sanhedrin in session, or any authorized assessor, or the culprit himself and at least one of the court. The pleading for the accusation must be done by one of the sitting judges, the day after the defense has closed its plea (8).

7. A plain majority of the judges, in their final vote, may acquit the culprit; the verdict of guilty must be pronounced by a majority of at least two, to be valid (9).

This Sanhedrin also established the rights, privileges and duties of the great and lesser Sanhedrin; the laws of social and domestic relations and protection; the laws of property; and many ritual laws, as preserved in the para-

---

(4) SIPHRI *Shophetim* 154; YERUSHALMI *Sanhedrin* vii. 3.
(5) MISHNAH *Sanhedrin* i. 4, 5.
(6) *Ibid* iii. 6 and Deuter. xxi. 9.
(7) MISHNAH *Sanhedrin* iv. and v.
(8) *Ibid*. v. 4.
(9) *Ibid*. v. 5.

graphs of the Mishnah (10). The Sadducean customs in the temple were abolished and the Pharisean introduced (11). Laws of Levitical cleanness, in which the parties disagreed, were established by senatorial enactment (12). Of the particular laws made and enforced להוציא מלבן של צדוקים "to counteract the opinions of the Sadducees," one is recorded which is characteristic of Juda b. Tabbai's tendencies and character. He ruled to impose capital punishment on one false witness out of two, who had testified against a man accused of homicide, in order to counteract a law of the Sadducees, who maintained that false witnesses should not be put to death unless the culprit had been executed in consequence of their false testimony. Simon b. Shetach maintained that his colleague had shed innocent blood; because the sages before them had established the law that false witnesses are not punished as the Laws of Moses prescribes, unless both of them have given false testimony. This was the cause that Juda b. Tabbai after that never decided an important case except in presence of Simon b. Shetach; and that he often sat upon the grave of the executed man and cried painfully on account of his fatal error (*Hagigah* 16 b).

5. THE REIGN OF QUEEN ALEXANDRA.

The nine years of Queen Alexandra's reign were a period of blessing to the Hebrews. There was peace, although she maintained two standing armies. No enemy crossed the borders. She held hostages from the petty nations around Palestine, who dreaded her power and popularity. The Pharisees who governed the country for her, gave her

---

(10) The main laws of these categories appeared finished and established to the sages of a later period, also in the controversies of the Hillelites and Shammaites.

(11) Graetz Vol. III. Note 9, B, counts seven particular points in this connection, of which the most important are that the Sadducees maintained that the daily sacrifices were to be made from the donations of private individuals, and the Pharisees maintained that they must be from the public funds; the former held Pentecost must be celebrated on the seventh Sabbath after the one in the Passover feast, and the latter maintained that it must be celebrated on the fiftieth day after the first day of Passover.

(12) MISHNAH, *Jedaim* iii. 5 and iv. 6, 7, 8. Most remarkable is the גזרו על כלי כתובת, in YERUSHALMI, *Kethuboth* viii. 10 and BABLI, *Sabbath* 15 b, viz., that metallic vessels of capacity having became Levitically unclean, if broken and recast, are unclean again. This question was so decided to Queen Salome, perhaps in order to discourage the use of golden and silver vessels.

considerable trouble by prosecuting and bringing to punishment those of the Sadducean leaders who were concerned in the persecution and bloodshed under the reign of her husband, and especially those who counseled the king to crucify the eight hundred prisoners of Bethome. Diogenes, and several more of those men, had been slain already. A deputation of Sadducees, headed by the queen's second son, Aristobul, came to the queen and begged protection. Most of the Sadducees having been Jannai's soldiers and civil officers, the queen committed all the fortresses, except three, to their care, where they were well protected against violence, and most likely the legal prosecutions were discontinued. She retained the fortresses of Hyrcania, Alexandrium and Macherus, where her principal treasures were. This arrangement secured domestic peace, and afforded the leading men the opportunity to restore respect for the law.

6. Capture of Damascus.

At Chalcis, a country at the foot of the Lebanon, Ptolemy was prince. He was a vexatious neighbor, and the queen resolved upon suppressing him. She sent her army, under command of Aristobul, to the north. He captured Damascus (71 B. C.), but made no further use of that victory. It was his object to gain the affections of the army, and having succeeded in this, he returned to Jerusalem to watch his chances.

7. Tigranes Before Ptolemais.

The Syrians, tired of the civil war and their native princes, who waged it, offered the crown to Tigranes, king of Armenia, who came into Syria (83 B. C.) and made an end of the Seleucidan dynasty. He took possession of the whole country except Ptolemais, where Queen Selen maintained dominion. Gradually she succeeded in adding several other cities to her kingdom. In the year 70 B. C., Tigranes came to Syria, governed by his lieutenant, and besieged Ptolemais. Queen Alexandra sent embassadors and presents to Tigranes and they were well received; perhaps, because he had no time to spare, the Romans having invaded his country, and the peace of Palestine was not disturbed.

8. Death of Alexandra.

Soon after this, however, Alexandra, being seventy-three years old, became very ill, and her recovery appeared improbable. Aristobul traveled rapidly from one fortress to the other to win the Sadducees in his favor. He was eminently successful, and the rulers in Jerusalem were alarmed. They took the wife and children of Aristobul and held them as hostages in the castle Baris. The members of the Sanhedrin, headed by the highpriest, came to the queen, and asked her decision as to who should be king after her. She delegated this power to the Sanhedrin, not wishing to disturb herself any more with worldly affairs, and died in peace. The country had been well pacified, but this uncertainty as to the succession precipitated it again into confusion, which ended with the loss of independence. All that is left now of that excellent woman is her place in history and a few coins extant bearing the inscription of " Queen Alexandra."

CHAPTER XVII.

The Brothers' Feud and Foreign Intervention.

1. STATE OF THE COUNTRY.

Salome Alexandra left Palestine in a flourishing condition. It extended from Macherus to Damascus, and from the walls of Ptolemais to Rhinocolura on the boundaries of Egypt, a land flowing with milk and honey. The public treasury was filled, and the army well organized (1). The temple was the center of piety for the Hebrews of all countries where they dwelt as well as in Palestine, and its treasury was replenished not only by the HALF-SHEKEL tax, but by the gifts sent from foreign lands in great abundance (2). The people were law-abiding, profoundly religious, and, in consequence of their religion and literature, highly intelligent, industrious and frugal. There were public schools, academies and synagogues in every town all over the land. The poor, the needy, the orphan, the widow, the stranger, were protected and supported as the Laws of Moses ordain. All were equal before God and the law, none stood above or beyond it. The ethical principles of the nation were purer, loftier and broader than those of any other. As the temple on Mount Moriah stood alone among all the temples of the world, a monument of Monotheism and pure humanity, so was Palestine a lone oasis among the countries and moral corruption of the Gentiles. Had that people been unmolested, it would have solved the highest problems of civilization, long before the European nations thought of them. But as one hundred years before that time the aristocracy of Jerusalem had brought misery on their

---
(1) Josephus' Antiquities xiii., xiv. 5.
(2) *Shekalim* in TOSEFTA II. and Talmud 6 *a* ; Antiq. xiv., vii. 2.

country, so they did again after the death of Salome Alexandra.

2. Hyrcan and Aristobul.

After the death of Alexandra, her eldest son and high-priest, Hyrcan, was crowned as her successor with the consent of the Sanhedrin and the Pharisean party. His brother Aristobul, however, with the Sadducees on his side, protested against the succession, and soon came at the head of an army to enforce his own claims. Hyrcan, with his army, marched out to meet him on the plains of Jericho. The hatred and fanaticism between Pharisees and Sadducees had subsided, and a martial spirit predominated. Aristobul was a soldier and Hyrcan was none; so many of his men went over to Aristobul. Hyrcan venturing a battle nevertheless was defeated, fled to Jerusalem, locked himself up in Castle Baris, and was besieged by his brother. Hyrcan being a good, peaceable man and averse to bloodshed, offered his resignation to his brother, which was at once accepted. Both brothers met in the temple, Aristobul received the crown and high priesthood, they swore solemn oaths of peace and friendship, embraced each other in the presence of the assembled multitude, and then Hyrcan retired into private life, and Aristobul II. assumed the reins of government.

3. The Reign of Aristobul II.—Shemaiah and Abtalion.

Six years and six months, from 69 to 63 B. C., Aristobul II. reigned over the Hebrews. His government was unpopular, as the sequel will show. The priests and the military chiefs, it appears, were his only friends; although nothing of importance against the will or interests of the people was done by him except, that he was accused by his enemies of violence and disorder, and especially of incursions made into neighboring countries and piracies committed at sea (3), which may have brought upon him popular indignation. It is certain that the democratic feeling spread rapidly under his reign (4), and the Asmonean name lost prestige among the multitude. The Sanhedrin was Pharisean and democratic. After the demise of Juda b. Tabbai and Simon b. Shetach, it was presided over by Shemaiah and Abtalion, called by Josephus Sameas and Polion

---

(3) Josephus' Antiquities xiv., iii. 2.
(4) *Ibid.*

(5), who were believed to be descendants of proselytes. An
anecdote preserved in the Talmud goes far to show the unpopularity of Aristobul. The Day of Atonement was very
solemnly observed in the temple. The highpriest, after
seven days' seclusion and preparation, presided in person
and performed all the ceremonies prescribed in the Law.
After the last sacrifice of the day had been made, he went
from the temple to his residence followed by a stately procession of senators, priests, state officers and other prominent people; and he gave a great feast to his friends,
because he had entered the *sanctum sanctorum* and
returned from it without an accident. Closing one Day of
Atonement, Aristobul left the temple, and so did the heads
of the Sanhedrin, Shemaiah and Abtalion. The people
left the highpriest and followed the heads of the Sanhedrin.
The highpriest felt offended, and said to the parting heads
of the Sanhedrin: "Farewell to the sons of Gentiles."
They replied, however: "The sons of Gentiles who do as
Aaron did may fare well; but the sons of Aaron, who do
not like Aaron, may not fare well." (*Yoma* 71 *b*.) According to another anecdote preserved in the Talmud, Aristobul
made himself obnoxious also to the students, by imposing
upon them a tax which had to be paid daily to the doorkeeper by every one on entering the academy (6).

4. THE INTRIGUES OF ANTIPATER.

The most intriguing and unscrupulous enemy of Aristobul was his brother's confiden t, an Idumean, whose name
was Antipater. He had been governor of Idumea under
Alexandra, and had lost his office under Aristobul. He
stirred up the most influential men of the nation against
Aristobul, whom he stigmatized as an usurper, and advocated
the restoration of Hyrcan to the throne. Hyrcan was too
kind and indolent to listen to Antipater's treacherous
schemes, although he told him repeatedly that his life
was in danger, as Aristobul's friends advised him to slay
Hyrcan. However, Antipater repeated his terrifying story
to the timid Hyrcan so often and so solemnly that he
began to believe it, and Hyrcan consented to flee from
Jerusalem to Aretas, king of Arabia, who had his residence
at Petra, provided that that king should promise him pro-

---

(5) *Ibid.* xiv., ix. 4; also xiv., xv. 1, and xv., x. 4, only that in the
two latter cases he puts the disciple of Abtalion, whose name was
SHAMMAI, in the place of the older Shemaiah.

(6) Joma 35 b וכ׳ הזקן הלל על אמרו.

tection against his brother. Antipater went stealthily to Petra, negotiated with Aretas, who promised protection to Hyrcan. In the early part of the year 65 B. c., Hyrcan followed Antipater at night, out of Jerusalem, and both of them arrived safely at Petra.

5. THE BROTHERS' WAR.

Hyrcan, now entirely in the power of Antipater and Aretas, was too pliable to resist the treachery of his friend. Antipater persuaded Aretas to invade Judea to restore the throne to Hyrcan, and promised him the twelve cities on the southeastern border which Alexander Jannai had taken from the Arabs, besides other valuable presents. Aretas invaded Judea with an army of 50,000 men to enthrone Hyrcan, who was with the army. In the first battle Aristobul was defeated, many of his men deserted and joined the ranks of Hyrcan. Aristobul fled to Jerusalem, the enemy followed him. He sought refuge behind the strong walls of the Temple Mount; the assault made upon it was repulsed, and a protracted siege followed, Aristobul within the temple inclosure and Hyrcan, with Aretas, without, in possession of the city of Jerusalem. Some of the principal citizens left the country and fled to Egypt.

6. BRUTALITIES COMMITTED.

Superstition and brutality almost always go together. The troops besieging the temple proved this. Onias (חוני הנחבא) grandson of the one mentioned in the fifteenth chapter (7) who also was believed to have moved heaven by his prayer for rain in a time of drought, was the man now in demand by those warriors. They believed that if he would curse the besieged garrison it would speedily perish. They sent for the saint. He hid himself, but was discovered and brought to Jerusalem, and the soldiers commanded him to curse the besieged garrison. The man, it appears, was neither an impostor nor a fanatic. He prayed: "O God, king of the whole world! since those who stand now with me

---

(7) *Taanith* 23 *a* and *b*. The family of this Onias, he and his two grandsons, Abba Helkiah and Onias the Hidden, were noted for working miracles by prayer. When rain was needed, they prayed, and it came. The grandfather was an older cotemporary of Simon b. Shetach. The grandson mentioned on this occasion was called *Hanechba* "the Hidden," for which Josephus gives one reason and the Talmud another. This story here refers not to the grandfather Onias, for if he had been slain he would not have become the hero of the legend, according to which he slept seventy years.

are thy people, and those that are besieged are also thy priests, I beseech thee that thou will neither hearken to the prayers of those against these, nor bring to effect what these pray against those." These words of peace and good will so exasperated the fanatical warriors that they assassinated the defenseless man. Another barbarity committed by those rude men was the following: The Feast of Passover approached, and those in the temple had no animals with which to make the prescribed sacrifices. They promised to the besieged as much money as should be asked for the required animals. They agreed, the money was sent, and the animals were not delivered. This impiety and breach of promise, like the death of Onias, brought down upon Hyrcan's friends the indignation of the people, so that Aristobul soon found better support. A hurricane swept over the whole country and destroyed the ripening cereals, and a modius of wheat was sold for eleven drachmas. This, of course, was looked upon as a just punishment for the barbarities committed. (Antiq. xiv., ii. 1 and 2.)

7. Roman Interference.

But another plague was soon to come worse than any endured before, and that was the interference of Roman usurpers, who succeeded in overthrowing the Roman republic and the independence of Palestine. In the year 66 B. C. Pompey was sent to the East to supersede Lucullus in the command of the Roman army operating against Tigranes and Mithridates. Meeting with decided success east and northeast of Palestine (65 B. C.), Syria was made a Roman province. Scaurus reduced Coelosyria and Damascus, and Gabinius, the eastern portion of that country as far as the Tigris. Scaurus, under Pompey, was the Roman commander, whose army was encamped nearest to Palestine. Therefore, both Aristobul and Hyrcan sent ambassadors to him at Damascus, praying for his support. Aristobul sent a bribe of four hundred talents (8) to the greedy Roman and three hundred to Gabinius, and thereby gained their favor. Scaurus sent imperative orders to Aretas to raise the siege at once. Had those petty kings had the good sense to form a coalition and present a united front against Scaurus, history would have taken another turn. But they lacked both patriotism and foresight. Aretas raised the siege and marched homeward with Hyrcan and Antipater and the small body of Hebrews sup-

---

(8) Compare Josephus' Antiquities xiv., ii. 3 and Wars i., iv. 3.

porting them. Aristobul, with his men, pursued them, his cause was espoused by many of the people who augmented his force, to chastise a barbarous enemy, and he defeated the retreating army with great slaughter at Papyron. Among the slain there was also Phalion, the brother of Antipater. Hyrcan remained in possession of a few cities on the southern line, and Aristobul was again master of the situation.

8. Pompey Annuls the Treaties.

Shortly after Pompey came into Damascus, Aristobul sent him the vine of gold, worth four hundred talents, which had ornamented the temple gate. This vine was afterward deposited in the temple of Jupiter, at the capitol in Rome. Pious Hebrews replaced it in the temple at Jerusalem under the reign of Herod (9). Pompey, being otherwise engaged, left Syria, and a year of peace followed. In 64 B. C., he returned to Coelosyria. Antipater, in behalf of Hyrcan, and Nicodemus, in behalf of Aristobul, appeared before the mighty Roman to plead the cause of their respective lords. Pompey heard their arguments, dismissed them with ambiguous promises, and ordered the two kings to appear in person before him. So another year of peace was secured, Pompey being still engaged in his war against Mithridates. Meanwhile, Aretas invaded Syria with decided success, Mithridates died on his way to invade Italy, and Pompey, in 63 B. C., came to Damascus, with the determination of invading Arabia. He took Petra and King Aretas, and then returned to Damascus, where both Aristobul and Hyrcan appeared before him to plead each his own cause. There appeared also representatives of the Hebrew people, who protested against both the pretenders and the monarchical form of government. In behalf of the nation, they demanded that their democratic theocracy be restored. But the Roman chief before whom they stood was the enemy of his own republic, and was even then prepared to usurp the highest powers of State at home; he hardly gave the representatives of the people a hearing, the less so since they had come without gifts or bribes. He listened only to the pleas of the two hostile brothers. They were no longer the people's choice. Once, in a similar critical moment, Jonathan appeared at Ptolemais, accompanied by the most prominent elders and priests. Now Hyrcan appeared with an intriguing politician, Antipater, to plead his cause; and

---

(9) Mishnah, *Middoth* iii. 8; Joseph. Antiquities xv., xi. 3.

THE BROTHERS' FUED AND FOREIGN INTERVENTION. 179

Aristobul was surrounded by a number of young and insolent fellows, clad in purple garments and decked with jewels. There was no Asmonean majesty in the appearance of either. The representative of Aristobul, a year before this, had provoked the ire of Pompey by charging his subordinates, Scaurus and Gabinius, with the crime of having been bribed, and Pompey himself never refused a bribe. Now, Hyrcan had brought him rich gifts, and Antipater was more submissive and pliable than Aristobul, whose violent temper afforded a good pretext for his removal, especially as Hyrcan, by the right of primogeniture, was the legitimate king of Judea. Aside, however, from all these considerations, Pompey had the ambition of carrying the Roman standards clear to the Red Sea, and any pretext sufficed him to annul all the treaties of Rome and Palestine, to break the solemn promises and pledges of former days, and to add one more country to his conquests. Honor, integrity and liberty were no longer the motives of Roman commanders. Selfishness and a boundless greediness of power and wealth had overcome all other considerations. Human lives and human rights had become equally worthless in their estimation. Therefore, Pompey, having heard the pleas of the two brothers, dismissed them with ambiguous words, promised to settle their dispute by the by, led each of them to believe that he was the favored man, and made preparations for the instantaneous invasion of Judea. Aristobul's conduct was the next pretext; for he had concentrated some troops at Delius and marched into Judea. Pompey, with his legions, followed him at once, marched through Galilee and Samaria without any resistance, and reached Corea, at the northern frontier of Judea proper; and there, in the fortress of Alexandrium, Aristobul was ready to dispute his progress.

9. POMPEY IN JERUSALEM.

By false promises, Aristobul was brought out of Alexandrium and persuaded to surrender it to Pompey. Aristobul retired to Jerusalem and prepared for war, and Pompey led his legions to Jericho. Aristobul, not certain of his people's support, repaired to Pompey as a penitent, promised him money and to receive him into the city of Jerusalem if he would do in peace all he wished to do. He consented, sent Gabinius, with a force, to take possession of the money and the city; but the people closed the gates of Jerusalem against both Gabinius and Aristobul, who was now cast into prison by his disappointed and treacherous protector. Pompey sent Piso, with an adequate force, to Jerusalem. An insurrection broke out in the city. The people, not caring much about the quarrel, resolved to receive Pompey's men and treat them hospitably, which the friends of Aristobul refused to accede to, because he was a prisoner. At last the Aristobulites gained possession of the temple, broke down the bridges and prepared for a siege; and the citizens of Jerusalem opened the gates to Piso, received and treated him well. He took possession of the royal palace, fortified the houses near the temple, and garrisoned all important points. He offered terms of peace to the besieged, which were refused. Then he commenced the construction of a wall to shut them up, in which Hyrcan assisted him, while Pompey came up with the main force and took his position north of the temple, where it was most vulnerable.

10. Capture of the Temple.

Three months the defenders of the temple defied the entire army of Pompey supported by Hyrcan and his friends, although they were provided with the best siege engines. A deep ditch which they had cut north of the temple protected it against the siege engines. This ditch, Josephus tells us, was filled up on the Sabbath days, when those inside the temple walls would not disturb the work, holding, as they did, to the Sabbath law established by Mattathia, which the Pharisees afterward abolished. Gradually the ditch was filled up, an embankment was raised, the engines placed in position, one of the two northern towers was battered down, a breech was made into the wall, and on a Sabbath day the Romans poured in, a terrible carnage ensued, twelve thousand Israelites lost their lives, Absalom, the uncle of Aristobul, was taken captive, and the temple, covered with the dead bodies of its defenders, fell into the hands of Pompey. The officiating priests, notwithstanding the carnage around them, remained steadfast at their respective posts, and performed their duties in the face of death, until their services were finished or they were dead.

11. The Temple Service Uninterrupted.

Pompey and his men went over the temple in all its apartments without regard to the laws and customs of the Hebrews; and this sacrilege was deeply regretted by his friends. Still he pleased them in another way. He took none of the numerous golden vessels, the costly spices, or the two thousand talents left in the treasury of the temple. He appointed Hyrcan highpriest. Next day the temple was cleansed and the services continued as heretofore. The priests and Levites who had escaped the slaughter were most likely few in number, and the slain were many; but Hyrcan II. went over their bodies, and was again highpriest.

12. The Loss of Independence.

After the friends of Aristobul had been slaughtered, sent as captives to Rome, or had left the country, the walls of Jerusalem and other cities had been demolished, the seashore cities and also the inland cities, taken by Alexander Jannai, had been made free cities and added to the Syrian province, and Judea reduced to its own limits, Antipater was appointed Roman procurator under the pro-consul of Syria, and Hyrcan was appointed Ethnarch or Prince of Judea, without the right of wearing the diadem, and an annual tribute was imposed on the conquered land, in violation of all existing treaties, and in spite of the fact that Pompey only conquered a small faction and one fortified point. Jerusalem had lost its independence, and Rome its integrity and honor. Antipater was a Roman servant and Hyrcan the shadow of a prince. This was the beginning of the end. Two hundred years of combat followed.

13. The Hebrews in Rome.

Aristobul, his son Antigonus, his two daughters, and his uncle, Absalom, like many other captives, were brought to Rome to grace the triumph of Pompey. Alexander, a son of Aristobul, escaped and returned to Palestine, where his mother also was. A large number of Hebrew captives were brought to Rome and set free by their wealthy co-religionists, who had established themselves in Rome long before the time of Pompey. The ransomed captives were called *libertines*, settled on an island of the Tiber, also on the left bank of that river, and upon the declivity of the Vatican. Being Roman citizens they soon made themselves felt among the multitude, especially as merchants, mechanics, soothsayers and the representatives of a religion, which had reached the most intelligent Romans by the Greco-Hebrew literature. One only of their prominent teachers, whose name was Theodorus, has become known to posterity. Although the Hebrews had established themselves all over Italy, still they were most numerous in

Rome. Four years later L. Valerius Flaccus was placed before his judges in Rome, by Laelius, for the oppression, robbery and violence practiced in his province in Asia, and one of the charges was that Flaccus stole the money which the Hebrews had collected for the temple in Jerusalem. Cicero was the advocate of Flaccus and was obliged to debase the Greeks and Jews in behalf of his client. He characterized the Greeks as faithless and unreliable, and the Jews as superstitious and seditious. We learn from this oration (10) that the Hebrews were numerous, united, and exercised a considerable influence in the public meetings, disliked the Romans, their laws and their power, etc.; but he never calls them faithless, immoral or unenlightened; because they were certainly the equals, if not the superiors, of the Romans in all these points as well as in bravery.

(10) Oratio pro Flacc. Secs. iv., v. and xviii.

V. Palestine Under Roman Vassal Rulers.

While the Roman Republic was shaken to its foundations by its matricidal sons, its power was extended over Europe to the Isles of Britain, over Egypt and Western Asia. The whole civilized world quaked under the footsteps of the Roman soldiery. The rights and liberties of nations were extinguished, and their religions superseded by the Greco-Roman idolatry and the worship of the emperor, as the son of God. Under the influence of conquest and military despotism, the Roman virtues gave way to moral corruption in its worst form. The highest officers, with rare exceptions, were sensual, ambitious, selfish, cruel and unscrupulous men. Their greed of power, wealth and sensual gratification were boundless. A haughtiness bordering on self-deification caused them to despise every person, thought or institution not in harmony with their prejudices and perverted conceptions of honor and religion. The governing class was supported by an army of automatons, recruited mostly among semi-barbarous nations and the lowest scum of civilized people, whose highest virtue was blind obedience. The governed class groaned helplessly under the towers of corruption, and the world appeared to have been given over to Roman soldiers. At the same time, however, in Rome, Latin literature reached its golden age, although her patricians were obliged to go to school to the Greeks, and Athens became the *alma mater*. And yet Rome became the reservoir to receive the various brooks of ancient cultures, to send forth the broad stream of modern civilization. How did the Hebrews resist that crushing power, and how were they affected? What did they learn of the Romans and the Romans of them? In the succeeding chapters we will answer these questions. The period before us is called Palestine under Roman vassal rulers, because the Hebrews maintained their independence in domestic affairs, while their rulers were vassals of Rome. It is divided into three ages:

1. The Last of the Asmonean Rulers (63 to 36 B. C.)*.
2. King Herod, the Idumean (37 to 3 B. C.)†.
3. Archelaus and the end (3 B. C. to 7 A. C.)‡.

CHAPTER XVIII.

The Last of the Asmonean Rulers.

1. Hyrcan II., Antipater, and their Antagonists.

Upon the throne of Judea, there now sat (63 B. C.) a prince without a diadem, governing a land without an army, and with a minister who was his superior in power and mind. Hyrcan II. was highpriest and ethnarch, who, with the Sanhedrin, could administer the domestic affairs of the Hebrews in Judea, as long as he paid the stipulated tribute to the Romans. His minister and friend, Antipater, was the Roman agent, the military governor of the land. Although he apparently did everything by command of Hyrcan, and in his interest; yet Hyrcan commanded that only which Antipater demanded. The policy of those two rulers was to be faithful to Rome, and to bear gracefully the foreign yoke. It was prudent, perhaps the best policy under the circumstances; yet large numbers of the people were not willing to submit to the wrong perpetrated by Pompey, and to give up the independence of their country. This class of dissatisfied patriots, irrespective of old party divisions and new geographical lines, was headed for the next twenty-seven years by the dethroned Aristobul II. and his two sons, Alexander and Antigonus.

2. Scaurus Invades Arabia.

Pompey left behind him Scaurus as the commander of the Roman troops. He had orders to invade Arabia and chastise Aretas. Antipater gave him permission to march through Judea, and furnished the army with provisions. But Aretas being the friend of Antipater, the latter was

---
*Josephus' Antiquities xiv., xvi. 4.
†Josephus' Wars I. xxxiii. 8.
‡Compare Antiquities xvii., xiii. 2 and Wars II. vii. 3.

used as a mediator by Scaurus. While the Romans pillaged the country, Antipater prevailed on Aretas to sue for peace, and he did so. He promised Scaurus three hundred talents, for which Antipater became surety. Scaurus left the country, went back to Rome, was elected Aedile, and a coin eternized his victory over the king of Arabia, although it had been obtained by diplomacy. The successors of Scaurus in Syria were Marcus Philippus and Marcellinus Lentulus, who were defeated by the Parthians, and then replaced by Gabinius, whom Cicero called a most infamous extortioner.

3. ALEXANDER'S FIRST EXPLOIT.

Meanwhile the dissatisfied patriots were quiet, although always ready to strike against the Roman party when an opportunity offered, as was the case when the Parthians had defeated the two Roman commanders and were ready to invade Syria. Alexander, the oldest son of Aristobul, who was about ten years old when, in 63 B. C., he escaped and came back to Palestine, was now the only Asmonean scion in the country about whom the patriots could rally. His mother, as well as his father, was an Asmonean. She was the daughter of Absalom, now a captive in Rome. How or when the patriots organized has remained a mystery. It appears, that on the line of Arabia beyond Jordan, this party had fortified Alexandrium, Hyrcanium and Macherus, and there was the center for that party. In the year 57 B. C., with Alexander at their head, they made an incursion into Judea, and succeeded in taking Jerusalem (1). They would have fortified it, if Gabinius and Marc Antony had not come in time to the rescue of Hyrcan. He had brought together a small force under Antipater, Pitholaus and Malichus, opposed by Alexander with ten thousand infantry and fifteen hundred cavalry. Alexander was defeated with the loss of half his army, and the rest retreated across the Jordan behind the walls of Alexandrium. Marc Antony besieged this fortress, and Gabinius fortified the cities inhabited by Gentiles, which were to hold the Hebrews in check, as in the time of the Syrians, and then he came with his forces to Alexandrium. Before an assault was made, the mother of Alexander, who stood in high esteem with the Roman, succeeded in obtaining amnesty for her son and his men, after he had capitulated and the three fortresses were demolished. Shortly after Alexander married his cousin, Alexandra, the daughter of Hyrcan.

---

(1) Josephus' Wars I. viii. 3, 4; Antiquities xiv. v.

4. Partition of the Country.

Gabinius again installed Hyrcan II. in his office of highpriest, but not as ethnarch. His power was altogether spiritual. In order to deprive the Asmoneans of all hope of restoration, he divided the country into five districts, and placed in each an executive council independent of the others. The five capital cities were Jerusalem, Jericho, Sepphoris, Gadara and Amatheus, which included all four provinces of Judea, Samaria, Galilee and Petrea. This was intended to satisfy the democrats, but it did not, and had certainly no practical consequences, and despite of them the people of Israel remained a unit, and the Sanhedrin in Jerusalem was the supreme judiciary and legislature, the expounders of the Law and the bearers of the traditions; and few, if any, had yet accepted the belief that the highpriest was not the lawful sovereign. All these were religious beliefs deeply rooted in the consciences of the multitudes, and a mere geographical division could not change them.

5. Aristobul's Abortive Exploit.

Gabinius, believing all matters in Judea to be settled, went with his army to Egypt. Scarcely had he gone, when Aristobul, with his son Antigonus, having escaped from Rome, appeared in Judea, and called his compatriots to arms. The democratic element, it appears, gave him no support; for although Pitholaus, one of Hyrcan's principal chiefs, came to him with one thousand men, he could not get together more than eight thousand men, nor had he the means to arm a greater number. He had come too late, after his son Alexander had been vanquished and the fortresses demolished. He succeeded in taking possession of Alexandrium and refortifying it, and then made the attempt of regaining Macherus. But on his way there he was overtaken by the Roman force under Marc Antony and the son of Gabinius, and lost in a battle five thousand of his men. And yet with the shattered fragments of his little army, Aristobul succeeded in reaching Macherus, and began to fortify it. When the Romans overtook him, he fought them desperately, until he was severely wounded and captured, together with his son Antigonus. They were sent back to Rome. Gabinius having informed the senate that he had promised to the mother the liberty of her two sons, Antigonus, who was (56 B. C.) a mere boy, was sent back to Palestine, and Aristobul remained a prisoner in Rome.

6. Alexander's Second Exploit.

Gabinius marched with his troops to the East to attack the Parthians. Meanwhile Ptolemy Auletes, King of Egypt, was dethroned. He promised Gabinius a large sum of money, and the avaricious Roman turned round to invade Egypt. Antipater furnished him men and provisions, and won in his favor the Hebrews below Pelusium who held the passes near the Isthmus. Alexander improved the opportunity and (55 B. C.) called the patriots once more to arms. He was more successful this time. A large army came to his banners. He slew and drove out the Romans and their compatriots in Galilee, and followed them to Mount Gerizzim, where they had intrenched themselves. Antipater was helpless. Gabinius returned from Egypt. He sent Antipater as a messenger of peace to the army of Alexander. By arguments and threats he succeeded in pacifying many. Still Alexander had left thirty thousand men to espouse his cause, and he ventured a pitched battle with the Romans near Mt. Tabor. He was too young a man to successfully handle an army of thirty thousand men against Roman veterans. The battle was lost, ten thousand of his men perished, and he fled into the mountains, where, it appears, he maintained himself as the ruler of a portion of Galilee to the year 48 B. C. Now peace was restored, Antipater was again master of the situation, and the friends of Aristobul were terrified. The same year Gabinius was recalled to Rome, was tried for his crimes and extortions, found guilty, and banished.

7. The Temple Ransacked by Crassus.

Marcus Lucinius Crassus, the triumvir with Pompey and Cæsar, the wealthiest citizen of Rome, was the successor of Gabinius in the province of Syria. His apparent object was to continue the war against the Parthians; but his actual aim was to gather as much wealth as could be found. He plundered towns and temples, and came also to Jerusalem. His object being known, the treasurer of the temple, Eleazar, came to him with the request not to disturb the temple, and promised him a piece of gold, which none besides him could find, weighing seven hundred and fifty pounds. Crassus consented, and swore an oath not to disturb the sanctuary. The gold was delivered to him, he took it, and then entered the temple, took two thousand talents from its treasury and vessels to the value of eight thousand talents, left the temple stripped of all its wealth and vessels, and left the city, in all probability, before its inhabitants knew what had been done. Then he marched against the Parthians, who slew him like a mad dog, and annihilated his army, of which Cassius, his quæstor, with five hundred cavalry escaped into Syria (53 B. C.).

8. The Extortions and Outrages of Cassius.

Cassius Longinus collected the fugitives from the army of Crassus in Syria and made preparations to receive the Parthians. He stood in need of money and extorted it from the various nations, also from the Hebrews. Having repulsed the Parthians, he came to Tyre, and went across Galilee to put down the friends of Aristobul. Pitholaus, with his men, held the city of Tarichæa, on the southern shore of Lake Tiberias. Cassius took the city, carried all its inhabitants and defenders (30,000) into slavery, and, at the request of Antipater, slew Pitholaus, because he had betrayed the cause of Hyrcan (52 B. C.). Still this did not bring the friends of Aristobul to terms; Alexander held his position, and must have lived in peace with his wife, the daughter of Hyrcan, who, prior to 48 B. C., gave birth to his two children, Mariamne and her brother, Aristobul, whose tragic end disgraces the history of Herod. We have to look upon Galilee as in a continual state of insurrection, kept up by Alexander and other friends of Aristobul. Still there was no particular disturbance from 52 to 48 B. C., because neither were the Romans nor was Antipater in a position to do anything effectual with those warlike mountaineers.

9. Julius Cæsar Changes the Situation.

While the Roman legions were defeated by the Parthians Julius Cæsar overthrew the independence of the various nationalities at the western end of Europe, from the Rhine to the Atlantic Ocean, Belgium and Britannia included. In Rome Pompey was all mighty, and he was no less hated there than in Palestine. After the death of Crassus he had but one rival, and that was Julius Cæsar. He was the expected savior of the Romans. When he had accomplished it, he was deified by his admirers, and the god Cæsar was the precursor of the god Jesus. In December, 50 B. C. Cæsar crossed the Rubicon and arrived in Rome. Pompey, with his warriors, fled across the Adriatic Sea to Epirus. Cæsar reduced all Italy, so that he was in possession of the western, and Pompey of the eastern half of the Roman

Empire. So the year 49 B. C. passed in making preparations.

10. THE END OF ARISTOBUL II.

Cæsar undoing in Rome all the measures of Pompey, released Aristobul II. from his prison, gave him two legions, and sent him back to Palestine to take possession of his kingdom. Had this expedition been successful, it would have restored the power if not the independence of the Hebrews, and outflanked Pompey in his rear. But it was not successful. Partisans of Pompey found means to poison Aristobul, and he died a sudden death. His body was preserved in honey, till several years afterward, when Marc Antony sent it to Jerusalem to be buried in the sepulcher of his fathers.

11. THE END OF ALEXANDER.

The news of Aristobul's change of fortune reaching Palestine, Alexander was ready to initiate the campaign against the forces of Pompey. Q. Metellus Scipio, the father-in-law of Pompey, had succeeded Bibulus as President of Syria, and he overpowered Alexander, captured him, brought him to Antioch, and there, by order of Pompey, he was beheaded (48 B. C.).

12. THE FAMILY OF ARISTOBUL.

The wife, two daughters, and one son (Antigon) of Aristobul II. resided at Ascalon, hitherto protected by the promise of Gabinius. But when Alexander had been slain in spite of that promise, they were no longer secure in Palestine. Ptolemy, the Prince of Chalcis, took the family to his residence, and his son Philip married Alexandra, one of Aristobul's daughters. Afterward Ptolemy fell in love with her, slew his own son, and married her. This event secured a place of refuge to the entire family.

13. CÆSAR IN EGYPT.

49 B. C. Cæsar was declared dictator, but resigned after eleven days, and was elected consul 48 B. C. He defeated Pompey at Pharsalia in Thessaly, who soon after was assassinated in Egypt before the arrival of Cæsar at Alexandria in pursuit of his dead enemy. When the news of Pompey's death had reached Rome, Cæsar was again appointed dictator. Still he was in a precarious condition

in Alexandria, where he had come with but 3200 infantry and 800 cavalry, and there enraged the people against him by rigorously exacting the payment of a heavy debt, and treating like a superior the two oldest children of the king, Ptolemy and Cleopatra, who were making war on one another about the succession. When at last he embraced the cause of the unchaste Cleopatra, the Egyptians made a fierce attack upon him, drove him into a perilous position, and it was only with the utmost difficulty and heroism that he maintained himself until reinforcements came from abroad.

14. Antipater Assists Cæsar.

Among those who came to reinforce Cæsar, there was also Mithridates, of Pergamus, who had arrived with his forces at Ascalon, but was unable to force his way into Egypt. Antipater came to him with three thousand Hebrews and a number of Arabians, followed also by a considerable number of Syrians. At Pelusium Antipater, with his men, were the first to break through the walls, and the city was taken. The Egyptian Hebrews of the Onias district were ready to stop Mithridates; but when Antipater showed them letters from Hyrcan exhorting them to cultivate the friendship of Cæsar, they fraternized with him and followed the host of Mithridates. By the same means the Hebrews of Memphis also came over to Cæsar's friends, and enabled the army to press on toward Alexandria. Near the Nile, at a place called the Jewish Camp, the Egyptian forces under Ptolemy were encountered. A battle ensued, in which Mithridates, commanding the right wing, was pressed back, and would have been routed, if Antipater, commanding the left wing, had not defeated the enemy and come in time to support Mithridates. Meanwhile Cæsar had been reinforced with a legion which came from Asia Minor by sea, and effected a junction with the forces of Mithridates and Antipater, and Hyrcan had also come there with 1500 men (2). The Egyptians were completely overthrown. Ptolemy lost his life in the Nile, Cleopatra was married to her second brother, who was thirteen years old, and was made Queen of Egypt with her brother as nominal king. The friendship of Hyrcan, the heroic conduct of Antipater, the wounds he had received in Cæsar's cause, and the services of the Egyptian Hebrews, endeared them to the great Roman. Before leaving Alexandria, he demonstrated his

(2) Josephus' Antiq. xiv., x. 2.

appreciation of the Alexandrian Hebrews by a public declaration that they were citizens of Alexandria. This decree was engraved on brass pillars (3).

15. Restoration of the Hebrew State.

Soon after Julius Cæsar came to Syria, where Antigonus, the son of Aristobul, appeared before him. He accused Antipater that by his instigation Aristobul was poisoned and Alexander beheaded; also that Antipater and Hyrcan governed the nation by violence, and did great injustice to him. He asked of Cæsar to be restored to the throne of his fathers. It was too late. Antipater and Hyrcan had rendered too valuable services to Cæsar in time of need to be abandoned by him. The remonstration of Antipater was brief. He accused Antigonus and his party of innovations and seditions, defended the punishment inflicted on Aristobul and Alexander, and then showed the scars of his wounds received in the Egyptian campaign. Cæsar's decision was that Hyrcan should be highpriest and ethnarch; that all the provinces and cities taken from him by Pompey and his successors in Syria should be restored and be governed henceforth by the laws of the Hebrews; and that he should have the right to refortify Jerusalem. Antipater was confirmed as Roman procurator (*Epitropos*), to govern the military affairs in behalf of Rome, with the additional title of a Citizen of Rome. Cæsar made his kinsman, Sextus Cæsar, President of Syria (47 B. C.), and left the country (45 B. C.).

16. Cæsar's Decrees in Favor of the Hebrews.

The decision of Cæsar was sent to Rome by an embassy of Hyrcan, for the ratification and publication by the senate and the consuls. In the various edicts bearing the name of Julius Cæsar, which Josephus has preserved (4), the following rights and privileges were granted to the Hebrews of Palestine:

1. That Hyrcan II., he and his heirs after him, shall be the hereditary highpriest and ethnarch of the Hebrews, "according to the custom of their forefathers;" and that he shall decide all questions concerning Jewish customs, consequently be the head of the Sanhedrin also.
2. That Hyrcan and his people shall be known as the

---

(3) Josephus' Antiq. xiv., xii; Contra Apion II.
(4) Antiquities xiv. x.

confederates of Rome and the particular friends of Cæsar; that no Roman commanders, under any pretense whatever, extort contributions from them; that the city of Jerusalem be fortified, and governed by the ethnarch's will only; that the tribute due to Rome shall not be let to farm, none be paid for any Sabbath year, nor should it always be as high as it was that year.

3. That all the land, towns and cities, excepting Joppa, shall be subject and tributary to Jerusalem, as heretofore, only the tribute of the city of Joppa to belong personally to Hyrcan and his heirs; and that no Roman officer shall have the right of raising auxiliary forces in Judea or of imposing a contribution.

4. The particular honors conferred on Hyrcan "and his sons," or the embassadors sent by him, were to be seated among the senators in the public games; when they desire an audience to be introduced to the senate by the dictator or by the general of the horse; and that any decree concerning them be made known to them within ten days after it had passed the senate.

5. But the most important of the Cæsar decrees was, that Hyrcan was appointed the highest authority of the Hebrews, to determine all questions about Jewish custom, with the same power over the Hebrews outside of Palestine, "to defend those who are injured;" and that the Hebrews outside of Palestine were declared Roman citizens, with the particular rights to live according to their laws and customs and to be free of military duty. Their public gatherings and common meals in Rome and the provinces were exempted from the decree against bacchanalian rioters.

17. Hyrcan Honored by the Athenians.

The services which Hyrcan rendered to the Athenians are not specified in the sources. They acknowledged, in general terms (5), that he bore good will to them in general, to every one of their citizens in particular. and treated them with all manner of kindness whenever they came to him, as embassadors or in any other capacity. Therefore, they voted him a crown of gold and a decree of honor, and erected his statue of brass in the temple of Demus and of the Graces.

---

(5) Ibid. xiv., viii. 5.

18. The Home Government.

In Palestine the government was restored as it was under Queen Alexandra, with the exception of the tribute paid to Rome and the military affairs governed by Antipater. The service in the temple and synagogues remained unchanged. The small number of priests and Levites who had escaped the massacre in the temple by Pompey, continued to conduct the temple service in the Pharisean style; and the *Sopherim*, whose numbers increased notwithstanding wars and seditions, conducted the synagogues, schools and courts. The Sanhedrin had undergone no change. It remained in the power of the Pharisees under the presidency of Shemaiah and Abtalion, while the Sadducees, with the other fighting men, ever since 63 B. C., were most of the time engaged in wars and seditions.

19. Shemaiah and Abtalion.

The policy and providentness of these two men is evident from their maxims left in Aboth I. Shemaiah said: "Love labor, hate domination, and remain unknown to the government." There are wealth, honesty and satisfaction in labor, the loss of all three of them in domination and threatening danger near the highest power, especially under the perpetual changes which that sage lived to see. Shemaiah cautioned his people to remain industrious and neutral, wealthy by their labor and free by not domineering over others, which was a blessing to thousands, and kept him at the head of the Sanhedrin. Abtalion, who was more of a teacher and less of a statesman than his colleague, said: "Ye wise men, be cautious with your words; perhaps ye might be condemned to exile, and driven to a place of stagnant water, and then the disciples succeeding you might drink (of your misunderstood words) and die, and so the name of heaven would be profaned." He saw thousands leave the country, compulsory or voluntary exiles; and among them were many of the *Sopherim*. In his time, the Derasha had its origin (6). The laws were completed. the doctrines established, and the doctors began to seek the origin of every custom, law or doctrine in the Bible, and this research was called *Derasha*. Shemaiah and Abtalion,

---

(6) תניא וגו' שמעיה ואבטליון ישהן חכמים גדולים ודרשנים גדולים וגי' (Guittin 57 b), למדו תורה ברבים (Pesachim 70 b). It is said of none before Shemaiah and Abtalion that he was "a great *Darshan*," who taught the Law to the public.

who stood at the head of the schools as well as of the Sanhedrin, withdrew the attention from politics and legislation and gave this direction to susceptible minds. There may have been advanced many an unripe thought in that research, and it is against this that Abtalion cautioned the wise men. No laws (*Halachoth*) bearing the names of these heads of the Sanhedrin are reported, and only a few are recorded by others in their name, viz., concerning the Sabbath (7), the posthumous child of a deceased priest (8), the bath of purification (9), and the equality of the freed woman with the Hebrew woman in regard to the "bitter water" (*Sotah*) (10). These few points show that the laws of the country had been completed before that time. Two of their cotemporaries, Juda b. Dositheus and his son Dositheus, retired to the south of Palestine, because they disagreed with Shemaiah and Abtalion (11). The names of their disciples, except Hillel and Shammai, have not reached posterity.

20. Pacification of the Hebrews.

The influence of the Sanhedrin and Scribes upon the excited parties was of great assistance to Antipater in restoring domestic peace. While in 44 b. c. the walls of Jerusalem were rebuilt, he traveled through the country and made known the present situation, that Hyrcan would be a father to the people and the Romans its friends, if the public peace were not disturbed; but Hyrcan would become a tyrant and the Romans the people's enemies if their authority was defied. This, it appears, had the desired effect everywhere except in Galilee, where the friends of the deceased Aristobul were not so ready to submit.

21. The Wife and Sons of Antipater.

Antipater had married an Idumean princess of the royal family of Arabia. Her name was Cypros (Zipporah?). She gave birth to four sons: Phasael, Herod, Joseph and Pheroras, and one daughter, Salome. These sons had spent most of their time in Arabia, and were estranged to the Hebrews by birth and education. After Cæsar had put

(7) *Beza* 25 *a*.
(8) *Jebamoth* 67 *a*.
(9) Mishnah *Edioth* i. 3.
(10) *Ibid.* v. 6.
(11) יהודה בן דורתאי in *Pesachim* 70 b.

Antipater in power, they were recalled from Arabia and appointed to the highest positions. Phasael was made Governor of Jerusalem and Herod Governor of Galilee. The latter was, in 44 B. C., about twenty-three years old. This was certainly an insult to prominent men, and a cause of dissatisfaction, which was aggravated by the lawless conduct of Herod in Galilee.

22. HEROD'S VIOLATION OF THE LAW. THE ROBBERS.

While Phasael was very cautious in the exercise of his authority in Jerusalem, and succeeded in gaining the people's good will for himself and his father, Herod started out a self-willed despot, careless of any law which interfered with his will. The partisans of Alexander being after his death without a leader, disbanded in guerrilla hordes, held the mountain passes and caverns of northern and eastern Galilee, and of Coelosyria, and subsisted on the booty which they could take from Hebrews or Syrians. These guerrillas were called robbers, and were a terror to the peaceable population. Herod pursued and captured many of them, together with Hezekias, one of their chiefs, and, instead of giving them a trial before a court of law, had them executed by his own authority and command. These summary proceedings alarmed many law-abiding citizens, although it gained him the applause of many, of Syrians especially, who had suffered from the incursions of those guerrillas.

23. HEROD SUMMONED BEFORE THE SANHEDRIN.

The chief men of the Hebrews gave utterance to their indignation before Hyrcan. They told him that he was no longer the ruler, but Antipater and his sons were. They demanded that Herod be brought to trial for his defiance of the law. Besides these, there were the mothers of Herod's victims, who had come to Jerusalem, and in the temple loudly clamored for justice in behalf of their slain sons. At last Hyrcan was compelled to bring Herod to trial, although he loved him paternally, and was sincerely attached to Antipater. By order of Hyrcan, Herod was summoned to appear before the Sanhedrin. His father advised him to appear with a body-guard sufficient to protect him in any emergency; and Sextus Cæsar wrote to Hyrcan that Herod must be acquitted.

24. The Trial and Flight of Herod.

In royal robes and decorations, and surrounded by a large body-guard, Herod appeared (43 B C.) before the Sanhedrin. This novel and audacious spectacle confused the high lords of law and peace, and their courage failed them. Hyrcan presided over a fear-stricken body. One, however, was bold enough to speak, and that was SHEMAIAH. He gave utterance to his indignation that a man accused of high crime should dare to appear before his judges in royal pomp, as this man Herod had come with his body-guard to intimidate the Sanhedrin; and then he turned upon his colleagues, upbraided them for their cowardice and subserviency, and closed thus: "However, take you notice that God is great, and that this very man, whom ye are about to absolve and dismiss for the sake of Hyrcan, will one day punish both you and your king himself." Now the trial was opened and the senators appeared ready to do justice to Herod. Hyrcan observing that his favorite's life was seriously jeopardized, adjourned the Sanhedrin to the next day. During the night Herod, as advised by Hyrcan, left the city and went to Damascus. The indignation of the Sanhedrin and the predictions of friends were in vain. They could not move Hyrcan to any decisive action against Antipater and his sons.

25. Herod Invades the Country.

Sextus Cæsar appointed Herod general of the Coelosyrian army, and he invaded Palestine. This placed his father and brother in Jerusalem in a precarious condition. They went out to Herod, and succeeded in persuading him to leave the country and to be satisfied with the demonstration of power and rank he had made in the face of his enemies. Herod retired with his army and remained in his office in spite of his being a fugitive from justice.

26. Cassius Again in Palestine.

Shortly after the return of Herod to Galilee, Cecilius Bassus, one of Pompey's partisans, slew Sextus Cæsar, and took possession of his province and army at Apamia. The generals of Julius Cæsar concentrated their forces near Apamia, and Antipater sent his sons with an army of Hebrews to assist them. Marcus was sent from Rome to succeed Sextus. Meanwhile Julius Cæsar was assassinated in

Rome (12), and one of his murderers, Cassius, came to Syria to take possession of the East and the armies stationed there. Both Bassus and Marcus made peace and went over to Cassius. A great war was pending between the two parties in Rome, the Cæsarians and the Republicans. Cassius prepared for it and needed large sums of money. He demanded of Palestine seven hundred talents; Antipater and Malichus were appointed to raise that sum. Herod was the first man who raised his share of one hundred talents in Galilee, which gained him the favor of Cassius. Antipater raised his full share, but Malichus could not do it. Cassius reduced to slavery the inhabitants of Gophna, Emmaus, Lydda and Thamna, and would have killed Malichus, had not Hyrcan given the missing hundred talents from his private purse.

27. Death of Antipater and Malichus.

Malichus and Antipater were Hyrcan's mightiest friends; only that the former believed the latter was becoming too powerful. Meanwhile, Herod rose high in favor with Cassius and Marcus, which confirmed Malichus in his belief that Antipater and his sons were dangerous to Hyrcan. The first attempt of Malichus to assassinate Antipater failed, and was strenuously denied. But the second attempt was successful. Dining in the palace with Hyrcan, Antipater was poisoned, and died (42 B. C.). His sons were informed that the misdeed was committed by Malichus, and Herod received permission of Cassius to avenge his father's death. He came to Jerusalem with a band of foreign soldiers, still he did not venture to slay Malichus there. Meanwhile, Cassius had taken Laodicea, his vassals came to congratulate, and among them was Malichus. On his way thither, before the city of Tyre, Roman assassins, sent by Herod, slew him. Hyrcan was speechless on hearing of the assassination of his friend; but Herod made him believe it was done by command of Cassius, because Malichus had intended to raise a revolt and dethrone Hyrcan. Hyrcan believed him.

28. Consequences of this Assassination.

Cassius and his army marched to Philippi and, with the exception of a small Roman garrison under Felix, in

---

(12) Suetonius narrates that the Hebrew residents of Rome, night after night visited the tomb of Julius Cæsar. *Lives of the Emperors* in C. J. Cæsar, chap. 84.

Jerusalem, the land was without foreign soldiers. A brother of Malichus took possession of several cities, and Herod was ill at Damascus. In Jerusalem, the Roman commander, supported by some of the citizens, attacked Phasael, and it appeared that the sons of Antipater would be overcome. But Phasael fought his opponents, shut Felix up in a tower, and then dismissed him from the city. Herod recovered, came with an army, in a short time retook the lost cities, and restored peace. Hyrcan was as weak as usual in this combat of the parties, and was accused by Phasael of ingratitude against the memory of Antipater. The weak highpriest could not rid himself of the sons of Antipater, and the next event delivered him entirely into their hands.

29. Antigonus in the Field—Herod Affiances Mariamne.

The absence of the Romans from Syria and the insurrection of a party against the sons of Antipater, encouraged a foreign coalition in favor of placing Antigonus, the youngest son of Aristobul II., upon the throne. The coalition consisted of Antigonus and his friends, Ptolemy, his brother-in-law, who was the Prince of Chalcis, Fabius, the Prince of Tyre, and Marion, the commander of the remaining Roman soldiers, who had been bribed by the princes. They invaded Palestine from the north, and succeeded in taking several cities. A general insurrection of the Hebrews which was expected, did not come to pass, and Herod succeeded in repelling the invasion. So Hyrcan was saved once more, and was so much more indebted to Herod, who, coming to Jerusalem, was received with demonstrations of gratitude and enthusiasm. Herod was married, the name of his wife was Doris, by whom he had several children. Still Hyrcan gave his consent to Herod's betrothal of the beautiful Mariamne, his and Aristobul's grand-daughter by Alexander and Alexandra. This made the Idumean a member of the Asmonean family.

30. Marc Antony in Syria.

Meanwhile (42 B. C.) the fate of Rome was decided in the battle of Philippi, in Macedonia. The republican army was vanquished, Brutus and Cassius were dead, Octavius Augustus and Marc Antony were the victors and lords of the Roman Empire. After the battle Augustus went back to Italy, and Marc Antony came into Syria. Having arrived at Bithynia, in Asia Minor, the princes and repre-

sentatives of many nations, and among them also the friends
of Hyrcan, came to win the favor of the mighty chief.
They complained that Herod and Phasael were, in fact,
their kings, and Hyrcan was an impotent figurehead. But
the sons of Antipater also had come to Bithynia, and
Herod had brought plenty of money for Marc Antony, who,
being a friend of the deceased Antipater, bestowed his
grace on Herod, so that the Hebrews found no hearing.
When Antony had reached Ephesus, he was met by the
ambassadors of Hyrcan and the nation, who presented him
with a crown of gold. They were graciously received.
Their petition was to restore the liberty and property of the
inhabitants of those cities which Cassius had confiscated.
The petition was granted, decrees to this effect were published, the Tyrians were commanded to restore all cities
and persons taken from the Hebrews; and all the decrees
of the senate under Julius Cæsar concerning the Hebrews
in and out of Palestine were renewed or reconfirmed by
Marc Antony and Dolabella (13); so that, as far as the
Romans were concerned, no cause of complaint was left to
the Hebrews. But the sons of Antipater had many enemies among the aristocracy; and one hundred of them
waited upon Marc Antony at Daphne, and in the presence
of Hyrcan, by their most eloquent orators, accused Herod
and his brother. Messala replied in behalf of the brothers,
and Hyrcan, interrogated by Marc Antony, decided in their
favor. The delegation was indignantly dismissed, and
fifteen of them were imprisoned. Herod and Phasael were
appointed tetrarchs (princes of a fourth of the land), which
merely added a title to their respective offices. This gave
rise to new tumults in Jerusalem, and a delegation of
one thousand men went to Tyre to meet Marc Antony.
Hyrcan and Herod had prayed them to abstain from the
demonstration, and accosted them again outside of Tyre
with the same prayer; but they insisted upon their plan.
By order of Antony a body of soldiers attacked the delegation, slew and wounded many of them. Still those who had
escaped raised their voices so loudly in Jerusalem, that
Antony was provoked, and he slew also the fifteen men
in bonds. However, while this struggle of the parties
was going on in Palestine, Hyrcan being the protector of
the Hebrews in the Roman Empire, succeeded in obtaining
for them the enjoyment of their rights as Roman citizens
and immunity from military service (41 B. C.).

---

(13) Josephus' Antiquities xiv., x. and xii.

31. Antigonus in Jerusalem.

Once more Syria changed masters. Pacorus, King of Parthia, drove the Romans out of Syria (40 B. C.) and left there Barzapharnes as governor. Lysanius, the son of Ptolemy, now Prince of Chalcis, and Antigonus succeeded, by a promise, to this governor, of a thousand talents and five hundred beautiful women, in inducing him to invade Judea in order to enthrone Antigonus in Jerusalem. The Parthian army invaded Palestine from two sides, half of it came down the coast of the Mediterranean, and the other half attempted to march through Galilee. The Galileans, however, checked its progress. They had no knowledge of the Antigonus scheme. A small corps of cavalry was given to Antigonus by the Parthian commander to reconnoiter in Palestine. He advanced with them to Mount Carmel, and was joined by a number of the inhabitants of that district. As he proceeded his corps grew, so that, unexpectedly, he appeared in force before Jerusalem, and entered it without opposition. Now, Herod and Phasael came out of Castle Baris to meet him, and a fight ensued. Antigonus was beaten, but managed to reach the temple and to exclude Herod. The priests and the embittered aristocracy, of course, favored Antigonus and strengthened his position, and they were supported by many of the citizens, as Herod had soon an opportunity to discover. He had placed a posse of sixty men in houses, from which the movements in the temple could be observed. A number of citizens set those houses on fire, and the men perished in them. Herod avenged this deed by an attack on the citizens, many of whom were killed; but it must have convinced him that he could not hold out much longer.

32. Hyrcan, Phasael and Herod Leave Jerusalem.

Herod made one more attempt to dislodge Antigonus. A large number of pilgrims came to the city to celebrate Pentecost, Herod attempted to win them to his cause, but they were divided into two parties; a great deal of fighting and bloodshed ensued, without any result, and Herod could no longer govern the enraged parties in the city. He was advised to admit the Parthian cavalry encamped outside of the city to restore peace, and he did so. Now he was persuaded to send Phasael as an ambassador to the King of Parthia, so that he might decide the matter. He suspected the honor and the word of the Parthians, still he consented to the proposition. Hyrcan and Phasael went to the King of Parthia. When they had reached the Parthian army of the north they were well received and courteously treated. Too late, however, they discovered that the Parthians were the allies of Antigonus. As soon as it was reasonably supposed that the other army might have reached Jerusalem, Hyrcan and Phasael were put in chains and sent to the King of Parthia. Herod being informed of their fate saw himself surrounded by enemies and his life in danger. His intended mother-in-law, Alexandra, a shrewd woman, convinced him that he could save himself and the whole family only by speedy flight. In the night, and with as many men as he thought were trustworthy, Herod took Mariamne, her mother and brother, his mother and brother, and a son of Phasael, with all their servants, and quietly left the city with them, to travel southward into Idumea. He was attacked several times by Parthians and Hebrews, especially at a spot eight miles from Jerusalem, where, in memory thereof, he built afterward the fortress of Herodium; but he always routed his assailants, and conducted his train of people and baggage to Massada. Having taken possession of that city, he left there eight hundred men under command of his brother Joseph, together with the whole family and their servants, provisioned the city, and then, in company with Phasael's son, set out for Rome.

33. ANTIGONUS KING AND HIGHPRIEST (40 B. C.).

Hyrcan and the sons of Antipater being disposed of, Antigonus was proclaimed king and highpriest. The Parthians, having received a thousand talents, had to leave without the five hundred beautiful women, who had escaped from the hands of their captors. The Parthians plundered the palace and the houses of the rich in and near Jerusalem, burnt down hamlets and towns, and then left the country. Apparently, all parties were satisfied, and peace would have returned to the unhappy land, after thirty years of incessant combats between the two branches of the Asmonean family, if the Romans had not interfered again. The Parthians had too many Hebrews in their provinces not to be well disposed toward those in Palestine; and Antigonus united in his person the glory of the Asmoneans and the anti-Roman feelings, which made him both popular and admired. The Parthians sent him Hyrcan and Phasael. He had Hyrcan's ears cut off so that he could be highpriest no more, and then he let him return to the Parthians.

Phasael was to be placed before a court-martial, but he committed suicide in his prison. Massada was besieged, but not assailed, and this certainly was a grave mistake. On the whole, Antigonus appears to have dealt very kindly with his enemies.

34. Herod Crowned King of Judea.

The deathless ambition of princes has brought on the nations most of the misery which they have suffered. Herod, with Phasael's son, left Massada, went to Arabia, whose king, Malchus, being a debtor to Antipater's family, did not permit him to enter it. He went to Rhinocolura, where he was informed of his brother's death, and thence to Egypt. Cleopatra wanted to keep him near her, but he insisted, notwithstanding the stormy season, on going forthwith to Rome. At Pelusium he took ship and set sail for Italy. The storm shattered his vessel, but he was driven on shore at Rhodus. Some of his rich friends there gave him another ship, in which he arrived at Brundisium in September, 40 B. C., and traveled by land to Rome. He found Marc Antony in Rome, informed him of the situation in Syria, and proposed Hyrcan's grandson, then thirteen years old, as king or ethnarch of Judea. Rome, however, needed the strong arm of a tried and faithful soldier in Judea against the Parthians, and Herod was the man. Antony and Augustus united on him, the senate gave its consent, and Herod was led in state to the capitol, and was solemnly crowned King of Judea. It was an outrage, but done it was, and eight days after his arrival Herod left Rome at the head of two legions, to return to Palestine, and to take possession of its throne.

35. Herod Relieves Massada and Besieges Jerusalem.

Near Ptolemais Herod landed his army, and the Hebrews of his party came to him in large numbers. While Ventidius commanded the Romans in Syria against the Parthians, Herod began his operations by the capture of Joppa, and the relieving of Massada. Meanwhile Silo, with several legions, sent by Venditius, appeared before Jerusalem. A plentiful bribe convinced the Roman that the cause of Antigonus was just, and he left Jerusalem. The Hebrews followed him and pressed him hard, when he was joined by Herod and persuaded to return to the siege of Jerusalem. Both armies took positions west of the city, where they were beaten repeatedly and with great losses by the defenders of the city. Herod addressed a manifesto to the people, in which he promised pardon to all and generous government to the country if he were placed on the throne. Antigonus replied in another document, in which he pointed to his inherited right and the usurpation of Herod, and added that if the Romans hated him they might appoint another Asmonean in his place, but not an Idumean half-Jew. Silo, being promised more money, discovered again that Herod was wrong, and acted accordingly. The Romans ransacked Jericho and became unmanageable, and Herod was obliged to raise the siege (39 B. C.) He sent his brother, Joseph, to Idumea into winter quarters with a portion of his army, and went with the remainder, and with his family, to Samaria.

36. Subjection of Galilee.

While Joseph occupied Idumea, and his brother, Pheroras, repaired the fortifications of Alexandrium, Herod placed his family and bride in safety at Samaria, and began the reduction of Galilee. He took Sepphoris without resistance, and was soon master of Lower Galilee. In Upper Galilee, however, there were numerous guerrilla bands, to which he had given the disreputable name of robbers. They dwelt in the caves of wild and craggy mountains, and could not be dislodged by ordinary means. The crafty Herod invented means to reach them. Large wooden boxes, filled with soldiers and provisions, were lowered by ropes from the top of the steep declivities to the mouths of the caves, and their inmates were dragged out with hooks fastened to long poles, if they could not be reached otherwise. Some surrendered, others were slain, again others, and among them, one who slew his wife and seven children, committed suicide, dying with imprecations on their lips upon Herod and Rome. Still he succeeded during the winter in the subjugation of all Galilee.

37. The Prospects of Antigonus Improve.

The summer campaign of 38 B. C. was opened by the Roman commander, Macherus, who, with two legions and one thousand cavalry, supported Herod, and marched to Jerusalem. Like Silo, Macherus also was not very eager to assist Herod, who, besides the favoritism of Marc Antony, had no claim on the throne of Judea, which, by decree of Julius Cæsar, was secured to Hyrcan II. and his heirs. So Macherus took as much money as he could get from Antigonus, and was ready to leave, when the defenders of Jerusalem fell on his legions and inflicted a severe punishment on them. The Romans retreated and slew Herod's friends as well as his foes, so that Herod was obliged to retreat into Samaria and to go once more to Marc Antony. He left his brother, Joseph, in command of the forces in Judea, with strict injunctions not to risk a battle. In violation of orders, however, he attacked Pappus, one of the generals of Antigonus, was defeated and slain with the legions of his command. Why Antigonus did not attack the forces of Herod before his return, is not known. It appears he did not inherit the Asmonean brilliancy of design and rapidity of strategetical movements. Also in Galilee, the enemies of Herod rose again, and cast many of his friends into the sea; but they received no succor from Jerusalem.

38. Herod Supported by Marc Antony.

While Venditius defeated the Parthians, slew their king and drove them out of Syria, Marc Antony revelled in Athens, and brutally indulged in all the excesses of that debased age and city, where art and learning had become the handmaids of the lowest sensuality. After a year of degrading debauchery, he was disturbed by Venditius, who called him to the front. He went to Samosatha, which the Romans besieged. Thither also went Herod, and brought with him the friends and adulators of Antony, who lacked the courage and skill to pass the hordes of Arabian robbers infesting the country. This secured a friendly welcome to Herod. Presents, promises and adulations reminded Antony that he had made Herod King of Judea, and Sosius was sent with a large army to support him. Before this army could reach Judea, Herod returned and, with his own men, attacked Pappus, defeated his army, and slew him with his own hands. When the winter approached, Antigonus saw himself confined to Jerusalem and its environs.

39. Jerusalem and Antigonus Captured.

Early in the spring of 37 B. C., the two large armies of Herod and Sosius united before Jerusalem. Preparations for a long siege had been made in the city, and one of the most bloody conflicts was incessantly carried on between the contending armies. Outside of the walls, there was the superiority of numbers and generalship, and inside death-defying bravery and infuriated hatred. However, there were not a few Pharisees and Essenes in the city, Abtalion and Shammai among the former and Menahem among the latter, who had prophesied the success of Herod, and wanted to open the gates to him. Still their counsel was disregarded by the warriors. A number of wonderful escapes from imminent danger were made use of by Herod's friends to show that he was heaven-sent and miracles had been wrought in his behalf. This, undoubtedly, pacified many and caused numerous believers in miracles to submit to the apparent decrees of heaven. Still the defenders of the city were resolved to fight to the last, and Herod was obliged to build up slowly three lines of siege works under incessant and bloody sallies from the city. While the siege works were constructing he married Mariamne, Hyrcan's grand-daughter, who was supposed to be the most beautiful woman in her country. Eleven legions and six thousand cavalry were encamped before Jerusalem. When the siege works were constructed and the engines in position, the battering and storming commenced, and it took sixty days of hard fighting before the city was taken. The Romans poured in like furies, massacred without discrimination, destroyed and plundered, and none could stop them, not even Herod, until he promised a special reward to each soldier for stopping the horrible work of destruction. Antigonus surrendered to Sosius and knelt before him praying for his life. The haughty Roman called him Antigona, the woman, and sent him to Marc Antony. After Sosius had received rich presents and had made sacrifices in the temple to the God of Israel, he left the city, and Herod, by the grace of Marc Antony, was King of Judea.

40. THE CRUCIFIED KING OF JUDEA.

Marc Antony intended to spare Antigonus and to bring him to Rome to figure in his triumph. Herod, however, was afraid the heroic and legitimate king might find friends in Rome to plead his cause before the senate. Therefore, he insisted that Antony should slay Antigonus, and the last of the Asmonean kings, by command of Marc Antony, was crucified, 37 B. C. Strabo says he was beheaded, but Plutarch, in his Life of Antony, and Dio Cassius (Book XLIX.), both state that he was crucified. Plutarch says that this was the first king thus put to death by the Roman victor. Dio says, "Antony now gave the kingdom to a certain Herod, and, having stretched Antigonus on the cross and scourged him, which had never been done before to a king by the Romans, he put him to death." The sympathies of the masses for the crucified King of Judea, the heroic son of so many heroic ancestors, and the legends growing, in time, out of this historical nucleus, became, perhaps, the source from which Paul and the Evangelists preached Jesus as "The Crucified King of Judea."

CHAPTER XIX.

Herod and Hillel.

1. DOMINEERING CIRCUMSTANCES.

The victor had many admirers and many more feared him. In the Sabbath year and on the Feast of Pentecost (37 B. C.), Jerusalem was captured. After all the carnage by the Romans, Herod slew forty-five of the principal men of the Antigonus party. The sons of Buta, kinsmen of the Asmoneans, were also condemned to death, but they were saved by one of Herod's officers (1). He gathered up all the treasures he could find among the living or the dead, and sent them to Marc Antony to secure to himself the throne in Jerusalem. Pious souls saw in Herod the man of destiny, but many more feared him, and trembled before Rome's threatening sword. His title had been improved through his marriage, for Mariamne and her brother were the legitimate heirs to the crown according to the decree of Julius Cæsar and the more ancient grant of the Hebrews to Simon and his heirs. But Hyrcan and his grand-son, Aristobul III., were still alive, and Herod's title was that of an upstart and usurper (2). He was either pious enough or sufficiently prudent to protect the temple against every violation, and to have it honored also by Sosius, who dedicated to it a golden crown; still the priests must certainly have been the enemies of him who caused the highpriest to be scourged and crucified like a Roman slave. The Sadducees and the entire aristocracy naturally hated and despised

---

(1) Josephus' Antiq. xv. 1. See Baba b. Buta; *Gittin* 57; *Baba Bathra* 3; *Nedarim* 66; *Kerithoth* 97.

(2) Josephus calls Herod "the Great," which means "the Elder," as then the רבא was understood to distinguish one from the זעירא, the second or third of the same name. Rapaport's *Erech Millin*, p. 132.

him who took the power out of their hands and bestowed it upon his favorites, most of them foreigners; and among the Pharisees the number of democrats and enemies of Rome was certainly considerable. According to rabbinical tradition, Herod slew all the rabbis, which is an exaggeration. Yet, among the forty-five friends of Antigonus, who were slain, there were, undoubtedly, also Pharisean senators. Under such circumstances Herod mounted the throne of Judea to govern a nation of democrats, soldiers and personal enemies of his. Under these circumstances only one form of government was possible, and that was absolutism. Herod's cardinal crime, the imposition of absolutism, was the dictum of circumstances.

2. Usurpations and Compromises.

Herod, as far as possible, usurped all the powers of the State. He took under his control the temple and the priests. He appointed a personal friend of his, Ananelus, an obscure Babylonian, highpriest, and organized a new Sanhedrin under the elders of Bethyra, who appear also to have been Babylonians (3). These elders were Pharisees, although the doctors never acknowledged their authority as bearers and expositors of the traditions, because they were not sufficiently learned (4), and, perhaps, also because they made a compromise with Herod in favor of absolutism, in order to save some authority for the Sanhedrin. There are on the Hebrew statute book three laws especially which could have been enacted only by this Sanhedrin:

1. The king can not be a judge, hence no member of a Sanhedrin, and can not be judged or tried for any crime; he can not be a witness in any case, nor can anybody testify against him (5). This placed the king above the law.

2. The king may condemn to death by the sword, or punish otherwise, without co-operation or interference of any Court of law, any man who rebels against him (מורד במלכות), disobeys his commands, or pays not the taxes; and may cause to be slain any murderer, cleared by a Court of justice on technical grounds (6). This justified the former crimes of Herod and conferred on him absolute power.

---

(3) Bathyra, Josephus' Antiq. xvii., ii. 2.
(4) הלכה זו נתעלמה מבני בתירה *Pesachim* 66 *a*, and paral. passages.
(5) Mishnah, *Sanhedrin* ii. 2.
(6) Maimonides, Mishnah Thorah, *Melachim* iii. 8, 10 and iv. 1, and sources *in loco citate.*

3. The property of those condemned to death by the king belongs to the king, while the property of all other condemned criminals belongs to the proper heirs (7). This justified all the robberies committed by Herod after the capture of Jerusalem.

There are on record derived laws of this Sanhedrin (*Halachoth*), but no legislative enactments (*Tekanoth*) (8).

Herod being thus in possession of the fourfold power, the executive, military, judicio-legislative and ecclesiastic, had no objections to the continuation of the usual discharge of duty by the Sanhedrin, scribes and priests, so long as none interfered with the political affairs of his government. Therefore all internal affairs of the country were apparently undisturbed, although, for the first time since the days of Antiochus Epiphanes, Judea was under the iron scepter of absolutism.

3. Hyrcan Returns from Parthia.

Herod's throne was not secured yet. In the East, a sister of Antigonus held Hyrcanium and the surrounding country (9), which had to be taken from her by force of arms. At home, his wife, her brother, and their mother were the lawful heirs of the crown which he wore. Worst of all, Hyrcan II., the king *de jure*, was in the power of the Parthians, who might place him on the throne of Judea, as had been done with Antigonus. The fact that the ex-king and highpriest was treated with kindness and distinction by the king and the numerous Hebrews of Parthia, increased Herod's suspicion. Therefore, by adroit management, Hyrcan was persuaded to return to Jerusalem, and he did so contrary to the advice of the Parthian king and Hebrews, although the latter furnished ample means to send him home in royal state. Herod received him affectionately, and showered on him all the honors he could bestow, while in his heart he must have maliciously triumphed in now having the whole family in his power.

---

(7) Maimonides *ibid* iv. 9 and sources *ibid*. It is evident that these laws did not exist before Herod, except No. 3, in the kingdom of Israel (I. Kings xxi.); also that they were not enacted under Hillel or any time thereafter.

(8) *Sabbath* 94 and 120; *Pesachim* 46 and 108; *Guittin* 59; *Zebachim* 12; *Menachoth* 6.

(9) Jos. Wars I. xix. 1.

4. Aristobul III. Appointed Highpriest and Slain.

Herod soon felt the influence of his mother-in-law, Alexandra. She took it as an insult to her family, that an obscure Babylonian was preferred to her son, who was the lawful heir of the high-priestly dignity. She conspired with Cleopatra, Queen of Egypt, and Herod was obliged to depose his highpriest and appoint Aristobul III. in his stead. When on the first day of the Feast of Tabernacles (36 b. c.) the youthful Asmonean appeared at the altar in the sacerdotal robes, the enthusiasm of the multitude broke forth in loud and imprudent demonstrations. Herod apprehended danger. He could not depose him, because the young man's beauty and lawful claims might have moved even Marc Antony in his favor. Herod kept Alexandra closely watched in his palace. She, nevertheless, found opportunities to communicate with Cleopatra, and was advised to come with her son to Egypt, to lay her grievances before Antony. Preparations were made to carry the mother and son out of Jerusalem in two coffins. This was betrayed, the coffins captured and brought before Herod, and when opened, Alexandra and her son stood before the king. The defense of Alexandra, confirmed by her tears, was received by Herod in good grace, although the doom of her son was sealed. He pardoned them and treated them well. However, shortly after that, Alexandra entertained the king and his courtiers at Jericho. The highpriest was among the guests. In the afternoon the young men went out to bathe in a fish-pond, the highpriest was among them, and, as Herod had arranged it, he was drowned by his companions. So perished Aristobul III., not quite eighteen years old. The lamentation of the family was profound; but Herod feigned to be the most afflicted of all, he shed tears and broke forth in loud lamentations over the irreparable loss. A magnificent funeral, with royal pomp, covered the villainy of the king; but Alexandra communicated the facts to Cleopatra, and she caused Marc Antony to take cognizance of the foul assassination. Antony's legions had been defeated by the Parthians, and he was obliged to join them in Syria; when he was before Laodicea, Herod was summoned to appear and defend himself.

5. Mariamne's Affection Alienated.

Guilty before his own conscience, Herod prepared (35 b. c.) for the possibility of a just punishment, which was death. He appointed his uncle, Joseph, regent in his absence, with the particular charge to slay Mariamne if Antony should slay him. Joseph betrayed this secret to the queen and her mother, who were amazed at the discovery. The honeymoon was passed, Aristobul's death and this horrid charge could only fill the queen's heart with hatred and contempt for her husband. The ladies were watched by the king's sister, Salome, who discovered their intimacy with Joseph, and the change in Mariamne's conduct. A rumor being spread in Jerusalem that Herod was tortured and slain by Antony, Alexandra desired Joseph to send them to the Roman camp outside of the city, to which he was not unwilling to give his consent; and this was also known to Salome (10). Meanwhile, letters from Herod arrived, informing the queen how well his gifts, adulation and plea were received by Antony, notwithstanding Cleopatra's hatred; and that Antony's decision was: "It was not good to require an account of a king as to the affairs of his government; for at this rate he could be no king at all, but that those who had given him that authority ought to permit him to make use of it" (11); furthermore, how Antony honored and distinguished him. Shortly after Herod returned to Jerusalem and was informed by his mother and sister of their suspicion. His sister accused Mariamne of criminal intercourse with Joseph. Being treated by the queen with cold indifference, and learning that she knew his secret orders to Joseph, Herod's jealousy and anger were roused to fury. He was at the point of killing her, and had Joseph executed without a hearing. His domestic happiness was gone forever. He loved Mariamne passionately, and she hated him no less, and her mother fully sympathized with her. On the other side, there were Herod's mother and sister with their deadly hatred to the Asmoneans, and unshaken fidelity to Herod, incessantly planning intrigues and poisoning the king's mind with malicious gossip.

6. Cleopatra Receives Jericho.

Cleopatra's friendship for Alexandra was not disinterested. She intended to get possession of Palestine. This failing, she obtained of Antony all the cities on the Mediterranean, except Tyre and Sidon, and also Jericho, with its

---

(10) Antiq. xv., iii. 9.
(11) Ibid. Sec. 8. These last words refer distinctly to the compromise laws mentioned in our Section 2 of this chapter.

balm plantations (12). Still, when returning from Syria, whither she had accompanied Antony on his way to Armenia, she was in Herod's power, he did not dare to kill her, and agreed to farm for her Jericho and her Arabian dominions, which proved a snare to cunning Herod, laid for him by a still more cunning woman.

7. War with Arabia.

Returning now to Herod, we find him in time of peace collecting men and money in order to be prepared for the threatened rupture between Antony and Augustus. Cleopatra, however, had laid a snare for him. The King of Arabia did not pay the imposed tribute. For some time Herod paid it for him, but then he informed Antony of that king's shortcomings. Cleopatra, hoping to become mistress of either Arabia or Judea by a war between the two kings, persuaded Antony to reject Herod's support, and to command him to invade Arabia, which was done, and Herod, with his usual good fortune, was not engaged in the battle of Actium. However, serious misfortunes were in store for him at home. He invaded the Arabian territory and defeated the Arabs at Diosopolis. When at the point of defeating them a second time in the battle of Cana, Athenio, the commander of Cleopatra's corps, unexpectedly turned against him, and he was routed. This raised the spirit of the defeated Arabs; they rallied and fought Herod with success, took his camp, slew many of his men, and forced him to retreat to the mountains, and then back to Jerusalem. At the same time the whole country was shaken by an earthquake, in which about ten thousand persons and a large number of cattle perished. The accounts of this event being exaggerated and embassadors having been sent to them by Herod to make peace, the Arabs presumed it was easy now to take the whole country. Therefore, they slew the embassadors and invaded Galilee. The Hebrews were discouraged. The earthquake was taken to be an indication of God's anger against his people. Some believed the whole war unjust. It was waged on the Arabs because they refused to pay a tribute to a foreign power. Herod addressed his men assembled in Jerusalem (13). He spoke like a bold warrior and prudent statesman, full of religious sentiment and patriotic feeling. Most remarkable in that

---

(12) Ibid. Chap. iv.
(13) Antiquities xv., v. 3. undoubtedly taken from Herod's own Commentaries.

speech, perhaps, is the statement, "Although it was not reasonable that Jews should pay tribute to any man living," etc., showing the position which he apparently occupied between his people and the Romans. When the sacrifices had been made in the temple, Herod marched with his army across the Jordan to meet the Arabs. He met and defeated them in several battles; seven thousand of them fell. The survivors at last were besieged in their own strongholds, and forced to surrender. The Arabs appointed Herod their governor, and he was made lord of the very country which had threatened his destruction.

8. Hyrcan's Death—Herod's Departure to Meet Augustus.

This victory and conquest gained Herod many friends and admirers, and made him so much more formidable to his enemies. Still his misfortunes were not all over. Meanwhile, Antony had been defeated by Augustus. This afforded the advantage to Herod, in that the surviving Asmoneans had no succor to expect from abroad; but it also put his crown in jeopardy, because he was the friend and supporter of Antony to the last, and was now exposed to the mercy of Augustus. His friends trembled at coming events, and his enemies rejoiced over the probability of a change. Fearing the latter might take advantage of the situation and proclaim the hoary Hyrcan king, Herod, improving the moment of his popularity, resorted to falsehood and forgery, produced a letter of Hyrcan to Malchus, the King of Arabia, written at the time that enemy had the advantage over Herod, in which Hyrcan proposed to leave Jerusalem and seek refuge with the King of Arabia. The letter was delivered to Herod by Dositheus, the confidant of Hyrcan. Alexandra was also implicated in the treacherous plot. The document was shown to the Sanhedrin, and must have called forth bitter indignation against Hyrcan from those who believed in its authenticity. But it was a forgery. Herod had cunningly appealed to prevailing feelings, and, without trial or ceremony, the hoary Hyrcan, who had been his and his father's benefactor, and had elevated them to the highest positions, was slain (14). Neither the Sanhedrin nor the people had the right to interfere in this case, as Hyrcan stood accused of high treason (15). With the

---

(14) Josephus' Antiq. xv., vi. 2 and 3.
(15) See Section 2, Point 2d, of this chapter.

blood of two highpriests and his own uncle on his conscience, Herod made preparations to meet Augustus and his own fate. He appointed his brother, Pheroras, regent in his absence, sent his mother and sister to Massada, his wife, Mariamne, and her mother, Alexandra, to Alexandrium, placed this castle under the command of his treasurer, Joseph, and Sohemus, of Iturea, and commanded them to kill both of them in case any mischief should befall him; then he started for Rhodes (30 b. c.).

9. Hillel and Menahem Elevated to the Presidency Over the Sanhedrin.

The Pharisean savants seized upon this opportunity to depose the Bethyra rulers of the Sanhedrin, and to elevate Hillel and Menahem to the presidency thereof. It was in the year 30 b. c., the first day of the Passover being on Sunday, the question arose as to the time when the paschal lambs should be slaughtered, which the Bethyra senators either did not know, or, what is more likely, they could give no reasons why the Sabbath might be profaned on account of that sacrifice. As Simon b. Shetach had done in the days of Alexander Jannai to the Sadducean senators, so the Pharisees did now to the Bethyrians: they forced them to resign. The elevation of Hillel and Menahem was another compromise with Herod. Menahem, the Essene, was the king's favorite (16), and Hillel was too meek and humane a man, a Babylonian without family connections in Palestine, to become formidable to Herod. Menahem held that position only a short time. He and his disciples were appointed to executive offices by the king (17). He was succeeded by another favorite of Herod, Shammai or Sameas, the disciple of Abtalion (18). These two men presided over the Sanhedrin, Hillel as *Nassi*, and Shammai as *Ab-Beth-Din*, to a time after the death of Herod. Hillel outlived Shammai (19), and, according to the Talmud, presided forty years. These two men opened a new period in the history of literature and religion, and became the founders of two schools called Beth Hillel and Beth Shammai, with whom begins the scholastic rabbinical

---

(16) Josephus' Antiq. xv., x. 5. Menahem was considered a prophet. Like Socrates to Alcibiades, he prophesied the crown to the boy Herod.

(17) Hagiga 16 *a* and *b*.

(18) Josephus' Antiq. xv., i. 1.

(19) Bezah 20 *a*; Hillel in Bruell's Mebo Hamishnah.

period, the source of rabbinical Judaism with its vast Talmudical literature, and of primitive Christianity with its New Testament Scriptures. Therefore, it is necessary to give some account of Hillel and Shammai.

10. Hillel's Origin.

Hillel became the ancestor of a line of princes of the mind, whose influence on the Hebrews to the fifth century, A. C., and, through them, on the civilized world, was very important. Yet we know nothing of his youth. He was by birth a Babylonian Hebrew (20), and a descendant of King David, by one of his daughters (21). He came to Jerusalem to study the Law under Shemaiah and Abtalion (22), and did so consistently, although he was very poor (23). Afterward his brother, Shabna, who was a merchant, supported him (24), and he became a great teacher in Israel. He went back to Babylonia and then returned to Palestine (25), as posterity said of him: "When the Law was being forgotten in Israel, Hillel, the Babylonian, came up and re-established it" (*Succah* 20), after the death of Shemaiah. In Palestine, he had eighty disciples, among whom Jonathan b. Uziel was most prominent, and Jochanan b. Saccai least, although the latter mastered all the learning of his age (*Succah* 28 a). Jericho, for centuries a priestly center, was now under the protection of Cleopatra, hence, not under the exclusive control of Herod. The men of learning met at Jericho and devised means to better the public affairs. They met in the hall of Ben Gorion. Most prominent among them was Hillel, the meek Babylonian, distinguished no less for profound learning than humility and humanity. One day, while the savants were assembled in that hall, so the rabbis maintain (26), the BATH-KOL announced to them that there was one among them worthy to receive the Shekinah, as did Moses of yore, only that his generation was unworthy thereof; and all turned their eyes upon Hillel. This signifies, in modern phraseology, that he was looked upon as the greatest man of his age, worthy to

---

(20) *Pesachim* 66 a.
(21) *Sanhedrin* 5 a; *Horioth* 11 b; *Sabbath* 56 a; *Bereshith Rabba* 98 הלל מדוד; YERUSHALMI *Taanith* II.; SEDER HODQROTH Art. Hillel.
(22) *Pesachim*, Ibid.
(23) *Joma* 34.
(24) *Sotah* 21.
(25) *Mebo Hamishnah* p. 34.
(26) Sanhedrin 11. בעלית בית גוריא בירחו ונחנה עליהם * * * בת קול מן השמים, etc,

be the *Nassi* of the Sanhedrin; and his generation stood in need of reforms.

11. Hillel as a Teacher.

With Hillel begins the humanitarian and logical school in Palestine, and he was its founder. The Hebrew mind had already been turned to the *Derashah*, by Shemaiah and Abtalion, *i. e.*, to discover all the truth embodied in the Hebrew Scriptures, traditions and history, and to find the Scriptural basis for the various laws, customs, doctrines and maxims handed down traditionally by the fathers. The first difficulty was to master the traditional matter which was too vast and unsystematical to be retained. It was preserved partly in the protocols of the Sanhedrin and partly in the private scrolls of teachers (מגלת סתרים), grouped, perhaps, about Bible passages, from which it was respectively derived, as is yet the case in the books Mechilta, Saphra and Siphri; but it was chiefly retained by the memory of the scribes. Hillel began the work of codification. He laid down the outlines of the code, as accomplished two hundred years later in the Six Orders of the Mishnah. He began the construction of general laws or paragraphs from a number of particular decisions and opinions in the syllabus form, called Halachah Peshutah, "an abstract law," or Mishnah, "a theorem," to serve as mementoes to the traditional matter and the groundwork to systematical codification (27). Whether and how any law, custom, doctrine or general principle was based upon the Bible, was a main question with the learned. Therefore, Hillel formulated the hermeneutics of the fathers in seven rules of interpretation (28), to be the touchstone for the existing material, and the guide for future interpretation. So he became the founder of the logical school.

12. The Humanitarian School.

With the death of Hyrcan II. the third phase of the Kingdom of Heaven closed. The first phase, with the prophet as the visible head of the Kingdom, closed with the prophet Samuel. The second phase, with a Davidian prince at its head, closed with Nehemiah. The third phase, with the highpriest at its head, closed with Hyrcan II. Herod represented a foreign power. Now the fourth phase, to-

---

(27) *Sed. Haddoroth* Art. Hillel.
(28) Yerushalmi Pesachim vi. 1. Tosephta iv. Babli *Ibid.* 66 a.

which Ezra had already laid the foundation, asserted itself in the minds of the people, viz., the Law governs the Kingdom of Heaven, and its legitimate expounders are the highest authority in the Kingdom of God. The Pharisean doctrine, with the religious idea to lead, and the political one to be secondary, gained the ascendancy. So it mattered not whether Herod or another person collected the taxes and fought the battles. But within the Law as man's sovereign guide, the question arose, Which is most important, its ritual or its humanitarian contents? Hillel preferred the latter. He maintained that the object of law is peace and good will; therefore, the principal law is, "Thou shalt love thy neighbor as thyself," which he expressed in the negative form, "Whatever would hurt thee thou shalt do to none," and added thereto the most expressive words, "This is the principal, the rest (of the Law) is its commentary; go and finish" (*Sabbath* 31 *a*). It is man's duty to overcome selfishness, to increase his knowledge, to guard against vanity and haughtiness, and to use well his time in perpetual self-improvement (*Aboth* i. 13, 14). He admonished his disciples not to seclude themselves from the community on account of Herod's government or the imagined wickedness of the world; not to place too much reliance in one's own virtue and piety before the very day of death; to condemn none before one has placed himself in the situation of the supposed sinner; and to speak clearly and intelligibly, not in dubious or deceptive language (Ibid ii. 4). He gave prominence to the ethical and humane contents of the Books of Moses and the Prophets as the eternal element, without opposition to the laws of the land and the customs of the people; and did so in practical life both as a private man and as *Nassi* (29). Therefore, he made many proselytes by mild suasion, without any attempt at miraculous or mystic practices and words, was venerated as a saint, and called by posterity a disciple of Ezra.

13. HILLEL'S LEGISLATION.

The Hillel Sanhedrin must have enacted the laws governing the appointed high priests (30), as after the death of Hillel, with the exception of a few years under Agrippa I. and from 67 to 69 B. C., no Sanhedrin existed; and the Pharisean customs ruled at the temple, and were cautiously

---

(29) *Sabbath* 30 *b* and 31 *a* ; *Kethuboth* 67 *b*.
(30) *Yoma* I; *Sanhedrin* II., and the like.

practiced also by Sadducean highpriests (31). To this category must be counted the games during the Feast of Booths (שמחת בית השואבה) (32). These games in the Court of Women, performed daily, except the first day of the feast, after the close of the evening sacrifice, under brilliant illuminations, music and song, in which gymnastics and the artistic flinging and catching of knives and flambeaux were prominent, all of which being of Greek origin, were introduced by Hillel, he, at least, is the first man connected with them in the traditions, as an offset to Herod's introduction of the Greek games in Jerusalem, and became very popular among all classes. Legislation for the temple led afterward to mortifying difficulties raised by the Shammaites against Hillel (33). Vowing animals and things, or their value, to the sanctuary having become too frequent, Hillel legislated against it, and it was established that none must vow anything to the sanctuary (*Korban*) (34), except at the sanctuary, where the vow was to be fulfilled at once (35). In regard to commerce two laws of Hillel are recorded: First, the PROSBOLE, protecting creditors by a legal instrument against the forfeiture of a debt in the Sabbath year, as prescribed in Deuter. xvi. (36); and the second, amending Leviticus xxv. 29, if one having sold a house in a city, and after a year, as was his right, wished to return the purchase-money and reclaim his property, but the purchaser could not be found, that the money be deposited with the legal authorities and the contract annulled (37). The Courts kept records of all titles and mortgages. A Sabbath law was also enacted by Hillel. There was a dispute pending, whether apparent labor (שבות) was prohibited on the Sabbath, and Hillel decided it was not, and so it was held after him in regard to the temple (אין שבות במקדש); although outside thereof four such apparent labors were prohibited on Sabbath and holidays, viz., to climb a tree, to ride an animal, to swim or to make a noise by dancing, striking or hand-clapping in

(31) *Yoma* 19 *b* מעשה בצדוקי א'.
(32) *Succah* iv. and Talmud *ibid.* 53 *a.*
(33) TOSEPHTA *Hagigah* II. closing passage and paral. passage.
(34) Marc vii., ii. *Nedarim* 25.
(35) *Nedarim* 9 *b.*
(36) *Guitin* 36 *a.*
(37) *Erechin* 31 *b.* There is also recorded that Hillel established the law that bills of divorce to be legal must have the consent of the woman to be divorced.

hilarious amusements (38). In regard to the ordination of judges and senators (סמיכה) the custom prevailed that qualified judges, teachers and senators in a Court of three could qualify others, who were then authorized judges and teachers, eligible to the said offices and qualified to advance from Court to Court up to the Sanhedrin (39). But in the days of Hillel it was established that such ordination could be bestowed only by the *Nassi*, or a person duly authorized by him, and in the presence of the *Ab-Beth-Din* (40). Physicians, however, could be licensed by the Court of their respective homes. One more institution of Hillel must be noticed; he gave legal force to documents informally written by laymen, and sanctioned the vulgar dialect in legal documents as well as in public teaching (41), which, up to his days, had to be done in Hebrew. Therefore, this was the time when the *Methurgam*, "the translator," was introduced in the synagogue to translate into the popular dialect the passage read from the Law, and Hillel's disciple, Jonathan b. Uziel, furnished a Syriac translation of the Prophets, and an anonymous scribe furnished a Syriac translation of the Law to assist the public translators (42). During the life-time of Hillel the decisions and enactments of the Sanhedrin were called after him, as he was the Nassi, and but a few differences between him and Shammai remained undecided. Not because Hillel had said so, but because the Sanhedrin established it so, it was a law. Some of Hillel's *Halachoth* were also rejected by his Sanhedrin (MISHNAH *Baba Mezia* v. 9) (43).

(38) *Baba Mezia* i. 6.
(39) *Hagigah* ii. 2, YERUSHALMI *ibid.*, and TOSEPHTA *ibid. Bezah* v. 2. All other additional Sabbath laws (שבות) are of a later origin.
(40) *Sanhedrin* 82 *b;* TOSEPHTA *Shekalim* end, and *Hagigah* ii.
(41) Maimonides in Sanhedrin iv. 5. *Baba Mezia* 104 *a; Aboth* i. 13.
(42) The translations mentioned must, of course, have been Syriac and not Aramaic. The original translations must be sought in the PESHITO, of which the Onkelos and Jonathan *Targumim* to Pentateuch and Prophets are later transcripts made for the Babylonian Jews in the beginning of the third century. The tradition that ONKELOS translated the Pentateuch in Hillel's time is old, and has found its way into SEDER HAD-DOROTH (See *Hillel Hazakan*), and to Azariah De Rassi's *Meur Enayim*. The word ONKELOS need not be a corruption of Aquila or Aquilas. It may have originally been אנקלמוס (*Baba Bathra* 68 *b* and *Tosephta* III.), which signifies "a writer," or ONMKLOS (שם טוב), which signifies "an anonymous person of a good name," in either case the MEM is dropped.

(43) TOSEPHTA *Hagigah* end of II.; *Edioth* I. and *Sabbath* 15 *a*. See *Mebo Hamishnah*.

After the death of Hillel the difficulties of the two schools had their beginning.

14. Shammai as a Teacher.

After the return of Herod, Menahem was replaced by Shammai, of whose youth nothing is known except that he was a disciple of Abtalion and a supporter of Herod. He was a representative of the inflexible, rigid and thorough-going Pharisees. He held to his master's maxim, "Let the Law penetrate the mountain" (44), and so, in his expounding the Law, he went to the extreme logical sequences (45) of the written Law and the hermeneutic principle applied. He held in his hand the twenty-four inch gauge (אמת הבנין) like a scepter, as the insignium of strict justice and his position among the highest of the *Bonim* or *Haberim* (46). In regard to the acceptance of proselytes, he was no less rigid than in other points, and went to the extreme in the laws on Levitical cleanness (47). Although he was high-tempered and prone to anger, he advanced this maxim: "Make thy (study and practice of) Law a fixed matter, say little and do much, and receive every man with a friendly countenance" (48). Shammai was of the opinion that the Law, strictly and logically expounded and rigidly enforced, was the only source of salvation, especially in his time, and insisted upon the literal application of every Law of Moses exactly as the terms of the Pentateuch suggest (49).

15. Hillel and Herod.

In temperament, Hillel was the direct opposite not only of Shammai, but also of Herod. The latter was impetuous, ambitious, high-tempered and haughty, while Hillel was so gentle that nothing roused his temper (50), so placid that men's whims never disturbed him (51), so meek, humble and pliable, that he rather yielded to antagonists than mortified them (52). Herod's ambition engendered in him that ever-vigilant suspicion which led him from crime to crime;

(44) Sanhedrin 6 b.
(45) Tosephta, *Erubin* III. and Babli *Sabbath* 19 a. עד רדתה.
(46) Tosephta *Demai* II.
(47) *Kelim* xxii. 4; *Edioth* i. 7 and 11.
(48) Aboth i. 15.
(49) *Yoma* 77; *Succah* 21; *Yebamoth* 15; *Nazir* 23.
(50) *Sabbath* 31 and 32.
(51) *Sabbath ibid.*
(52) *Erubin* 13.

while Hillel's meekness made him extremely confiding in
God and man (53). Hillel's ambition was learning for the
benefit of his fellow-men, and Herod's ambition was to acquire power and glory (54). Therefore, Herod was under
the dire necessity of grasping large sums of money from
the people's wealth, and Hillel, always content, stood in
need of nothing (55), and yet could always afford to be un-
commonly charitable (56). Herod represents the animal
intellect and Hillel the purest ethical intelligence. They
were natural evolutions of two parties among the Hebrews.
Herod was the product of the party of war, conquest, military glory and dominion; and Hillel was an offspring of
the Law, the party of the historical mission to the nations,
whose sole object was Monotheism, justice, charity and intelligence, the preservation, exposition and promulgation
of the Law.

16. Herod's Return.

All the reforms mentioned in the previous sections were
effected in the reign of Herod. He returned to Jerusalem
confirmed in his dignity and power, his possessions enlarged by the cities of Gadara, Hippos, Samaria, Gaza, Anthedon and Joppa, and with Cleopatra's body-guard, presented him by Augustus. His friends rejoiced, his enemies
were silenced. He accepted the changes made by the Pharisees, appointed the Essenean Menahem and his disciples
to high executive offices; and Shammai was placed, with
Hillel, at the head of the Sanhedrin, so that, apparently, all
parties were satisfied. In the temple, too, it appears, he
made a compromise with the Pharisees. After the death of
Aristobul III., he reappointed Ananelus to the high priesthood, but removed him from office, and appointed in his
place Joshua (Jesus), a son of Fabus, and this was a Pharisean family of distinction. So Herod opened the second
period of his government evidently with the intention to
become just and give satisfaction to his people.

17. Death of Mariamne.

Mariamne made no secret of her hatred to her husband,
for Sohemus had divulged to her the secret orders of Herod

(53) *Berachoth* 60 *a*.
(54) *Aboth* i. 12, 13, 14.
(55) *Bezah* 16.
(56) Kethuboth 67 *b*.

when he had left her and her mother prisoners at Alexandrium. His love, however, was as violent as her hatred. The king's sister and his mother never ceased irritating his wrath against his wife, and his domestic peace was lost forever. In a fit of madness, to which he was subject, Herod had Sohemus slain, convoked his slavish courtiers to a council, and the sentence of death was passed on Mariamne, which the king, under the evil influence of his sister and his mother, executed. Alexandra, to save her own life, reproached and insulted her innocent daughter as she went forth to meet her fate. But the last daughter of the Asmoneans, in greatness of soul and firmness of mind, equal to her most valorous ancestors, died "without changing the color of her face" (Josephus). Aristobul II., his sons, Alexander and Antigonus, Hyrcan II., and their grandchildren, Aristobul III. and Mariamne, rested now in peace; and Herod lived the miserable life of a wretched criminal in remorse and self-contempt (29 B. C.).

18. Death of Alexandra and Castoborus.

Shortly after Mariamne's death a terrible pestilence broke out in Palestine, Herod left Jerusalem and went to Samaria. Some of his best friends died. Remorse, violent affection for his murdered wife, misery and superstition tormented and reduced him to a raving skeleton. Alexandra, hearing of his critical condition, schemed a plot to save the kingdom for Herod's children, as she said, and demanded of the respective commanders possession of several fortresses, which was at once reported to Herod. He slowly recovered his health, but never again his temper, returned to Jerusalem, and, without trial or delay, ordered the execution of Alexandra, and the last head of the Asmoneans was laid low (28 B. C.). Then Herod raged furiously against his own friends, and slew also his brother-in-law, Castoborus, the husband of Salome, from whom she had, contrary to law, divorced herself, and then accused, together with other friends of Herod, of plotting against him with Cleopatra. Besides, Castoborus had rescued the sons of Buta, who were also of the Asmonean race; they were now betrayed by Salome and slain with Castoborus (28 B. C.), except Baba b. Buta, who, being a disciple of Shammai, was spared, but was deprived of his sight.

19. Innovation and a Revolt.

Having disposed of all the Asmoneans, and believing himself secure on his throne, Herod began to imitate

Menelaus and Jason by the introduction of foreign customs and games. He built a theater in the city and an amphitheater on the plain, and appointed solemn games every fifth year in honor of Cæsar. He promised royal prizes for the victors in chariot races, in the contests of gladiators and naked wrestlers, beast fights and beastly combats of condemned criminals, and to the best musicians. He displayed Cæsar's trophies and inscriptions of his valorous deeds, invited all nations by proclamation to come to the games, and spent the people's money most pompously and audaciously. But it all came to nothing; the childish and barbarous ostentation and brutality of the Greeks would not take root among the Hebrews. They were too earnest and too manly for it. The citizens of Jerusalem rose against the innovations. When they had been pacified or overawed, ten men conspired against Herod's life, and would have assassinated him in the theater, had not one of his spies informed him in time, and kept him out of harm's reach. The conspirators were arrested and put to death, but soon after the spy was also caught and torn to pieces by the populace, which led to the torture of women and the extermination of whole families by the king, in his bloody revenge. Still the Grecian games were suppressed in Jerusalem in spite of Herod's power and wealth.

20. HEROD'S ARCHITECTURE.

Unable to Romanize his people in Jerusalem to please his mighty patrons, Herod did it abroad at the expense of his people, and especially by monuments of architecture, while at home he gave to every new structure, also to the rooms in his palace, an Augustan name. Providing first for his own safety, he strengthened the fortifications of Jerusalem, built himself a new palace at Acra, near its northern wall, rebuilt three northern towers of Zion, and called them respectively Hippicas, Mariamne and Phasael, with another palace adjoining this latter tower, and enlarged the old castle Baris in the north-eastern corner of Mount Moriah, which he called Fort Antonio. These buildings placed Jerusalem and the temple under his control. Apprehending that, nevertheless, he might one day be ejected from his capital, he provided for the emergency. He rebuilt and strongly fortified the city of Samaria, which he called Sebaste, and did the same with Guba in Galilee, which was the place of rendezvous for his cavalry. He also enlarged and fortified Strato's Tower with its harbor, on the

Mediterranean, and called it Cæsaria. He placed in all those new cities a large Heathen population, to rely upon in case the Hebrews should reject him. Thus secured behind strong walls and citadels, commanding the respective cities, surrounded by a standing army and a host of vigilant spies, he considered himself safe at home, and feared no attacks from abroad except from Rome, where Augustus and his wife were his mighty patrons. In the erection of all these structures, however, Herod was guided by an excellent taste and sense of the beautiful. He erected for himself architectural monuments. He also built Herodium, a fortress near Jerusalem, Antipatris on the plain, and Castle Cypros near Jericho. But he spent much more money in foreign countries in the erection of architectural monuments, water-works, fountains, parks, groves and arcades, and encouraging the Olympian games, which made him famous among foreigners for taste and munificence, although his people had to pay oppressive taxes and derived no benefit from the vast sums squandered in foreign lands. Syrians and Greeks praised him as a benefactor, and Augustus said of him, that he was worthy to wear the crown of Syria and Egypt. He gave no little offense to his people by the erection of Heathen temples in Palestine and outside thereof, while Hebrew soldiers under Alexander the Great, at the risk of their lives, refused to assist in the rebuilding of a Baal Temple. To please and appease the Hebrews, Herod also rebuilt the temple of Jerusalem in the grandest style, as we shall narrate further on.

21. The Famine.

While Herod was thus engaged in squandering the people's money (24 B. C.), a prevailing drought destroyed the fruit, and a distressing famine prostrated the whole country, and swept away many victims. The public treasury was exhausted and Herod was obliged to sell all the silver and gold vessels he possessed to purchase grain in Egypt for his starving people. He did it most munificently and also assisted the Syrians, who suffered by the same calamity. This benefaction, says Josephus, wiped out the old hatred which his violation of the nation's customs had procured for him (57), and the famine turned out to his great advantage.

---

(57) Antiq. xv., ix. 2.

22. He Assists Augustus and Marries Again.

The same year Herod sent five hundred chosen men of his guard to assist Aelius Gallius in a war against the Arabs, few or none of whom ever returned. Meanwhile, the king fell in love with a priest's daughter. Her name was Mariamne, her father's name was Simon, son of Boethus, hailing from Egypt. Herod deposed the high-priest of the house of Fabus and placed the Boethite in the lofty position, and then married his beautiful daughter. The Boethites were Sadducees. Four of them were high-priests between 24 B. C. and 42 A. C., and they became the theological expounders of Sadduceeism on Helenistic principles. Therefore, the Sadducees were frequently called Boethites (ביתוסים) (58). The Sadducees, deprived of political power, became, through the teachings of the Boethites, a religious sect.

23. Three Provinces Added to Palestine.

Herod's three sons by Mariamne, the Asmonean, were his special favorites. He lavished all possible care and tenderness upon them. He sent them—Alexander, Aristobul and Herod—to Rome to be educated. The last-named died, and the survivors were placed in the house of Pollio, one of Herod's intimate friends. But the emperor took them to his palace, and afforded them all the advantages of a princely education. He was so favorably impressed with the lads, that he wrote to Herod that he might choose either one of them as his successor, and his choice was confirmed in advance. At the same time, Augustus added to Herod's kingdom the three provinces of Trachonitis, Auranites or Iturea, and Batanea, which included the largest portion of Coelosyria up to Damascus, and then north-east beyond the 34° n. l. to the Mediterranean, including the seaport of Berytus (22 B. C.). One Zendoborus had been farming part of these provinces for the Romans, after Antony had slain Lysanius, its prince; but that man had made common cause with the numerous robbers who infested those mountains. Herod overcame them and kept the country under his iron sway, although Zendoborus was always busy in stirring up sedition among his party. The dissatisfied ones reached Augustus, and gave utterance to their grievances. The emperor sent his friend, Agrippa, to the East to govern the Asiatic provinces and to look into

---

(58) YERUSHALMI, *Yoma* i. 5; TOSEPHTA, *Ibid.* I.

into the affairs of the Coelosyrians. He took up his residence at Mitylene, on the Island of Lesbos and Herod went there to defend his course. He succeeded well with the Roman, who was his personal friend and returned to Jerusalem. When he was gone, ambassadors of the people of Gadara came to Agrippa to seek redress; but he sent them in chains to Herod, who had the moderation this time to let them go unpunished (21 B. C.). Next year Augustus came to Syria. Again the parties complained, and again in vain. He received Herod like a brother, and when shortly after Zenodohorus died, the emperor presented the estates of the deceased, Ulatha and Panias, to Herod. It was in this latter place that the Hebrew king erected a temple to Augustus, the god-emperor. It was not in Palestine proper, and the Hebrews could not oppose it; although Herod's hypocrisy and adulation must have rendered him contemptible among honest men.

24. The Temple in Jerusalem Rebuilt.

Baba b. Buta, whom Herod had blinded, gave him the advice to rebuild the temple on Mount Moriah, in order to atone in part for the wrongs he had inflicted on his people (59). Although he had been eminently successful with Augustus, who also bestowed a tetrarchy upon Pheroras, Herod's brother, he nevertheless knew that his people was dissatisfied, and could not be governed altogether against its will. He released his subjects of a third part of the taxes without gaining in their favor. He prohibited all public meetings, surrounded them with spies, imprisoned many in the citadel of Hyrcania, where not a few were put to death; but it did not change the outspoken antagonism against him. He demanded an oath of allegiance from his subjects. However, not only the principal Pharisees, to the number of six thousand, and among them also Hillel, Shammai and their disciples (60), and all the Essenes refused to take the oath; but even his own brother's wife secretly paid the fines imposed on them (61). He had ample cause to know that something of extraordinary importance had to be accomplished in order to overcome the popular indignation. He obeyed the counsel of Baba b. Buta to rebuild the temple. The people were neither ready nor willing to assist him in this work. He made a very

---

(59) *Baba Bathra* 3 b and 4 a.
(60) Josephus' Antiq. xv., x. 4.
(61) Antiq. xvii., iii. 4.

flattering address to them, and yet many feared his craft and hypocrisy. He promised not to tear down the old building till the materials for the new were on the spot. In one year and six months the priests built a new temple upon the spot of the old, which was looked upon as the most gorgeous and most costly building of the age (19 to 17 B. C.), and then the cloisters, corridors, towers and arcades were rebuilt in the same magnificent style, all much larger and loftier than in the old temple. Herod did not forget to build a subterranean passage from Fort Antonio to the eastern gate of the temple, and to put up a golden eagle over the main portal to please Rome, and to have easy access to the temple in case of need. It did not rain at daytime, as long as the work was progressing, says Josephus (62), so well was the Almighty pleased with that sacred enterprise. However, neither this historian nor Nicholaus, of Damascus, Herod's historiographer, tells us of any particular enthusiasm among the people when that gorgeous structure was dedicated to the service of the Most High. The holy reminiscences connected with the old building, now over five hundred years old, could not be replaced by a profusion of marble, gold or architectural beauty, produced by the will of a despot. The spirit of piety was missing in the beautiful forms of the new temple. Herod decorated the interior of the temple with all the gold and silver he could find, and replaced the golden vine at the entrance. The anniversary of his ascension of the throne was appointed as the day of dedication, the people and numerous foreigners were invited to the gala day, hecatombs were slaughtered, the altar was crimsoned with blood, and the guests were royally entertained; but no fire came from heaven, no enthusiasm from the heart of the dissatisfied people; the new temple was a mass of cold marble and gold. Still thousands, and especially the priests, were well pleased with the gorgeous structure, which was admired by all (63).

25. The Foreign Hebrews.

No Israelite was considered a foreigner in Palestine. It was his country, and he was a citizen thereof, whenever he claimed that right, although he was also a Roman, Alexandrian or Parthian citizen at his respective home. The term "Foreign Hebrews" must be understood in regard to

---

(62) Antiq. xv., xi.
(63) *Dibre Malchuth Baith Sheni.*

domicile. Those Israelites who lived outside of Palestine looked upon the new temple with the same veneration as they did upon the old one. They sent their annual contributions as heretofore (64), and came to Jerusalem, especially on Passover, in very large numbers. Still, all over the Roman Empire they maintained their rights as Roman citizens, with freedom of worship, as Julius Cæsar had granted to Hyrcan II., and Marc Antony had confirmed after Cæsar's death. Augustus also found occasion to reconfirm their privileges, especially to those of Ionia, Libya, Cyrene and elsewhere, when the Greeks, disliking the Monotheism of the Hebrews, attempted to interdict their worship and to prevent their sending of money to Jerusalem. But the edicts of Julius Cæsar were also enforced by Augustus. In one case the decision was rendered by Agrippa in Ionia, in presence of Herod, Nicholaus, of Damascus, pleading the cause of the Hebrews. The other cases were decided in Rome on presentation of the case by a deputation of Hebrews from Cyrene (65).

26. A Settlement of Babylonians.

Herod was no less hated in Trachonitis than in Palestine. The robbers and guerrillas there, in sympathy with the Arabs and with their own people, gave him much trouble. When he was in Rome for a short time it was given out that he was dead, and that whole province rose in an insurrection against his authority. Returning from Rome, he drove the robbers and guerrillas into their mountain fastness, where they defied him. He slew the relatives of those men all over the country, which made the evil worse. This also involved him in a quarrel with Obedas and Aretas, his successor, King of Arabia, and finally led him to rashly invade that country. Augustus being informed thereof was very angry at Herod, and it took all the eloquence of Nicholaus, of Damascus, to restore Herod in the favor of Augustus (66). In order to keep

---

(64) Josephus' Antiq. xvi., ii. and vi.
(65) Remarkable in the decree of Augustus, preserved by Josephus (Antiq. xvi., vi. 2), is the passage, "That the Jews have liberty to make use of their own customs according to the laws of their fathers, as they made use of them under Hyrcan, THE HIGHPRIEST OF ALMIGHTY GOD," etc., these last words being a wonderful admission by a heathen emperor, unless they refer to the title assumed by John Hyrcan כהן לאל עליון.
(66) Josephus' Antiq. xvi., ix.

Trachonitis quiet Herod invited Zamaris, a Babylonian Hebrew, and his followers, to settle down in a position which enabled them to keep the Trachonites peaceable. This Zamaris was an expert horseman and archer, and so were all his followers, as well as most of the Parthians. He had come with a hundred men to Syria, and the Roman governor, Saturninus, had given them a new home at Valatha, near Daphne. Herod invited this man and his followers to settle in or near Trachonitis, in order to protect the pilgrims to Jerusalem from the East. They were given land in Batanea free of taxes and with considerable autonomy, and built there the fortified village of Bathyra, which they held to a time long after the fall of Jerusalem, a people famous for valor and candor, no less than for expert horsemanship.

27. Death of Mariamne's Sons.

Having narrated the public acts of Herod, we return to his domestic life. This was a series of intrigues, cabals, conspiracies, malicious accusations, hatred, torture of servants and friends, of misery and wretchedness to Herod, horror and death to his courtiers and three of his sons. In the year 16 B. C. Herod went to Rome and came back to Jerusalem with his two sons by the Asmonean Mariamne, Alexander and Aristobul. Thereupon Alexander married Glaphyra, daughter of Archelaus, King of Cappadocia, and Aristobul married Bernice, Herod's niece, the daughter of Salome. The hopes of the nation were centered in these two young princes. Therefore, they were hated by Herod's family; for Salome, no less than Pharoras, entertained hopes of securing the succession. On the other hand, there were Herod's first wife, Doris, and her son, Antipater, who, by right of primogeniture, was the future King of Judea. Nor was the second Mariamne, with her son, Herod, inactive in her own behalf. So the intrigues, treacheries and mutual denunciations began in Herod's palace. The two princes, who were mere children when their mother was beheaded, had, nevertheless, learned of it in Rome, and looked upon their father as the murderer of their mother and her whole family, and disliked him heartily and frankly. This roused Herod's suspicion against them, and he saw the specters of his own guilt in his sons. Salome understood the diabolical art of poisoning Herod's mind, and he soon saw nothing but fratricides and regicides. Herod having again taken Doris and Antipater into his palace, the conspiracies of the women and the wickedness of Antipater were unbounded, till he accused Alexander, the heir apparent, of having attempted to poison his father. Herod took Alexander to Rome before Augustus, who declared him innocent, and reconciled the father and son. The ingenuity of the conspirators was not yet exhausted. Again they found means to arouse Herod's suspicion, and Alexander was put in chains again after Pheroras and Salome had been pardoned for their part in a plot against the king. Archelaus, the father-in-law of Alexander, came to Judea, and by his prudent management he succeeded in reconciling father and son, and in persuading Herod that his evil inclination to suspect everybody and to give credence to every malicious gossip was the cause of all his troubles. It did not last long. A wicked man, Eurycles, conspiring with Antipater, being well paid by the latter, ingratiated himself with the king, won his confidence, and cautioned him against his sons, Alexander and Aristobul, who, he said, were anxiously awaiting an opportunity to assassinate their father. They were arrested and put in bonds. Augustus gave permission to have them tried at Berytus, where a Court of Roman and Syrian dignitaries heard Herod's violent accusations. The sons and their advocates were not heard, and the Court condemned them to death. An outcry of horror shook the land. An old soldier, Tero, had the moral courage to tell the king that justice was trampled under foot, truth was defied and nature confounded. But he and many others were arrested, and another plot was spun by the three furies, Salome, Pheroras and Antipater, a number of soldiers, and Trypho, the barber, were slain. The two princes were sent to Sebaste, and there put to death by strangulation, and their remains were sent to Alexandrium (6 B. C.). So Herod destroyed first the Asmonean and then his own dynasty; for with the death of these princes the hopes of his family among the Hebrews were destroyed.

28. PHERORAS AND HIS WIFE BANISHED.

One of the conspirators at Herod's Court was his brother, Pheroras, and his wife, who had paid the fines for the Pharisees. They had prophesied to her and her successors the crown of Judea, which had cost their lives. Herod demanded of his brother to abandon his wife, which he refused to do. The king then commanded his son, Antipater, and his mother, to hold no intercourse with Pheroras and his wife, and enjoined upon the latter to avoid the company of the women at Court. Still Antipater and Pheroras, with his wife, frequently met at the rooms of Antipater's mother, and it was given out that he had criminal intercourse with his aunt. The actual cause of their intimacy, however, was not yet known. Antipater, at his own request, was sent to Rome with rich presents and the last will of Herod, which appointed Antipater his successor, and in case of this prince's untimely death, the throne should be inherited by Herod Philip, the son of the second Mariamne. Pheroras and his wife were banished from Jerusalem, and he swore never to see the king again. Shortly after, however, Pheroras fell sick and Herod came to his residence. Soon after the banished prince died, and Herod brought back his remains to Jerusalem, and had them interred with high honors. The death of Pheroras became the cause of Antipater's downfall.

29. THE FALL OF ANTIPATER AND THE HIGHPRIEST.

Antipater was his father's equal in wickedness, and on a level with Salome in designing intrigues and plotting conspiracies. When the three conspirators had succeeded in disposing of the sons of the Asmonean Mariamne, the conspirators operated against one another; this time Salome against Antipater and Pheroras. The end was the journey of Antipater to Rome and the banishment of Pheroras. His death was unfortunate for his wife, for she was accused of having poisoned him. A searching investigation followed, the torture was applied, and the discovery made, that Doras and her son, Antipater, hated the king, and were anxiously awaiting his death; and that the poison discovered in possession of Pheroras' wife had been sent to her by Antipater, while on his way to Rome, to be administered to Herod. These facts being established, Doras was driven from the palace, and epistles dispatched to Rome to bring back Antipater, under the pretense that the king was very sick and desirous of seeing him. Also the second Mariamne was found guilty of conspiracy and driven from the palace, her son was disinherited, her father removed from the high priesthood. This office was given to Matthias, son of Theophilus, who was replaced shortly after by Eleazar, son of Boethus. Antipater returned, was arrested and tried before Quintilius Varus, then President of Syria. Nicholaus, of Damascus, was the accuser and prosecutor, and Antipater was condemned to death. He was bound and sent to the royal castle at Jericho, and the whole matter was referred to Augustus. Augustus said he would rather be Herod's swine than his son. The last will of Herod was changed, and he himself approached his end.

30. Special Sins of Herod.

A special sin of Herod was that he took it upon himself to sell burglars as slaves to foreign countries, which, like the eagle upon the temple, violated the laws of the country (67). This, being a direct interference with personal rights and freedom, was considered one of his most unpardonable sins. His next special sin was that he opened and entered the sepulchre of King David (68). He stood in need of money, had heard that there were treasures in that sepulchre, part of which only John Hyrcan had taken out, and went down to secure the remainder. Naturally enough, he found nothing except a few golden ornaments, which he took, and escaped with empty hands and a distressing fright. He built a propitiatory monument of white stone at the entrance of that ancient structure, which did him no good, for the people were convinced that his domestic miseries, which made him the most wretched man in Israel, came upon him with renewed violence in consequence of that sacrilege. Polygamy, which had become extinct, at least among the kings and princes, was reintroduced by Herod, who had no less than nine wives, six of whom were blessed with children. Another of his special sins was the reintroduction of the Olympian games, this time in the heathen city of Sebaste (8 B. C.), when all the buildings of that city were completed. Under the most disgusting pomp, ostentation and extravagance, to which also Julia, the wife of Augustus, contributed her share, the revolting displays of naked brutality tainted by Grecian art were enacted before a hilarious company of foreigners and domestic adulators and slaves (69). The games were established by the king, to take place every fifth year, but it did not come to pass. If anything more had been necessary to disgust the people with the hoary sinner these games would certainly have been sufficient.

31. The End of Herod.

Herod had grown old. Although he spent much of his time in corporeal exercises, dyed his hair and beard, painted

(67) Antiq. xvi. 1.
(68) Antiq. xvi., viii.
(69) Antiq. xvi., v.

his face and changed domicile frequently, his health and
strength failed. The baths of Callirhoe afforded him no
relief. His disease grew on him. He was always hungry,
and every bite of food gave him terrible pain. His body
was swollen, and emitted a pestilential stench. The bath
of perfumed oil did him no good; there was no relief for
him either bodily or spiritually; he was the most wretched
man in his country. All his crimes loomed up in his mind
and tormented him, while he suffered the most intense physical pain (70). Yet the list of his crimes was augmented
in the last days of his life. Two Pharisean teachers, Judas
b. Saripheus and Matthias b. Margoloth, falsely informed
of the king's death, excited their disciples to a rash act of
public disturbance. They threw down the golden eagle
from the temple gate. The two teachers and forty young
men were arrested and condemned to death by Herod for
sacrilege. They died heroically on the pyre, and left to
Herod's successor a terrible legacy of popular hatred.
Shortly after, Herod, under the influence of tormenting
pains, attempted suicide, which was thwarted by his servants. The noise to which this event gave rise in the
palace at Jericho, reached Antipater's prison. Believing
his father dead, he made seductive promises to his jailer to
set him free. Herod learning how his son rejoiced over the
news of his father's death, ordered his immediate execution, Augustus had decided not to interfere, and the head
of plotting Antipater fell five days before the death of
Herod. The last villainy of Herod was, that he had captured many of the most prominent men, kept them captives in the hippodrome at Jericho, to be slain after his
death, so that the nation should mourn for them, as he
knew none would mourn for him. But this act of barbarity

---

(70) Matthew's story of the massacre of the babes in Bethlehem
can not be true. No other book of the New Testament or outside
thereof mentions this atrocious deed. Herod's misdeeds were not
committed in direct violation of Jewish law, and that slaughter
would have been an exception so shocking in its nature that it must
have been recorded. The story of Matthew is based upon an astro-
logical superstition, with a star moving from east to west. Matthew
misinterprets a passage of Jeremiah and then turns it to a fact, so
that his intention to write a legend for public use can not be misunderstood. Besides all this, Luke directly contradicts Matthew's genealogy of Jesus and the story of his nativity, which he replaces by
another legend; so that John rejected both, and no other New Testament writer refers to the birth of Jesus or any circumstances connected with it. Perhaps Matthew intended to refer (like Luke) to
Archelaus, who was also called Herod.

was not executed. A few days after (3 B. C. (according to Jewish count 4 B. C.), in the year 751 of Rome), on the second day of SHEBAT (71), after a reign of thirty-four years (72), and at the age of seventy, died the most wicked and most wretched king of the Hebrew people, cursed by many and lamented by none. Herod was great as a soldier and statesman. He enlarged the boundaries of Palestine, improved the country, advanced the arts of civilization, and gained Rome's respect and good will for the Hebrew people. But he was the assassin of the Asmoneans, the executioner of his kinsmen and friends, the heartless despot of his antagonists, as all Roman rulers of his time were, and a most abominable fury in his old age. Yet he respected the religion, worship, laws, customs and private rights of his people; so that aside of his family and courtiers, none but political offenders were maltreated by him, and the complaints against him rose not only from the heavy burdens of taxes which he imposed, as they had also risen against King Solomon after his death; they rose chiefly from the offense which he had given to the moral feelings of many, the general antagonism against the foreign power and the imposition of despotism on the Hebrew people, which made his name odious among his people. And yet there was in Judea a party of Herodians after his death who gratefully remembered the great services he had rendered to his country.

(71) MEGGILLATH TAANITH xi., which was made a half holiday.
(72) Josephus' Antiq. xvii, viii. 1; Wars I. xxxiii. The Evangelist Matthew was the only cause why Christian writers, contrary to all sources, gave to Herod a reign of thirty-seven or thirty eight years, so that he must have died in the year after the birth of Jesus of Nazareth. But there are the following objections: 1. The beginning of the Christian era fixed by the Dionysius Exiguus, in the sixth century, is now generally admitted to be inaccurate by four years (See Chronology in Harper & Bros.' Cyclopædia of Biblical Theology, etc.), so that it is supposed Jesus was born 4 B. C., which is no less an error, while it is certain that the eclipse of the moon in the year of Herod's death was March 13, 4 B. C. (Josephus' Antiq. xvii., vii. 4). 2. According to Luke, Jesus being born in the year of a Roman census, it must have occurred in the year 6 or 7 A. C., when the census described by Luke was taken (See Prideaux's Old and New Testament, etc., in Anno 5 B. C. and 8 A. C.).

CHAPTER XX.

The Fruits of Despotism.

1. HEROD'S LAST WILL AND BURIAL.

Herod left by his nine wives, besides the grandchildren of the Asmonean, Mariamne, also the following children: By Mariamne, daughter of the highpriest, Herod, Philip, and three more children; by Malthace, Archelaus and Antipas; by Cleopatra, Philip and two more children; by Pallas, Phedra and Elpis, one child each; and three of his wives were childless. Archelaus married his deceased half-brother's (Alexander's) wife, Glaphira, whose children by Alexander were Alexander II. and Tigranes. Herod's last will was that Archelaus should inherit Judea, Idumea and Samaria; Philip should receive Auronitis, Trachonitis, Paneas and Batanea; and Antipas, Galilee and Perea; the income of the cities of Jamnia, Ashdod and Phasaelis, with a sum of 500,000 drachmae, he willed to his sister Salome. He also made provision for the rest of his children, and willed most all his money, precious vessels and garments to Augustus and his wife. Herod Philip, the son of the second Mariamne, was given a legacy but no claims in the succession. Therefore, immediately after the death of Herod, Archelaus assumed the royal authority. When Salome's husband, Alexa (1), had dismissed the captives in the hippodrome at Jericho, and Herod's letter to the army had been read, arrangements were made to bury, in royal pomp, the half rotten body of the deceased king; and it was carried out with all the barbarous luxury and ostentation, as if Herod himself, with all his vainglory, had ar-

---

(1) This Alexa, called in the Talmud אלכסא or אכסא, an abbreviation of Alexander, died at Lydda, where great honors were bestowed on him by the savans of his day (*Chagiga* 18 a).

ranged the matter. He was buried at Herodium, and then followed seven days of mourning. The patriots declared the day when the captives were dismissed from the hippodrome a half holiday (*Meguillath Taanith* xi.).

2. ARCHELAUS ACCEPTED.

The Hebrew people were willing to submit to Archelaus, and expected reforms. When after the days of mourning he went to the temple, he was received with demonstrations of loyalty. A throne of gold had been placed on a platform in the temple court, which Archelaus mounted and was received with popular acclamation. He returned thanks, and informed the multitude that he could not accept the diadem before it was granted him by Augustus. He expressed his hopes that this would be done and his promise to be "better than his father." The people believed him, and demanded the release of all political prisoners, and a reduction of taxes. Archelaus promised all this and much more, in order to keep them attached to his cause.

3. THE DISSATISFIED PARTY.

The two teachers, and their forty disciples, slain by Herod and buried like brutes, had left too many friends and disciples in the city to be forgotten in so short a time. The teacher had become the highest and most sacred personage. He was the highpriest of his disciples, their living library and prophet, who was to be honored above all men; as the sage was considered higher in authority than the prophet, and the learned bastard preferable to the ignorant highpriest. The head of a school was looked upon as the highest of all mortals. But Herod had two of them and forty of their disciples slain and buried like condemned rebels; and the survivors demanded retribution. They assembled in groups and lamented their loss, till many sympathized with them. Then they demanded of Archelaus the punishment of those who were connected with that execution, and the removal of the Boethite highpriest, Joazar, whose theology was abominable to them, and whose predecessor in office, Matthias b. Theophilus, was removed on account of his complicity in that affair, which cost those teachers' lives (2). Archelaus was embarrassed. He did not like to

---

(2) Antiq. xvii., vi 4; ix. 1. Matthias, the teacher, had been burnt alive, and that very night there was an eclipse of the moon. Did not the Evangelists imitate this situation?

exercise any sovereign authority before he had obtained the Roman sanction to his father's testament; and had a sedition before him in Jerusalem. Therefore, he promised to do all they had demanded as soon as he should be confirmed in his office by Augustus. But these men did not care for promises, they demanded speedy action. They would not listen to the king's messengers, and continued their public meetings and clamors in the temple, and the number of sympathizers grew rapidly, augmented by the usual number of seditious persons. They kept up the excitement to the Passover Feast, when they found numerous sympathizers among the pilgrims. Archelaus sent soldiers to the temple inclosure to arrest the leaders, but they overpowered the troops He ordered an attack in force upon the pilgrims inside the temple inclosure, while those outside thereof were prevented by cavalry from assisting them. Three thousand of the multitude were slain, and the rest fled in dismay, carrying all over the land the tidings of the bloody deed, which was the signal for one of the worst insurrections in the history of the Hebrews.

4. All go to Rome.

The city being quiet again, Archelaus appointed his half-brother, Philip, regent, and left Jerusalem accompanied by his mother, Nicholaus, of Damascus, and other friends and advocates, to go to Rome. At Cæsarea he met Sabinus, the treasurer of Augustus, who had come to take possession of Herod's treasury. This was momentarily prevented by Varus, the Governor of Syria. Now Archelaus started for Rome. But he was followed by Salome and her children, Antipas and his mother, with his advocates, each claiming the crown from the hands of Augustus. Besides, there came afterward to Rome fifty ambassadors of the Hebrew people encouraged by Varus, and they were supported by eight thousand Hebrew residents of Rome, to remonstrate against the whole Herodian family, and to obtain the liberty of living according to their own laws (3), or to be joined to the province of Syria (4). This embassy was also followed by Philip, who had some hopes of receiving the crown. The greatest orators of the age were engaged by the contesting parties, and all sorts of intrigues were enacted. It took Augustus a long time before he could decide. The people's

---

(3) Antiq xvii, xi. 1.
(4) Wars II. vi. 2.

ambassadors, of course, were overruled in Cæsarian Rome. At last the various parties were disappointed and Herod's last will was confirmed, although it was also partly opposed by Varus and Sabinus. Achelaus was confirmed as ethnarch of Judea, Idumea and Samaria, with the exception of the three cities of Gaza, Gadara and Hippose, which being inhabited by foreigners, were taken to Syria. Galilee and Perea were given to Antipas. Philip received the four northern principalities. Salome received what Herod had bequeathed to her and a royal palace at Askalon. The money willed to Augustus was given to Herod's daughters, and he gave them in marriage to the sons of Pheroras. Before this decision was rendered the following bloody drama was enacted in Palestine:

5. A Second Cause of Rebellion.

Varus had accepted the task of keeping Jerusalem quiet. He came to the city and found its citizens peaceable. He left a Roman legion there and returned to Antioch. A few days later Sabinus, contrary to his promise given to Varus to await the decision of Augustus, seized the citadels of Jerusalem and searched for money, wherever he thought there was any to be found, to satisfy his notorious avarice. This outrage on the rights of a people roused a bitter hatred in the country against the foreign robber. The Feast of Pentecost approaching, people from all parts of the land came in large numbers, and an organization was effected. Divided in three corps, they took such positions that Sabinus and his soldiers were beleaguered. Sabinus fled to the tower of Phasael, wrote urgent letters to Varus, and then commanded an attack on the Hebrews. The latter were defeated, but immediately rallied again and drove the Romans and Herodians from their positions. Sabinus succeeded in setting fire to the temple cloisters, so that the whole building was in danger. This carried confusion and death into the ranks of the Hebrews. The Romans rushed into the temple, seized its treasury, and achieved a momentary victory. The Hebrews rallied again, a number of Herod's soldiers fraternized with them, and they pressed Sabinus into the royal palace, where they besieged him. They demanded that he and his men should leave the city, or else all of them should be burnt in the palace. Expecting the arrival of Varus, he did not capitulate, and the siege was vigorously pressed until the approach of Varus, several weeks after, terrified the multitude, which left the city and afforded the citizens of Jerusalem the opportunity of denying every connection with the rebels.

6. Detached Rebellions.

The people all over the land were exasperated by the bloody work done in Jerusalem during Passover and Pentecost, and the whole land was ripe for rebellion. It broke out simultaneously in all parts of the country, without fixed design or unity of action. In Idumea, two thousand of Herod's veterans, most likely those who had fraternized with the people in Jerusalem, raised the standard of rebellion, forced Achiabus, Herod's cousin, with his corps to retreat into the fastnesses of the mountains, and succeeded in organizing a force of ten thousand men with relations of Herod among their commanders. The real object of this party is unknown. Meanwhile a slave of Herod, Simon, excited an insurrection in Perea, collected a considerable force of fighting men and crossed the Jordan. He burnt the royal palace at Jericho and other royal edifices, after he had plundered them, and had been proclaimed king by his followers. In the north two disconnected parties rose in rebellion and did terrible execution. One was the gigantic shepherd, Athronges, with his four brothers, who was proclaimed king. He came down from the Upper Jordan, defeated the Romans, and drove them as far as Sebaste. Meanwhile the Galilean democrats raised their standard under Juda, of Gamala, the son of the so-called robber, Ezekias, whom Herod had slain. He took Sepphoris with the arms and treasures stored there, and earnestly strove to restore the republic. Besides these, smaller parties of guerrillas rose and ransacked the country. All these parties fought the Romans and Herodians, although they also afflicted many non-combatant citizens, and plunged the whole country into misery, without hope of success, on account of the selfishness of the various leaders. Had Juda, of Gamala, been the man to unite the rebellious factions, a new epoch might have opened. The reign of absolutism had demoralized the Hebrews.

7. The Campaign of Varus.

The Roman legion and the royal troops were helpless amid those commotions. Varus, on receiving the letter of Sabinus, immediately concentrated his two legions and the auxiliary troops at Ptolemais, and marched with three columns into Palestine. The various parties were successively overthrown or checked, Sepphoris was burnt and its inhabitants sold into slavery, Emmaus and other cities suffered a similar fate, and Varus arrived at Jerusalem in time to save Sabinus with all his stolen treasures. Besides all the cities burnt and the people sold as slaves, two thousand Hebrews were crucified, and the relatives of Herod engaged in the rebellion were punished in Rome. Still the insurrection was not entirely overcome. Athronges held out a long time after that event. Now Varus gave his permission to the popular party to send an embassy to Rome, as mentioned above. But a nation's woes and a dynasty's crimes did not weigh much in Cæsarian Rome, where selfishness and sensuality over-balanced every ancient virtue. The brief and bloody campaign (*Polemus*) of Varus not only cost thousands of lives, and millions of property destroyed and stolen by Romans and marauding Arabs, but also a portion of the archives in the temple were destroyed with the burning cloisters (5). The nation bled from a thousand wounds. Now the sons of Herod could return to take possession of the down-trodden country.

8. Dissolution of the Sanhedrin.

The campaign of Varus, which was twenty-six years after Egypt had been a Roman province, and the last vestige of the Greco-Macedonian supremacy had disappeared (6), closed also the Hillel Sanhedrin, and opened in the history of Rabbinism the eighty years of the two schools of Beth Hillel and Beth Shammai (רבנן של שמונים שנה). No Sanhedrin is mentioned any more in the sources, except under Agrippa I. and during the war before the fall of Jerusalem. The Shamaites began their opposition to Hillel and his school by re-enacting the laws of Jose b. Joezer, declaring all foreign countries and imported vessels unclean, as a barrier between Hebrews and Gentiles, and an inducement to immigration from foreign countries. Hillel had yielded to Shammai and his school in many points relating to Levitical cleanness (7), and was obliged also to yield to that extreme measure, for the Shamaites were in the majority, and so fanaticized that the sword was drawn, and Shammai proposed measures still more extreme. But Hillel left his seat, and, like an humble disciple, sat down at

---

(5) Joseph. Contra Apion i. 7. See Gractz Vol. III. Note 21.
(6) *Abodah Sarah* 8 *b* and paral. passages.
(7) *Sabbath* 14 *b* שמאי והלל גזרו טומאה על הידים

the feet of Shammai, which assuaged the excited champions, and the Sanhedrin quietly dissolved itself into two schools. "This day," says the chronographer, "was as unfortunate to Israel as was the one when the golden calf was made" (8). Shammai died three years and a half after this event (9), hence 2 A. C. Then the *Bath-kol* announced that the laws should be practiced according to the Hillel decisions; but the Shamaites did not yield (10). It is not ascertained how long after that Hillel died. The connection of these violent disputes with the rebellions after the death of Herod is certain. The Shamaites were partisans of Juda of Gamala, and ready to initiate a revolutionary movement as in the time of Mattathia and his sons; while the Hillel men were the advocates of peace and moderation.

9. THE SONS OF HEROD.

In the same year (2 B. C.) the sons of Herod returned from Rome. Archelaus took up his residence in Jerusalem. Herod Antipas rebuilt Sepphoris and Bethramphta, calling the latter Julius, and making the former his residence, till after the death of Augustus, when he built the city of Tiberias on lake Genesareth. There and in the neighboring Emmaus were the hot springs. Tiberias being built upon a spot of many sepulchres, the Hebrews refused to dwell there, so that Antipas was under the necessity of populating it with foreigners, and forcing Hebrews to take up their residence in that unclean city (11). Philip took up his residence at Paneas, at the fountains of the Jordan, where he built the city of Cæsarea (Philippi). He also made a city of Bethesda, at the head of lake Genesareth, and called it Julia. Among these princes Philip proved to be the best and Archelaus the worst.

10. THE GOVERNMENT OF ARCHELAUS.

Archelaus, on his return to Jerusalem, divorced his wife Mariamne and married Glaphyra, his brother's widow, who had children by her first husband. This, although no direct

---

(8) *Sabbath* 17 a. TOSEPHTA *Ibid.* I. refers to a later date as the time when those extreme measures were adopted, as a momentary compromise of the two schools.

(9) שלש שנים ומחצה נחלקיי שמאי והלל is the correct version, *Erubin* 13 b.
(10) *Bezah* 20 a.
(11) Antiq. xviii., ii. 3.

violation of law, was detestable to the Hebrews (12). He removed from office the highpriest, Joazar, and appointed in his stead his brother, Eleazar Boethus, who was also deposed in a short time and replaced by Jesus, son of Sie. It appears, however, that he also was removed, and Joazar was reappointed (13), so that the respect for the temple and its ancient culte was weakened, and decreased steadily. The highpriests were Sadducees and the people Pharisean. Like the Sadducean magistrates, they were obliged to conform to Pharisean customs and laws (14) and to play the hypocrite. Archelaus made an end of the rebellion. He overpowered Athronges, captured him, and his brother surrendered. He also had a plantation of palms, for which he stole the water from the village of Neara, and built a town on his plantation which he called Archelaus. But this is all that is known of him, except that he was a barbarous and licentious despot, hated by many and loved by none.

11. A Spurious Alexander.

A young Hebrew, brought up in the house of a Roman freedman at Sidon, resembled Mariamne's son, Alexander. On the strength of this resemblance he claimed to be that very man, and maintained that he was saved when his father had condemned him to die with his brother. He now claimed the crown of Judea. Many believed his story and gave him support, especially the Hebrews of Crete and Melos, who enabled him to make his appearance in Rome, where also the Roman Jews gave him their support and received him with royal honors. Anybody but Archelaus was acceptable to the Hebrews in and outside of Palestine. Augustus, however, did not believe the story. Investigation, and finally self-confession, exposed the spurious Alexander, who was sent to an imperial ship "to row among the mariners," while those who had designed the plot were put to death, and the deluded people escaped with a mere disappointment.

12. Archelaus Banished to Vienna.

Nothing, however, could save Archelaus, who continued his despotic misrule and barbarity in Jerusalem. His own

---

(12) Antiq. xvii., xiii. 1. It appears that Glaphyra died shortly after this marriage, in consequence of a dream, in which her first husband severely rebuked her faithlessness; although the dream may have been a popular invention.
(13) Antiq. xviii., i. 1.
(14) Antiq. xviii., i. 4.

kinsmen, together with an embassy of prominent men from Judea and Samaria, gave utterance to the people's grievances before Augustus, which must have been very aggravating and conclusive; for Augustus ordered Archelaus, by his Roman resident, to appear before him immediately. Archelaus had a dream, as despots do, and Simon the Essene, interpreted it, as Essenes, informed of current events, knew how to interpret dreams (15); and the dream of wicked Archelaus proved a prophecy. The message of Augustus was delivered to him while feasting with his friends, and he was obliged to leave the country without adequate preparations. Arrived in Rome, Augustus heard his case and found him guilty. He was banished to Vienna in France, his treasures were confiscated by Augustus, and the three provinces of Judea, Samaria and Idumea were added to the Roman province of Syria, nine years after Herod's death (6 A. C.). Herod's murderous policy bore its legitimate fruit. Sixty-nine years after the capture of Jerusalem by Pompey, the Hebrew people were sufficiently demoralized by military despotism, that its aristocracy surrendered the independence of a liberty-loving people to Rome without offering any resistance. It was not the people, it was its aristocracy, that betrayed it, which surrendered to Rome.

---

(15) It is reported in the Talmud (*Berachoth* 55 *b*) by Rabbi Banah, most likely Banus, the teacher of Josephus (Life 3), that there were in Jerusalem twenty-four interpreters of dreams. He once went to all of them, told them the same dream, and received twenty-four different interpretations, each of which was fulfilled in his after life; simply, we add, because he interpreted the interpretation.

VI. Period---The Rule of the Procurators.

During the reign of the five emperors, Augustus, Tiberius, Caligula, Claudius and Nero (7 to 68 A. C.), thirteen Roman Procurators, under the President of Syria, governed Judea and its annexed provinces, excepting only the short period under Claudius, when Agrippa I. was king. All Roman provinces, organized by Augustus, were either senatorial or imperial, the former of which were governed by the senate and the latter by the emperor, *i. e.*, the latter were under direct military rule. So was Syria and so was Judea, where the legions engaged in making war on Parthia, or watching it, were stationed. A military government is always despotic. The rights of man are of secondary consideration. The will or whim of the commander is law. Therefore, Syria, hence also Judea, was one of the most oppressed provinces of the Roman Empire. Besides, the wealth of Syria, and especially of Judea, was another cause of continual oppression, bloodshed and irritation of the masses to riots, in order to have a pretense for slaying the rich and confiscating their property, or despoiling public institutions. The Hebrews, with their democratic laws and institutions, and their inflexible attachment to law and liberty, were not easily bent under the lawless foreign yoke. Therefore insurrections, on a small or large scale, were perpetual during this period, and led at last to a general war of independence. There were in the provinces three superior officers: First, the Proconsul, or President, whose power, except in senatorial provinces, was absolute, and who was responsible to the emperor only; second, the Praetor, who was the actual civil governor and chief justice of the province under the Proconsul; and third, the Procurator, who governed a part of the province under a Proconsul. The governors of Judea under the Proconsul of Syria had different titles at different times, but were always the commanders of the troops, the financial agents of the emperor and the chief judges of the country. The people had no share whatever in its own government. How this irritated and demoralized the Hebrews, will be narrated in the following chapters:

CHAPTER XXI.

The Messianic Commotion.

1. THE CENSUS.

Rome began its dominion in Judea with the confiscation of the property and treasures of Archelaus, and taking a census of all people and property to be taxed. Coponius was appointed Procurator and P. Sulpicius Quirinus (Cyrenius), was sent to take the census (1). It took the whole influence of the highpriest, Joazar Boethus, to persuade the majority of the people to submit quietly to this innovation, which changed independent Palestine into a Roman province. A minority, however, viewed it in its proper light, as an introduction of slavery. Juda of Galilee (2), supported by a Pharisean teacher, whose name was Zadok, stood at the head of this party and counseled resistance to that aggression. They met with no success in regard to the census, which was taken anyhow, but they succeeded in establishing the party of Zealots (קנאים), which

---

(1) According to Luke this was the time when Jesus of Nazareth was born (Luke ii.), while according to First Gospel of the Infancy, first chapter, he was born 309 of the s. E., ten years before this. But Luke's date is also uncertain, because: *a.* The narrative is connected with the appearance of an angel to some shepherds, and reports other miracles, which, if true, Matthew or other evangelists must have narrated. *b.* It makes Jesus a son of David, which he denied being (Mark xii. 35 to 37). *c.* The whole story of Jesus being born in Bethlehem and not in Nazareth is spurious, in order to fulfill a Scriptural passage, misunderstood alike by Jews and Gentiles (Micah v. 1. See *Targum Jonathan*). It is not known when or where Jesus was born; although Matthew, referring to Herod, may have meant Archelaus, as all successors of Herod were also called Herod.

(2) Judah the Galilean, Judah the Gaulanite, and Judah of Gamala, are identical. It appears that he was born in Gamala, west of lake Genesareth and lived in Galilee.

never submitted, but nourished and promulgated implacable hatred of Rome, its agents and partisans. Included in these hated classes were all those who held office under the Romans, as well as the publicans and their collectors, foreign harlots and abused men, called "sinners," together with all other camp-followers of the Romans.

2. The Sects.

Political parties, in consequence of the reign of absolutism, degenerated into sects and schools. The Sadducees, under the tuition of the Bœthites, gradually denied immortality, future reward or punishment and Providence. They became Stoics, who adhered to the Laws of Moses and some of the ancient traditions and practices. The Essenes had become sanctimonious mystics, who maintained they knew all about the angels and secret arts, to heal the sick, to expound dreams, and to prophesy. They cultivated the soil, raised medicinal plants, wore the Levitical garments, practiced the entire Levitical laws in their private lives, baptized themselves every morning by immersion, and washed their hands before every meal as the priest did on entering the sanctuary, looked upon their tables as altars, their meals as sacrifices, and each imagined himself to be prince, priest and prophet. They sent gifts to the temple, but made no sacrifices, and kept aloof from all other Israelites whose food and persons they considered unclean. They had introduced in their order secrets of three grades, subjected new-comers to hard probations and tutelage, and were extreme Pharisees with severe practices and sanctimonious mysteries. They claimed to be in possession of ancient traditions reaching up to Moses, which was certainly not the case, as they originated in the Maccabean revolution, and remained unnoticed to the time of Jonathan. They believed in the existence of angels, the immortality of the soul, and the exclusive control of Providence over all human actions. They had nothing in common with any class of Gentile philosophers, grew out of the Hebrew mind entirely, and were the extreme asceticists given to a contemplative life and mystic and allegoric expounding of Scriptures. With them the *Kabbala* originates, but the precise nature of their teachings is unknown. Besides the Sadducees and Essenes, there were the Herodians, who, perhaps, were merely a political party that wanted a Herodian at the head of the Hebrew monarchy. But all these sects were mere abnormities, whose influence upon the Hebrew people in Palestine and outside thereof was insignificant. The Hebrew people were Pharisean (3).

3. THE TWO PHARISEAN PARTIES.

The Sanhedrin being dissolved the Pharisean scribes were divided into the two schools of BETH HILLEL and BETH SHAMMAI. There was no authority left to decide their controversies or to ordain teachers, and each school did it on its own account, so partisans, unprepared for this dignity, received the ordination (4). Although, in the main, they did not impose upon the people, or even upon themselves, the laws on which they differed (5); nor did they discuss laws of vital importance to the public. They were chiefly engaged in scholastic discussions to find Scriptural grounds for existing customs. Still they promulgated uncertainty in private life, especially in religious observances and formulas, marriage laws, and the all-important question of Levitical cleanness (6). With the census under Quirinus, the two schools, already divided in political opinions, assumed the character of two political parties. The Hillel Pharisees were the men of peace, humanity and patience. Like their master, they looked upon humanity as the main object of the law, and like the older Pharisees, they did not care too much about the political affairs of the country. The profane business of governing the State and collecting the taxes was with them a question of minor importance. The maintenance of the peace, the mission of Israel to preserve and promulgate the Kingdom of Heaven, the study of the Law and the practice of humane deeds, were paramount with them. Therefore, with the Sadducees and Essenes they maintained the peace when the census was taken. The Shammai men, however, who took the whole Law and traditions with all their remote logical sequences as the Israelite's divine guide, the preservation and promulgation thereof as his paramount duty, looked upon every submission to foreign rulers, and every payment of tribute or

---

(3) Josephus' Antiq. xiii., v. 9; xviii., i. 2. Wars II. viii. 2. J. J. Bellermann's Essaer and Therapeuten. Dr. Zachary Frankel's MONATSSCHRIFT 1846, 1855; Dr. Ab. Geiger's URSCHRIFT p. 104, a'so his Pharis. and Sadd. J. Wellhausen's Pharisaeer and Sadducaeer.

(4) *Sanhedrin* 88 *b*, historical report of R. Jose משם כתבו ישלחו refers to the abolition of the ordination by the *Nassi* and his associates.

(5) MISHNAH *Yibamoth* i. 4.
(6) *Darkei Ham-mishnah* p. 55.

taxes to a foreign prince, as a flagrant violation of the Law, which must be resisted with all means at the nation's command, at all hazards and sacrifices. Therefore, they identified themselves with the democrats led by Juda of Galilee, and also resisted the taking of the census, as the introduction of a foreign government and the abolition of the Kingdom of Heaven. Failing in this attempt, they still remained a political party of distinct and stern principles, whose main object was the restoration of the Kingdom of Heaven, also in its political principles; God to be the only Ruler and Lord of Israel, and His Law the sovereign guide of all. The loss of property or life could be of no consideration in the combat for the highest and holiest treasure of Israel; as the Kingdom of God is in heaven and eternity as well as in time and on earth, and death is a mere transition from time to eternity. This doctrine made of them champions of liberty, death-defying heroes, glaring fanatics and uncompromising patriots, whose hatred against foreign customs, laws, languages and persons grew violently with the progress of the Roman oppression and the incursions of Syrians. Therefore they were called Zealots (קנאים), although, like the Hillel men, they were Pharisees.

4. THE TEMPLE AND ITS OFFICERS.

The temple was entirely in the power of the Roman procurator. He held Fort Antonio, which commanded the temple and contained the sacerdotal vestments of the highpriest as a sort of hostage. If the highpriest was to preside over the services, his official vestments had first to be obtained of the commander of Fort Antonio. Besides, the procurator appointed and removed the highpriest, hence all the offices in the temple were under his control and dependent on his will, and could have been Roman tools only. Traditions concerning the highpriests and chiefpriests of this period are very severe. With the exception of the house of Fabi, they were denounced as wicked men (7); although there certainly were some good and faithful men among them and their subordinates. In consequence of their ignorance, they surrounded themselves with scribes learned in the laws and customs, and were watched by the "Commoners" (אנשי מעמד), who were Pharisees. Therefore, the authors of the New Testament story group together in the temple priests, scribes and Pharisees. These

---

(7) SIPHRI, *Phineas;* YERUSHALMI, *Yoma* i. 1; *Pesachim* 57 a from TOSEPHTA.

Pharisean Commoners, however, were replaced every week by other colleagues. The sanctuary and the sacrificial culte gradually lost their influence so that a short time after Hillel the temple was frequently without any visitors (8). In the same ratio, however, the authority of the scribes grew among the people; the teacher took the place of the priest (9) and the study of the Law replaced the sacrifices (10). Still, during the high feasts, the pilgrims crowded the temple, the city and suburbs, and the priests, as also did Josephus Flavius, continued to consider themselves, the temple, and the sacrificial culte the soul of Israel; and their power and influence were great to the very last, especially among the pilgrims.

5. Procurators Under Augustus.

Augustus (from 7 to 14 A. C.) sent three Procurators to Judea—Coponius (7 A. C.), M. Ambivius (10 A. C.) and Annus Rufus (14 A. C.). No acts of particular violence by these Procurators have been recorded. The country was quiet. This was also the case in the other provinces of Palestine under the government of Antipas and Philip, who spent their time and treasures in building cities, as we have mentioned before. Under the administration of Coponius some sectarian Samaritans played a malicious trick on the Hebrews. It was customary that on Passover the priests opened the gates of the temple shortly after midnight. Some of those Samaritans came early to the temple and threw human bones about the cloisters. This did not disturb the divine service, as the Samaritans, perhaps, believed it would; still it gave rise to the unjust mandate on the part of the priests to exclude all Samaritans from the temple. Under the administration of Ambivius, Salome, the sister of Herod, died (12 A. C.). She willed her possessions to Julia, the wife of Augustus, and to her countrymen she left the memorial of her infamy.

6. Procurators Under Tiberius.

In August, 14 A. C., the emperor Augustus died, and on the nineteenth day of that month his stepson, Tiberius

---

(8) YERUSHALMI, *Hagigah* ii. 3 and TOSEPHTA *ibid.*

(9) YERUSHALMI, *Berachoth* end תלמידי חכמים מרבים שלום בעולם; *Peah, Mishnah* i; *Aboth* iv. 12 and iii. 2 to 9; *Baba Meziah* ii. 11.

(10) TOSEPHTA, *Demai* ii., ובזמן שאין (הכהנים) עושין רצוני של מקום וג'; MECHILTA, *Bachodesh* ראוין היו כל ישראל לאכל בקדשים וג'

Nero, the son of Julia, succeeded him as Roman Emperor. Like Julius Cæsar, the dead Augustus also was deified, priests were appointed to worship him, and his statue was erected everywhere among the other idols (11). However vile, profligate and despotic Tiberius became during the second period of his reign, he started out with noble intentions. "In the provinces no new burdens were imposed, and the old duties were collected without cruelty or extortion. Corporal punishment was never inflicted, and confiscation of men's effects was a thing unknown" (12). Therefore, the first Procurator he sent to Judea, Valerius Gratus, was a man of probity, who left no record of maladministration, nor was there any sedition among the people during the eleven years of his official term, although he appointed and deposed no less than five highpriests. But after a few years of a tranquil reign, Tiberius threw off the mask. By acts of cruelty he harrassed the people of Rome as well as of the provinces, and by his authority encouraged the tyranny of his subordinates. A wicked man, Aelius Sejanus, ingratiated himself in the emperor's favor and confidence, and rose to supreme power as his prime minister. Sejan put in power his own coadjutors and most obedient tools, both in Rome and the provinces. One of the latter was Pontius Pilate, supposed to have been a native of Vienna in France, whom he sent to Judea to replace Gratus as Procurator of that country (25 A. C.). With this Sejan-like representative of the foreign ruler the misfortunes of the Hebrews in Judea increased rapidly.

7. Character of Pontius Pilate.

A cotemporary of Pontius Pilate was the Hebrew philosopher, Philo, of Alexandria. He left the following description of that Procurator (13): "One day representations were made to him (Pilate); but as that man was of an impetuous and stubborn disposition, he would not listen. He was then told, with suggestive stress, to desist from irritating to sedition and war, abstain from making peace impossible. It is the will of Tiberius that our laws be respected. If thou art in possession of a new edict or epistle, let us know it, and we will instantly send a deputation to

---

(11) Tacitus Annals I, liv., lxxiii. and lxxiv.
(12) Ibid. iv., vi.
(13) Philo, De virtut. et legat. Cai.

Rome. These words provoked the Procurator so much the more, since he apprehended that an embassy to Rome must expose all his crimes, the venality of his sentences, his rapacity, the ruin of whole families, all the infamies whose author he was, the execution of many persons without process of law, the excess of cruelties of all descriptions." No law was in his way, no principle of honor or integrity incumbered him, treaties and secured rights were no limitations to him; he did anything to satisfy his greed and rapacity, to abolish or override the laws and customs of the land, and to irritate seditions for the sake of pretenses for carnage and confiscation, and for demoralizing and bending the popular will to servile submission.

8. Abolition of the Law.

Pontius Pilate began his administration in Judea with an attempt "to abolish the Jewish law," exactly as Tiberius, or his minister, Sejan, did in Rome. The religion and laws of the Hebrews had rapidly spread over the Roman Empire by the Greco-Hebrew literature and by the numerous Hebrew colonies all over the empire, to whom the edicts of Julius Cæsar had secured the Roman citizenship and the free exercise of their religion. The influence of Judaism upon declining Heathenism became evident everywhere and especially in Rome, by the large numbers of proselytes who publicly or privately confessed Judaism, and the numerous "devout Gentiles" all over the empire. The more one class of Gentiles inclined to Judaism, the more, on the other hand, the fanaticism and jealousy of the Pagans were aroused against the Hebrews and their laws. This spirit broke forth in various cities, as we have seen before, and became afterward the source of calamity to the Hebrews, especially in Alexandria, and other centers of ancient Paganism Hitherto the Roman emperors and the Jewish kings (Hyrcan and Herod) had protected the foreign Hebrews. But Tiberius turned against them, and none was left to protect them. Therefore, Pilate initiated his administration in Judea with the attempt to abolish the Jewish laws (14). He removed the army from Cæsarea to Jerusalem, and it entered the city in the night time, and displayed all its ensigns with the effigies of the deified Cæsars,

---

(14) Josephus' Antiq. xviii., iii.

the crucified man (15) and the various symbols of idolatry. The citizens of Jerusalem were amazed and exasperated at the audacious affront and violation of law and treaties. In large numbers they went to Cæsarea to remonstrate with Pilate, but he would not listen to them. On the sixth day of their remonstrance, when they appeared again before Pilate, they were surrounded by soldiers, and immediate death was threatened to the petitioning multitude if they would not leave instantly. "But they threw themselves upon the ground, and laid their necks bare, and said they would accept death very willingly, rather than see the wisdom of their laws transgressed." Pilate yielded. He commanded the images to be carried back from Jerusalem to Cæsarea. The garrison, it appears, remained in Jerusalem, and the laws of the land remained suspended as long as Pilate was Procurator. This is the period called in the traditions, "Forty years before the destruction of the temple," when the administration of the penal law was taken entirely out of the nation's hands and held by the Procurator and his officers; when the two lesser Sanhedrin also left the temple mount. No Sanhedrin existed any longer, although Simon, Hillel's son, may have been the recognized head of the Hillel school, and considered by that party the *Nassi* and expositor of the traditions. The destruction of the temple was then prophesied by those who understood the political situation, as did Rabbi Jochanan b. Saccai, and knew that in the struggle thus initiated, either Judaism or Heathenism would have to succumb at last; and Rome was all-mighty (16).

9. A Massacre of Non-Combatants.

The hatred of Pilate and the people was mutual and violent. He missed no opportunity for massacre and confiscation, and drove people to seditions because each offered him a fine harvest. Private estates being insufficient to gratify his rapacity, he seized the temple treasures under the pretext of improving the water-works of Jerusalem;

---

(15) See our "Martyrdom of Jesus of Nazareth," p. 101. "Your victorious trophies not only represent a simple cross, but a cross with a man upon it" (Reeves' Apologies Vol. I. p. 139), a Christian teacher said afterward to the Romans. Rebels were crucified, therefore, the cross and the man on it was one of the Roman trophies, which was in aftertimes adopted as a Christian trophy. This must have been especially repugnant to the Hebrews, because it reminded them of the fate of the last Asmonean king, Antigonus, crucified by Marc Antony.

(16) *Yoma* 39 *b*.

although that money did not belong to the city, and he, in his official capacity, had no right to interfere with either. The people loudly remonstrated against the sacrilege and abuse of authority. When he came to Jerusalem, many appeared before his judgment seat, and gave free utterance to their grievances. Pilate responded by another crime. He commanded his soldiers and spies to wear the national cloaks, to hide under them heavy clubs, and use them freely at a given signal. When next day the multitude again approached the judgment seat, the signal was given, and the clubs were freely used upon the unarmed and unprepared multitude. A large number of them were trampled to death under the feet of the amazed and terrified multitude, and another number of them died in consequence of the blows received (17.)

10. SLAUGHTER OF SAMARITANS AND GALILEANS.

The outrages perpetrated by Pilate gave rise to many a prophet and savior besides John the Baptist and Jesus of Nazareth. One of them, a Samaritan, whose name is not recorded, (18), roused the people, "not in order to revolt against the Romans, but to escape the violence of Pilate," as his advocates maintained. He called the patriots to Mount Gerizzim, and promised them as a proof of his divine mission, to show them the sacred vessels and the ark made by Moses, which, according to the Samaritan tradition, were buried on Mount Gerizzim (19). Many of them, both Samaritans and Galileans, came thither armed, and met at the village of Tirathaba, with the intention of ascending Gerizzim in a grand procession. Pilate sent to the spot his soldiers, who took possession of the strategic points, attacked the pilgrims in the village while they made sacrifices, slew a number of them and put the others to flight. Many of them were captured, and the principal men were executed by order of Pilate. This, however, was one of the last of Pilate's crimes. An embassy of Samaritans (20)

---

(17) Wars ii., ix. 4. Antiq. xviii., iii. 2.
(18) Compare Josephus' Antiq. xviii., iv. 1 to Luke xiii. 1.
(19) According to II. Maccabees ii 4 to 7 the Prophet Jeremiah hid the ark in the cave upon Mount Nebo. Other opinions on this subject in the Talmud Yoma 53 b.
(20) Josephus mentions in this connection a Samaritan senate, a body of which neither he nor any Samaritan source has an account. Then he drops the embassy and speaks only of the "accusation of the Jews" against Pilate. It appears, therefore, that the embassy came from Sebaste, which was inhabited by Pagans, who supported the Hebrews in their accusation against Pilate.

supported the Hebrews before Vitellius, the president of Syria, and Pilate was ordered to Rome to answer before the emperor for his outrages (21). But it was not his very last crime, as we shall narrate below, after we shall have reviewed the fate of the Roman Hebrews under Tiberius.

11. Expulsion of the Hebrews from Rome.

The number of Hebrews in Rome had been largely augmented by captives of war sent there, who were ransomed by their brethren, and by immigration from the various provinces; so that there were actually two classes of them, citizens and freedmen. They made use of the privileges granted them by Julius Caesar, not only in adhering to their religion and laws, but also in making proselytes from among all classes of Romans; so that Horace speaks of "proselytizing Jews," and of their Sabbath which his friend, Fuscus, would not violate because he was "one of the many" who observed it. Ovid also, in his ART OF LOVE, speaks of the Jewish Sabbath as being largely observed by Roman women; and Seneca found it necessary to censure the observance of the Sabbath as a useless institution, although he felt bound to admit of the Hebrews, "the conquered have given laws to the conquerors." It was no rare case with Roman women of high rank to send gifts to the temple at Jerusalem. It will not appear strange that with the great number of Hebrews coming to Rome there were also hagglers, chaffers, beggars, soothsayers, interpreters of dreams, men and women who worked miracles, and other mercenary impostors. One of them, says Josephus (22), who had been driven out of his country by charges for transgressing the Law, assumed in Rome the airs of a great teacher of the Law, and, in company with three other rogues, persuaded Fulvia, a Roman proselyte, to send purple and gold to the temple at Jerusalem; but the impostors kept those gifts. The husband complained to

---

(21) Tiberius died March 16, 37 A. C., before Pilate reached Rome, hence the latter left Palestine in the fall of 36 A. C. He was ordered to Rome by Vitellius after the massacre at Tirathaba, and partly in consequence thereof. According to Luke xiii. 1, Jesus heard of that massacre, which must have taken place in the autumn of 35 or early in the spring of 36 A. C.; consequently the death of Jesus must have occurred in the spring of 36 A. C., when he, according to Luke, was about thirty years old (Luke iii. 23), for there can be no doubt that he was put to death shortly after his disciples had proclaimed him the Messiah.

(22) Josephus' Antiq. xviii., iii. 5.

Tiberius, and this, says Josephus, was the cause of the Hebrews' expulsion from Rome. But this narration does not agree with those of Suetonius and Tacitus (23). With them the cause was simply the rapid spread of Judaism by Palestinian and Egyptian Hebrews, which caused the senate to enact a decree against them. Four thousand of the young Hebrews and proselytes were sent to the pestilential Island of Sardinia, and the remaining worshipers of Jehovah were ordered, at a certain day, to depart out of Italy, unless before that time they renounced their religion, and burnt the vestment and vessels used in their sacred rites. Slavery was threatened to all who violated the mandate. So the decrees of Julius Cæsar were set at naught in the capital, and the Hebrews all over Italy, together with all their proselytes, were outlawed. This fact must be taken in connection with the malicious attempts of Pontius Pilate in Judea to abolish the Law and to crush the people, in order to comprehend the popular perturbation caused by John the Baptist and Jesus of Nazareth.

12. Causes of Rigid Asceticism.

The Kingdom of Heaven being thus assailed and endangered from without and within, its sanctuary being the citadel of the invader and its priesthood the tool of foreign rulers, its laws defied by soldiers and publicans, and its faithful children reviled and oppressed both abroad and at home; the self-conscious spirit of the Hebrews broke forth in many violent eruptions. The first question naturally was, Why does God bring all this misery on His chosen people? On account of its sins, was the first reply of rigid teachers who held the doctrine, "No death without sin, no pain without iniquity." The restoration of the Kingdom of Heaven, therefore, depends on repentance and the extinction of sin; so that the cause of the present afflictions be removed, the grace of God regained, and His kingdom be restored. The religious enterprise of rousing people to repentance of misdeeds and atonement of sins was of a patriotic origin. The Levitical priesthood and the sacrifices being no longer considered efficient, other means were adopted; and those other means were practices of stern righteousness and asceticism, rigidness in devotions and mortifications, to which the Hebrews always inclined in times of public calamities.

---

(23) Suet. in Tiber xxxvi. and Tacitus in Annals II. lxxxv.

13. JOHN THE BAPTIST.

One of those who preached this doctrine was John the Baptist (24). He was of priestly extraction, and had his home at Bethabra, beyond Jordan. There in a retired spot he taught his dire asceticism as the means of restoring the Kingdom of Heaven. He prayed and fasted much, wore coarse garments, and taught his disciples to do the same. Bathing in cold water was considered one of the mortifications by which sin is overcome (טבילת בעלי יובה). Bathing in the Jordan had the particular advantage of having been recommended to the leprous Naaman by the prophet Elishah, and the man was healed of his disease (II. Kings v.). Besides, all pious men of that age, Essenes and *Haberim* (25), all who adhered to the laws of Levitical cleanness, frequently bathed their bodies in water. Some did so every morning, and were called *Toblei Shacharith*. Therefore, one of John's ascetic practices was baptism, bathing in the Jordan. Like many other men of the same secluded and ascetic life, John became known and renowned as a prophet, which signified with them an austere man who renounced the charms of life and spent his time in practices of devotion and mortification—a saint. With the hostile measures against the Kingdom of Heaven in Rome and Jerusalem, the resistance of the Hebrews and the number of John's disciples increased. Galilee, under the government of Herod Antipas, enjoying a certain degree of independence and liberty under the Law, the meetings of those patriots, supported also by Roman proselytes (26), were held there. The bulk of the Hebrews, however, and especially the Hillelites, were no ascetics and no visionaries. They did not admit that they were sinners worse than their fathers, or that by any fault of theirs Tiberius, Sejan and Pilate were hostile to the Kingdom of Heaven as they were to the liberties of the Roman people; and looked upon John with his followers, their prophecies and their austerity, as the outgrowth of a morbid imagination. This irritated John to harsh words, and he called his opponents a genera-

---

(24) Josephus' Antiq. xviii., v. 2. JOSEPHON, chapter 63, and SEDER HAD-DOROTH, Art. R. Gamliel *Haz-zaken*, copied their John story partly from the Gospels

(25) ASSOCIATES, who ate their common food in the same state of cleanness as that in which the sacrificial meat was eaten.

(26) Roman proselytes to Judaism (גרים רומיים) are frequently noticed in the Talmud; for instance, YERUSHALMI *Pesachim*, end of Section 8 and TOSEPHTA *ibid.* Section 7.

tion of vipers (27). Mutual denunciations only increased the influence and popularity of the ascetic teacher, and the religious revivals at the Jordan assumed the aspect of a threatened rebellion. This alarmed Herod Antipas, who, for his own sake, had good cause to dread seditious demonstrations in his territory. In order to prevent this, John was captured and sent to Machaerus, which now belonged to the King of Arabia, the father-in-law of Antipas, and there, outside of the Hebrew territory and beyond the reach of his friends, the innocent fanatic was put to death. The people condemned the bloody deed, but had no power to prevent it. However, the commotion thus started was not decapitated with John at Machaerus The sect that believed in John's teachings remained (Acts xviii. 25, and xix. 2 to 4), and Jesus of Nazareth continued in his spirit.

14. Misalliance, War and Defeat.

One of the grand-daughters of Herod I. and the Asmonean Mariamne, Herodias, was married to her uncle, Herod Philip, who was the son of Herod I. and the Boethite Mariamne. They lived in Rome in retirement, which Herodias disliked. She was ambitious, was desirous of wearing the diadem, but her husband made no attempt to obtain one. It happened that her other uncle, Herod Antipas, came to Rome and fell in love with her. She consented to leave her husband and marry Antipas. In consequence of this secret understanding, she sent her husband a divorce, contrary to Jewish law, although according to Roman law, without his consent. Meanwhile, Antipas had returned to Galilee, and there his wife, who was the daughter of Aretas, King of Arabia, happened to receive information of her husband's intended faithlessness. She begged his permission to go to Machaerus, which he granted. She went to Machaerus and from there to her father, and informed him of the faithlessness of Antipas. Antipas married his brother's wife, and Aretas made war upon him to avenge the honor of his daughter (28). The armies of Antipas and Aretas met in battle, and Antipas, by the treachery of some of his men, was disastrously defeated. People said

---

(27) Matthew iii. 7; Luke iii. 7.
(28) The Elijah character of John which is given him in the Gospels is unhistorical, because neither Josephus nor any other ancient source had any knowledge thereof, and the former fully reports in the account of his career the cause of his death. The story of John sending from his prison messengers to Jesus is no less spurious

the defeat was God's punishment to Antipas for the innocent blood of John the Baptist. Antipas, however, wrote to the emperor that Aretas had made war upon him, and the emperor commanded Vitellius to invade Arabia and bring to Rome Aretas or his head.

15. First Teachings of Jesus.

John the Baptist had sent forth a number of active disciples, who preached his doctrine of repentance, asceticism and baptism, to restore the Kingdom of Heaven. Prominent among these disciples was one Jesus of Nazareth, in whose mind the religious patriotic idea had taken deep root. Neither the place nor the year or day of his birth were known to his biographers (29), except that in rabbinical sources he is always called (נוצרי) *Notzri*, "one born at Nazareth," a town in Galilee. In fact, if it were not for those rabbinical notices of Jesus, and especially one (30), there would not be any evidence on record that such a person ever lived. Nothing is known with certainty of his parentage and his youth. Contrary to his own statements (31) his biographers made him a son of David, and, in their eagerness to make him also a son of God, they branded him as a bastard, according to modern conceptions,

---

as the captive was sent away out of the country to prevent a sedition, which was certain y done hurriedly and secretly before his disciples could save him. The whole story of John rebuking Antipas on account of his misalliance with Herodias, together with the dancing of her daughter, etc , is fictitious; because John was dead before Antipas married Herodias. Macherus belonged to Aretas (Antiq. xviii , v. 1). The wife of Antipas and daughter of Aretas left her husband on discovering his intended faithlessness, before he brought Herodias to Tiberias. This was the beginning of hostilities on the part of Aretas. Antipas could not have had John beheaded in a city which belonged to, and was garrisoned by, his enemy. Consequently John must have been beheaded before that second marriage of Antipas.

(29) The four canonical Gospels were written between 120 and 170 A. C. in the following order: Mark, Matthew, Luke and John, and the Apocryphal Gospels were written much later. Compare Dr. Sepp's *Leben Jesu*, Dr. F. Mul er's *Briefe ueber die Christliche Religion*, Dr Karl August Credner's *Zur Geschichte des Kanons*, and our Martyrdom of Jesus of Nazareth.

(30) Yerushalmi *Sabbath* xii. 4, also in Tosephta and Babli. R. Eliezer b. Hyrcan, a cotemporary of the apostles, says: והלא ב סטרא (סטרא) רביא כשפים ממצרים אלא בכך

(31) Compare Mark xii. 35-37 and paral. passages with Epistle of Barnabas, London, 1820, in the Apocryphal New Testament xi. 13.

although among Pagans it was no rare case that a woman was supposed to have conceived by some imaginary deity (32), or that such distinction was claimed for or by some hero like Alexander the Great. According to the Talmud, Jesus spent some years in Egypt with a teacher called Rabbi Joshua, and learned there also the art of necromancy (33). If the healing miracles of Jesus, recorded in the Gospels, are based upon any facts, he must have learned in Egypt the art of Horus and Serapis, as practiced there by the priests, which the Hebrews could call Egyptian necromancy only (34). He came back to Palestine as a physician, and was by nature an enthusiast and Hebrew patriot. When John's preaching excited idealistic minds, Jesus also went to that teacher and was inspired by him to promulgate his doctrine, notwithstanding his youth and lack of experience (35). Jesus started out as a public orator and teacher with the doctrines of John, and in that capacity referred exclusively to his authority, as every public teacher then had to be ordained by some acknowledged authority (36).

16. Jesus in Galilee.

As long as John was at large, Jesus, in the capacity of an itinerant teacher and physician, roused the people of Galilee to repentance of sin, to bring about the restoration of the Kingdom of Heaven. He met with the same opposition that John did, from those who would not admit that they were more sinful than their progenitors or neighbors, or that asceticism was the proper means for the restoration

---

(32) Josephus' Antiq. xviii., iii. 4.
(33) See Matthew ii 14 and Gospel of Pseudo Matthew, chapters xvii. to xxiii. in Cowper's edition xxii., c. 8
(34) Compare Dr. Joseph Ennemoser's *Geschichte der Magie*, the chapter *Magie bei den Egyptern*, with Sueton in Vespasiam vii. 1; Tacitus History iv. 8, and *Talmud Sabbath* 108, about healing by touch, contact, sleep, spittle, etc., which were all Egyptian superstitions.
(35) We can only adhere to Luke's dates, viz.: that Jesus was born 6 or 7 A. C., after the banishment of Arche aus, and was executed 36 A. C., when he was scarcely thirty years old. John viii. 57: "Thou art not yet fifty years old," reads in several MSS. "forty," and refers to the Jewish adage: בן ארבעים לבינה "With the fortieth year reason begins to ripen." The Jews told Jesus that he was not old enough to be very wise.
(36) Mark i. 14, 15; xi. 27 to 33. Matthew iv. 17; xxi. 23 to 27 and paral. passages.

of the Kingdom. He met with some success among the lower classes, also among foreign harlots, Sodomites, publicans and other Roman agents; but the intelligent portion remained cold to his enthusiasm. The cures which he performed appeared miraculous to the vulgar, impious to the religious, and ridiculous to the intelligent. While they were aggrandized by the believers, they proved repulsive to the sober and reflecting minds (37).

17. The Religion of Jesus.

Soon, however, Jesus rose above the narrow standpoint of John, and embraced that of the Hillelites, presenting most conspicuously the humanitarian contents and cosmopolitan spirit of Judaism; and he did it in almost the same words as Hillel had done it (Mark xii. 28 to 34, and Matthew vii. 12). Like all Hillelites he believed in one eternal God, His general and special providence (38), the resurrection of the dead being taught in the Law (39), in future reward and punishment (40), in the revelation and the divinity of the Law and the Prophets (41), in the election of Israel by the Almighty (42), in the eternity of God's laws and promises (43), in the superior importance of the humanitarian over the ritual laws and doctrines, without wishing to abolish the latter or even the traditional laws (44). The natural result of these first principles was, that he disregarded the laws of Levitical cleanness, which were so important to Shammaites and Essenes, and so unimportant to Hillelites, and ate with unclean sinners, publicans and lepers, and permitted harlots to touch him, while his disciples also did not wash their hands before meals (45). Furthermore, he looked upon the whole Levitical institution, temple, sacrifice and priesthood included, as being necessary no longer, and not worth the blood shed about and around the temple (46). This was certainly also

---

(37) Mark iii. 21 to 23; Matthew ix. 3, 4; xii 24.
(38) Mark iv. 24; Matthew vii. 2; x. 29, exactly like the Talmud; Luke vi. 38.
(39) Mark xii. 19 to 27; compare *Sanhedrin* 90 *b*.
(40) Mark ix. 43 to 48.
(41) Matthew v. 17 to 19; Luke xvi. 17.
(42) Which was the Kingdom of Heaven to be restored.
(43) Mark x. 18 to 21.
(44) Mark i. 44; Matthew xii. 7; Mechilta, *ki-Thissa*; Matthew xxiii. 1 e. s.
(45) Mark ii. 15.
(46) Mark xi 15; John ii. 13; see our "Jesus Himself," chapter iv. in *Israelite* of 1869.

the opinion of the most prominent Hillelites, who prophesied the speedy destruction of the temple, and placed the repentance of sin, the study of the Law, the practice of charity and benevolence, the education of the young, and good will to all, above all Levitical observances (47). He abandoned the asceticism of John, lived, ate and drank like other men, was cheerful among the cheerful, sympathetic among the suffering, loved the company of women, who were among his most faithful disciples, and became a popular man among his people (48). Now he had ample opportunity to chastise those to whom rigorous observances and outward performances were more holy than the humanitarian laws and practices, and the quibbling scholasts whose wisdom consisted of wit and sophism; to convince them of their blindness, sinfulness and self-complacency; to admonish them to sincere repentance, and the restoration of the Kingdom of Heaven (49).

18. Style and Contents of his Speeches.

Jesus spoke in the sententious and parabolic style, always relying on Scriptures as the highest authority, as was the *Midrash* style of the Scribes of those days, viz.: a maxim expressed in the style of Solomon or Sirach's son, based upon a verse of Scriptures and illustrated by a parable, without resort, however, to the allegoric method of the Egyptian Hebrews. He uttered many good and wise sayings, which were not new to the learned, being taken from the so-called floating wisdom of the nation, found abundantly in the ancient rabbinical literature (50); but they were new to his disciples and audiences, who admired them exceedingly. Jesus was not distinguished for either learning or originality, and this enabled him the more easily to make himself intelligible and acceptable to his audiences. He was distinguished for ardent sympathy with his people and its cause, strong convictions and moral courage to utter them, and that

---

(47) *Yoma* 86; חביב עלי צדקה ומישפט מכל הקרבנות *Shekalim*; *Succah* 49 b; *Meguillah* 16 b.

(48) Mark vii.; ii. 18 e. s.; Matthew xi. 18, 19; Luke vii. 33 to 35.

(49) The Anti-Pharisaic speeches in Matthew xv. and xxiii. are productions of the second century A. C.; compare to Luke xi. 37 e. s.; xiii. 34 and Mark vii.

(50) The numerous parallel passages of the New Testament and the Rabbinical literature were compiled by Lightfoot, *Hora Hebraicæ et Talmudicæ*, etc.; F. Nork, *Rabbinische Quellen und Parallelen*, etc.; Zipser, *Die Bergpredigt in Talmud*; Wunsche, *Neue Beitrage*, etc. Gruenebaum, Isidor Kalisch, and in our Origin of Christianity.

nervous eloquence which inspires confidence. Irrespective of even common politeness or any social forms, he cared not for his own mother and brothers, traveled in company of eccentric women, subsisted with his disciples on his friends' property, upbraided men of learning and prominence, and evinced not the slightest regard for the practical affairs of man, which, under the prevailing excitement, only increased his popularity.

19. The Policy of Jesus.

Success matured the belief in Jesus that the Kingdom of Heaven was at hand, and he changed his tone from the promise to the fulfillment, opening thus the third phase of his biography. He assumed the prophetic title of the "Son of Man," as Ezekiel and Daniel (viii. 17) had called themselves, and as the latter had called the head of the restored Kingdom of Heaven (vii. 13 *Bar Anosh*). According to the Laws of Moses (Deut. xviii. 15 to 22), it was not the king of the house of David or of any other dynasty, nor the highpriest who was to be the head in the Kingdom of Heaven; the prophet was to be the chief ruler, who must be obeyed. Jesus presumed that the Kingdom of Heaven was re-established and himself its chief ruler. He had the peculiar idea of going back in history one thousand years and resuming its form of government as left by Samuel. This met with approbation among his disciples and followers, who were visionary enough to apply ancient Bible conditions to modern emergencies; but it roused the opposition of those who did not believe in the authority of the Paraclete or Bath-Kol, had no faith in a form of government overcome in history, and had enacted stringent laws against prophetical pretenders (51). Jesus preaching in this sense, and sending out some of his disciples with the same message to the people, his policy was attacked more than his doctrine. Here are the Romans, the lords of the land, was the main question, how will you overcome them? Jesus replied with the ancient Pharisees and the Hillelites, it matters not who holds the political power and collects the taxes, you pay at any rate nothing but Caesar's money, money unlawful to you on account of its idolatrous effigies. If the Kingdom of Heaven and God's grace are restored to Israel, He will also settle your political affairs. You can not conquer the Romans, convert and love them

---

(51) Sanhedrin 89 *a;* Yerushalmi *ibid.* xi. 7; Siphri 177 and 178.

and they are your enemies no longer. Their administration of the laws is unjust and oppressive; have nothing to do with their judges, and they can not wrong you. "If any man will sue thee at the law, and take away thy coat, let him have thy cloak also," etc. (Matthew v. 40-47) (52). Have patience and faith, wait till God changes this state of affairs. Your temple is in the hands of Roman soldiers and Hebrew hirelings; stay away, pray in your closets, understand what it means: "I delight in grace and not in sacrifice." This is a time of affliction and tribulation; bear it with patience as the punishment for your sins. All depends on the restoration of the Kingdom of Heaven and God's grace to Israel; this accomplished, Providence will heal all wounds. It is the same policy which Jeremiah in his time advanced and advocated, and to which the Hillelites adhered to the very last. But the party of action and the Zealots no less consistently and patriotically opposed this policy as visionary and unmanly. Therefore, while it placed Jesus in conflict with the officiating priests, Sadducees, Shammaites and Zealots, it certainly met with the indorsement of thousands whose feelings and aspirations were less political and more religious.

20. Jesus a Fugitive.

The arrest of John was a warning to Jesus. Herod Antipas had good reason to believe him as dangerous as was John, who had been beheaded, of which Jesus, it appears, was never informed (Matthew xiv.). Jesus, perhaps, cautioned by his mother (Mark iii. 21), or by the Pharisees, who were his friends (Luke xiii. 31), became a fugitive. He was now among the Gadarenes, east of Galilee (Mark v. 1), and then "departed privately into a desert place by ship" (*Ibid.* vi. 32). We find him in Bethsaida, in Philip's territory (*Ibid.* vi. 45), then in the borders of Tyre and Sidon (*Ibid.* vii. 24), in the coasts of Decapolis (*Ibid.* viii. 31), inhabited chiefly by Gentiles, then again at Dalmanutha (*Ibid.* viii. 10), east of Galilee, and at last at Caesarea Philippi (*Ibid.* viii. 27), at the extreme north of that

---

(52) The Sermon on the Mount was never delivered. No man ever delivered an address on so many different subjects. Therefore, none besides Matthew has that sermon, and the other Evangelists have various portions of it in different places and times. It is entirely misunderstood. It contains maxims of Jesus in reference to that particular age and those particular circumstances, which have been changed into moral principles.

country. He spent his time as a fugitive, now in the desert then on the lake, now at this and then at the other border of Galilee, nearly always in Philip's territory, which had become (34 A. C.) a Roman province under the mild government of Vitellius; and he never appeared again in the populous centers of Galilee. He exclaimed, " The foxes have holes, and the birds of the air have nests; but the Son of man hath not where to lay his head" (Matthew viii. 20). Some of his disciples, it appears (Luke ix. 54), lost their patience and were ready for acts of violence, but Jesus told them, " The Son of man is not come to destroy men's life, but to save" (lives). However, persecution is an incitement to enthusiasm, and martyrdom rouses the compassion and sympathy of the multitude. So also in this case, the martyrdom of John and the supposed persecution of Jesus by Antipas only increased the popularity of the Son of man, elevated him in his own convictions and in the opinion of his disciples, and brought about the fourth epoch in his history.

21. Jesus Proclaimed the Messiah.

Early in the year 36 A. C. (53), when Jesus and his disciples were sojourning in the towns about Cæsarea Philippi, Peter proclaimed Jesus the Messiah or Christ. Jesus protested emphatically against that royal title, rebuked Peter,. "Get thee behind me Satan, for thou savorest not the things that be of God, but the things that be of men," and charged his disciples not to tell any man, as the assumption of that title must bring on him great suffering, he would be rejected by the Hebrew authorities and killed (crucified) by the Romans (Mark viii. 27 to 33). But the word was out, the disciples seized it, and against his will, with inevitable death before his eyes, Jesus was proclaimed the Messiah. Messiah or Christ signifies " the annointed one" (54), and in the Hebrew records only the highpriest or his proxy (Levit. iv. 3; v. 16), the king of all Israel (55) and Cyrus were called Messiahs. The Hebrews then and always thereafter, who believed in the coming of a Messiah, expected him to be the King of Israel, who would gather

---

(53) See Section 11 Note 3.
(54) From משח to annoint.
(55) Compare 1. Samuel ii. 10, 35; xii. 3, 5; xv. 6; xxiv. 7, 11; xxvi. 9, 11, 23; 11. Samuel i. 14, 16; xix. 22; xxiii. 1; Isaiah xlv. 1; our Origin of Christianity, p. 180, and our Jesus Himself, chapter 3 in *The Israelite*, August 13, 1869.

the Hebrews from all lands to Palestine, and there reign over them as their political king. The expectation of a coming Messiah was not a doctrine of the Hillelites, so that one of their last representatives, Hillel II., declared directly against that belief (אין משיח לישראל). In the Palestinean literature there is no evidence at all that the Hebrews, prior to the final destruction of the temple, entertained such a belief or held such a doctrine; although some enthusiasts may have believed in the future restoration of the Urim and Thumim and true prophecy, but their number was certainly insignificant. There existed, however, such Messianic hopes and speculations among the Greco-Roman Hebrews, who expected a Messiah would come and regather the Hebrews from all lands. These hopes and speculations were also imposed on the Septuagint, found expression in the Sybiline poems of that and subsequent ages, and formulation in the semi-mystic speculations of Philo (56). The Roman edict against the Hebrews, under Tiberius and Sejan, may have excited again, among the Greco-Roman Hebrews, the hope and expectation of a Messiah. Thousands of them undoubtedly came to Palestine, and other multitudes were expected to come to Jerusalem, as usual, to celebrate the Passover. Those were the main persons, upon whose belief and support Peter and the other men of action among the disciples of Jesus, relied when they proclaimed him the Messiah.

22. The Failure.

Being completely in the hands of over-excited enthusiasts, Jesus followed them down from Cæsarea Philippi to Jericho, crossing and recrossing the Jordan at various points, being proclaimed the Messiah, and performing feats of Thaumaturgy which his followers magnified and aggrandized. Death was constantly before his eyes, and it was inevitable. Still his enthusiastic and patriotic disciples could not imagine that the contemplated rising of the people, supported by publicans and other Roman agents, could prove a failure. They came with him to Jerusalem shortly before the Passover feast, roused the enthusiasm in the suburbs, where most of the pilgrims were encamped, and then entered Jerusalem in triumph. He rode on an ass as the coming Messiah was expected, and, under the acclamations of the excited multitude, he was proclaimed the

---

(56) Philo, *De Excrationibus*.

restorer of the Kingdom of David (Mark xi. 10). He was lead to the temple, where another popular demonstration greeted him, and he began with exercising sovereign authority and accusing the priests of having made of the temple a den of thieves. He argued with priests and scribes, addressed the masses, reviewed in brief his entire scheme of salvation; still he was no longer the same enthusiastic and self-confident man. No angels and no miracles came to his aid, and his chosen disciples were helpless as children. The learning of Jerusalem and the prevailing unbelief in paraclete, new prophets, supernatural aid, Messiahship and other products of enthusiasm, undeceived and confused him, so that he denounced them all, and prophesied misery and affliction to all. His disciples would not let him stay over night in Jerusalem, fearing he might escape them or be captured, and so he was kept in secluded quarters on Mount Olive among lepers. He must soon have discovered that the Hebrew authorities afforded him no protection, and that Pontius Pilate certainly would not spare the man who had been publicly proclaimed the King of the Hebrews.

23. Capture and Death.

Caiphas, the highpriest, was not merely a Roman tool, which he must have been, or else he could not have maintained himself in his office all the time with Pontius Pilate. He was also the mediator between the people and the Roman authorities. He and all responsible men in Jerusalem must have dreaded an insurrection in the city, and especially during the feast, which would have afforded to Pilate a welcome pretext for carnage and plunder. Therefore, he and his few coadjutors concluded upon abandoning Jesus into the hands of Pilate without exciting the multitude, and disavowing every sympathy with the Messianic commotion (John xi. 45 to 50). The disciples, however, had Jesus formally annointed, and kept him well secluded and secured at night time, so that he could not well be captured without exciting the tumult which was dreaded. The insurrectionary demonstration was ripe, and ready to break out on the Passover feast. Jesus was well aware that this would cost the lives of thousands without effecting any good. Bloodshed and worldly power were contrary to his teachings and repugnant to his nature. Therefore, he resolved upon delivering himself into the hands of the authorities and dying the martyr's death before the demonstration could take place, in order to save his own friends and followers, with hundreds of others, from certain death. By prudent hints he encouraged Judas Iscariot, one of his disciples, to betray his secret retreat to the priests, and Judas did so without supposing that Jesus would be put to death. In the night of Passover the soldiers of Pilate surprised Jesus and his companions in their secret retreat, and early in the morning, without ceremony or trial, Pilate ordered him to be put to death as the "King of the Jews," before his friends could have the least knowledge of his fate (57). He died a martyr to save his friends and many more innocent men. The Messianic drama ended with the death of its hero, and his disciples, dismayed and disappointed, left Jerusalem to be quiet for some years (58).

24. Pontius Pilate Banished.

If the crucifixion story of the Gospels is true in regard to the end of Jesus, then it is certain that Pilate treated him with special cruelty. He not only imposed on his victim the worst of all Roman punishments, viz.: crucifixion, but also scourged him, and then had him mocked by his soldiers before he was crucified. Scourging and crucifixion were inflicted in Rome only in exceptional cases and on slaves only, and on rebels in the provinces. But this was Pilate's last outrage committed in Judea. We have no doubt this execution was one of the points advanced against him by the Hebrews and Samaritans before Vitellius (59). In the fall of 36 A. C., Vitellius sent Marcellus

---

(57) See our Martyrdom of Jesus of Nazareth.
(58) Jesus was no Essene, did not allegorize Scriptures, had no intention to establish a new religion, or even to oppose the Hillelites. He was too young to see his mistake in time, that a nation can not go back a thousand years to reinstitute a form of government which had outlived itself. Stern realities wi l not submit to idea's, however lofty. His disciples proclaiming him the Messiah, forced him into the embrace of death, and Pi ate was the executioner. His martyrdom, like his teachings, was gravely misunderstood.
(59) To which Philo refers in his charges against Pilate "the execution of many persons without process of law" (See Section 8 of this chapter). It appears that Josephus did mention this fact in Antiquities xviii., iii 3; but some time between 250 and 325 A. C. that paragraph was changed into its present form, of which Origenes in 250 A. C. had no knowledge, and Eusebius in 325 A. C. mentions for the first time. The same appears to be the case with Antiquities xx, ix. 1, where the words "who was called Christ" were made of the phrase "whom his disciples called Christ." Forgeries of that kind were not uncommon at that time, when quite a number of

to Judea to take charge of that country, and commanded Pilate to go to Rome and defend himself before the emperor. Pilate left his post in disgrace and hastened to Rome. But before he reached it Tiberius died (March 16, 37 A. C.). Still Pilate was tried, found guilty, and banished to Vienna, where he ended (some say in Switzerland) in suicide.

25. VITELLIUS IN JERUSALEM.

The next Passover (37 A. C.) Vitellius came to Jerusalem and made a successful attempt to pacify the Hebrews, which quelled the Messianic commotion. He restored the highpriest's vestments to the custody of the priests, and removed Caiphas from office. Jonathan, the son of Ananus, was appointed in his place (60). Another evidence of his good will was this: According to the command of Tiberius, he made ready to invade Arabia, and intended to let his legions march through Judea. The Hebrews prayed him not to do it on account of the idolatrous ensigns, and he changed the route of march for the soldiers. Next Pentecost he came to Jerusalem with Herod Antipas, removed from office Jonathan, who, it appears, did not wish to be highpriest, and appointed in his place his brother, Theophilus. While in Jerusalem, Vitellius was informed of the death of Tiberius, and in consequence of which he did not invade Arabia, but returned to Antioch. For a short time there was again peace in Palestine.

pseudonimic books were forged, with the avowed intention to prove the existence of Jesus and his crucifixion, which were denied by heretics and others, and to settle the responsibility of the master's death upon the Jews (See Gospel of Nicodemus and the others following in Cowper's edition).

(60) Josephus' Antiq. xviii., iv. 3.

CHAPTER XXII.

Agrippa I. and his Time.

1. AGRIPPA'S YOUTH.

One of the grandson's of Herod I. by the Asmonean Mariamne, was Agrippa, son of Aristobul and Berenice, the daughter of Salome. Berenice being a particular friend of Antonia, the mother of Germanicus, sent her son to Rome, and he was educated there in the imperial family with Drusus, son of Tiberius. Extravagance was one of the vices which young Agrippa contracted at that Court, and levity was another. Although he married a very affectionate and prudent scion of Herod, Cypros, these vices had the mastery over him all his life. As long as his mother lived he was kept within bounds. When she was dead he continued borrowing and squandering large sums of money, till at last he was obliged to leave Rome in order to escape prosecution by his creditors. At Malath in Idumea, he contemplated committing suicide, an intention which his wife frustrated. She wrote to his sister, Herodias, the wife of Herod Antipas, and he appointed Agrippa his minister of commerce with a considerable salary. Agrippa could not long be his uncle's servant, he soon left him and went to Flaccus, where his brother, Aristobul, whom he disliked, also was. He also soon lost the favor of Flaccus, and went to Ptolemais with the intention of going back to Italy. His freedman, Marsyas, obtained the money for him, he went to Anthidon, hired a ship, but was arrested for debt to the imperial treasury. Released on parole he sailed to Alexandria, where a rich co-religionist, Alexander Lysimachus (1),

---

(1) He was alabarch of the Alexandrian Hebrews and President of the Imperial Salt-works; he had been before the steward of Antonia (Josephus' Antiq. xix., v. 1).

the brother of the philosopher, Philo, furnished him with the means to reach Italy, where he provided him with other sums of money. Drusus was dead, and Agrippa went directly to Caprea, where the emperor resided temporarily. He was kindly received, but when the emperor was informed of his debt to the imperial treasury, he refused to receive him again till that debt was paid. Antonia and a freedman of Tiberias, Thallos, helped him this time with large sums of money, and he was reinstated at the Imperial Court. Tiberius wanted him to befriend especially the son of Germanicus, Caius Caligula, and so he became associated with one of the most extravagant and most extraordinary fools of Rome.

2. Reduced to the Extreme.

Agrippa was now one of the most envied favorites of the emperor, and an intimate friend of the Cæsar. But the tenure of such fortune is very uncertain. One day he was alone with Caius, as he supposed, and told him that he considered him more competent than the cruel Tiberius for the throne, and wished that the emperor would soon vacate it. His freedman, Eutychus, had heard this, and being afterward accused of theft by Agrippa, reported to the emperor Agrippa's words with aggravating additions. Agrippa was put in chains and sent out before the palace to stand there among other captives. A slave, Thaumastus, was the only person who gave him a drink of water, for which he promised him liberty, and he kept his word. A German captive prophesied that Agrippa would yet mount the throne, although he would die a sudden death five days after having seen an owl over his head (2). The prince in purple and chains was sent to a prison, where Antonia took good care of him. One day a report reached Rome that Tiberius was dead, and Marsyas carried the tidings at once to Agrippa, and told him in Hebrew, "the lion is dead." His jailer observing that something very fortunate had occurred, persuaded Agrippa to tell him the news. He took off the chains of his prisoner, and they sat down to a royal banquet, when suddenly the news of the emperor's death was

---

(2) The Germans, like other heathens, were also very superstitious before they embraced Christianity. The fact that Josephus makes such extensive use of his owl story and the prophecy connected with it, proves that he had embraced Roman notions of soothsaying and augury, a fact which must be taken into consideration wherever he speaks of prophets.

contradicted. The terrified jailer again put his prisoner in chains and forced him back into his gaol. Next morning, however, the death of Tiberius was officially announced. Agrippa was freed of his chains and sent to his own house to await there the orders of Caius Caligula.

3. From the Prison to the Throne.

After a few days Agrippa was called before Caligula, who placed the crown upon his head and made him king of Philipp's tetrarchy (37 A. C.), in the north and northeast of Palestine, which had been for three years part of Syria. Agrippa remained in Rome one year longer, the boon companion of the emperor, before he returned to Palestine, and then at the express desire of the emperor he took his way home via Alexandria, where the following melancholy events transpired (Josephus' Antiq. xviii., vi.):

4. Rise of the Pagans Against the Hebrews.

The conflict between Heathenism and Judaism was a literary feud no less than a sanguinary combat among its respective champions. While the Hebrews employed their pens and the Greek language to expound and promulgate their religion, laws and history, Pagans, by the same means, attacked and derided them. Foremost among the latter were Apollonius Molo (90 B. C.), Posidonius of Apamea (70 B. C.), who was one of Cicero's teachers, Chaeremon (50 B. C.), Lysimachos (30 B. C.), and Apion of Alexandria, in this period, besides the Latin writers noticed. Apion was notorious as a malicious demagogue, whose main fort was in impudent lying, bragging and glittering sophistry (Josephus *contra* Apion). The ancestors of the Hebrews were defamed as a number of leprous slaves driven out of Egypt. Moses was aspersed as a rebel priest of Heliopolis, the Hebrews were denounced as atheists who worshiped no gods and had an ass in their *sanctum sanctorum*, and the enemies of all men who would not partake of the Heathen banquets (3). As long as the edicts of Julius Caesar were in force and a Hebrew monarch enthroned in Jerusalem insisting upon their execution, the conflicts in the various cities between Heathen and Hebrew were brief and easily settled by Roman authority. The edict of Tiberius against the Italian Hebrews and Pontius Pilate's scornful oppressions

---

(3) John Gill's Notices of the Jews and their country by the classic writers of Antiquity, London, 1872.

in Judea gave a fresh impetus to the hostility of the Pagans. This was the case especially in Alexandria, where the native Egyptian element always looked with hatred upon the favored foreigners, and especially upon the Hebrews, who, by their superior intelligence and their numerous connections in all foreign lands, were the most skilled artisans and most successful merchants, held the most responsible public positions (4), and counted among their men some of the finest and most cultivated minds. A natural consequence of all these advantages was their wealth, which irritated the lower classes to envy and ripened in them bloody designs. The evil grew when Flaccus, another creature of Sejan, was sent to Egypt with the same policy with which Pilate had been sent to Judea; and Egypt, like Judea, groaned under the barbarous despotism of Rome. This threatening fire under the ashes began to break forth, when in July, 38 A. C., Agrippa came to Alexandria, and was enthusiastically received by the Hebrews. The row began with a farce and ended in terrible bloodshed. The populace congregated about the gymnasium, took hold upon an idiot, whose name was Carobas, dressed him up fantastically with purple, crown and scepter, placed him high upon a throne, and saluted him as king, calling him by the Syriac title of *Maran*, "our lord," and played a royal farce with the fool, a burlesque of Agrippa and the Hebrews. This feeler being successful, the populace rushed next morning into the synagogues and erected there the emperors' statues, and Flaccus, in imitation of the Tiberius edict, by proclamation, deprived the Hebrews of the rights of citizenship, so that he need protect them no longer. Now the bloodshed and robbery began. The Hebrews were driven from the four quarters of Alexandria into the Delta quarter, which was besieged and their houses ransacked. None could bring any provisions there, and those who did venture out were slain or barbarously maltreated. Women also were abused and tortured. Thirty-eight men of the Council, by command of Flaccus, and on the emperor's birthday were publicly scourged (August 31st), and a centurion with soldiers was sent to the Delta quarter to search the houses for arms, which was another pretense for violence and plunder. In the middle of September, however,

---

(4) Alexander, the Alabarch, was at this time the chief officer of the salt-works, one of Rome's most important sources of wealth in Egypt. He covered the temple gates of Jerusalem with gold and silver, wrought in Alexandria.

Flaccus was relieved by Bassus, and was afterward tried and in exile put to death. Order was restored in Alexandria; but the question of rights could be settled by the emperor only, who was now in distant Germany and France (Philo *contra* Flaccus).

5. Banishment of Herod Antipas.

Agrippa left Alexandria and arrived soon after in his kingdom. He was well received, and, like his uncle and predecessor, Philip, he governed with justice and generosity. His sister, Herodias, ambitious and envious as she was, persuaded her husband also to obtain the crown and title of king from Caligula. Antipas gave his best support to Vitellius when he invaded Parthia, and then made his application in Rome, where he was opposed by both Vitellius and Agrippa, the crown of Judea and Samaria being the object of Agrippa's own ambition. Antipas was charged with conspiring with Artaban, King of Parthia, and Agrippa, who had come to Rome, informed Caligula that his uncle had accumulated arms enough for 60,000 to 70,000 men, hence must have treacherous designs against Rome. Antipas confessed that he had collected the arms, and this, without any further investigation, was taken as a proof of his treacherous intentions. He was banished to Lyons in France, and his wife was given a pension by the emperor and the liberty of choosing her future place of residence. Herodias, however, would not desert her husband, and went with him into exile to Lyons and then to Spain (39 B. C.), after Antipas had governed his provinces thirty-one years. These provinces were now added to the kingdom of Agrippa. It is evident that neither Archelaus nor Antipas went alone into exile; a considerable number of the Hebrew nobility must have gone with them to France and Spain, where Hebrew colonies existed before this period.

6. The Alexandrian Embassy to Caligula.

The madness and arrogance of Caligula grew steadily upon him, till at last he proclaimed himself god and exacted of his subjects divine worship. The dead Julius Cæsar, Augustus and Tiberius were also gods, but he was the highest. The Pagan conceptions of Deity were so low and crude that the lord of the empire was also accepted as the highest god. The head of the Olympian Jupiter was cut off and that of Caligula placed on the statue. The imperial edict was obeyed everywhere in the Roman Empire, except, of course, by the Hebrews, and the slightest opposition to this crazy whim roused Caligula to fury. The Egyptian Hebrews were the first victims of this new phase of despotism. The Hebrews of Egypt, and of Alexandria especially, having been robbed of their rights as citizens, were continually maltreated and scorned by their Pagan neighbors. Personal combats, riots and bloodshed were the order of the day. The Pagan citizens of Alexandria sent an embassy to Rome, under the leadership of wicked and brilliant Apion, to obtain the emperor's consent to the edict of Flaccus disfranchising the Hebrews. The Hebrews on their part also sent an embassy to Rome under the leadership of Philo, the philosopher, whose depth of thought and sentiment was equaled only by his elegance of diction and nobility of character. He was born 1 A. C. (and died 60 A. C.) in Alexandria, a scion of the highest aristocracy. His brother, Alexander, was the highest officer of the Egyptian Hebrews, whose son, Tiberius, was afterward Procurator of Judea, and occupied the highest offices of the empire. Alexander was also among the embassadors. In a country seat which he was inspecting, Caligula received the two embassies in a most unbecoming manner. Running from one apartment to the other, criticising this and that, and the embassies following him, he wanted to be informed of the nature of their controversy. The Procurator in Egypt had already informed him that the Hebrews refused to acknowledge his divinity, and he had no ear for their pleas. His first address to the Hebrew embassadors was: "So you are the contemners of the gods, who would not acknowledge my divinity and prefer to worship a nameless being, while all besides you worship me?" Then he cursed and blasphemed God in terms which Philo would not write down. Being accused that the Hebrews made no sacrifices for him, Philo showed that they did, and Caligula ejaculated: "That may be, but what good does it do me, that you make sacrifices for me and not to me?" He gave them no chance to speak, asked them questions and ran to the next apartment before an answer could be given, behaved like a crazy man, so that he excited laughter, and at last dismissed them with these words: "These men appear to be less wicked than stupid, because they deny my divinity." No decision followed, Alexander was thrown into prison, and the embassy returned broken hearted to Alexandria. Philo wrote in five books "The Embassy to Caius," of which but two fragments are extant. The conduct of that crazy emperor appears now very ludicrous and barbarous; and yet it was no worse than that of many a high prelate or prince in after times to those who refused to acknowledge the divinity of Jesus of Nazareth; and yet Jesus was no more a god than Caligula.

7. Caligula's Attempt to Supersede the God of Israel.

Caligula was determined to be acknowledged and worshiped as the highest God. The Hebrews, refusing to grant him that honor, he appointed Publius Petronius President of Syria to succeed Vitellius, and charged him with the special duty to invade Judea, to carry the emperor's statue to Jerusalem, and to erect it in the temple. Petronius concentrated his army at Ptolemais and made due preparations to invade Judea the following spring. The Hebrews came by the thousands to Ptolemais to convince Petronius that he could not carry out the emperor's mandate as long as any of them were among the living; that they would fight to the last for the honor of God and His laws. Petronius replied that he was sent to Syria to enforce the emperor's will, which he could not change, and the Hebrews insisted that they would not see their laws transgressed from fear of death, so that a war of extermination appeared inevitable. Perhaps this was the determination of the Hebrews of Judea only, those of Agrippa's kingdom might be of another opinion, Petronius thought, and went to the city of Tiberius. However, he found there the same determination; they would not permit the imperial statue to be erected even in their city, much less in the temple at Jerusalem, and told him: "We will die rather than see our laws transgressed." Aristobulus, the brother of Agrippa (Agrippa was in Rome), and other prominent Hebrews, persuaded Petronius to appeal to the clemency of Caligula, and to present to him the state of affairs as it was, the death-defying determination of the Hebrew people in defense of their laws, and the dire necessity of depopulating the whole land before the emperor's will could be carried into effect. This was a dangerous enterprise for Petronius, it might have cost him position, liberty and life; yet he yielded, and sent a message to the emperor to acquaint him fully with the state of affairs, and to inform him that he was awaiting his instructions before commencing active hostilities. The Hebrews were persuaded to return to their peaceful occupations, and this advice and assurance by Petronius and the leading men at Tiberius were supported in Jerusalem by the chief priest, Simon, son of Boethus, also called "The Just." He admonished the people to keep quiet and to trust in God, who would perform miracles for them as he had done for their fathers (5). A *Bath-kol* afterward confirmed his prophecy, and was recorded among the wonderful occurrences (6). Meanwhile Agrippa was not idle in Rome. As the boon companion of the emperor, he understood how to win his particular favor. He prepared for him a most luxuriant banquet with royal pomp, and when Caligula's stomach was well filled, and his senses half benighted, he praised the excellent taste and royal generosity of his extravagant friend, and desired him to ask any favor of him, which he promised unconditionally to grant. Agrippa apparently had nothing to ask for; but being repeatedly and urgently encouraged by Caligula to ask of him something, he asked of Caligula to revoke his command given to Petronius. The emperor promised he would, although it was the very worst that could have been asked of him. When, however, the message of Petronius arrived informing Caligula of the determined resistance of the Hebrews to his will, and the apparent weakness of Petronius, which looked like disobedience and treason, his wrath was boundless, and his command to Petronius to place the emperor's statue at the temple of Jerusalem was renewed, even were it necessary to exterminate half of that rebellious nation. The ship bearing these dispatches sailed slowly, another sailed faster, and this other bore to the east the news of the assassination of Caligula in his own palace, by the hands of Charea and his conspirators (January 24, 41 A. C.). The second ship arrived first. With the godhead of Caligula the miseries of the Hebrews were overcome once more for the time being. The twenty-second day of *Shebat*, the date when this news reached Jerusalem, was made one of the national half-holidays.

8. Agrippa King of Palestine.

The pretorian guard seized upon the son of Drusus and Antonia, Claudius, and proclaimed him emperor, while the senate deliberated as to how to restore the republic and abolish the imperial office. Agrippa was now the most important man in Rome, and it was by his diplomatic intercession be-

---

(5) Megillath Taanith xi.
(6) *Ibid.* and Talmud *Sotah* 33 a.

tween the two parties that Claudius was acknowledged
emperor. He thus paid part of the debt to his patroness,
Antonia. Agrippa was now overwhelmed with honors and
power. The senate bestowed on him the consular dignity,
Claudius restored to him the whole kingdom of Herod I.,
adding to it the province of Abilene on the Lebanon, and
made a league with him, which was confirmed by oaths on
the forum in the city of Rome. The Alabarch of Alexandria, Alexander Lysimachus, was released from his prison
and sent to Egypt, followed by the imperial decree which
restored to the Egyptian Hebrews all the rights and privileges they had been granted before, and especially "that
they might continue in their own customs." A similar
edict was published reinstating the Hebrews all over the
Roman Empire in their rights and privileges as citizens
with special immunity "to keep their ancient customs without being hindered so to do," and the command that the
edict be engraved and everywhere exposed to the public for
thirty successive days. Agrippa gave his daughter, Berenece
to Marcus, the son of the Alabarch, who, however, died before he married her. The Hebrew government being restored, and the edicts of Tiberius and Caligula revoked, it
appeared that a new era of prosperity to the Hebrews had
opened (Josephus' Antiq. xix., v.).

9. A LAW-ABIDING KING.

The grandson of Herod I. was a law-abiding king—notwithstanding the nugatory impressions he had received in
Rome, and the precedents set by his ancestors—and grateful to his friends who had stood with him in hours of
adversity. Arriving in Jerusalem he "offered all the sacrifices that belonged to him, and omitted nothing which the
law required." So did he afterward mixing with the multitude that had come to offer up the first fruits in the temple; bearing his own basket, like every peasant, he appeared
with them before the altar as the law ordains (7). When
in the year 42 A. C. the Sabbath year closed, on the Feast of
Booths, he read the Law to the assembled people according
to ancient custom. When he came to the passage which
ordains that no foreigner should be king of the Hebrews,
he wept on account of his Idumean extraction. But the
voice of the multitude exclaiming, "thou art our brother,"
assured him that he was not looked upon as a non-

---

(7) MISHNAH *Biccurim* iii. 4.

Israelite (8). The highpriests whom he appointed were
men of known piety and patriotism. He appointed first
Simon Boethus, the man who had consoled and encouraged
the people in the time of calamity; but soon removed him
again, perhaps because he was a Sadducee, and appointed
the worthiest priest of his days, Jonathan, son of Annas,
who had held that office a short time under Vitellius. But
this man declined the high honors, because, as he said,
"God hath adjudged that I am not at all worthy of the
high priesthood." He recommended his brother, Matthias,
of whom he said, that he was pure from all sin against God;
and he was appointed highpriest. It is not stated why he
was removed, and his successor, Elioneus, son of Cantheras,
was appointed; but it is recorded that the latter also was a
pious and patriotic man (9), who was the first after John
Hyrcan to sacrifice again the red heifer. Agrippa re-
established the Hebrew State upon the national laws, consequently the Great Sanhedrin also, after a suspension of
thirty-five years (6 to 41 A. C.), was reconvoked to the temple under the presidency of Gamliel (or Gamaliel), the son
of Simon, who was the son of Hillel, called RABBAN GAM-
LIEL HAZ-ZAKAN.

10. THE GAMLIEL SANHEDRIN.

The restoration of the Sanhedrin with its political and
judicial powers was the main event in the reign of Agrippa,
because it was the restoration of the national form of government with all its civil and religious liberty, and made
him the most popular ruler in Israel since the days of John
Hyrcan, so that the rabbinical sources like Josephus are
profuse in his praise. It was a Hillel Sanhedrin, hence
liberal, reformatory and peaceable. The grandson of Hillel
presi led over it and an immediate disciple of Hillel, Rabbi
Jochanan (John) ben Saccai, was its chief justice, because
Akabiah ben Mahalalel, who was considered the most
worthy man of his time, disagreed with the school in some
minor points, and perfect unanimity was considered essential (10). The two scribes of this Sanhedrin were John
and Nahum (11). There were among the prominent mem-

(8) *Sotah* 41 *a*. See also *Kethuboth* 17 *a*.
(9) אֱלִיהוֹעֵינִי בֶּן הַקּוֹף *Mishnah Parah* iii. 5.
(10) *Edioth* v. 6, 7; *Aboth* iii. 1; *Berachoth* 19 *a*; *Sanhedrin* 88 *a*.
His HALACHOTH are *Sanhedrin* 77; *Sebachim* 88; *Bechoroth* 26; *Niddah*
19; *Negaim* 72 and 78.
(11) *Sanhedrin* 11 *b*; *Nazir* 56; *Peah* ii. 6.

bers of this Sanhedrin Ishmael b. Fabi (Elishah) and Joshua b. Gamala, afterward highpriests, Hanina (Ananus), highpriest proxy, afterward the head of the moderate party, and many of those teachers who were afterward counted among the FIRST AGE OF TENA'IM. It is with them that the titles of Abba, Rabbi and Rabbon or Rabbenu begin. The latter title, "Our Teacher," was conferred on the lawful *Nassi* only, because he was considered the teacher of all teachers.

11. THE GAMLIEL LEGISLATION AND TEACHINGS.

Little is known of the legislation of the Gamliel Sanhedrin on account of its brief existence. Laws were enacted "for the preservation of society" (משום תקון העולם) in the very spirit of Hillel; such as, a widow may marry again if any one witness testify to the death of her husband (12). Orphans' funds loaned out need no PROZBOL-contract to set aside the law of release (13). Persons who have gone beyond the Sabbath way on the day of rest in order to perform a higher duty, may then, like other people, walk two thousand cubits in any direction (14). Bills of divorce must be so written that no mistake can occur in regard to names, place or date (15). A widow's dowry must be paid at once after her husband's death (16). Sadducees and Boethites lose none of their rights by their difference of opinion (17), which included also the primitive Christians (18). The law may be written in Greek characters as well as in the Assyrian (19). Public schools must be supported in every district, besides the high-schools in the district towns, and all children between the ages of six and seven up to sixteen or seventeen years must frequent them (20). The first reforms in Jewish calendation belong to this Rabban

---

(12) *Jebamoth* 115 *a*.
(13) *Guittin* 37 *a*.
(14) *Rosh Hashanah* 23 *b*.
(15) *Guittin* 32 *a* and 34 *b*.
(16) *Ibid.*
(17) *Erubin* 68 *b*.
(18) Acts of the Apostles v. 35 to 39.
(19) Compare MISHNAH *Meguillah* i. 8 with *Debarim Rabbah* i. מותר לכתוב ספר תורה יונית
(20) *Baba Bathra* 21 *a*. where this enactment is ascribed to Joshua b. Gamala before he was highpriest, but it must naturally have been enacted by the Sanhedrin, although it may have been proposed by Joshua b. Gamala.

Gamaliel (21). Like the Chaldeans the Hebrews counted 223 synodical revolutions of the moon in 6585 1-3 days, which made a lunar moon of 29 355-669 days (established by the rabbis in 29 days 12 793-1080 hours); nor were they ignorant of Menton's luni-solar cycle, and the discoveries and corrections by Hipparchus of Bithynia (160-125 B. C.). The fractions of the lunar moon were intercalated by a thirtieth day of the month, so that some months had 29 and others 30 days; and the luni-solar years were adjusted by the intercalated thirteenth month of *Adar Sheni* in seven out of every nineteen years. (Established by the rabbis to be the 3, 6, 8, 11, 14, 17 and 19 years of the cycle). This work of establishing years and months, hence also the feasts, was done by the Sanhedrin, and from and after Rabban Gamliel by the president thereof, assisted by some colleagues. According to ancient custom, the new moon had to be seen, and the witness to testify to the fact before the *Nassi* or his colleagues, before the new moon day of any month could be established, which gave rise to much confusion. Rabban Gamliel introduced the astronomical tables with the presentation of the various phases of the moon, made use of a sort of telescope (22), and had an observatory on the temple mount (מעלת הר הבית) not only to control the witnesses, but to establish months and years according to astronomical calculations, called afterward (סוד העבור) "the secret of intercalation " (23). This Rabban Gamliel, who was so favorably disposed toward the Greek language and literature, was, nevertheless, opposed to the Syrian translations of Scriptures, and commanded a Syriac version of the Book of Job to be so disposed of (Sabbath 115 a) that it be not put into public circulation. He was an opponent also of the sacrificial polity, and maintained, as he also did in practice, that the laws concerning the priests were given to all Israel, and every one is his own priest, and must live like one, according to the Law. (Bruil's *Mebo*. p. 51). His controversies with Sadducees, Gentiles, philosophers and unbelievers, as well as his enactments, extending the charity

---

(21) The second R. Gamliel, in all chronological matters, refers to traditions which he received from his grandfather: מקובלני אני מישום מיקובלני מבית אבי אבא, *Rosh Hashanah*, 23 and 25 a.

(22) That the ancient astronomers knew the telescope and its use, has been established by the anonymous author of the book "On Mankind, their Origin and Destiny," London, 1872, pp. 704, 705.

(23) *Rosh Hashanah* ii. 8; *Sabbath* 115; *Erubin* 43; *Sanhedrin* 11 and paral passages.

laws to the Heathens, shows that he was a liberal representative of the Hillel school, who sought peace and conciliation (24). As the cause of all the misfortunes under which his generation suffered, he laid down this: "The increase of false judges increases the number of false witnesses. The increase of calumniators increases confiscation. The increase of insolence diminishes reputation, honor and glory. By the corrupt doings of the nobility before their Father in Heaven, a hypocritical government is raised over them to punish them" (25). It is supposed that Rabban Gamliel lived to 52 A. C., and when he died, the honor of the Law, purity and piety, died with him.

12. The Reign of Agrippa.

The Kingdom of Heaven was restored in Israel, at all events, to the satisfaction of all parties, except the extremely vigorous Shammaites and zealots. The national laws were in full force, the temple was under the superintendency of pious and patriotic highpriests, peace prevailed, and the good old times appeared to return. The young heathens of Doris carried a statue of the Emperor into the synagogue, and erected it there, to the chagrin of the Hebrews. Agrippa was prompt in suppressing the riot. He demanded speedy action of Petronius, the President of Syria, and he at once issued a decree against that Pagan enterprise, commanding peace and order in behalf of the Emperor, which settled the matter. Agrippa paid close attention to the fortifications of Jerusalem, and especially to its northern walls, now separating Bezetha from the city. He was disturbed, however, in this enterprise, by Marcus (or Marsus), the successor of Petronius, who suspected Agrippa's motives, and, perhaps, justly so, as his chances for more liberty were favorable. Agrippa having inherited the building passion of his grandfather, erected palaces and beautified cities. He built also a grand and elegant theater, and a bath with magnificent porticos, in the city of Berytus, and at heavy expense introduced the games and shows in the Greco-Roman style, in Berytus, Caesarea and other Gentile cities. Although this may have been done for political purposes only, as will appear from the sequel, yet it gave offense to the extremists, who would not tolerate any Heathen per-

---

(24) *Sabbath* 30; *Abodah Sarah* 54 and 55, with the captain of Agrippa's host, as it should read, viz.: Silas, see Josephus' Antiq. xix. 7.; *Sanhedrin* 39 and 92; *Guittin* 59 b. 61, and *Yerushalmi ibid.* v.

(25) *Esther Rabba* i.

formance. One Simon (HAZ-ZENUAH?) (26), who was a distinguished teacher, congregated a number of rigorous men about him, and while Agrippa was in Cæsarea, accused him of an unholy and unworthy life. Being informed thereof, the king sent for his opponent, and on his arrival in Cæsarea had him given a seat in the theater next to the monarch, and there asked him, "What is done in this place that is contrary to the law?" This moderation and kindness of the king overcame Simon's wrath and zeal. He begged the king's pardon, and received it. So he disarmed his opponents, except one, Silas, the general of his horse, who had been his faithful boon companion in former days, and would now treat the king as he did formerly the frivolous and fast-living prince. This man would not change his tone and deportment, was exacting and insolent; so that after repeated attempts to change his tone, Agrippa was obliged to keep him in prison (27). His reign was prosperous, his income was no less than 12,000,000 drachmæ a year, although he had remitted all taxes upon houses in Jerusalem.

13. FRUSTRATED COALITION.

Herod, the brother of Agrippa, and by his intercession, King of Chalcis, had married Berenice, Agrippa's daughter. Most of the kings in the neighborhood were of Herodian descent, or related to that family by marriage; and there existed a good understanding among them. A great entertainment given by Agrippa at Tiberias, brought many foreign guests thither, and among them also the kings of Commagena, Emesa, Lesser Armenia, Pontus, and Chalcis, all relatives of Agrippa. They had come, as they maintained, to witness the games, and to enjoy the royal entertainments. But Marcus, who was an enemy of Agrippa, had his suspicions. He unexpectedly appeared at Tiberias, and had those kings advised to leave, which was done, and Agrippa felt offended at this rude interference. Still, it appears, Marcus had good reason to apprehend the intimacy of those six kings, headed by a monarch who was popular among his people, and known in Rome as a shrewd and successful statesman. There were in their rear two other friends of the Hebrews, Izates, King of Adiabene, and a

---

(26) Not Simon ben Hillel, who was certainly dead before his son Gamliel, was made *Nassi*, and, according to the notices in the Talmud of Agrippa's standing with the Pharisees, would not have opposed him so rigorously and public'y.

(27) Josephus' Ant. xix., vi. and vii.

new Hebrew State in Mesapotamia under two warlike brothers at Neerda (Nehardea). A coalition of those eight States, backed, perhaps, by the Parthians, might have proved too strong for Rome.

14. THE ALLIES IN THE EAST.

There were two strong and populous cities on the Euphrates, Neerda (or Nehardea) and Nisibis, inhabited entirely or principally by Hebrews. These were central points for the Hebrews on both sides of the river. They deposited there their half-shekels for the temple in Jerusalem. Two brothers, Asineus and Anileus, weavers by trade, of Nehardea, succeeded in collecting about them a number of armed young men, who gradually became a terror to the province through daring depredations. The Governor of Babylonia, then a Parthian province, led a considerable force of Parthians and Babylonians against those freebooters, attacked them, and met with a very disastrous defeat. Artabanus, King of Parthia, on being informed of the valor of those Hebrews, appointed Asineus Governor of Babylonia. This upstart and his brother proved eminent warriors. Asineus built fortresses and governed Mesapotamia fifteen years with the best success. Mesapotamia was, to all intents and purposes, a Hebrew State (28). North of it was Adiabene. There Izates, the son of King Monobaz, had reigned since 37 A. C. Queen Helen, the wife of Monobaz, had embraced Judaism. When he died his and Helen's son Izates was his successor, and he also embraced Judaism, first secretly, but then openly after he, his sons and his brother, Monobaz, had been circumcised. Queen Helen and her son Monobaz went to Jerusalem, in order to worship in the temple of God. They became afterwards great benefactors of the Hebrews. Izates, a pious and faithful man, occupied the throne of Adiabene, and was one of the mightiest vassals of the King of Parthia. He restored Artiabanus to the Parthian throne (51 A. C.), when his governors conspired against him, and fought with success against the rebels in his own country. He reigned twenty-four years, and after his death was succeeded by his brother Monobaz (29); so that Adiabene also

---

(28) Josephus' Ant xviii., ix.

(29) This Monobaz resided in Jerusalem before he mounted the throne, and became famous among the Hebrews for his munificent charity. *Yerushalmi, Peah* i. 1; *Tosephta ibid.* iv., and BABLI *Baba Bathra* 11 *b.*

could be counted among the Hebrew States (30), which might have been united under the lead of Agrippa, whose statesmanship and patriotism certainly inspired confidence.

15. The Death of Agrippa.

The festivities at Tiberias having been rudely disturbed by Marcus, Agrippa prepared another grand entertainment at Caesarea in honor of Claudius. That city, and that particular time had been selected for the shows and games, because then and there Agrippa's friends had arranged a festival " to make vows for his safety;" "at which festival a great multitude of the principal persons was gotten together, and such as were of dignity throughout his province," Josephus remarks. Then and there, by the interference of Blastus, the king's chamberlain, Agrippa was reconciled to the Tyrians and Sidonians (Acts. xii. 20), who had been supplied with food at the king's expense. It was a popular demonstration, faintly covered by the shows and games in honor of the emperor. On this occasion, when Agrippa appeared in royal attire, the Heathens among his admirers exclaimed: "Thou art a god" (equal to the emperor), and he resented it not. Shortly after he saw the fatal owl, or rather he was poisoned. Violent pain prostrated him. The people lamented, and prayed in sackcloth and ashes, still Agrippa died after five days of violent pains, in the fifty-fourth year of his life (44 A. C.) Superstition expounded this event to please itself; but preceding and subsequent events confirm the suspicion that Agrippa, having grown too mighty for Rome's interests, was poisoned, as was quite usual at the time, when vile Messalina, the infamous wife of Claudius, with her freedmen, shed the best blood of Rome, sold her charms and the offices to the highest bidders, and had in Marcus, the President of Syria, one of her most obedient servants. Perhaps it was an act of revenge on the part of Marcus, who was shortly after removed from office by Agrippa's influence over the emperor. When the king was dead and buried, the Pagan inhabitants of Caesarea and Sebaste gave vent to their hatred and brutality. The soldiers entered the king's palace, stole the statues of his daughters, and deposited them in the brothels, celebrated public feasts to Charon, drank, and conducted themselves in a beastly manner. The wrath of the Pagans had been stifled, and broke forth with renewed fury after the close of this brief period of national revival and glory. A

---

(30) Josephus' Antiq. xx. 2 to 4.

large number of coins is extant bearing the inscription, "Agrippa, the Great King, Friend of Cæsar," around the crowned bust of Agrippa; with a standing Fortuna, bearing the cornucopia, and leaning on an anchor, inscribed with "Cæsarea," or a flying Victoria, bearing a crown with both hands, on the reverse. Coins of Herod of Chalcis, with similar effigies and inscriptions, are also extant (31).

16. THE ACTS OF THE APOSTLES.

Under the reign of Agrippa and the Gamliel Sanhedrin, when civil and religious liberty was again respected, the Disciples of Jesus of Nazareth had ample opportunity for uniting and forming the nucleus of the future society of Christians. The book, however, which contains the first acts of the Apostles, is legendary (32). It appears that the capture of Jesus, and his sudden death, made temporarily an end of the Messianic drama and excitement (33). His disciples fled to Galilee, and, perhaps, remained there to the year 41 A. C. (34). Recovering from their consternation, the impressions which their master had made upon them, and the lessons he had taught them, revived in their minds, together with the boundless veneration then felt for one's teacher and his words. Every word of Jesus which they could recollect became an oracle to them, as the words of Hillel, Shammai, or any other teacher, had become to his respective disciples; and every word was carefully considered and expounded, to be understood or misunderstood. They had, besides, the conviction that Jesus had died for them; that he had voluntarily sacrificed his life to save them and many more, who would have become victims to the Roman sword, if the sedition had not been prevented by

---

(31) *Lenormant's Numismatique de rois grecs*, and the cabinet in the Paris Library.

(32) Among the books of the New Testament, "The Acts of the Apostles" is the least reliable as a historical source (See our Origin of Christianity, Cincinnati, 1868). Its author, supposed to be Luke, contradicts the Gospels in his accounts of Judas Iscariot and the ascension; contradicts Paul's Epistles in the life of that Apostle; contradicts the Pentateuch in his Stephen speech; and contradicts Josephus in many points. The book is doctrinal and harmonizing in its tendency, to cover over the differences existing between Peter and Paul, the Jew and Gentile Christians; it was written in the second half of the second century, partly from Church traditions and partly from notes of Paul's travels, marked "we;" and was not finally accepted as canonical until the fifth century.

(33) Tacitus. Annals xv., xliii.

(34) Matthew xxviii. 16; John xxi.

the self-sacrifice of Jesus. These two feelings, combined in men of simplicity, enthusiasm, credulity and many eccentricities, must have wrought up their minds to a state of mourning which is bewildering in itself; of ecstacy and visions, which solves the most difficult problems as satisfactorily to the excitable as the solution is unsatisfactory to reason. The Bible, which was to the Hebrew the book in which all and everything must be contained, was consulted in order to discover therein the words of Jesus, the incidents of his life and death. Illiterate as those disciples were, and in that peculiar state of mind, they naturally found in the Bible what they did seek; especially as they did not distinguish between facts and tropes, and where incidents did not exist they were easily developed by amplification and personification, or existing ones shaped " to fulfill Scriptures." The disciples of Jesus applied the peculiar methods of expounding Scriptures allegorically, superseding facts or laws by exotic precepts; severing any passage from its context, and imposing a foreign sense on it; making facts of poetical tropes; and above all, changing the political history of the ancient Hebrews into a new semi-divine fabric of government, a fantastic-political application of a form of government, defunct for ten centuries. All of which was illegitimate, unscientific, and contrary to the juridical exegese of that age. Still, by this method, they succeeded in discovering in Scriptures their own ideas and wishes concerning their martyred master, and came to these conclusions:

1. Jesus actually was the Messiah, who did die the death of a malefactor in order to rouse the survivors to repentance of sin, so that by sincere repentance the remission of sins and the restoration of the Kingdom of Heaven might come to pass.

2. Jesus, though slain, is not dead; he has been caught up to Heaven, and will shortly return to occupy the throne of David in the restored Kingdom of Heaven.

3. Those who repent their sins, believe in Jesus, and faithfully wait for his second advent, will be the first and highest in the Kingdom of Heaven.

When Agrippa had mounted the throne of Judea, some of them, styling themselves Apostles and witnesses of the Messiah, could venture to Jerusalem, and eleven of them did come, elected a twelfth man (Matthew), and established a communistic and cenobitic society without a name, in imitation of similar Essene colonies. A number of men and women, said to have been one hundred and twenty lived together in one house and ate at one table, in a state of ecstacy and paroxysm, which they called Holy Ghost, Paraclete or Bath-kol. The twelve apostles were the rulers of the society in its infancy, till afterward stewards and evangelists were appointed to assist them. Those men, preaching repentance, prophesying the speedy restoration of the Kingdom of Heaven and the throne of David, and leading a retired and ascetic life, must have been looked upon as benighted fantasts by the enlightened citizens of Jerusalem, although the simple and ignorant among the citizens and pilgrims must have considered them saints. Anyhow, they were unmolested during the reign of Agrippa, and as long thereafter as they did not interfere with the laws of the land. That one of the Apostles, James, was slain, and Peter was arrested by Agrippa (Acts xii.) is, therefore, not true, because the miracle and the massacre of the soldiers connected with the release of Peter can not be true; the names James and Simon (Peter) are taken from another story, reported by Josephus (Antiq. xx., v. 2); and besides, this is reported as the last persecution of the Apostles (Acts xii. 17), when the first took place under the highpriest Ananias (Acts iv. 6), who was the second highpriest after the death of Agrippa (Josephus *ibid.*). The author of the Acts, in writing that notice, made a mistake of several years; for in the year 62 A. C., James, the brother of Jesus, was slain, as we shall narrate hereafter. Agrippa and the Gamliel Sanhedrin were certainly not guilty of the persecution of any religious sect.

CHAPTER XXIII.

Military Despotism and its Effects (45 to 66 A. C.).

1. THE PROCURATOR AGAIN.

Agrippa left three daughters and one son. Bernice, sixteen years old, was married to Herod of Chalcis; Mariamne, ten years old, had been espoused by Julius Archelaus Epiphanes, and Druscilla, seven years old, by the King of Commagena. The son, Agrippa II., seventeen years old, was then in Rome, where he was being educated under the care of the emperor. Claudius, in a decree, called Agrippa Junior " my friend, whom I have brought up and now have with me, and who is a person of very great piety " (1). The friendship of Claudius for Agrippa I. and his family appears to have been sincere and consistent. Informed of Agrippa's death and the shameless conduct of the soldiers of Cæsarea, he recalled Marcus from Syria, as Agrippa had requested him to do, and sent him in his place Cassius Longinus; commanded that the legions of Cæsarea and Sebaste should be sent to Pontus; and was willing to send to Palestine Agrippa II. as successor to his father, and to reconfirm the existing league by oath. But Claudius was no longer the lord of Rome; his wife and freedmen governed, and they knew how to persuade the weak emperor not to intrust so important a kingdom to so young a man. The policy against the Hebrews was not changed, the soldiers were not sent to Pontus and not punished otherwise; Cuspus Fadus was appointed procurator of Judea, and military despotism again assumed its iron sceptre over unhappy Palestine (45 A. C.). No reason is assigned for the assassination of Silas, the late king's master of horse, in

---

(1) Josephus' Antiq. xx., i. 2.

his prison by order of Herod, King of Chalcis, except personal enmity (*Ibid.* xix., viii. 3).

2. Doings of Fadus.

The Hebrews, for a number of years, had been used again to the blessings of free government and the supremacy of their national laws. These being suddenly replaced by the military rule under a foreign master, dissatisfaction and insurrection were sure to come again. Even at the beginning of this administration, seditions broke out at two different points. Some people at the eastern boundary of Perea, having a quarrel with the Philadelphians about a certain village on the line, seized it and defeated the Philadelphians. As in Cæsarea and Sebaste, so also at this point, Fadus sided with the Pagans against the Hebrews, had three of their leaders arrested, slew one of them, Hannibal, and expatriated the two others, Amram and Eleazar, without calling the Philadelphians to any account. Insurrectionary bodies forming again in various parts of the country, whom Josephus calls robbers, Fadus put them down by force of arms, captured and executed one of their chiefs, Tolomy, although others escaped. Having thus struck terror among the country people, Fadus began his usurpations in Jerusalem. He demanded the sacerdotal vestments of the highpriest and the king's crown to be deposited again under his control in Fort Antonio, which signified not only the assumption of the regal powers, but also exclusive dominion over the temple and its treasury. Longinus, the President of Syria, had come to Jerusalem with a sufficient military escort, to enforce the demands of Fadus. The people, determined not to submit to the usurpation, finally prevailed upon the Roman rulers to grant them permission to send an embassy to Rome to have this matter decided. Hostages were given to the procurator and the embassy departed for Rome.

3. The Theudas Sedition.

The popular indignation was roused by the usurpations of Fadus; the belief in miracles had received a fresh impetus by the Messianic commotion under Jesus of Nazareth and the teachings of his disciples; and so, another prophet could rise with pretensions to work miracles and save the people. His name was Theudas. He congregated a number of credulous admirers at the Jordan River, which he promised to divide for them, and do other great and marvelous things. The number of his admirers was only about four hundred (2), and their pretensions, it appears, were not very dangerous (3). Still Fadus embraced this opportunity, sent a troop of horsemen to the Jordan, slew and captured many of the deluded visionaries, and among the latter, also Theudas, who was beheaded, and his head exhibited in Jerusalem. The second Messianic drama ended as did the first, ten years before.

4. HEROD OF CHALCIS, CHIEF RULER OF THE TEMPLE.

The embassy of the Hebrews was successful in Rome. Agrippa interceded with Claudius in behalf of his people; an imperial decree was issued addressed to the "magistrates, senate (4) and people, and the whole nation of the Jews," in which the emperor said: "I would have every one worship God according to the laws of his own country," and granted the request of the Hebrews, as had been done ten years before by Vitellius. Herod, the King of Chalcis, was appointed chief ruler of the temple, and after his death Agrippa II. exercised that authority. Fadus was recalled and Tiberius Alexander succeeded him. Herod began the exercise of his authority by appointing highpriest Joseph, the son of Camus or Camydus (46 A. C.) to supersede the last highpriest appointed by Agrippa. However, the son of Camus was not long retained in office; Herod appointed as his successor, Ananias, the son of Nebedus (5).

5. ADMINISTRATION OF TIBERIUS ALEXANDER.

The successor of Fadus was Tiberius Alexander, the son of the Alabarch of Alexandria, who had embraced Paganism and advanced to the highest positions in the empire. He began his administration with the capture and crucifixion of James and Simon, sons of Juda, of Galilee. But then Palestine was visited by a great famine, and the land was as quiet as a graveyard. It was during this distressing famine that Queen Helen, of Adiabene, who resided in her own palace in Acra, as well as her sons, King Izates, and his

---

(2) Acts of the Apostles v. 36.
(3) Josephus' Antiq. xx., v. 1.
(4) Hence the Sanhedrin had not been dissolved again.
(5) 47 A. C. Josephus *Ibid.* xx., v. 2, under whom the first prosecution of the Apostles took place.

brother, Monobaz, distinguished themselves as the benefactors of the poor. She imported large quantities of corn and dried figs from Alexandria and Cyprus which were distributed among the needy. King Izates sent large sums of money to Jerusalem for the poor, and his brother distributed all he had (6).

6. CONFLICT OF THE APOSTLES WITH THE AUTHORITIES.

The conflict of the disciples of Jesus of Nazareth with the authorities at Jerusalem took place after the Theudas sedition (7) and when Ananias was highpriest (8), hence in the year 47 A. C. The massacre following the Theudas commotion must have caused those authorities to watch carefully all pretended prophets and workers of miracles, whose enterprise endangered the lives of credulous multitudes. This was certainly also to the disadvantage of the Apostles, who pretended to work miracles, and appealed to those very masses whose credulity and excitability were most to be apprehended. Those Apostles practiced thaumaturgy and necromancy. They cured the sick, drove out evil spirits in the name of Jesus, as others did in the name of King Solomon (9), and healed wounds and sores by whispering over them magic spells (10). All this was contrary to the Law of Moses (11), although in time of peace and order, it was not strictly enforced, so that Essenes and other thaumaturgists were looked upon as harmless men. The Apostles, on their part, were obliged to procure the means of subsistence for a whole congregation, and the year 47 A. C. was one of distressing famine. They did no kind of work, and were obliged to exercise their practice of thaumaturgy and necromancy for a living, as other Hebrews did in Rome and elsewhere. Therefore, and not on account of preaching any doctrine, Peter and John were arrested and placed before a council of priests. The judges treated the prisoners very leniently. They merely warned them not to excite the people and not to practice thaumaturgy and necromancy (Acts iv.), and then dismissed them.

---

(3) Josephus' Antiq. **xx.**, ii. 5; YERUSHALMI *Peah* i. 1, and parallel passages.
(7) Acts v. 36.
(8) *Ibid.* iv. 6.
(9) Josephus' Antiq. viii., ii. 5 · Wars vii., vi. 3.
(10) לחש של רמיכה See the story of the Apostle James and the nephew of Rabbi Ishmael, *Abodah Sarah*, 27 b.
(11) Deut. xviii. 9-14.

But the Apostles did not desist from the forbidden work, and all of them were arrested. This time it was Rabban Gamliel who defended them before their judges (Acts v. 34), and they were dismissed with the most lenient punishment that could be inflicted for contempt of law after a forewarning; they received stripes and another warning to stop those practices (Acts v.). The Apostles, however, looked upon that humiliation as a sacrifice to their cause, and not only continued glorifying their martyred master and proclaiming loudly their new doctrine, but also practicing thaumaturgy and necromancy. They addressed themselves mostly to foreign Hebrews sojourning in Jerusalem (Acts ii. 9; vi. 9), who were more inclined to believe in a coming Messiah than were the Hebrews of Palestine. They continued their work in spite of all forewarnings, until it led to a riot, in which one of the evangelists or stewards of the congregation, whose name is said to have been Stephen, lost his life (12). This man's blood innocently shed, it is maintained, became the cause of Paul's conversion, to which we refer in another paragraph of this chapter. It stopped the work of the Apostles in Jerusalem, and broke up the communistic society; although many of them remained in Jerusalem and in close communication (Acts xii. 11). The Apostles and evangelists, however, began their work outside of the city, and with more success, especially at Caesarea, Joppe, Sebaste, Damascus and Antioch. "They spake with tongues and prophesied," not only the Apostles, but also all baptized by them, which was a sign of having received the Holy Ghost. This is explained by Paul (13) to have been so; the proselytes claimed or were persuaded to believe they possessed "gifts of grace" by their conversion, superior faith, wisdom or eloquence, the gift of prophecy, the power to work miracles, to heal the sick, to drive out evil spirits, to speak diverse tongues or to expound them. This speaking with tongues or diverse tongues was a peculiar superstition. The medium, supposed to be under the influence of the

---

(12) The historical nucleus of Acts vi. and vii. can not possibly be more than a vulgar row, as the numerous mistakes in those chapters show, and as it is a matter of impossibility that the highest authorities of a civilized country should conduct themselves in the manner described there. Besides, the name Stephen throws suspicion on the whole story; for, like Simon and James, it is taken from a narrative of Josephus (Antiq. xx., v. 4), that name occurs nowhere else in Hebrew records: and from a rabbinical legend referring to the conversion story of Paul, as does also this story. See our Origin of Christianity, Chap. viii.

(13) Corinthians xii.

Holy Ghost in a state of violent ecstasy, did not speak intelligible words to his audience; he ejaculated inarticulate groans or shrieks, accompanied by wild gesticulations, and then either he or another of the company expounded the supposed revelation. Paul opposed this superstition among his proselytes in Corinth. It is not difficult to see that pretensions of this kind could find credence among the illiterate only, and how dangerous such practices are to that class. Reason and intelligence are set at naught, imagination and self-delusion are wrought up to an uncontrollable point, to believe or even see anything almost in the realm of impossibilities. And yet, if Paul is to be trusted, the Apostles and Evangelists were engaged in giving such seances, and made use of these pretensions and practices to convert people to their own belief; only that the Holy Ghost could not be brought upon the proselytes except by one of the Apostles themselves, and this alleged fact laid the foundation to a new hierarchy. Nascent Christianity was a small sect, and would have gone under with all the other sects in the catastrophe, if it had not been for one young man, known to us under the assumed name of Paul, "the small one," who seized upon this commotion and turned it into an entirely different channel. But we can not review his work here. We must first narrate the development of facts in his age.

7. Agrippa II., King of Chalcis.

In the eighth year of Claudius, hence toward the close of 48 A. C., Herod of Chalcis died. Although he left three sons, Claudius gave that kingdom to Agrippa II., who remained in Rome and had that little country governed by others. Four years later, Claudius gave Chalcis to the oldest son of Herod, Aristobul, and appointed Agrippa king of the tetrarchy of Philip, together with Batanea, Trachonitis and Abila. He was also the chief ruler of the temple. The four original provinces of Palestine, Judea, Galilee, Samaria and Perea, remained an imperial province, and Cumanus was sent there as procurator (48 A. C.).

8. Crushing Slaughter on Passover.

To maintain the peace was the first object of the Roman procurators, only they did not know how to do it among an intelligent but dissatisfied people. They attempted it by the usurpation of power and the application of brute force, which made the evil worse with every passing day. Cumanus held the same erroneous views, which led to the following horrible catastrophies. A vast number of pilgrims assembled in Jerusalem to celebrate the Passover (48 A. C.). Cumanus was frightened by the immense concourse of people, and apprehended mischief. He placed a regiment on guard duty in and upon the temple cloisters, which innovation must have chagrined the pilgrims. Still everything passed off peaceably for three days. On the fourth day, however, one of the soldiers outraged common decency by making an indecent exposure of his body to the multitude in the temple court. This enraged the worshipers, who construed it as an affrontery offered to God more than the Hebrews, and loudly maintained that Cumanus had instructed his soldiers to insult the community. Cumanus, instead of punishing the soldier and appeasing the people, sent his whole garrison up to Fort Antonio, and exposed the lives of tens of thousands to the hostile arms. Before an attack had been actually made upon the people, the multitude fled, panic stricken. The temple gates were narrow, the crowd large, with the Roman arms glittering behind it, thus one of those horrible catastrophies ensued which has so often repeated itself among horrified masses. The multitude, crazed and unmanageable, crowded, thronged and trampled one another under foot in a wild stampede, which cost the lives of twenty thousand innocent men, women and children, and threw the city into a state of indescribable sadness and mourning. This, perhaps, better than any other event, tells the cause why Jesus of Nazareth was arrested before the feast, and why his disciples, together with all innovators and impostors, were so much dreaded by the authorities in Jerusalem. The lives of tens of thousands depended on the maintenance of peace, and those eccentric saviors, prophets, Messiahs, thaumaturgists naturally created excitement, uproar and imprudent sedition, although their motives may have been religious and patriotic.

9. THE TRUE STEPHEN STORY.

As though the cup of woe had not been filled to the brim, Cumanus added another outrage to the first. A man was robbed near Jerusalem. His name was Stephen, and he was a servant of Cæsar, who, perhaps, carried the booty to a place of safety. That this must have been done by the pilgrims who denounced the soldier's indecency in the temple, was the supposition of Cumanus. Instead of arresting the guilty parties, he sent his soldiers to the neighboring

villages to plunder them and to arrest their principal men.
The soldiers did terrible execution; they took or destroyed
all they could find, and one of them seized a scroll of the
Law and, with imprecations and scurrilities, tore it in
pieces before the horrified villagers. This sacrilege was
worse than the first in the estimation of the people, and
Cumanus was obliged to have that soldier beheaded, in
order not to appear implicated in those outrages.

10. THE QUARREL WITH THE SAMARITANS, 51 TO 53 A. C.

The decline of power in Jerusalem always encouraged
the enemies abroad to acts of violence. This time the
Samaritans were the aggressors. Pilgrims from Galilee
were attacked at Ginea, a Samaritan village, and many
of them killed. In vain did the Galileans demand justice of Cumanus; the Samaritans had bribed him, and he
was on their side. The injured men, however, resolved
upon taking the matter into their own hands and effected a
military organization under the lead of Eleazar ben Dineus,
a guerrilla chief of that neighborhood; invaded Samaria,
plundered and burned several villages. Cumanus marched
against them with an adequate force. In the first conflict
many of the Galileans fell and others were captured. But
this might have served as a mere signal to a general insurrection, which the authorities in Jerusalem dreaded. They
sent some of their most eminent men to the Galileans to
beg for peace in behalf of the nation and the temple, whose
existence was threatened by the Romans. They succeeded;
the Galileans laid down their arms. It appears that Cumanus also, perhaps by bribes, was persuaded to drop the
matter at that point. This again displeased the Samaritans. They went to Tyre, where they met Quadratus, now
President of Syria, and accused Cumanus of bribery and
neglect of duty, and the Hebrews of defying the authority
of Rome. Quadratus adjourned the case until he came to
Samaria, and there, without giving a hearing to the Galileans, he sentenced their captives in the hands of Cumanus
to be crucified. Next he went to Lydda and gave this matter a second hearing. On the testimony of the Samaritans
against Dortus, and four more principal men of the Hebrews, that they had urged their people to rebellion against
Rome, he condemned them to death; sent in chains to
Rome, Ananias, the highpriest (14), and Annas, the cap-

---

(14) Ananias, the highpriest, is called in the Mishnah (*Parah*)
הגמאל המצרי, who also sacrificed a red heifer, and a few years later

tain of the temple, and ordered the representatives of both the Hebrews and Samaritans, together with Cumanus and Celer, the tribune, to appear before the emperor for a final settlement of their differences. Next he went to Jerusalem with the intention of continuing his bloody work. But there he found the multitude peaceably assembled to worship God on one of the high feasts.

11. The Emperor's Decision.

There was an abominable regime at the imperial court, although Messalina had been publicly executed. Claudius had married a second wife, Agrippina, the mother of Nero. This woman and the freedmen ruled the emperor, and they were enemies of the Hebrews, and friends of Cumanus and the Samaritans. Still, Agrippa II., yet in Rome, succeeded in winning the good will of Agrippina, so that she persuaded the emperor to give a hearing to the contesting parties. Claudius decided the controversy in favor of the Hebrews. The Samaritan representatives were slain, Cumanus was banished, and Celer, the tribune, was sent back to Jerusalem to be dragged through the city and then to be slain (53 A. C.). Still the priests remained captives in Rome for several years after.

12. Felix, Procurator (53 a. c.).

For the time being, the Hebrews were relieved and avenged, but it was only for a short time. Claudius, it appears, wished to be just to the Hebrews, but his courtiers, who hated and feared them, always prevented him from doing the right thing. Now, certainly, was the proper time to give to Palestine its legitimate king, Agrippa II., who was the only man to restore order and law in that country. But instead of that, he sent there Felix, the brother of Pallas, and gave to Agrippa the northern kingdom. However, Claudius was no more mistaken in the man he sent to Judea than was the highpriest, Jonathan (15), the immediate successor of Ananius, who recommended Felix for the procuratorship, although Jonathan's candor and patriotism were subject to no doubt. The procuratorship of Felix was a fresh source of calamity to the Hebrew.

---

another was sacrificed by Ishmael b. Fabi, which shows how generally the laws of Levitical cleanness must have been observed, if they needed the ashes of three red heifers in less than two decades.

(15) Josephus' Antiq. xx., viii. 5.

13. THE AGRIPPA FAMILY (54 A. C.).

Claudius also, and shortly after his son, Britannicus, like Agrippa I., were cut off by poison. His wife, Agrippina, in order to secure the throne of the Cæsars to her son (Domitian), the horrible Nero, disposed of her husband, as afterward her son disposed of her and his own wife, Octavia, and Nero was proclaimed emperor by the soldiery of Rome (54 A. C.). In the first year of his reign, he appointed Aristobulus, King of Chalcis, Governor of Lesser Armenia, and added to the kingdom of Agrippa II. portions of Galilee and Perea, including Tiberias and Terichea west of the lake, Julias, Gamala, and thirteen other places east of the lake. The daughters of Agrippa I. also occupied high positions. Mariamne deserted her first husband and married Demetrius, the alabarch of the Hebrews of Alexandria. Berenice, after the death of her husband, Herod of Chalcis, in order to escape scandalous reports, married Polemo, King of Cilicia, who had embraced Judaism, but she afterward left him and he left her religion. Drusilla was married to Azizus, King of Emesa. But either shortly before or after the death of her husband, she was persuaded by Simon, the Cyrian magician, to marry Felix, the Procurator, who was a Heathen, and this was considered a transgression of the laws of her forefathers (16).

14. INTERNAL DISSOLUTION OF THE COMMONWEALTH.

However prosperous the aristocratic families and the populous cities looked, the commonwealth was fatally poisoned by the military despotism of the foreign master. Ever since the Romans had imposed their iron scepter upon Palestine, the Hebrew democrats protested and opposed it: first, as patriots, then as zealots; first, as guerrillas, then as robbers, and in alliance with assassins. Three generations of patriots had been slain by Roman executioners, viz.: Ezekias, his son Judah, of Galilee, and his sons, James and Simon, and this is the index to the fate of the party. Those men fought lion-like on the battlefield; when defeated, they retired to their natural fortresses in the clefts and caverns of the mountains or inaccessible retreats in the wilderness, and, hard pressed there for sustenance, they were forced to live on booty taken from foes or friends, as necessity compelled them. The hatred against Rome and the habits of the guerrilla having been inherited from sire to son, a large

---

(16) *Ibid.* xx., vii. 2.

portion of the fighting population, branded as robbers and
outlaws, defied the laws and undermined the groundwork
of society. The profound religious feelings of the Hebrews
and firm trust in Providence, tried by reverses, scorned by
heathens, and offended by impious tools of the foreign government, deteriorated into fanciful superstitions and blind
fanaticism. In the land of law and juridical speculations
there rose all sorts of theopathic and theo-romantic necromancers, thaumaturgists, prophets, Messiahs, saviors and
redeemers of all kinds, and brought anarchy and dissolution into the religious feelings of the people. The rabbis
of Beth Hillel and Beth Shammai quibbled and quarreled
over unimportant minor topics. The whole fabric of society
was in a state of dissolution. As the corruption and degeneration grew in Rome, despotism and cruelty, with their
horrors and dissolving efficacy, progressed in Palestine.
The speedy restoration of the Hebrew government and the
national laws was the only means to arrest the onward
march of dissolution; but instead of that, Felix was sent
to Judea to make the evil incurably worse.

15. Treachery, Crucifixion and Assassination.

Felix began his career (54 A. C.) in Palestine with a campaign against the robbers, captured many of them and had
them crucified. Like all other despots, he believed ideas
could be crucified or crushed by a reign of terror. He
promised amnesty to the Galilean chief, Eleazar b. Dana,
who capitulated, but Felix, instead of keeping his promise,
sent him in chains to Rome. Still, during the first years
of Nero, the country was quiet. The highpriest, Jonathan,
whose influence upon the people and the Roman authorities was equally potent, kept both Felix and the dissatisfied
people under control. Felix grew tired of that man of stern
righteousness who had brought him from Rome, and
Agrippa certainly would not remove him from the high
priesthood. As was then fashionable among the Roman
grandees, Felix resorted to assassination. By the wickedness of a citizen, Doras, a number of robbers were hired,
who came to the city with concealed arms and assassinated
the highpriest. No arrests were made, and the last bonds
of society were rent in twain. The procurator in conspiracy with assassins and the highpriest dead—this taught
many a malicious man how to rid himself of his enemies
in the Roman style, and assassinations soon became as

common in the streets of Jerusalem as duels afterward in Christian communities.

16. Another Highpriest and Other Impostors (57 to 60 A. C.).

Agrippa II. now appointed as highpriest Ishmael b. Fabi (Elishah), who was a man of learning and patriotism. Still the assassination of a highpriest was a burning sore in the heart of the nation. A large number of prophets, saviors, redeemers, Messiahs and impostors, under different titles, rose to make an end of misery by miracles and fantastic enterprises. Felix knew of no better remedy against the evil than the sword and the cross. He had all those deluded visionaries slain as fast as they could be caught, which certainly made the evil worse. One of those impostors, an alleged prophet from Egypt, succeeded in congregating a multitude on Mount Olives, where he promised to perform miracles. Felix sent out his soldiers, who slew four hundred and captured two hundred of the duped multitude. The prophet luckily escaped, or else history might have had another crucified savior. All those impostors, however, as well as the robbers, were patriots; only that the latter appealed directly to the sword, and the former did it indirectly through the religious feelings. Therefore, with the commotion of the impostors, the robbers also renewed their activity; stirred up the people to war with the Romans and inflicted dire punishment on those who preferred peace (17).

17. The Sedition of the Highpriests.

The murderous executions by Felix did not restore respect for law and order; it could only foster violence and anarchy, and it did that to so alarming an extent that the city of Jerusalem, and in it the various ex-highpriests, were seized by the destructive current. A feud of the various ex-highpriests, wealthy and mighty men, was a novelty in the holy city. They had each their partisans, armed servants and ruffians who, although not as bloodthirsty as the knights and prelates of medieval christendom or the Guelphs and Ghibellines, insulted and attacked one another in the streets of Jerusalem, and there was no government to stop them. Some of those parties went so far in their

---

(17) Josephus' Ant. xx., viii. 6.

lawlessness as to send their ruffians into the country to take the tithes out of the hands of the husbandmen, so that the peaceable priests got nothing and were reduced to starvation (18).

18. Disfranchisement in Cæsarea.

Under such conditions it is not surprising that the Heathens again raised their heads and ventilated their hatred against the Hebrews. This time it was in Cæsarea, where the Syrians and Hebrews collided. The Hebrews claimed something in preference to the Syrians, Josephus does not tell what, and this started a feud among the parties. The ringleaders on both sides were punished and the quarrel stopped. But soon after the wealthy Hebrews started the same quarrel, which led to fights. Felix embraced the favorable opportunity to exercise his authority. He sent his soldiers, who slew some, captured others, and plundered the houses of the rich, which was the main object in quelling disturbances. Shortly after that, Felix was recalled to Rome, and both Hebrews and Syrians followed him to lay their grievances before the emperor. In Rome, however, money and friends could accomplish anything, justice, nothing. Pallas protected his brother, Felix, and he escaped unpunished. Money purchased Nero's tutor, Burrhus, who obtained a decree from Nero to disfranchise the Hebrews of Cæsarea, the city built by Herod and beautified by Agrippa with the money of the Hebrews. This, when a few years after it became known in Cæsarea, exasperated the Hebrew citizens, and they became so much more seditious till, at last, they became the very first cause of the outbreak of the war.

19. Calamities of the Babylonian Hebrews.

Worse than all this was the calamity of the Babylonian Hebrews. Asineus and Anileus, though feared as warriors, soon lost the confidence of the Hebrews, because they led profligate lives, and were hated by the Babylonians, whom they oppressed. Anileus had married a Pagan woman, against which the Hebrews loudly remonstrated. Fearing the judgment of Asineus, the woman poisoned him, and Anileus governed the province alone. He made marauding

---

(18) Josephus' *Ibid.* xx., viii. 8, and Talmud *Pesachim*, 57 *a*. Ishmael b. Fabi himself is described there as a good man, but his family was involved in the same feuds and acts of violence with the others.

expeditions into the adjoining provinces of Mithridates, the son-in-law of King Artabanus, who came with an army to chastise him. This army was defeated and Mithridates captured. He was spared and sent back to the king; but his wife, ashamed of his defeat, pressed him hard to renew the fight, and he did so. This time Mithridates was victorious, and Anileus retreated to Nehardea. A band of marauders, gathered about him, did great damage to the Babylonians, until finally, Anileus and his men fell into their hands and were slain. Now the Babylonians turned their arms against the Hebrews in the country, who were obliged to seek protection in Seleucia. They lived there in peace for five years, but then, in the sixth year, the Greeks and Syrians of the city combined against them and slew about fifty thousand of them; those who escaped sought shelter in the city of Ctesiphon, but not being sufficiently protected there they went to the cities of Nisibis and Nehardea. So it appears that the Hebrews of all Mesopotamia were driven to those two large, strong cities. The chief authority of Nisibis was the Tana, R. Judah b. Bethyra, who resided there till he died, some years after the fall of Jerusalem (19).

20. Administration of Festus (61 a. c.).

Porcius Festus was sent to Judea as the successor of Felix. He found the country exposed to bands of guerrillas and robbers, and the city infested with assassins. Especially terrible were the sicarians, men armed with short, bent swords, somewhat like sickles, who did terrible execution. The patriotic excitement of those zealots ran very high. Whoever was loyal to the Romans was considered an enemy and treated accordingly. Villages were burnt and plundered, men were driven from their homes and their land was sold or otherwise disposed of. Another pretending savior was at work, and promised freedom and deliverance to his followers (20), and the procurator, like his predecessors, could only wield his authority by military executioners, by slaughter and confiscation, which could but increase the evil. Nothing would convince the Roman authorities that the Hebrews could be governed by their own laws and institutions alone, and the military despot-

---

(19) Josephus' Antiq. xviii., ix; Talmud Pesachim 3 and 109; Sanhedrin 32; John b. Bag-Bag was his cotemporary (Kiddushin 10).
(20) Josephus' Antiq. xx., viii. 10.

ism displacing them gradually and surely, produced the entire demoralization and dissolution of society.

21. THE QUARREL OVER AGRIPPA'S DINING ROOM.

Agrippa II., in possession of the royal palaces in Jerusalem, spent much of his time there, although he had two capitals, viz.: Tiberias and Cæsarea Philippi. The old Asmonean palace was so situated on the Temple Mount that it afforded a prospect of the city and the temple. Agrippa built there a dining-room, from which he could look into the inner court of the temple. This was considered unlawful, and the rulers of the temple built an addition upon the western wall of the inner court to intercept the prospect from that dining-room, and of the western cloisters of the outer court, where the Romans kept guards during the festivals. Agrippa was displeased, and Festus demanded of those rulers to take down the wall. A deputation was sent to Rome consisting of twelve men, headed by the highpriest, Ishmael b. Fabi, and Helkias, the treasurer of the temple. Poppea, the wife of Nero, who, notwithstanding her wickedness, "was a religious woman," embraced the cause of the embassadors, and Nero decided in favor of the new wall. Ten of the embassadors were sent back to Jerusalem; Ishmael and Helkias were held as hostages by Poppea. The particular remark of Josephus, that Poppea was a religious woman, conveys the information that, like many more Roman women of high rank, she admired Judaism. However, the personal beauty of that highpriest is highly lauded in the Hebrew legend of the Ten Martyrs.

22. ISHMAEL'S DOCTRINE OF ATONEMENT.

This Ishmael b. Fabi or Elisha, who must not be mistaken for Rabbi Ishmael b. Elisha, of the second century A. C., taught in Rome the doctrine of atonement without the medium of sacrifice, priesthood, redeemer, mediator, or ransom of any kind, contrary not only to the teachings of Paul, but also to the theories then generally accepted. Based upon Scriptural passages, he advanced four degrees of atonement, always connected with sincere repentance of misdeeds. He maintained (21) that there were four degrees of sin. If one neglects the performance of a duty commanded in the Law, and then sincerely repents his negli-

---

(21) MECHILTA, *Bachodesh* vii., and parallel passages in both Talmuds.

gence, his sin is forgiven. If one violates a prohibitory law of Scriptures, and then sincerely repents, it will ward off the punishment, and the Day of Atonement will bring him remission of sins. If one presumptuously transgresses a law connected with the Scriptural threat of death or " to be cut off," and then sincerely repents his misdeed, repentance and the Day of Atonement will ward off the punishment, but afflictions only will bring him remission of sins. If one profanes the name of Heaven and then sincerely repents this most grievous sin; repentance, Day of Atonement, and afflictions will only ward off the punishment, and only his death in repentance can bring him atonement. This doctrine of atonement, after the destruction of the altar and the spread of Christianity, became so important to the teachers that the principal rabbi of Rome, Matthia b. Harash, went all the way to Palestine (to Lydda) in order to ascertain of the then Associate Nassi, R. Eleazar b. Azariah, whether this doctrine had been accepted, and he was told it was (22). The pretensions of this highpriest, made by or for him, are the same as those made by or for Paul. The latter maintained that God revealed to him "His Son;" and Ishmael conversed with "Suriel, the Prince of the Countenance" (23), which is the same idea. Paul alleged that he was caught up to the third Heaven, or paradise, and there heard unspeakable words (24); Ishmael saw AKATHRIEL JAH JEHOVAH ZEBAOTH, "the crown and full glory of the Lord of Hosts," upon a high and exalted throne in the *sanctum sanctorum*, and the vision encouraged him to pray. He prayed that God's mercy for His children might predominate over all His other attributes, and the vision nodded assent, viz.: That this is the nature of the Deity, and such should be man's prayer (25). Strange is the remarkable coincidence that this highpriest, being a hostage, was slain in Rome (26) at the outbreak of the rebellion in Palestine, and was counted second among the " Ten Martyrs " (27), the one who went up to Heaven alive

---

(22) Maimonides' MISHNAH THORAH, *Teshubah* i. 4.
(23) *Berachoth* 51 a.
(24) II. Corinthians xii. 1, etc.
(25) *Berach t'h* 7, a.
(26) קרקפלי של ר' ישמעאל כונח ברומי (Chulin 123 a), is the correct reading according to Aruch, "Ishmael's skull lays in Rome." The Romans used skulls for purposes of necromancy, and many were carried along by the legions on the march.
(27) The first is the NASSI, Simon b. Gamliel, and Simon and Peter are again synonymous, and Peter is the second martyr in Rome of the Christian legend also.

to hear the decree of the Almighty; and Paul, according to post-Evangelical legends, also died a martyr in Rome. It is difficult to say which is the original and which the copy. Sure it is that those two men preached the opposite forms of the doctrines of divine mercy, atonement and redemption, as held since their days in Christianity and Judaism.

23. Death of James and His Companions.

While the embassadors noticed above were in Rome, Festus, the Procurator, died, and Nero appointed Albinus as his successor. Three months elapsed between the death of Festus and the arrival of Albinus in Palestine, during which time the highpriest was Governor of Judea. Agrippa II., in consequence of the opposition offered to him by the Pharisean authorities of the temple, appointed first the Boethite, Joseph Cabi, son of Simon Boethus, and after a few days, the Sadducean highpriest, Ananus, son of Ananus. This Ananus, himself highpriest, had five sons successively in that responsible office. This new highpriest, Ananus, was very insolent, of a bold temper. and, like all other Sadducees, "very rigid in judging offenders above all the rest of the Jews" (28). When Festus was dead and before Albinus arrived, Ananus convoked a criminal court or Minor Sanhedrin at Lydda (29), accused James, the brother of Jesus, and some of his companions, of "leading astray to idolatry" (Deut. xiii. 7), to which effect the doctrines of Paul were understood. The accusation, it appears from the Talmud, was produced by spies in an insidious manner. James and his companions were found guilty, condemned and put to death. This execution roused the indignation of the law-abiding citizens. Hitherto the Roman procurators only had slaughtered so-called impostors, to the chagrin of the Hebrews; but now a highpriest and a *quasi* Sanhedrin committing the same crime, the laws of the land were outraged. They sent a deputation to Agrippa II. demanding him to stop the highpriest in his work of bloodshed, and when Albinus came into the country, prevailed with him to threaten punishment to Ananus for his unlawful convocation of a Sanhedrin, and Agrippa was obliged to remove Ananus from his office (30) and appoint as his successor Jesus, son of Damneus.

(28) Josephus' Antiq. xx., ix. 1.
(29) *Yerushalmi* Yebamoth xvi. and Sanhedrin vii. 16, and parallel passages.
(30) This is the fact which misled the author of the Acts of the Apostles to report James slain by Agrippa I.

24. Administration of Albinus (62 and 63 a. c.).

Albinus began his administration, like his predecessors, with a chase after the so-called robbers and sicarians, whose number and violence had not decreased. He slaughtered many and imprisoned many more, without changing the *statu quo*. Their number increased as the resolution of resistance against Rome grew in the popular mind. Those sicarii knew how to take advantage of the situation. The ex-highpriest, Ananus, one of those who robbed no less than the robbers did, bribed both the procurator and the highpriest, and was second in power to none in Jerusalem. His son, Eleazar, was the principal scribe of the temple. The sicarii knew this, and on the evening before the feast, captured him in the heart of the city, took him to one of their retreats, and sent word to Ananus that they would exchange Eleazar for ten of their imprisoned men. Ananus urged Albinus to accept the proposal, and Eleazar was exchanged. The consequences were that every now and then servants and friends of Ananus, or other men of influence, were captured by the sicarii to release their prisoners by exchange, till the city and the country alike were terrorized by them. Money purchased anything of Albinus; so the chief priests bribed him to allow them to go on with their schemes of violence and robbery; and the heads of robber bands paid their shares to go on with their business undisturbed. Heavy taxes were imposed on the country and rigorously collected. Wealthy men were robbed unless they purchased immunity of this procurator. So while on the one side all bonds of society were weakened, the number of the dissatisfied increased daily, and a tremendous rebellion was rapidly preparing. Albinus enriched himself and dragged the country to the abyss of destruction. Before he left his post he took out of the prisons all his victims, killed those who could not pay and set those free who ransomed their lives, irrespective of the crimes committed.

25. Unpopularity of Agrippa II.

No less unfortunate, at that particular time, was the growing unpopularity of Agrippa II. He squandered in foreign cities his people's money and his country's treasures of art. He, like his predecessors, was plagued with the building mania. He enlarged Cæsarea Philippi, and called it Neronias in honor of Nero. He built a theater in Berytus and amused the people there with shows, at heavy expense, distributed corn and oil in foreign towns, and transferred thither the ornaments which belonged to his country. Since his quarrel with Ishmael b. Fabi about the dining-room, he had appointed three unworthy highpriests, and now bribed by a woman, Martha, a daughter of Boethus, he made her husband, Joshua (Jesus) b. Gamala, highpriest. He was a worthy man, yet the other chief priests were opposed to him. This led to brawls and riots in the city, of which also kinsmen of Agrippa took advantage. A state of anarchy prevailed among the men in power; the aristocracy had become riotous. Still Joshua b. Gamala sustained himself in the highpriestship for some time. Agrippa added to all this an innovation which was unpopular with the priests and conservative laymen. With the aid of a special Sanhedrin, he bestowed upon the Levites, who were the singers in the temple, the right to wear the same white linen garments that the priests wore. Nothing was more offensive to the Hebrews than innovations in the temple. It appears, however, that a labor question was the principal cause of Agrippa's unpopularity. Eighteen thousand workmen had been engaged to finish the buildings about the temple, and their work was completed this year (64 A. C.). It was the desire of the workmen's friends to take down and rebuild the immense but very old structure called the porch of Solomon, with its cloisters, built of white, square stones, twenty-one cubits square, and resting upon solid masonry work clear down to the valley. The main object was to give employment to those eighteen thousand artisans; to which Agrippa refused to give his consent. The artisans were partly engaged in paving the city with white stone; but this gave them scanty employment, and the dissatisfaction was general among them. Agrippa also removed the highpriest, most likely on account of his siding with the laborers, and appointed as his successor, Matthias, son of Theophilus, who was the fourth in two years.

26. Paul of Tarsus.

Under these circumstances, the growing demoralization and despotism among the Heathens and the rapid advance of political dissolution among the Hebrews, Paul laid the foundation to Gentile Christianity, *i. e.*, he remodeled the Messiahism of the Apostles, afterward called Jewish Christianity, to be made acceptable first to foreign Hebrews, and then also to the Gentiles, whose Paganism had been demolished by advancing Judaism. Paul traveled and taught

under the fictitious name of " The Little Man." His proper
name has not reached posterity. The author of " The
Acts," by changing P into S, gave him the name of Saul.
The rabbis called him ACHER, " another," or properly " an
anonymous man " (31) or Elisha b. Abujah, which is also
fictitious and expressive of Paul's theology (32). He was
born in Jerusalem (28 or 29 A. C. ?), of wealthy parents of
the tribe of Benjamin (Romans xi. 1), who afterward emigrated to Tarsus, in Cilicia, where his father became a Roman citizen (33). After he had received his first education,
also in Greek, he came to Jerusalem to sit at the feet of
Gamliel, as he says, which means to study the national
literature and traditions. In the academy at Jerusalem he
was noted as paying more attention to Greek poetry and in-
fidel books than to his studies (34); and disputing the
supernaturalism of Gamliel in regard to the future or post-
Messianic state of the world (35). Like many other
young men of his days, he studied little, believed less, and
was inclined to innovations. In consequence of his aversion to supernaturalism he was opposed also to the Messiahism of the Apostles, and says he persecuted them and
their disciples; although he overdid his own wickedness
before the Gentiles in order to prove the magnitude of his
conversion. This gave rise to the overwrought stories in
the Acts. It must always be borne in mind that the Gospels and the Acts of the Apostles were written from different traditions before different authors, but chiefly from the
epistles and traveling notes of Paul; and many an acci-
dental expression of his has been modeled by those writers
into an incident of his life or in the life of Jesus and his
disciples (36).

27.   TURNING POINT IN PAUL'S LIFE.

The transition from the orthodox Pharisean school to
Gentile Christianity was started by the wrongs and woes

(31) The identity of PAUL and ACHER has been established in our
book, " The Origin of Christianity," p. 311, etc.
(32) אל-ישע בן אבו-יה signifies " The godly savior, son of the
Father—God."
(33) YERUSHALMI HAGIGAH ii. 1; RABBAH to *Ruth* v.; YALKUT
Shimoni 974.
(34) *Hayigah* 15 *b*: זמר יוני לא פסק מפומיה * * * ביטעה שהיה
עומר מבית המדרש הרבה ספרי טועין נושרין מחיקו
(35) לנלג עליו אותו התלמיד *Sabbath* 30 *b*, and elsewhere.
(36) See *Die Entstehung der vier Evangelien und der Christus des
Apostels Paulus*, Berlin, 1876.

of that age. He saw the innocent Stephen stoned, says the author of the Acts; he saw the tongue of the slain Judah Nachtum dragged about by dogs, narrates the Babylonian Talmud; he saw a man on the plain of Genesareth fulfill both commandments, to which Scriptures add the promise of long life, fall down from the tree and meet with instant death, the Jerusalem Talmud reports, and so he was forced to the conclusion, "There is no justice and there is no judge" (לית דין ולית דיין). All those anecdotes convey the same idea: He saw the wrongs and woes of his generation and his people, and no retribution, no redress from on high, and, like many others of his age, he became a skeptic. Minds like Paul's can not remain long in that painful state. They seek an outlet from the labyrinth. When they have knocked in vain on every portal of eternity which the philosophy and theology of the age point out, and none is opened, no answer is given to the momentous question: Why is it? Wherefore is it so? then, like King Saul, under similar circumstances, many resort to superstition. So did some of the best men under the pressure of public calamities, resort to GNOSTICISM, the belief that knowledge can be obtained from high Heaven by other than natural means, by ecstatic meditation, the Paraclete the Holy Ghost, the *Bath-kol;* or by fasting, praying and tarrying on a burial ground, in order to contract a prophesying evil spirit; or by transporting oneself into Paradise in order to learn there the mysteries of existence. This latter state of ecstasy was reached by seclusion and meditation, bathing, fasting and praying, till the nerves were unstrung; and then by sitting flat on the ground with the spine curved and head bowed down between the knees, which excited the circulation of the blood to madness; then the gnostic saw opened before him the small and the large palaces of Heaven, and at last imagined himself transported into Heaven or Paradise, where he saw the angels or even the throne of glory, and heard answers to his questions; to return then to the earth instructed in the mysteries of Heaven and gifted with superior wisdom. The Talmud mentions only four who thus went to Paradise, and one of them was Paul, who tells the same story of himself (37), viz.: that he was caught up to Heaven "in the body or out of the body," and there in Paradise, he heard unspeakable

---

(37) ארבעה נכנסו לפרדס: HAGIGAH, II. *Perek*, in both Talmuds; RABBAH to Canticles; compare to II. Corinthians xii. i., and Haya the Gaon to the first passage.

words. So, through skepticism and gnosticism, Paul arrived at his Christianity. He calls that "God had revealed his Son to him," of which the author of The Acts made a story, of how Jesus appeared to Paul on his way to Damascus, of which Paul himself never speaks. He went through these visions in Arabia, says Paul, as then the land east of Perea, full of wild and secluded spots, was called.

28. THE END AND THE MESSIAH.

In that state of mind, Paul invented nothing new; he combined and remodeled existing schemes and paradoxes to a new fabric of salvation. The miseries and woes of the age appeared to him incurable under the prevailing circumstances, hence the end of that cycle of the earth and its inhabitants must be at hand and might come to pass any day (38). The end is nigh, was his keynote. Before the end and the resurrection of the dead, the Messiah must come. This was believed by those who believed in the coming of a personal Messiah, although the two great epochs of redemption were kept far apart by some. Paul, believing the end and the resurrection nigh, convinced himself that the Messiah must have come. Among all the pretenders to that dignity who had loomed up in those days, he considered Jesus of Nazareth to be the most eminent, and so he became Paul's Messiah, as he was Peter's and the other Apostles', although from entirely different motives. Why was the Messiah slain?

29. THE CORPOREAL RESURRECTION OF JESUS.

Why was the Messiah slain? That he resurrect again and prove thereby that he actually was the Messiah, that the dead resurrect, that the universal resurrection is nigh, and Jesus has arisen to forewarn all of the speedy approach thereof. With Paul the corporeal resurrection of Jesus has its beginning (Corinthians xv. 4 to 9), and on his authority it was accepted in the Gospels. The original Apostles taught merely a spiritual and personal conservation of Jesus, and not his resurrection in the body (39). The idea

---

(38) I. Corinthians i. 7, 8; iv. 5; xv. 19 to 51; x. 11; Titus ii. 13; Philippians i. 6; iii. 20; Ephesians i. 5 to 11; II. Timothy iv. 8; compare to PIRKAI R. ELIEZER, chapter 51, where Rabban Gamliel is named as the originator of that doctrine; also MECHILTA to שׁי אין שׁ׳ תחת and רבי אליה אמ SANHEDRIN 92 a and 97 a, bottom of the page, and R' A' B' D', in Teshubah viii. 8.

(39) This is evident from "Revelations" and all epistles besides

of vicarious atonement, that the blood of Jesus was shed to atone for the sins of the believers, never ripened in Paul's mind, although some of his expressions led to that doctrine, and to statements of that kind in the Gospels. The idea of human sacrifice was anti-Jewish and anti-Scriptural (40). Those who have died with the Messiah, figuratively, and are dead to sin, resurrect with him to eternal life, and thus escape death in the approaching catastrophe, was Paul's doctrine. All who believe his doctrines, and also their deceased relatives, will, at the approaching end, either resurrect in incorruptible bodies or, if still living on earth, their bodies will be so changed. Paul certainly did not preach his resurrection doctrine to Jews, who were not used to so unnatural a belief. He preached it to Pagans, who knew of several such resurrections in their mythologies.

30. The Metathron—Son of God.

In the mind of Paul, another mystic doctrine of Gnosticism was blended with the Messiahism of the Apostles; and this was the *Metathron* or *Syndelphos* speculation. The highest of all angels, who is the prince of this world and prince of the countenance, stands or sits before God, whose name is also in that angel, receives the prayers of man shaped into crowns, to place them on the head of the Almighty, and is permitted to enter the merits of Israel in the book of memorial; this highest angel, whose name is METATHRON, SYNDELPHOS, SURIEL or otherwise, was a man on earth, viz., Enoch or Elijah, and was transported to Heaven. Elijah-Metathron's appearance on earth, they maintained, was promised to precede the great and terrible day of judgment; and Paul added, this Metathron has appeared on earth in the person of Jesus of Nazareth, because the great and terrible day of judgment is nigh; and he has returned to Heaven to be the prince of the world and the mediator for his believers; to conduct the catastrophe on the last day of judgment. But after that his office ends and his dominion ceases, and God will be again all in all. While the Gnostic Hebrews called that Metathron *Syndelphos*, God's confrere, or *Jeshajahu*, God's

---

Paul's, in none of which is the bodily resurrection of Jesus mentioned; and especially from II. Peter i. 16. Peter argues against unbelievers and testifies in favor of the Messiah, but never mentions his resurrection, which he must have done, as being his best point, had he believed in it.

(40) Genesis xxii.; Exodus xxxii. 32, 33.

savior, or *Suriel*, God's first one. Paul, to suit Gentile ears, called him Son of God, with all the above epithets. The theories were precisely the same. Paul's Christology and the Hebrew Kabbalah originated from the same source (41). Paul, like every other Hebrew, believed in one God, and his "Son of God" was a superior angel, commissioned to announce, by his death and resurrection, the speedy approach of the end of this world, the resurrection of the dead, and the day of judgment; to save those who believe from the coming destruction, by their faith and his intercession; and to conduct the last judgment day by the power vested in him by God's appointment (42). It can not be ascertained from Paul's Epistles or the Acts, how long it took him to build up this departure from orthodox Judaism, or at which particular time it was finished. It certainly ripened in him gradually, while at work preaching Gentile Christianity.

31. PAUL EVANGELIZING THE GENTILES.

With these and similar doctrines, Paul went forth to preach Jesus crucified. He had no proofs, no evidence to advance in support of his doctrines and allegations. He had learned them of no one, not even of the Apostles, nor was he appointed by anybody to be an Apostle; it was all revelation, as he called it, addressed simply and exclusively to uninquiring faith, an absurdity to the Greeks, and a stumbling-block to the Hebrews, as he characterized it. Where he referred to Scriptures in support of his teachings, it was done in a novel manner, and without foundation in rational exegese. He had nothing to do with reason, logic or philosophy, nothing even with common sense; he told a story and preached a doctrine to those who believed it, and no opportunity was offered them to ascertain whether Paul believed his own story. He commenced preaching in Damascus and failed utterly (II. Corinth. xi. 32), although most of the women of

---
(41) *Hagigah* 15 a, * * חוא מיטטרון דאתיהבא ליה רשותא למיתב שמא ח'ר' שתי רשויות הן. *Sanhedrin* 38 b, read for צדוקי Christian, and for Metathron, Jesus.

(42) Acts xvii. 22 to 29; Romans i. 9; ii. 16; vi. 10; viii. 11; I. Corinthians v. 15 to 17; iii. 23; xi. 3; xv. 21 to 28; Origin of Christianity, p. 332, etc.; compare to PIRKE R. ELIEZER III. and PESACHIM 54 a, about the name of the Messiah preceding the world's creation; and PIRKE R ELIEZER xi.; also YALKUT to I. Kings, Sec. 211, "the ninth king is the Messiah;" then, as the tenth and last king, God will reign alone as in the beginning, etc., exactly as Paul maintained.

Damascus were Judaized. The Apostles would not acknowledge him, and the Hebrews did not believe him (Gal. ii. 1). He went to Antioch, and, in company of Barnabas, started out to evangelize the Gentiles. He called his new religion Christianity, and himself the Apostle to the Gentiles. In Syria and Asia Minor, he found many devout Gentiles; such men and women who knew Judaism and the Bible, and had been estranged to Paganism. It was chiefly to them that he addressed his Messiah-Metathron doctrine. He inspired terror by his earnest and emphatic prediction of the approaching end of the world, the fearless rehearsal of the crimes and corruptions among the Pagans, and the certainty of their sudden destruction and annihilation. Having thus crushed them, he opened for them the mysteries of the Messiah-Metathron drama, a gospel of his own, which promised salvation and happiness; and many believed. He made it easy for them, for he declared the Law abolished with the coming of the Messiah, and all that was required of them was love, hope and faith: faith in his doctrines, hope in the speedy approach of the Son of God to make an end of the present misery and this world, and love to one another in these last days. He poured out for them the great truths of the Bible and the floating wisdom and profound ethics of the Hebrews, which edified and converted them. Like the other Apostles, he persuaded his converts that they had received the Holy Ghost and the other gifts of grace, and succeeded in rousing that unreasoning enthusiasm which believes blindly and works itself up to a state of ecstasy, where all arguments and human speculations fall dead to the ground. He organized congregations, appointed bishops, presbyters and deacons, and he was their Apostle, their demi-god and mediator. He introduced among them the common meals of the Hebrews, with a form of divine worship (43), replacing the sacrificial meals of the Pagans; and added to it that at each of those meals they should eat of the body and drink of the blood of Jesus (figuratively) in memory of him, as he had so ordained at his last supper, so that they should eat, drink, be merry and worship simultaneously. In fourteen years he laid the foundation to Gentile Christianity, a peculiar amalgamation of Hebrew ethics and denationalized theology with Gnostic mysticism and Pagan conceptions, destined, however, to overthrow and supersede Greco-Roman Pagan-

---

(43) Josephus' Antiq. xiv., x. 8; *Mishnah*, BERACHOTH vii.; I. Corinthians xi. 20; Martyrdom of Jesus, etc., p. 46.

ism, to be then itself overthrown in its turn by the Logos speculations of the Alexandrian Christians.

32. Paul's Troubles with the Apostles.

Paul, of course, was grossly abused and maltreated by orthodox Pagans and orthodox Hebrews, although he kept himself on good terms with the Roman authorities by preaching submission to those who bear the sword, of the wife to her husband, and the slave to his master. He never spoke of liberty, human rights or such other subjects which might have done him injury with the men in power. Denationalizing Judaism and condemning the Jewish laws as he did, he had nothing to say, not a word, of the woes and afflictions of his people; and, representing the present state as a mere preparation for the approaching end of the world, he could bestow no care and no reflection on matters and things appertaining to this sublunar life. Still he was maltreated and abused by those who did not take him to be a harmless and visionary fanatic. His greatest difficulties, however, were with the Apostles and their flock in Palestine. Although he glorified their Messianic master, and built up their church among the Gentiles, he collected money for them and sent it to them to Palestine, as the Pharisees did to their teachers in the Holy Land (44); he was a man of brilliant mind and rare energy, and they were humble fishermen; nevertheless, they could not consent to his teachings and would not acknowledge him as one of their own (Galatians i. and ii.). They could not do it; for they obeyed and he abolished the Law. Like Jesus, they were sent to the House of Israel only, and he went to the Gentiles with the message, that with the death and resurrection of the Messiah the covenant and the Law were at an end, and a new dispensation, a new covenant, begins. They glorified their master, whom they had seen and heard as a human being, and he proclaimed a phantom, half-man and half-angel, entirely foreign to the common man's conception. They had one Gospel story and he had another. They spoke of the miracles and teachings of Jesus, he never mentioned either, always referred to the Old Testament and his own wisdom, and condemned "their fables and endless genealogies" in the strongest terms (II. Timothy i. 3, 4) (45). They prophesied the speedy return of their master from the realm of death to

---

(44) YERUSHALMI HORIOTH iii. 7, מעשה וגו׳; *Pesachim* 53 *b*; I. Corinthians xvi. 1 to 3.

(45) See our Origin of Christianity, p. 363.

restore the throne of David in the Kingdom of Heaven, and he prophesied the end of the world and the last day of judgment to be at hand. They preached repentance and baptized penitent sinners, and he preached faith and was not sent to baptize (I. Corinthians i. 17). They spoke of Jesus hanged on a tree (Acts v. 30; x. 39; xiii. 29), and he insisted on preaching him crucified (46). They forbid their converts to eat unclean food, and especially of the sacrificial meals of Pagans, and he made light of both, as well as of the Sabbath and circumcision (I. Corinthians viii.). They, like Jesus, believed in one God, the Almighty, and he preached a God and a demi-God (שתי רשויות), having divided the dominion among themselves. The Apostles, more so than the other Hebrews, must have considered Paul an innovator and heretic, who made their beliefs odious with the masses and criminal before the Law. To endeavor to abolish the entire Law is certainly rank rebellion, and undoubtedly cost the lives of James and his compatriots. The Apostles made repeated attempts to avert this danger and to silence Paul. They held councils, adopted rules for the conduct of proselytes, sent messengers after Paul to undo his innovations and to reconvert his converts. Paul retaliated forcibly against the brothers of Jesus, Peter and the other Apostles (47). He accused them of not leading the most pure and pious lives, and was as fierce against his colleagues in Jerusalem as he was in his denunciations of the Law and circumcision. These difficulties increased with Paul's successes, and so damaged both parties that he at last found it necessary to go to Jerusalem and attempt a reconciliation of the embittered parties.

33. PAUL IN JERUSALEM.

Paul arrived in Jerusalem at that very dangerous time when James, the brother of Jesus, and his compatriots, had been put to death, and the nascent congregation was presided over by the other James, supposed to have been a cousin of Jesus, the man who wrote the Epistle in which Paulism is radically denounced. This James, called in the Talmud, Jacob of Kaphersamia, was an orthodox Pharisee who believed in the Messiahship of Jesus and his second advent, practiced necromancy with the name of Jesus, and spent most of his time kneeling in the temple and praying "till his knees were become as hard and brawny as a

---

(46) The cause was stated above, end of Chapter xviii.
(47) I. Corinthians ix.; II. Corinthians xi., and elsewhere.

camel's." The situation of Paul was painful. He stood before a synod of opponents, meeting in the house of James, "and all the elders were present." He explained to them his Gospel to the Gentiles, and informed them that he had also another Gospel which he preached "privately to them which were of reputation." But the reply of the synod was this: The Jew-Christians believe and are zealous of the Law, and Paul teaches to forsake Moses and abolish circumcision; were the multitude informed of his presence in Jerusalem, he would not be safe among them (Acts xxi. 20 to 22). Therefore, they bid him recant, practically, this pernicious doctrine, to go through, with four of their Nazirites, the ceremonies of purification in the temple, "and be at charges with them, that they may shave their heads; and all may know that those things whereof they were informed concerning thee, are nothing; but that thou thyself also walkest orderly, and keepest the Law" (*Ibid.* xxi. 24). Paul submitted to the hypocrisy inflicted on him. He went to the Temple Mount with the four men, to pass through the whole ceremonial which he had denounced and condemned so emphatically. Paul, under this pressure of imposed hypocrisy, keenly felt the humiliation. Speaking of that synod (Galatians ii.), he calls the heads thereof "those who seemed to be somewhat, whatsoever they were," and says of them that they added nothing to his knowledge. The rabbis describe his feelings thus: ACHER, or Paul, tells of himself: "I once rode behind the temple, and I heard the *Bath-kol* exclaiming: Return all ye froward children, except ACHER, who knows my glory and rebels against me." However, a number of Asiatic Jews recognized Paul on the Temple Mount, a disturbance ensued, and the Roman soldiers arrested him under the impression that he was the Egyptian prophet who had made his escape sometime before. Being a Roman citizen and appealing to Cæsar, he was, after a few days, taken to Cæsarea, to be sent to Rome with other prisoners. Paul was certainly glad to escape from the hands of his friends, and to go to Rome and before his Gentile converts as an expatriated and persecuted man, no longer one of the Jew-Christians. Three of the Apostles acknowledged him an apostle to the Gentiles; not, however, an apostle to the Hebrews.

34. Paul Sent to Rome.

Not before Felix, but before Albinus, Paul must have had a hearing in Cæsarea, since the highpriest, Ananus, who appeared as prosecutor against him, had been appointed,

62 A. C., by Agrippa II. No very aggravated accusation was preferred against Paul, especially as he had preached his doctrines outside of Palestine, so that Agrippa II., who also heard his case, did not find him guilty of any punishable deed. Like all other prisoners who came into the hands of Albinus, Paul also was held in Cæsarea without any further notice to the close of that governor's administration, two years, 62 and 63 A. C. (Josephus' Antiq. xx., ix. 5), and then he was sent to Rome with other prisoners. In Rome, where no Christian congregation was at the time, Paul was again a Hebrew among Hebrews. They had received no letters out of Judea concerning him, nor had they any information to incriminate him, and so they treated him well, as one of themselves. There was a tradition in the church that Paul stood twice before Nero (II. Timothy iv. 22), but it is uncertain. It is sure that he was in Rome two years (64 and 65 A. C.) in his own hired house, and was not included among the Christians persecuted by Nero, because he was known there as a Hebrew and not as a Christian. It is also certain that he returned from Rome to Asia, traveled in Italy and Illyricum (Romans xv. 19), wrote his Epistle to the Romans and other epistles after his return from Rome and after the destruction of Jerusalem (Galatians iv. 25), when his main work commenced. When Paul came to Rome he was no older than thirty-six years, and he had already done the work of a man. During the four years of his captivity in Cæsarea and Rome, many of his converts turned from his teachings. Some of them embraced Judaism, like Priscilla and Aquila (Romans xvi. 3), while others embraced Jew Christianity; so that on his return he found much to correct, much to repent, and many opportunities to amend what he had done or said in the days of youth, zeal and eccentricity. After the fall of Jerusalem, when Paul was about forty years old, his main work as Apostle to the Gentiles was done. The stories of his and Peter's martyrdom are certainly fictitious.

Period VI.—The Catastrophe.

This period, comprising less than six years, is, nevertheless, one of the most remarkable chapters in history. A down-trodden people, deserted by its own aristocracy, rises, lion-like, to fight for its independence and bids defiance to mighty Rome. Death-defying deeds, bravery and heroism, which the utmost suffering could not bend, characterize the unequal combat of the Hebrew patriots pitched against Rome's mighty legions and her numerous allies. The mighty ones fell buried under the ruins of the cities which they defended to the last; Jerusalem and its glorious temple, crimsoned with the blood of their champions, are laid waste by a raging and barbarous enemy; all the furies of destruction are let loose, over a million of lives are sacrificed, and tens of thousands are sold into slavery, expatriated, or otherwise driven into foreign lands, and the political existence of the Hebrews is drowned in the blood of its patriots. No nation closed its political career more heroically than Israel did, none was more patriotic; because none had holier treasures to guard or more glorious reminiscences by which to be inspired than Israel had. Liberty or death was the parole in this mighty struggle; death was victorious and liberty was buried under the ruins of Jerusalem.

CHAPTER XXIV.

Preludes to the War.

1. The Last of the Procurators (64–66 A. C.).

The last of the thirteen Roman Procurators in Judea, Gessius Florus, was also the worst. By a series of villainous outrages he forced the Hebrews into the rebellion and war which ended with the destruction of Jerusalem and the political death of the Hebrews of Palestine. The Roman government in the orient had become so much more despotic and intolerable under Nero's misrule, and the maladministration of his President of Syria, Cestius Gallus, on account of the threatening attitude of the Parthians, and the prediction and wide-spread apprehension that the orient was seeking predominancy over the occident and Rome. So Palestine also was subjected to continual suspicion and martial law. The boundless and shameless avarice and malice of Gessius Florus and of his wife, Cleopatra, intensified the despotism to an unbearable degree. He treated the Hebrews as though he had been sent to them as an executioner to punish condemned malefactors, says Josephus, and Tacitus (History x., v.) confirms it.

2. The Situation.

What Albinus had done under the cloak of dissimulation, Florus did openly and pompously, to secure all the money of private persons or public institutions which could be extorted by an abuse of authority, the aid of marauders, and the menaces of expatriation or death. Whole districts ransacked by the Procurator's soldiers or robbers were impoverished. No man of wealth was safe at any time or place. There was no protection of life or property. The situation was aggravated by the despotism of the President of Syria, who would not permit an appeal for redress to him. He came to Jerusalem on Passover (65 A. C.) and was there petitioned by the representatives of three millions of people, said to have been assembled then in and about Jerusalem. He promised much, did nothing, and left Florus to give vent to his wrath against those who had dared to complain. Many of the wealthy citizens left the country, but many more gave support to the Zealots, determined to expel Florus from the land. Among the latter there was the youth of the land, the flower of the fighting population, inspired with a glowing patriotism not impaired by considerations of probabilities, dangers or death. With the oppression the enthusiasm grew, and prudence gradually lost its influence.

3. The First Conflict.

Interests, pride and principles tied many aristocratic families, and among them also many Hillel Pharisees, to the Roman government. They still desired peace, and might have succeeded in frustrating the rebellion, if Florus had not committed one treacherous outrage after another, apparently with the avowed intention of forcing the Hebrews into rebellion and war, in order to fill his coffers, to cover or justify his atrocities, and to satisfy his bloodthirsty disposition. An outrage was committed at Cæsarea. The Hebrews of that city, built by Herod I. with the money of his people, had been ostracized by an edict of Nero, as noticed above, and at this time the embassadors returned from Rome with the edict. The Gentiles did their worst to mortify the Hebrews. The latter had a synagogue in the city, around which the ground was owned by a Greek. He hemmed in the sanctuary by low shops and left but a narrow passage to it. The young Hebrews made a demonstration against the outrage, but they were restrained by military force. Eight talents were collected and given to Florus in order to obtain justice from him. He took the money, promised redress and protection, and then left the city for Sebaste. His absence encouraged the enemies of the Hebrews. On Sabbath, while they were assembled in the synagogue, a Greek sacrificed a bird at its door to insult them, by insinuating, as in Manetho's and Apion's story, that the ancestors of the Hebrews were leprous. A fight ensued which was stopped by military intervention. The Hebrews took their Scrolls of the Law and retired to the neighboring town of Narbata, while a deputation of thirteen went to Sebaste to remind Florus of his duty and promises.

He threw them into a prison, did nothing for the outraged Hebrews, and sent men to Jerusalem to bring him seventeen talents of silver from the temple treasury.

4. THE SECOND CONFLICT.

The people of Jerusalem, exasperated by the conduct of Florus at Cæsarea and Sebaste, peremptorily refused his demand for money. Some, to shame his avarice, went round with charity boxes to collect money for the greedy Procurator. He instantly came to Jerusalem and demanded the surrender of the men who had insulted him. This being refused, he ordered his soldiers to ransack the residences of the rich at the Upper Market. A horrible scene of bloodshed and rapine ensued. Those who were caught alive were scourged and crucified, among them women and children, and also citizens of the equestrian rank. Three thousand and six hundred persons fell on that sixteenth day of *Iyar*. In vain did Berenice, the sister of Agrippa II., humiliate herself before the bloodthirsty man, suing for mercy for the innocent; nothing would arrest his fury. The next morning the horrified multitude gathered at the Upper Market, lamented over the slain ones, and cursed their villainous murderer. The rulers and priests, dreading a repetition of the scenes of the previous day, besought and persuaded the people to disperse and keep quiet. Then Florus sent for them and told them that, unless the people turn out to salute the troops coming in from Cæsarea, as a token of submission to the Roman authority, he would continue the massacre and rapine. They exerted their utmost influence to persuade some of the multitude, for the sake of their city, country and sanctuary, to deprive the villain of every pretext for the opening of a war, which might end in utter disaster. Many went out to salute the cohorts who, according to instructions, treated the Hebrews with contempt. Some of the multitude giving vent to their disappointment, the soldiers rushed upon the crowd of unarmed men and assaulted them with clubs. A stampede and a horrible slaughter followed, at the suburb of Bezetha. The race for the Temple Mount made by the people and the soldiers simultaneously, was won by the former. From those positions the Hebrews turned against the Romans, galled them sorely and forced them to retreat to the palace. Now the connection between the temple and Fort Antonia was broken down, and Florus was convinced that his way to the temple treasury was barricaded. Seeing the main object of his villainies beyond his reach and himself in imminent danger, he left a small garrison in the city and returned to Cæsarea, followed by the curses of the mourning multitude.

5. AGRIPPA II. AS PACIFICATOR.

Florus, eager to bring on the war, wrote to Cestius that all the Hebrews were in a state of revolt against Rome. However, the rulers of Jerusalem and Queen Berenice also, wrote letters to Cestius and informed him of the true state of affairs. It was resolved in the council of Cestius to send Neopolitanus to Jerusalem to ascertain the truth. He went to Lydda to meet Agrippa II. The rulers of Jerusalem, and members of the Sanhedrin also, came to Lydda to welcome King Agrippa, who had just returned from Alexandria. The representative men of the Hebrews maintained that the people were not rebellious against Rome; it was against Florus that arms had been taken up, and persuaded both, King Agrippa and Neopolitanus, to go with them to Jerusalem in order to convince themselves of the peaceful disposition of its citizens, and their devotion to Rome. Sixty furlongs distant from the city they were received by a stately procession of people and escorted to the palace. The city was quiet, orderly and under the complete control of law. The popular men asked the privilege of sending an embassy to Nero to prove that they were not disposed to revolt, and that Florus was the cause of the prevailing dissatisfaction. Instead of granting this reasonable request, Agrippa called the multitude together and addressed them in a most elaborate speech, which Josephus has preserved (Wars II. xv. 4). With his sister, Berenice, he appeared before the people, described to them the vastness of the Roman power, which to withstand successfully they could have no reasonable hope. He predicted to them the destruction of the temple and the city, the ruination of the entire country and the overthrow of the Hebrew nation, if they insisted on war with Rome and be the losers in the end. He closed thus: "Have pity, therefore, if not upon your children and wives, yet upon this your metropolis, and its sacred walls; spare the temple, and preserve the holy house, with its holy furniture, for yourselves," etc. "I call to witness your sanctuary and the holy angels of God, and this country common to us all," he said, "that I have not kept back anything that is for your preservation," etc. Then he and his sister wept. The response was that they would not fight against Rome, but against Florus. Agrippa told them that they were already in a state of revolt against Rome by non-payment of the tribute and the demolition of the galleries between the temple and the fort. His words impressed the people; the rebuilding of those galleries was commenced at once, and messengers were dispatched to Florus to send a collector to receive the tribute. It appeared momentarily, that the danger of an immediate war with Rome was averted.

6. Two Hostile Events.

It was too late to reason with outraged men, who valued liberty higher than life. The treatment received from the Procurators after the death of Agrippa I. had driven many to desperation, and changed law-abiding men into lions with hearts of flint. They saw only the bloody wrong committed by Rome, and their right to be free. The politicians and statesmen of Jerusalem could contemplate chances, interests and probabilities; the multitude felt the wrongs and would not reason. Therefore, while momentary pacification was achieved in Jerusalem, a party of Zealots took Masada, the armory of King Herod, massacred its Roman garrison and replaced it by their own men. Plenty of arms were captured. Menahem, the grandson of Juda the Galilean, was the leader of that party. He represented the fourth generation in revolt against the Roman usurpation. This victory re-echoed in the temple at Jerusalem. Its governor, Eleazar, son of the ex-highpriest, Ananus, persuaded the officiating priests to receive no gift or sacrifice for the temple of any Gentile, and they rejected on this account also the usual sacrifice for the emperor. This, says Josephus, was the beginning of the war. It certainly was an unmistakable declaration of it. This appears to have been the time when the stormy meeting of the Shammaites and Hillelites took place in the hall of Ananus b. Chiskiah, over one of the temple cloisters. Then the Eighteen Interdictions were enacted, one of which was to refuse all sacrifices and gifts of Gentiles for the temple, while the others prohibited the purchase of oil, wine and other articles of luxury of the Gentiles, to intermarry with any of them, or to speak any of their languages, and laws concerning Levitical cleanness. The Shammaites, with swords in hand, forced the Hillelites to sanction those laws, with the proviso that they should never be repealed, in order to keep the Hebrews entirely and forever separated from the Heathens (1).

7. THE OUTBREAK OF CIVIL WAR.

The moderate party called a meeting to the inner court of the temple, and made one more attempt to maintain the peace. It was proved by men of learning that the gifts and sacrifices of Heathens had always been accepted by the rulers of the temple, and that Heathens had largely contributed to its splendor and wealth. The contemplated war with Rome was denounced as a national calamity, certain to bring destruction upon the nation, its capital and temple. However, the leaders of the war party were determined to shake off the Roman yoke or to die in the attempt, and gave expression to their resolution in unmistakable words. Unable to change the death-defying determination of the war party, and knowing that vengeance would be meted out first on the rich and the men in power, they sent embassies to Florus and Agrippa, praying them to send sufficient military forces to the city to crush the rebellion at once. Florus, who wanted war, took no notice of the petition; Agrippa sent three thousand men to assist the moderate party. This started the civil war in Jerusalem. The war party seized upon the Temple Mount, and the peace party, with the three thousand soldiers, took possession of Mount Zion; active hostilities were begun and continued for seven days with bloody results, without advantage to either party. Meanwhile, the fifteenth day of AB, the principal Xylophory (קרבן עצים) approached; a large number of pilgrims, and with them also many SICARII, arrived, and augmented the ranks of the war party. The partisans of the peace party were rigidly excluded from the Temple Mount, which roused their indignation, and brought on an action in force on the fourteenth day of AB. The men from the Temple Mount, led by Eleazar b. Ananus, sallied forth in force, routed the soldiers and drove them into the king's palace on Mount Zion. Now the victorious party began its work of destruction; the palaces of Ananus, Agrippa and Berenice, and the city archives, were burnt, together with all the documents therein, so that every

---

(1) *Sabbath* 13 *b*; YERUSHALMI and TOSEPHTA 1. The captain of the temple, who took the lead in this matter, is called in the MISHNAH *Orlah* II. 12, יועזר איש הבירה, who was a Shammaite. Josephus reports only as much of those Eighteen Interdictions as referred to the temple and public business. The Talmud reports the others.

evidence of indebtedness was wiped out. The leaders of the peace party were slain, except those who retreated with the soldiers to the palace, and some others, like Ananus, who sought refuge in vaults under the ground.

8. From the Fifteenth Day of Ab to the Sixth of Ellul.

Next day, Fort Antonia was taken by Eleazer b. Ananus, the garrison was slain and the citadel set on fire. Then the palace was attacked, but could not be taken at once. The war party was now reinforced by Menahem, the Galilean, with his well-armed band of Zealots from Masada. He seized upon the chief command, and began his operations with the siege of the palace. He pressed it vigorously, and the besieged capitulated. They were permitted to leave the city, except the Romans, who mistrusted Menahem. With considerable loss they reached the towers of Hippicus, Phasaelus and Marianne, leaving their camp equipage and war engines in the hands of Menahem. The city, with the exception of the three besieged towers, was now entirely in the hands of the war party.

9. The Death of Menahem.

Previous to that day, a party of miners, digging under the wall of the palace, captured the ex-highpriest, Ananus, and his brother, hid in the aqueduct. Menahem had both of them slain, although Eleazar was the massacred man's son. After his victories, Menahem was also accused of behaving like a king, endangering the liberty just won. Eleazar, at last, succeeded in raising a sedition against him on the Temple Mount; he and his men were overpowered, many of them were slain; some, under Eleazar b. Jairus, escaped to Masada. Menahem fled to Ophel and was slain there, leaving Eleazar b. Ananus master of the situation.

10. Treachery and Massacre.

Eleazar b. Ananus continued the siege of the towers, and the Romans at last capitulated and left the city unarmed. Outside of the walls, however, all pledges and promises were set at naught by the infuriated Zealots. They fell upon the Romans and brutally massacred them. The men of peace were no longer permitted to raise their voices. The priests of the peace party heard a voice from the temple, "Let us remove hence," and the terrible prophet of woe who had raised his voice already in the time of Albinus, cried aloud: "A voice from the east, a voice from the west, a voice from the four winds, a voice against Jerusalem and the holy house, a voice against the bridegrooms and the brides, and a voice against this whole people" (2). The victors shouted in Jerusalem, but many were the patriots who mourned. Once more Jerusalem was free.

11. Massacre of Hebrews and Gentiles.

The very same day and hour, says Josephus, when the Roman soldiers were slain before the walls of Jerusalem, the Gentile inhabitants of Cæsarea slew all the Hebrews of that city. Twenty thousand men, women and children were massacred in one day, and nothing was done by the Roman authorities to prevent or avenge the horrid slaughter. The Hebrews, enraged by this bloodshed, rose in large numbers all over the land, attacked the Syrian and Tyrian cities, including Ptolemais, Cæsarea, Sebaste, Anthedon and Gaza, demolished, burnt and plundered them and the villages protected by them, and took summary vengeance. On the other hand the Gentiles committed the same barbarities. All over Syria, except in Antioch and some smaller cities where they were too numerous, a war of extermination was waged against the Hebrews and the Judaizers that dwelt among them. Thousands were slain and other thousands put in chains. Two races raged against each other in boundless fury. The corpses lay in the streets unburied. In Scythopolis, the Hebrew inhabitants had made common cause with the Gentiles, and the hostile Hebrews who attacked the city were defeated. But scarcely was the danger averted, when the Gentiles of Scythopolis, in a most treacherous manner, destroyed all their Hebrew fellow-citizens, about thirteen thousand. On this occasion a terrible man and heroic warrior, Simon b. Saul, distinguished himself in a horrible manner by slaying his whole family and then committing suicide, in order not to fall into the hands of the treacherous enemy. Also in Agrippa's dominion seventy distinguished men of Batanea were slain by his regent, Noarsus; but Agrippa was informed in time, and, deposing Noarsus, prevented further bloodshed. In the southeast of the land, the Hebrews succeeded in taking Machaerus which they garrisoned, and also

---

(2) Josephus' Wars vi., v. 3.

Cypros, near Jericho, which they demolished; so that the Romans had no foothold in the southern part of the land. The worst treachery, however, was committed on the Hebrews of Damascus. The women of that city were mostly attached to the religion of Israel, and their husbands fearing a conspiracy with the resident Hebrews, fell treacherously upon the latter and cut the throats of about ten thousand of those who were unarmed and could not defend themselves.

12. The Massacre in Alexandria.

The Alexandrian Hebrews were most violently hated by their Gentile neighbors, because they were more prosperous. The bloody scenes in Syria re-echoed in Egypt. The Alexandrian Gentiles became seditious against the Hebrews. At a public meeting in the theater, to send a deputation to Nero, a number of Hebrews were present. The populace declared them spies, fell on them and killed several of them. Three Hebrews were captured and dragged to the pyre. Meanwhile, the others had been thoroughly alarmed and came in large numbers to rescue their co-religionists, which they did, and then threatened to set the theater on fire. A bloody affray ensued and all the furies were let loose. The Hebrews were numerous and valiant, and the populace mad, bloodthirsty and greedy for booty. The Gentiles were reinforced by five thousand Lybian savages. There were two Roman legions stationed in the city, and they might have restored order, but they were under the command of Tiberius Alexander, the renegade, who sided with the populace. He sent peacemakers first, and when they were unsuccessful, the two legions reinforced the populace, and a terrible conflict was fought out in the streets of Alexandria first, then in the Delta quarter, inhabited by Hebrews exclusively. Those Hebrews fought for several days that whole furious crowd, but were finally overpowered and slain without mercy, till the place was drenched with blood, and fifty thousand dead Hebrew men, women and children covered the streets of that city, half of the Hebrew houses were ransacked and destroyed, and the fury and greed of the populace had been satiated.

13. Cestius Attempts to Vanquish the Hebrews
(66 a. c.).

This bloody conflict of the races might have been suppressed either by securing to the Hebrews what they wanted and had the indisputable right to ask, viz. : free government, as their laws, traditions, institutions, state of civilization, and historical character required; or, by giving them, with the foreign government, also the benefit of its protection, as Julius Cæsar had done. But Nero occupied the throne of the Cæsars, and every idea of justice was defunct in Rome. Cestius Gallus governed Syria as Tiberius did Alexandria, and as Gessius Florus tyrannized over Judea. Instead of thinking of concessions and reforms to pacify the excited multitude and assist the peace party in Palestine, Cestius resolved upon making a speedy end of the rebellion by terror and slaughter. He concentrated the forces of the petty princes, among them also Agrippa II., to reinforce the Roman legions, and made an excursion from Ptolemais into the northern country. The beautiful city of Zabulon was the first to be surprised, but its inhabitants had fled to the mountains. The city was ransacked and partly destroyed. He overran the whole northern country and gave it up to his bloodthirsty and rapacious hordes, and then returned to Ptolemais, believing he had terrified the victims of his bloody despotism. The fugitive Hebrews in the mountains, however, seized upon the favorable moment, returned to their homes, especially at Zabulon and Berytus, and slew two thousand of the invaders. Now Cestius marched with his whole force from Ptolemais to Cæsarea, sent one detachment to Joppe, another, of horsemen, into the populous district of Narbatene, and a third, under Gallus, the commander of the Twelfth Legion, into Galilee. Joppe was surprised, captured, ransacked, burnt, and eight thousand four hundred of its inhabitants were slain. The same implacable barbarities were enacted at Narbatene. In Galilee, however, the peace party predominated at Sepphoris, and its gates were opened to the Romans, who were received with acclamations of joy. The rebels fled to the mountains, and concentrated about the Asamon range. Gallus defeated and scattered them, and returned to Cæsarea.

14. THE DEFEAT OF CESTIUS GALLUS BEFORE JERUSALEM IN THE FALL OF 66 A. C.

Now Cestius, again concentrating his forces, marched on Jerusalem. He stopped at Antipatris to fight those who had sought refuge in the tower of Aphek, but they had fled and dispersed before his arrival. Then he stopped at Lydda, which he found deserted; its inhabitants had gone to Jerusalem to celebrate the Feast of Tabernacles. This, however, did not prevent him from ransacking and burning the city, and slaying the forty men who had been left behind to guard the homes of the pilgrims. Then he marched to Gabao, thirty-five thousand feet distant from Jerusalem. It was on the Sabbath and a high feast, and Cestius thought he might take the city without trouble. But the citizens and pilgrims rushed to arms, made a daring and impetuous attack on the forces of Cestius, and routed them. The cavalry saved them from utter destruction, still they lost five hundred and fifteen men. Among the most valiant leaders on that occasion were Monabaz and Kenedius, kinsmen of the King of Adiabene, Niger, of Perea, and Silas, of Babylon; the latter had been the commander of cavalry in King Agrippa's army. The Hebrews were obliged to retreat back to the city, because they had no cavalry; and Cestius marched back to Beth-Horon. His rear, however, was attacked by Simon b. Gorion's band, who captured many beasts loaded with arms. The Hebrews inside of the city and on the eminences around it, now prepared for resolute resistance. Agrippa II., who was with Cestius, tried once more to persuade the people to submission, and sent two embassadors to the city; one of them, however, was killed outside of the walls, and the other fled, severely wounded, which roused the anger of the people against the murderers, who were beaten with stones and clubs and driven into the city. Next day Cestius attacked and repulsed the Hebrews and advanced to Scopus, forty-nine hundred feet distant from the city. Four days later, the thirtieth day of *Tishri*, he took Bezetha, and set it on fire, and had arrived before the northern wall, opposite the royal palace. His adjutants advised him not to attempt the assault, and he desisted. An invitation from some leaders in Jerusalem under Ananus b. Jonathan, to take possession of the city by a gate to be opened for him, was also refused. The intended treachery of Ananus was discovered, and he was hurled down over the wall. After considerable delay, an attack was made on the wall, and repeated on five successive days without any effect. On the sixth day an attack on the northern wall of the temple was also unsuccessful. The Romans had commenced to undermine that wall, which created a momentary panic in the city. However, Cestius, weakened as his army was, began to retreat to his camp at Scopus. He was immediately pursued by the besieged, and attacked in the rear and flanks by archers. So the Romans were fought all the way back, also to Gabao, where they arrived in disorder after a severe loss in men and baggage. Their mules were killed, and the march continued to Beth-Horon, which they reached in despair; half of the Roman army had been slain and destruction threatened the other half. It was by strategy that Cestius outwitted the Hebrews and, during the night, got a considerable distance ahead of them before they discovered his flight. They pursued the wreck of the invading army to Antipatris and then returned in triumph to Jerusalem. Nearly ten thousand Romans had lost their lives in a few days, the whole camp equipage, war engines, arms, provisions and money, which Cestius had in his train, fell into the hands of the Hebrews. The whole land re-echoed their shouts of triumph, the victory was great, the land was apparently rescued from the clutches of a hated invader.

CHAPTER XXV.

The First Period of the War (67 and 68 A. C).

1. The Moderate Party Victorious.

After his defeat, Cestius Gallus returned to Antioch, reported his disaster to Rome, and fell sick. An embassy of loyal Hebrews was sent to Achia to defend the party of obedience before Nero, and to lay all the blame on Florus and his outrages. But the emperor was most ridiculously engaged in public games, and a momentary suspension of hostilities followed in Judea. The victory achieved over the Romans made the Zealots, for a while, masters of the situation. They insisted upon raising the standard of independence. The doctrine of Judah of Galilee, that it was a shame and crime to be subject or to pay tribute to any foreign potentate, was the parole of the party, and its resolution was to fight the enemy to the bitter end of liberty or death. They pointed to numerous events, especially to the records of the Maccabees, when God protected Israel's cause by a mere handful of resolute and patriotic warriors, and maintained that what had happened so often might occur once more to men of courage and patriotism, if they put their trust in the same God and in the holy cause of Israel. But if the worst should come, it is better to die for a holy cause than to live a slave or a renegade. The Romans, they maintained, had defied the Hebrews' laws, rights, liberties and religion; the worst that could possibly be done was to submit any longer to the oppressive usurpation. The other extreme party, however, fearing the vengeance of Rome, followed the defeated Romans to Antioch or went to the distant western settlements of the Roman Empire, especially to Spain (1). The moderate party could no longer prevent

---

(1) Mishnah *Baba Bathra* iii. 2. Any vacant estate of such emi-

the war, and opposed only its main object. A defensive war, to obtain more favorable conditions from Rome for the Palestinean Republic, and to remain, nevertheless, loyal to the empire, was their object. This party comprised most of the priestly and lay aristocracy, the prominent statesmen and doctors, and all those who liked to be Romans and Israelites. Under the prevailing excitement and roused spirit of liberty, it was dangerous to express moderate views; and so this party was obliged, momentarily, to submit to the Zealots. Still those leaders understood how to manage the populace so well, that the most important offices were filled by the men of their choice. The doctors of the Hillel and Shammai schools contributed largely to the patriotic enthusiasm by enactments and harangues, and especially by writing popular books on the Maccabees and their combats against Syria; so that the heroic figures of a glorious past loomed up in the excited imagination, and stimulated emulation.

2. Organization of the Defense.

The reorganization of the Sanhedrin as the central authority was the first step taken to govern and defend the country. Simon b. Gamliel, the great-grandson of Hillel, had been at the head of that body since 52 A. C., although it had been powerless. It was now restored to its lawful place and powers under its legitimate Nassi. The country was divided into seven districts, viz.: 1. PEREA, east of the Jordan, from Macherus in the south to Gadara in the north; 2. UPPER AND LOWER IDUMEA, between the Dead Sea and the Mediterranean in the extreme south. North thereof were: 3. DISTRICT OF JERICHO, 4. OF JERUSALEM, and 5. OF THAMNA, between the Jordan and the Mediterranean. North thereof were: 6. DISTRICT ACRABATENE, covering the pass between the Jordan and the central mountains, the communication with Galilee; on the other side of which was the part of Samaria held by the Romans; and 7. UPPER AND LOWER GALILEE, which had revolted from Agrippa II., and made common cause with the nation. The following governors were appointed for the various districts: Ananus and Joseph b. Gorion, both descendants of highpriests, were appointed Governors of Jerusalem with the special charge

grants the law secured to the occupant after an undisputed possession thereof of three consecutive years, provided the owner was in any foreign country or the property was not at all claimed within the three years.

of fortifying and provisioning the city. Ananus (2) was the actual President of the Sanhedrin and chief-ruler of the land. Manasseh was appointed for Perea. Eleazar b. Ananus, the principal agitator and soldier, and Jesus b. Sapphias, both descendants of highpriests, were sent to Idumea to govern the district conjointly with Niger, its officiating governor. Joseph b. Simon was appointed for Jericho, and John, the Essene, for Thamna, which included Joppa, Lydda and Emmaus. Joseph (Flavius, the historian) b. Matthias was appointed Governor of Galilee, and John b. Matthias, of Acrabatene. The chief men were aristocratic priests of no military fame and, perhaps, like Josephus, young men without practical experience. All these military governors were charged with the duties of enforcing the law, organizing the militia, fortifying the cities, and obeying the Sanhedrin and central authority in Jerusalem. The leaders of the actual Zealots and extreme war party, it appears, were excluded from the highest executive offices (3) or put under the control of colleagues, as was the case with Eleazar b. Ananus. The moderate party was master of the situation. Still the governors and people of Jerusalem went to work with energy and enthusiasm. The fortifications of the city were repaired, strengthened and enlarged; provisions were stored in the city; arms were forged in all shops, and all able-bodied men were armed and drilled, so that the whole city became one large fortified camp, where hoary men, women and lads vied with valiant men in patriotism, enthusiasm and love of liberty (4).

(2) This R. Hananiah is also reported in SIPHRI (*Naso* 42) to have said: "Peace is as weighty as the rest of God's creation." גדול השלום שׁשׁקול כנגד כל מעשה בראשית.
(3) Josephus does not mention the name of Simon b. Gorion, who was appointed to some lower command, it appears, at Acrabatene.
(4) It is not known who had a seat in that Sanhedrin. Besides Simon b. Gamliel, Jochanan b. Saccai, President and Vice-President, none is mentioned by name except Aristeus of Emmaus, who was one of its scribes (Josephus' Wars v., xiii. 1). The disciples of R. Jochanan could have no seat in the Sanhedrin with their master. Ananus, the principal Governor of Jerusalem, and virtually the head of the Sanhedrin, appears to be identical with R. CHANINAH SEGAN HAK-KOHANIM of the Mishnah, whose policy is expressed in his *Mishnah* (ABOTH iii. 2): "Pray for the peace of the government." His son, R. Simon b. Has-segan, was prominent in the next generation. Joshua b. Gamala, ex-highpriest (Josephus' *Life*, 41), R. Zadok, who fasted forty years that the temple might not be destroyed, R. Nechunia b Hak-kanah, Nachum Ham-modai, and all the prominent teachers which are counted among the "First Generation of the

3. Defeat at Ascalon.

The governors repaired to the various districts to carry out the orders of the Sanhedrin. To recover the seaports was the first object to be achieved. Therefore, three valiant leaders, Niger, of Idumea, John, the Essene, and Silas, the Bablylonian, led an expedition to capture Ascalon. Their intention was betrayed, and the Roman commander in that city, Antonius, gave them a warm reception. The impetuosity and valor of the Hebrews in the open field proved inadequate against the armament, tactics and coolness of Roman veterans, especially the cavalry, against which the Hebrews could not protect themselves; so they were disastrously defeated under the walls of Ascalon. John and Silas, with several thousand of their men, lost their lives in that battle, and Niger retreated into Sallis in Idumea. Shortly after he made another attack upon Ascalon and was defeated again. He and many of his warriors sought refuge in the tower of Bezedel, which the pursuing Romans set on fire and then withdrew. Niger and some of his men were saved, however, in a subterranean passage. This was the first disaster, and a very ominous one, because it proved the inability of the Hebrews to cope with the Romans in the open field or to wrest the seaports from them.

4. Simon b. Gorion.

Shortly after, one of the most daring and violent partisans, Simon b. Gorion, who, like others of his party, suspected and disliked the men in power, succeeded in collecting a band of guerrillas in Southern Idumea, and moved northward to put himself and his party in power, ravaging the country as he advanced. Ananus sent an adequate force from Jerusalem to check him. He evaded it and succeeded in reaching Masada, near the Dead Sea west, which was in the hands of the extreme Zealots, commanded by Eleazar b. Jairus. This was another ominous disaster. It roused the suspicion of the extremists against the moderates and opened the horrid fountain of civil war and self-destruction. The hostilities of Simon b. Gorion were effectively continued from Masada, as shall be narrated hereafter.

5. Josephus in Galilee.

Galilee was, at this moment, the most important portion of Palestine, because it was the most populous and most

---

Tena'im," may have been members of that Sanhedrin, but it is not stated expressly that they were.

loval district, and the enemy was obliged to come through
that mountainous country, which a skilled and experienced
general could have defended longer than the Romans were
prepared to wage war. One telling victory in Galilee might
have roused the Parthians and the petty princes of the East
to espouse the cause of the Hebrews. But Galilee was governed by Josephus, who was too young for the position, had
no experience in warfare, was the friend of Agrippa II., and
an admirer of Rome. He tells us in his autobiography that
he was a descendant of Jonathan the Asmonean, by one of
his daughters, hence of the highest aristocracy of the land;
that his father, Matthias, was a distinguished citizen of
Jerusalem; and that he was very successful in the schools
of all sects, especially of the Pharisees, whose cause he
espoused at the age of nineteen. He was born 37 A. C., and
up to his twenty-sixth year had done nothing to distinguish himself, although he was one of the most accomplished scholars in the Greek as well as in the national literature. In the year 63 A. C., he went to Rome to liberate
the priests sent there by the Procurator and kept as captives. He was shipwrecked, and with eighty men out of
six hundred, saved his life and reached Puteoli. A Hebrew
stage actor, Aliturius, introduced him to Poppea; and he
succeeded in liberating those priests and in being deeply
impressed with the glory and power of Rome. On his return to Jerusalem, he always sided with the peace party
and the friends of Rome. After the defeat of Cestius Gallus and the slaughter of the Hebrews in the various cities
of Syria, he, like his compatriots, disguised his real opinions and intentions and espoused the cause of the moderate party. When he was about thirty years old, without
having any military record, he, with two legates, was sent
to Galilee as governor of that important province, and came
to his post more with the intention of disarming the veteran enemies of Rome and Agrippa II., in order to obtain an
honorable peace, than to win the independence of his people.
"My first care was," says Josephus, "to keep Galilee in
peace" (Life 14), in which he proved a shrewd and resolute
man, a man of courage and circumspection. He made
compacts with the so-called robbers, and paid them wages
to remain inactive in their mountain fastnesses and make
no expeditions; also not against the Romans, unless called
upon to do so. He asked seventy hostages of the principal parties in the revolt, kept them about himself as a sort
of Sanhedrin, and established the authority of the law in
the revolted districts and cities. He succeeded admirably

in making peace, and was always eager to imitate Moses and to enforce his laws. He was soon suspected of treason. For, arrived at Sepphoris, he sided at once with the Roman party in that city, protected it against the threatened attack of the patriots from without, left both the city and its fortifications in the hands of Roman partisans; and this was one of the most important strategic points of Galilee. Here the first blow was struck in the coming war. He did no better in Tiberias, near which, in Bethmaus, he had fixed his residence. This city having but recently declared against Agrippa II. and embraced the national cause, had its political parties, one of which was opposed to the innovation, and with the leaders of that very party Josephus consulted first. He had brought the decree of the Sanhedrin to the people of Tiberias to take out of Agrippa's palace all the ornaments and furniture, as some of them represented idols. Still finding the Agrippa partisans opposed to it, he proposed to send all valuables taken from the palace to Agrippa, who was then the declared enemy of the country. The people of Tiberias revolted, the governor ran away to Upper Galilee, and a number of Agrippa partisans were slain before the decree of the Sanhedrin was enforced. Worse than this he behaved in the Dabaritta case. A lady of Agrippa's court had the affrontery to travel through the revolted district in royal pomp and display. The soldiers of Dabaritta captured her, took all her valuables, and let her go in peace. The spoil was brought to Josephus and he promised to send it to Jerusalem to be applied to the fortification of the capital; but he at once informed the king's confidants that he would send him the whole spoil. This being betrayed, became the cause of a formidable revolt, and might have cost the life of Josephus, if he had not extricated himself by a cunning fabrication of falsehoods, and finally, by a villainous treatment of his fiercest opponents. He protected those who were considered spies and enemies of the country (Life 31), although it was known that the partisans of Agrippa were in continual correspondence with him, and Josephus boasts of sixty-three letters of Agrippa to himself. He betrayed his own inclination and feelings too freely to escape detection, so that all Galilee was filled with the rumor, he narrates, that their country was about to be betrayed by him to the Romans (Life 27). His intentions, like those of his party, to prevent the war, were certainly patriotic in his and their opinions. But he was not in sympathy with the cause and its champions, which he had officially espoused; was obliged to play a double game, and could not escape suspicion and hatred. The military preparations of Josephus proved a decided failure. He fortified, as he narrates (Life 37), Gamala on the Lake, a number of places in Gaulonitis, which had revolted from Agrippa, and built walls around Seleucia and Soganni. He also built walls around cities and villages in Upper Galilee, especially Jamnia, Meroth and Achabare. In Lower Galilee he fortified, or rather permitted the fortifying of Tarichæa, Tiberias, Gischala, the cave of Arbela, Bersobe, Selamin, Jotapata, Caphareccho, Sigo, Jepha and Mount Tabor. However, notwithstanding the death-defying heroism of the defenders of those places, not one of the hurriedly-constructed fortifications withstood, successfully, the Roman attacks. When the enemy approached in force, Josephus provided the cities with arms and provisions and organized the militia. Two hundred thousand men were enrolled and four hundred thousand men could have been enrolled; half of them were kept in garrisons and drilled in the use of arms and submission to discipline. That which was most necessary, to organize and drill an army to cope with the Romans in the open field, and to make proper use of the advantages of the Galilean terrain, was not at all attempted; on the contrary, those so-called robbers, the most available forces for this purpose, and the veteran fighting men of the country, were partly disarmed and partly kept under pay and oath not to fight. When the enemy did come, the defending forces were scattered all over the land in the fortified places, without any plan of co-operation. The military preparations of Josephus were intended to make peace and not to make war. It will always be difficult to decide whether it was inability or unwillingness to defend the country efficiently, which must be charged on Josephus and his party in Jerusalem (5).

---

(5) However eminent a scholar and historian he was, and his erudition was great, like his historiographic talent, he was not honest in his narrative of the last war and the presentation of his opponents. When after his "Wars," etc., had been written under the eyes of Titus and Agrippa in Rome, and Justus of Tiberias and several others (Life 65) had also written the same history without being under obligations to Titus or Agrippa, Josephus wrote his "Life," in which many of his statements in his "Wars" are considerably modified, and appear in an entirely different light. Those works must have considerably damaged the narrative of Josephus and his partisan standpoint. The student must control his statements made in his "Wars" by those made in his "Life," and must bear in mind that he wrote in the palace of the Cæsars.

6. The Opponents of Josephus.

Most prominent among the opponents of Josephus in Galilee was John of Gischala, called John b. Levi. He was the friend and companion of the Nassi, Simon b. Gamliel (Life 38), and the most competent man of the war party (Wars ii., xxi.). He, perhaps, was not the first to suspect the want of ability or fidelity of Josephus, still he was the first to say so to the Sanhedrin in Jerusalem, and to propose the removal of Josephus from the responsible office. John sent his brother, Simon, with Jonathan b. Sisenna and one hundred armed delegates, to Jerusalem. They succeeded in convincing the Nassi, who was already opposed to Josephus, that Josephus should be removed from office. The Nassi convinced Ananus and his advisers that this ought to be done speedily. A commission of four distinguished men was appointed, sufficient money and an armed force placed at their disposal, to send Josephus to Jerusalem, if he would obey voluntarily, or to kill him if he offered resistance to the decree of the central authority. Josephus, informed of the decree, refused to obey. Both parties fearing the outbreak of a civil war if an attempt should be made to settle the matter by the force of arms, maneuvered against each other for a considerable time. Josephus outmaneuvered the commission, and it failed to enforce the decree. Josephus and his party in Galilee were now virtually in a state of rebellion against the central authority in Jerusalem. He went to Tiberias and assembled his friends to a Sanhedrin (Life 66) and consulted as to what he should do to John of Gischala. They advised war upon him, which Josephus was not prepared to undertake. He offered amnesty to all of John's men who would at once return to their allegiance to him, which necessitated John to remain quiet in Gischala, and Josephus remained Governor of Galilee by usurpation. However, not all submitted quietly. A party in the two capitals, Tiberias and Sepphoris, made the attempt to have Josephus deposed. The people of Tiberias were determined that the decree of the central authority in Jerusalem should be enforced. Justus b. Pistus, known as Justus of Tiberias, the historian, it appears, was the prime mover in this matter. However, Josephus came, with eleven thousand men, against the city to enforce his authority; a civil war was feared by its rulers, and they submitted to his authority. Shortly after, however, the king's party got the upper hand in that city; chosing the least between two evils, Agrippa was invited by

Justus to take possession of the city. The king was too slow, his messenger was caught and brought before Josephus, who, by strategy, took Tiberias and again enforced his authority; then he let the king's messenger escape unpunished. In Sepphoris, too, no sooner had it become known that Josephus was deposed by the central authority than the rulers sent messengers to the President of Syria, and asked of him to come instantly or to send them a protecting garrison. Cestius Gallus could, at that moment, do neither, and Josephus took Sepphoris; his men ransacked the city till he got them out of it by a false alarm of approaching Romans. Josephus, in his autobiography, narrates all this in his own defense against Justus and the other historians, and certainly reported the facts as favorably to himself as he possibly could. Nevertheless, they proved conclusively that he was lawfully deposed, that a large portion of the people wanted him to obey, and he, by unlawful means, continued to hold the office for which he had neither the ability and experience nor the heart and sympathy, and became, as Justus said of him, the main cause of Israel's disaster. Before the legates of the Sanhedrin came back to Jerusalem to report, it was too late; for the war had been commenced by Josephus himself. Cestius Gallus had sent Placidus, with seven thousand men, to assist Sepphoris, and Josephus attempted to take the city by storm. After he had partially succeeded in this attempt, he was driven out again and forced to a battle in the plain, which he lost, and the Romans remained in possession of Sepphoris. At the same time, some of Agrippa's forces, under Sylla, approached the northern shore of the lake, and encamped before Julias, holding the roads to Cana and Gamala. Josephus attacked and routed the king's forces, but could not follow up his victory because he was thrown from his horse and had to be brought to Capernaum. He was then removed to Tarichæa, where he was attacked and routed by Sylla. He saved his men and himself by a sudden move on Julias, to come into the rear of the enemy, who was thus obliged to retreat. So the war had commenced with two defeats for Josephus, and meanwhile, Vespasian had come to Tyre ready to take the field. It was too late either for Josephus to resign or for the Sanhedrin to remove him from office. Justus of Tiberias, was with Agrippa in Tyre. He was accused before Vespasian by people of Decapolis for having burnt their villages and condemning many to death; but Agrippa saved him and he was put in irons for some time.

7. Defeat of Placidus before Jotapata.

From Sepphoris, Placidus made expeditions into the country, slaying the defenseless, plundering and burning as he proceeded. The people fled into the fortified cities. He proceeded as far north as Jotapata, which he schemed to take by surprise. The defenders of that city, however, received him outside of their fortifications, gave him battle, and forced him to retreat with considerable loss. The heavy armament of the Romans saved them. They marched back to Sepphoris, and Josephus had no army there to molest them. Sepphoris and the rich plain at the sea side were lost to the national cause, although the people of Jotapata heroically defended their city, and the fate of Galilee was virtually decided before the arrival of Vespasian.

8. Vespasian and Titus in Palestine.

When Nero had learned the defeat of Cestius, he was alarmed. The loss of the Asiatic portion of the empire appeared certain, if the Hebrews overthrew the Roman power in their land. He summoned the man whom he most disliked among his generals, because he had fallen asleep when Nero recited his own poetical productions, Titus Flavius Vespasianus, and appointed him commander-in-chief of a large and picked army to subject and crush Palestine. The founder of the second Roman dynasty was of humble origin. He had distinguished himself as a soldier in Thrace, Africa, Germany and Britain, and especially in forcing the Roman yoke on free-born men. With Vespasian, came also his son, Titus, to Ptolemais (in the spring of the year 68 A. C.), where the army of invasion was organized, while Mucianus succeeded Cestius Gallus as President of Syria. The army consisted of the Fifth, Tenth and Fifteenth Legions, with a large quota of cavalry, augmented by the armies of the surrounding petty princes, Agrippa II. included, to the number of 60,000 regulars, and a large number of irregulars, who always went with the Roman armies as traders of all kinds when their military service was not needed. It was supported in Palestine by the Heathen population and many Hebrews who remained loyal to Rome. The main strength of that army was in its heavy armament and scientific discipline, the skill and experience of its officers, the utter heartlessness, brutality, rapacity, bloodthirstiness and blind obedience of its soldiers, and the hatred of the Heathens against the Hebrews. But all these combined forces might have been overcome, if the Hebrews had been united in the resolution to shake off the Roman yoke, and the men of decisive action, instead of those who wanted to win a patched-up peace, had been from the start at the head of the revolution. Their patriotism, zeal and bravery were certainly adequate to the emergency.

9. THE FALL OF GADARA.

Without any molestation, Vespasian marched from Ptolemais to Gadara (Gabara), situated between Giscala and Jotapata, and took it without resistance, because its defenders had left it at the approach of the enemy. The defenseless inhabitants, lads, women, children and old people, were mercilessly massacred, the city and the villages around it were pillaged and burnt. Only those persons were spared who were considered saleable as slaves; all the others perished (*Nissan* 68 A. D.). The barbarities of the invader roused the Zealots to fury and prompted Josephus to leave his post in Tiberias, as under the circumstances, his life must have been in danger. He locked himself up with his men in Jotapata, which he must have known to be the next objective point of the enemy, simply because it was necessary for him to win, surrender or die. He sent messengers to Jerusalem to inform the central authority that unless they sent him an army he could not successfully defend Galilee. The army was not sent and Galilee was lost.

10. JOTAPATA AND JOSEPHUS TAKEN.

Early in the month of *Iyar*, Josephus had arrived in Jotapata, and shortly after, Vespasian surrounded the city. It offered a desperate and well-conducted resistance. During the siege of Jotapata, one detachment of the Roman army took the neighboring city of Japha (25th of *Sivan*), and another defeated the Samaritans on Mt. Gerizzim (27th of *Sivan*), pillaging, burning and slaughtering or selling into slavery without regard to age or sex, as had been done in Gadara. Meanwhile, the defenders of Jotapata, by a siege of forty-seven days, were so exhausted that they could offer no effectual resistance to an attacking army. A deserter informed Vespasian thereof, and during the next night, which was foggy and dark, his men succeeded in scaling the wall, taking the citadel and cutting down all who were in the city (1st of *Tamuz*). The city was demolished and its fortifications burned. Forty thousand Hebrews lost their lives in and about Jotapata. However, among those who had sought refuge in subterranean hiding-places, there was also Josephus, with one hundred men, in a den adjoining a deep pit. Escape being impossible, those hundred men and Josephus resolved to slay one another. Josephus knew how to manage the affair so that he and Nicanor were to die last. Ninety-nine died the voluntary death, then Josephus and Nicanor escaped and delivered themselves up to Vespasian. Before Vespasian, he played the *role* of a prophet, he says, predicting to him that he would be the next emperor of Rome (6), which prophecy the Talmud claims for R. Jochanan b. Saccai. It is not difficult to see why Vespasian spared the man who had always been a friend of the Romans, and had done his best to deliver Galilee up to their authority. From and after this day, Josephus remained among the Romans as an informer, the Hebrews maintained; in chains and as a pleader and pacificator, he maintains. His foes and friends at home denounced him as a traitor, who had never intended to fight the Romans. He went to Jotapata to be captured, as he could no longer maintain himself in Galilee, and could not return to Jerusalem. He made such a heroic defense there, because he dared not do otherwise, as he feared his own warriors. He prophesied the fall of the city many days before it took place, hence he knew the object of his coming to Jotapata.

11. Joppa Taken and Tiberias Surrendered.

Vespasian left the depopulated region with its corpses and ruins, and pressed on westward. In Joppa, however, the Hebrew mariners were organized and carried on a maritime war against the Romans and Syrians. A band of Romans, sent by Vespasian, surprised the city at night and many of the inhabitants fled to their ships. A storm dashed the vessels against the rocky shores and many perished. Joppa remained in the hands of the Romans and the patriotic enterprise of the mariners was frustrated. Many of them, undoubtedly, fled to European and African shores. Meanwhile, Vespasian went to Agrippa's capital, Cæsarea Philippi, to be feasted and lauded there. Then he marched to Tiberias to retake it for Agrippa. After some resistance, the Zealots and their compatriots were obliged

---

(6) He certainly did not dare to predict this before the death of Nero had been known in the camp. That death occurred June, 68 A. C., about the same time, and could not have been known yet in Palestine.

to leave the city and seek refuge in the neighboring Tarichæa. Tiberias surrendered to the Romans and submitted again to the authority of Agrippa II.

12. Fall of Tarichlea—Bloody Treachery of Vespasian.

Tarichæa, at the south-western end of the lake, was well fortified and favorably located for defense. It was now the center of fugitives from all the destroyed and surrendered cities, reinforced by patriotic men from all parts of the upper country. Between this city and Tiberias, the Romans constructed a fortified camp. Jesus b. Saphat, commanding the fugitives from Tiberias, provided with boats, came upon the Romans from the coast, drove away the working men, destroyed the walls of the camp, and retired to the vessels. The Hebrews retreated before the enemy, approaching in force, far enough into the sea that their projectiles could reach the enemy, who could make no attack on them. At a distance, the Hebrews were superior to the Romans with their heavy armament. Titus commanding there, was obliged to send for reinforcements. When a part of them had arrived, he attacked the Hebrews outside the walls of Tarichæa, and forced them to retreat. Vespasian prepared a fleet to fight the Hebrews on the lake, and succeeded in destroying their whole fleet, and the sea was full of dead bodies and destroyed vessels. The engagement was a most desperate one and cost many lives on both sides. Meanwhile, Titus had taken the city with the assistance of its original inhabitants, who had been promised pardon by Vespasian. Still, after the victory had been secured, the mighty Roman gave permission to his brutal hordes to kill one thousand and two hundred old and disabled people, sent six thousand of the young and strong to Nero " to dig through the Isthmus " (Wars iii., x. 10), and sold 30,400 of them into slavery, besides those whom he presented to Agrippa (*Ellul*, 68 A. C.). Only a Roman could be so treacherous and barbarous. Every feeling of humanity and every sense of justice had been suffocated among the brutalized Heathens of that age; and among all Heathens, the worst were, undoubtedly, the Roman Grandees.

13. The Last Stronghold's Fall.

After the fall of Tarichæa, the cities of Galilee surrendered to the Romans, and the rest of the fighting men fled to Mt. Tabor, which was well fortified, to Gischala and to Gamala, west of the lake, besides those who escaped into Judea and Perea. Mt. Tabor was taken by Placidus, who had made treacherous promises to the warriors, to bring them down to the plain, where they were massacred in cold blood. The defenders of Gamala, however, offered the most heroic resistance to the entire Roman army. Agrippa had been beaten before the walls of the city, and Vespasian, with his whole force, besieged it. Many Romans lost their lives there while erecting siege works, and in the first assault upon the city they sustained such terrible losses that the entire army was in danger, and Vespasian saved his life by personal bravery. The city was short of provisions and water, so many were obliged to leave. When half the population was gone, another assault was made on the city and then on its citadel, which would not have been taken had not a violent storm on the top of that mountain favored the Romans. The twenty-seventh day of *Tishri*, the city and its citadel fell, and those of its inhabitants who had not escaped by subterranean passages were massacred. With Gamala, the last hope of the patriots in Galilee vanished. Gischala capitulated, after John and all his men had left. Galilee was conquered, Agrippa II. was again lord of his kingdom, the heroes of Jotapata, Tarichæa and Gamala were in their graves, and, as far as Galilee was concerned, the war was over.

14. STATE OF AFFAIRS IN JERUSALEM.

The central authority in Jerusalem, under Ananus, Joseph b. Gorion and the Sanhedrin, gave no assistance to Galilee, and during the years 67 and 68 A. C. did nothing to prepare for the war, besides the abortive attack on Ascalon, the fortifying of Jerusalem and some other cities, arming the defenders of those cities and storing provisions in them, exactly as Josephus had done in Galilee (7). While the Roman army was engaged in Galilee and Samaria, nothing was done in Judea, Perea and Idumea to weaken the enemy, to divert his attention or to divide his forces. Therefore, it

---

(7) The Talmud *Guitin*, 56 a, and the Midrash Rabba to Lamentation, furnish the story of the four rich men in Jerusalem, Ben Zizith, Ben Gorion, Ben Nakdimon and Ben Kalba Shebua, who had laid up provisions enough to last the city ten years or longer. However, when the Zealots took possession of the government they, by one of their captains, Ben Batiah, a nephew of R. Jochanan b. Saccai, burnt all the provisions in order to force the population to fight or starve.

could not be doubtful to anybody that the policy of the central authority was precisely the same as that of Josephus, to keep the peace, and to obtain favorable conditions. The conquest of Galilee and the comfort of Josephus in the Roman camp could not fail to convince the Zealots that they were betrayed by the party in power, although they had not the strength in Jerusalem or the provinces to supersede their opponents. But after the conquest of Galilee, there came to Jerusalem John of Gischala, with all his armed men and the fugitive Zealots from all Galilee, and they were received with enthusiasm by their compatriots. They imbued many of the young men with the idea that fighting in the weak cities of Galilee after the strongest places had been lost, was a waste of lives, which had to be saved for the defense of Jerusalem, the impregnable city, never to be taken by the Romans. In a short time the Zealots were in possession of sufficient power to take the reins of government into their own hands. They began (68 to 69 A. C.) by taking possession of the temple. They deposed all the old officers, and in order to overcome the historical right of primogeniture in filling those offices, they went back to the old practice of deciding by the lot. Having accomplished that, they deposed also the highpriest, Matthias b. Theophilus, and appointed as his successor, one of their democratic men from the country, Phanneas (Pinchas) b. Samuel. The temple was now the headquarters of the Zealots. The aristocratic party was roused to appreciate the danger of the situation by the eloquence of Ananus, Joseph b. Gorion, Simon b. Gamliel, and other men of the highest authority. In a public meeting, it was resolved to set bounds to the dominion and excesses of the Zealots, and a body of militia volunteered to effect that purpose.

15. Outbreak of Civil War.

The Zealots being informed of the resolution of Ananus, met on the Temple Mount, and John of Gischala, who had a seat in the council of Ananus and was sent to pacify the Zealots, roused them to speedy and energetic resistance to the lawful authority. He impressed upon them two points, viz.: that they need expect no pardon from their opponents, and that the latter were about to call in the Romans to their assistance. He counseled resolute resistance to the authorities and the speedy invitation of armed succor from other parts of the country. His counsel prevailed. The leaders of the Zealots, who were the priests, Eleazar b.

Simon and Zachariah b. Phalck, gave the alarm, "Ananus has imposed upon the people and was betraying the metropolis to the Romans." They dispatched secret messengers to Idumea, asked instant reinforcement, and made ready for self-defense. The militia led against them was superior to them in number and alacrity, but they were superior in arms and discipline. The first conflict was very obstinate and murderous on both sides, until the citizens of Jerusalem were thoroughly aroused; but then they overpowered the Zealots, took the cloisters, and drove the Zealots into the Court of Women, which the latter closed and defended from the parapets. Ananus did not wish to break through the gates or to lead his men into the interior of the temple courts without being first Levitically cleansed, and submitting to ritualistic prejudices, he stopped short with the work half done. He selected six thousand men to besiege the Zealots in the interior courts, and thought the work was done. So the citizens of Jerusalem thought, and the rich sent paid substitutes to the temple cloisters to prevent the escape of the Zealots. But unexpectedly, twenty thousand armed men from Idumea, well organized, under four zealous leaders, John and Jacob b. Sosas, Simon b. Cathlas and Phineas b. Clusothus, appeared at the gates of Jerusalem to reinforce the Zealots.

16. THE IDUMEANS IN JERUSALEM.

When the messenger of the Zealots had come to Idumea with the exciting message, the rulers of that province alarmed the impetuous mass of patriots, and twenty thousand of them rushed to arms at once to save the metropolis and the republic. Ananus closed the gates of Jerusalem against them, which only enraged and confirmed them in their belief that he was a traitor whose intention it was to deliver the metropol's into the hands of Rome (8). In vain did Joshua b. Gamala address the Idumean warriors to make them understand the situation and to persuade them to keep the peace. Neither his age and dignity nor his eloquence and argumentation changed the minds of those champions of independence. Simon b. Cathlas answered in their behalf: "You are traitors and we have come to protect liberty, and will hold to our arms until you repent of what you have done

---

(8) In fact it is difficult to ascertain what was, at that time, the actual intention of Ananus and his party. It is not unlikely that a speedy peace with Rome was their programme, believing that the fall of Galilee must have changed the popular mind.

against it." The Zealots in the temple took advantage of a very stormy night; some of their boldest men, provided with proper implements, made their escape from the temple, reached the city gate, and quietly opened it for the Idumeans, whom they persuaded to proceed quietly and rapidly to the Temple Mount and to raise the siege. This they did; they took the six thousand men there by surprise; the Zealots in the temple sallied out, and a terrible conflict and carnage ensued. The besieging militia fought bravely, the city was thoroughly alarmed, and the fight became general and furious. At last the citizens were overpowered, the outer temple was drenched in blood, and the Zealots were in possession of the entire mountain. Now the victorious party turned against the city, plundered and massacred indiscriminately, cut down the principal men of the party in power, and slew both Ananus and Joshua b. Gamala. Then they convoked a Sanhedrin of seventy of their compatriots, drove the lawful Sanhedrin out of the temple (9), tried and executed those who were suspected of conspiracy with Rome, and committed all the barbarous excesses of fanatical and enraged partisans. Eight thousand and five hundred men fell that day. Terror reigned in Jerusalem, and the beginning of its final destruction was made.

17. Reign of the Zealots in Jerusalem—Escape of R. Jochanan b. Saccai to Jamnia.

The fury of the Idumeans being spent, they began to see

---

(9) Josephus does not report Simon b. Gamliel among the slain of that terrible day, although he was certainly one of the principal leaders of the moderate party, and the rabbis maintain that he was slain by the Romans after the fall of Jerusalem which is not confirmed by Josephus, although it is so adopted by Josephon (chapter xcvii.). Still his name is mentioned no more in any of the records. Josephus merely records that the Zealots set up "fictitious tribunals of justice;" that among the most eminent men who were slain at that time was Zachariah b Baruch; "Moreover, they struck the judges with the backs of their swords, by way of abuse and thrust them out of the court of the temple." An ancient tradition recorded in the last section of Megullath Taanith, maintains that on the twenty-fifth day of Sivan, there were slain Simon b. Gamliel, Ishmael b Elishah an I Haninah Segan Hak-kohanim. The latter being identical with Ananus and Ishmael to be amended by Joshua b. Gamala it would appear that Simon also was among the victims of that bloody twenty-fifth day of Sivan in the year 69 A. C., of which it is said also in Dibrei Malchuth Bayith Sheni, that many of the most pious men in Israel (חסידי ישראל) were slain that day.

the wickedness of their doings. Repentance came too late, the dead could not be reanimated. No enemy approaching the capital, and the accusation of treason against the slain men lacking evidence, the Idumeans quietly left the city to the surprise of the parties left behind. The Zealots being now in undisputed possession of the power, continued the bloody work by cutting down all prominent men whom they suspected of loyalty to the overthrown party. Among the latter, there were two men of great prominence, viz.: Gorion and Niger, the ex-Governor of Idumea, whose body was full of scars of wounds received in the service of his country. The rich people fled, although the Zealots guarded every passage out of the city, and slew the fugitives; yet their guards were bribed by some, while others escaped their vigilance. Among the latter, there was also R. Jochanan b. Saccai, the Chief-Justice and Vice-President of the Sanhedrin. His disciples, Eliezer b. Hyrcan and Joshua b. Hananiah, carried a coffin out of the city for burial, in which, instead of a corpse, there was the venerable and hoary disciple of Hillel. Ben Batiah, the nephew of R. Jochanan, being on duty at that gate, the coffin was not searched. They succeeded in reaching the Roman headquarters, and R. Jochanan obtained a hearing of Vespasian, to whom he prophesied both the downfall of Jerusalem and its temple, and Vespasian's elevation to the throne of the Cæsars. The Roman general being well disposed to the fugitives, and especially to the hoary savan who represented the intelligence of his country, the rabbi asked of him the favor to be given Jamnia (JABNEH) as a place of refuge for himself and his disciples, to continue there, in peace, the teaching of the Law, as he had formerly done at BERUR CHOL. This being granted, the rabbi and his disciples went to Jamnia, re-opened its ancient academy, and there laid the foundation to the reconstruction of Judaism out of the ruins of its ancient polity and politics. In Jerusalem, however, with the death and flight of her most eminent citizens, a reign of terror was maintained by men, of whom Josephus reports (Wars iv., vi. 3), that they trampled upon all the laws of man, laughed at the laws of God, and ridiculed the oracles of the prophets as the tricks of jugglers; although it can not be doubted that he exaggerates, in order to defame his enemies and to justify, partially, the Roman barbarities.

18. Vespasian's Further Conquests.

Meanwhile, Vespasian continued his conquests in the north and west of Jerusalem almost without resistance. He had reduced all Acrabatene, also Jamnia and the whole sea coast down to Gaza. His captains wanted him to march at once to Jerusalem and take it, as he had been invited, and he would certainly have been welcomed as a redeemer by the bulk of the population. But he refused to do it, and thought the partisans of the capital would destroy one another fast enough. While the Zealots were doing nothing for the protection of the country, and their compatriots all over the land imitated their acts of violence in various cities, the inhabitants of Gadara, east of the Jordan, a resort of a large number of very rich people, called on Vespasian for protection. Placidus came with sufficient force to frighten the Zealots out of Gadara. But the fugitives, reinforced by the country people fleeing before the approaching enemy, took a stand at Bethenrabris, and gave battle to the enemy. Their courage and enthusiasm were counteracted and overcome by the strategies of the Romans, their superior tactics and arms, and the fighting Hebrews were defeated and their stronghold burnt. They fled toward the Jordan, followed by many thousands of the terrified country people, and pursued by the Roman cavalry. The massacre and destruction of property were horrible. The Jordan being impassable, another disastrous battle was fought, and only those who swam the Jordan or fled to the wilderness, escaped. 150,000 of the defenders of Perea lost their lives and 2,200 were taken prisoners. Perea down to Macherus was again subjected to the Roman sway. Macherus and the country around it could not be taken by Placidus. Meanwhile, the best part of Idumea was also overrun, the cities burnt, the inhabitants slain without mercy, and whatever could not be carried off by the brutal invaders was destroyed. Like the city of Gerasa, which was totally ransacked and destroyed by L. Annius, cities and villages, whatever their population professed, were swept away and their population massacred like wild beasts or sold to slave dealers. Trajan was the name of the hyena that raged in Idumea. He boasted of having slain 10,000, and bringing 1,000 prisoners. Near Jericho, he met Vespasian. That city capitulated without resistance. All these slaughters, however, did not secure the country to Vespasian. The mountains, with their natural fastnesses, caverns, steep and narrow passes, were as so many dangerous points for the invader, and Vespasian was obliged to build forts and castles in many points of the land to secure himself against the concentration of the patriots and the surprise of his army on the plains, as had been done often before. Finding the whole land swarming with rebellious patriots, who, defeated in their cities, sought refuge in the mountains, he could not venture the siege of Jerusalem before he was master of the land, which was a difficult task, and took considerable time. Meanwhile, Nero had made an end of his miserable life and reign (June 11, 68 A. C.), and a period of confusion followed in Rome under the successors of Nero—Galba, Otho and Vitellius—all in one year (68 A. C. to July of 69). Meanwhile, the armies of the East proclaimed Vespasian Emperor of Rome. From Jericho, he, in company with his son Titus, and also Josephus, released from his chains, went to Alexandria, and some of the best legions followed them. The struggle for the throne of the Cæsars against Vitellius and his party was conducted on the part of Vespasian from Alexandria, and ended with his victory; so that in July, 69 A. C., he was proclaimed emperor in Rome. He became the founder of the Flavius dynasty, which name Josephus was also given, in addition to his Hebrew name. He remained in Alexandria till the Judean war was over, in order to return as victor and conqueror of the Orient.

CHAPTER XXVI.

The Destruction of Jerusalem.

1. JERUSALEM BEFORE ITS DESTRUCTION.

Jerusalem was, after Antioch, the largest city of the East. It had within its walls over 600,000 inhabitants, and was capable, with its suburbs, to give shelter to two millions and even three millions of people, a number which did sometimes assemble, including the pilgrims from all parts of the then inhabited earth. The city embraced now within its walls Zion in the south-west, Acra directly north thereof, and Bezetha directly north of Acra, the suburb of Bezetha east of Bezetha, the Temple Mount south thereof and Ophel south of the temple. The city, with its one hundred and sixty-four towers, rising thirty-two feet above the wall, with its numerous cupolas and minarets within, presented a most picturesque and imposing prospect from the highest point of Mt. Olives. The streets of Jerusalem were narrow, paved with white stone, well drained and extremely clean; but besides one rosary, there was neither garden, park nor tree in the city. Its fortifications were no mean evidence of the Hebrews' achievements in architecture and mechanics. No city was better fortified than Jerusalem before its fall. It consisted of six fortified places with citadels in each, and the temple was a citadel within a citadel, with all possible obstacles to an advancing enemy, with its brass gates, its parapets and towers. Rich people occupied cloisters and lodges about the temple, where they not only came to worship, but also deposited there their treasures for safe keeping (it never occurred that anything was stolen in or about the temple, that a building was struck by lightning, or that a fire broke out accidentally); so that an immense wealth was gathered around and in the temple treasury. The city was well-provisioned until the

Zealots destroyed the provisions to force the citizens to starve or fight. It was supposed that Jerusalem was impregnable, and besides, it was believed by many that God would not permit the holy city and temple to be taken, although others had prophesied its destruction long before.

2. The Zealots in Jerusalem.

After the death of Ananus and the victory of John of Gischala and the Idumeans, many citizens fled from the city. Still the expeditions of Vespasian north and west of Jerusalem, also in Perea and Idumea, drove so many more fugitives to the capital, some to save their lives and treasures, and others to fight for the city and the temple. The fugitives increased the forces of the Zealots and augmented, especially, the number of John's adherents, while the Zealots of Jerusalem acknowledged Eleazar b. Annus as their head. No Sanhedrin and no central authority are mentioned any longer. The most propitious time, when Vespasian and Titus, with the best portion of the Roman legions had left the country, and the whole Roman Empire was shaking under the violence of its armies and emperors, was wasted by the leaders in Jerusalem in fortifying their own power and holding the peaceable citizens in subjection. Now was the time either to strike a decisive blow or to win the favor of Vespasian, neither of which was done, and the year 68 A. C. passed away without anything being done except sending messengers to Mesopotamia and Parthia to obtain succor from that side, which proved a failure.

3. Simon B. Gorion.

Simon b. Gorion, prominent among those who had fought Cestius Gallus, and afterward among the opponents of Ananus, had been driven with his men into Messada. He was a patriot and soldier of uncommon courage, bodily vigor and military talent. The men of Messada did not trust him, and after they had been driven out of Jerusalem, were unwilling to engage again in any warfare except in defense of their city. After the death of Ananus and the fall of his party in Jerusalem, Simon left Messada, retired into the mountains, proclaimed freedom to the slaves, and succeeded in collecting an army about him. He fortified a town called Nain and the caves in the valley of Pharan. The Zealots of Idumea being alarmed by the progress of Simon, met him at their borders, and gave him battle. Without being defeated, Simon went back to Nain, reorganized his army and marched to Thecoa, from whence he sent an embassy to the garrison of Herodium, demanding the surrender of that place. His embassador, Eleazar, was killed. Still one of the Idumean chiefs espoused Simon's cause, and he succeeded in taking Hebron and overrunning Idumea from that point. The Zealots of Jerusalem, jealous of Simon's growing power, and unable to give him battle, laid ambushes in the passes, and succeeded in capturing his wife, whom they took to Jerusalem. Instead of bringing Simon to terms, as the intention was, it made him furious. He marched up to the very walls of Jerusalem, maltreated or killed whomsoever fell into his hands, and threatened destruction to everybody, until the frightened Zealots liberated his wife. He returned to Idumea, driving the people before him to seek refuge in Jerusalem.

4. SIMON B. GORION IN JERUSALEM, AND THE ARMY OF DEFENSE.

When Vespasian was gone and the danger of an immediate siege averted, the Zealots in the city behaved themselves outrageously against the citizens and pilgrims, not only by vulgar and immoral conduct, but also by constant feuds, fights and bloodshed. Some of them mixed among the crowd in women's attire, and assassinated their enemies. They appropriated for themselves the first fruits and tithes brought to Jerusalem, and lived in high glee on other people's property. At last a fight broke out among the Zealots, the Idumeans attacked John's men and broke into the Grapta palace at Ophel, where John had his treasury and headquarters. While John rallied his men on the Temple Mount, the priests and citizens embraced the cause of the Idumeans, and sent for Simon b. Gorion to come to their assistance. He came and took possession of the city, and the Zealots held the temple. The two parties attempting to dislodge one another, destroyed houses and magazines, so that the Temple Mount was environed with ruins. Many warriors and non-combatants lost their lives, and many a store of provisions was consumed by fire. At last the Zealots on the Temple Mount also disagreed. Eleazar, who had started the war, saw himself under the command of John of Gischala, whom he disliked. He persuaded a number of leaders to revolt against John, and they followed him to the interior of the Temple Court, in which they were secure against attacks from John, and took the material stored near by for raising the temple wall twenty cubits, and constructed four towers to protect themselves against attacks from Simon b. Gorion. Now citizens and pilgrims coming to the temple ran the risk of being plundered twice, once by John's and once by Eleazar's men. All attempts to make peace among the three factions, in which the late highpriest took the lead, proved a failure; each of the three chief men claimed the highest authority, and they jealously watched each other's movements. So the most precious time, from 69 to the spring of 70 A. c., was wasted, men, buildings and provisions were destroyed, many of the citizens were forced to leave, while others wished for the approach of the Romans in order to direct the warriors' attention abroad. There were now in the city 24,000 warriors: 3,000 under Eleazar and Simon b. Jair, 6,000 under John of Gischala, 5,000 Idumeans under Jacob b. Sosa and Simon b. Cathla, and 10,000 under Simon b. Gorion. Had those 24,000 impetuous heroes, together with the Zealots of Massada and elsewhere, been in the field when Vespasian marched into Galilee, which could have been the case, and their number could have been largely increased, if the moderate party had been earnest in their purpose to make war, history would have taken quite a different turn; but now it was too late. One city with but a small strip of country around it could not effectually resist the Roman colossus, had every man, woman and child therein been a Maccabean hero; as Rome, to save its honor and its dominion in the East, was obliged to crush the Hebrews.

5. Titus Approaches Jerusalem.

Vespasian having secured the throne of the Cæsars, Titus was appointed commander-in-chief of the army in Judea. The festivities over in Rome and Alexandria, Titus came with an army to Cæsarea. His legions and auxiliaries amounted to no less than 80,000 men, provided with all war engines known in Rome and every facility which science had invented. Two distinguished Hebrews were in his camp, the apostate Tiberius Alexander, who was a general under Titus, and Josephus, supposed to have been used as a mediator between Romans and Hebrews, although the latter considered him a renegade, traitor and spy. It was possible yet to save the city and temple. Titus was madly in love with Berenice, the sister of Agrippa II., although she was ten or fifteen years his senior and had been the wife of two husbands. She was not without patriotism and piety. It was easy to win her for the cause of her people, and it was in her power to influence Titus in its favor. But this circumstance, perhaps, was unknown, and the Zealots would not have violated their oath of liberty or death. So Titus marched without any molestation from Cæsarea to Jerusalem.

6. The Zealots' First Victory.

Titus, on approaching the city, went with six hundred cavalry from the main body of his troops to reconnoiter the northwestern corner of the fortification. When he approached the tower of Psephinus, suddenly a number of Hebrews rushed forth from the places called the Women's Towers and surrounded Titus and his men, so that the commander of the army saved his life only by his personal bravery and the skill of his cavalry. After this lesson, Titus knew he had to deal with a valiant enemy, and began to be cautious. Three camps were to be fortified for the besieging army, one at Scopus, opposite the northeastern wall of the suburb of Bezetha; another camp was to be laid out at the other end of the fortifications, viz.: behind the sepulchre of the Kings of Adiabene, opposite the northeastern wall of Bezetha; and another camp for the Tenth Legion, coming via Jericho, was to be located on Mount Olives. When the Tenth Legion went to work to construct the camp, the Hebrews sallied forth from their fortifications and attacked them with such impetuosity that they were thrown into a state of disorder and confusion, from which they recovered but slowly, to turn and attack the Hebrews. But the latter fell on the Romans with renewed fury, and would have crushed the Tenth Legion, if Titus had not come with succor from the northeastern camp. So the beginning was made and it augured success to the besieged, who had thus twice worsted the over-confident enemy, whose approach had suddenly united all the factions in the city, although they did not give up their respective positions within, and watched each other with the same jealousy as heretofore.

7. Assassination in the Temple.

The beginning of the siege occurred a few days before Passover, with a vast concourse of pilgrims in the city. On the Feast of Passover, Eleazar opened the temple for the worshipers. Among them there came also the men of John, with arms concealed under their garments, and suddenly appeared in armor among the crowd of pilgrims. The

Eleazar men discovering the treachery, leaped down from the battlements and sought refuge in the subterranean passages of the temple. The pilgrims stood amazed, were driven from place to place, many were beaten, trampled upon, and not a few were slain. After the pilgrims were out, John seized upon all the engines which Eleazar had constructed or captured, and began an attack on Simon and the city. Many lost their lives on that last Passover in the Temple; still the two factions on the Temple Mount were reunited, and Jerusalem had only two factions under Simon and John.

8. The Romans Beaten Again.

This state of affairs becoming known in the Roman camp, Josephus was sent to invite the parties to surrender, but he could get no decisive answer from anybody. The besieged made the best use of the information obtained from the enemy. Titus being engaged with moving the camp down Mount Olives, in an air line with the walls of the temple, and leveling the valley between, a party of Hebrews came out of the walls and behaved as if they had been ejected from the city, and those upon the wall apparently attacked those below to drive them hence. The Romans were deluded into the belief that one hostile faction had driven the other out of the city, and rushed to the attack. When the Romans had been drawn near enough to the fortifications, the Hebrews, reinforced from the city, attacked them and drove them clear back to their old fortifications. Titus, after this third defeat, would have been inclined to a reasonable peace. One Nicanor, together with Josephus, approached the wall near enough to discourse with the sentinels, and to offer terms of peace to the leaders. The answer was a shower of darts and stones. Nicanor was wounded, and Titus was forced to prepare for a long and tedious siege.

9. Another Successful Sally.

The siege progressed steadily. Places were leveled, embankments thrown up, engines put in position and three towers were erected to overlook the walls. Once more the Hebrews sallied out in force and engaged the enemy with the intention of destroying the siege works and burning the engines and towers. It was a desperate struggle. engaging the entire Roman force to save the engines; still a large portion of the siege works was destroyed, and one of the three towers came down at night with a terrible crash, alarming and frightening the whole camp. This last sally, however, exhausted largely the strength of the Hebrews in the city, especially as on the same day they lost one of their principal captains, the Idumean John, and they could no longer prevent the rams from battering down the northeastern wall of the suburb of Bezetha.

10. The First Wall Taken.

On the seventh day of *Iyar* (70 A. C.), the first wall was taken by the Romans, without much resistance, which placed the suburb of Bezetha in their power. The camp was moved to that suburb, where once the Assyrians had been encamped. The wall between that suburb and Bezetha was now defended vigorously by Simon's men, and John's force attacked the enemy from Fort Antonia and the temple wall. The Hebrews roused from a momentary lethargy, defended that wall most persistently, and made such impetuous sallies on the Romans that they worked and fought under constant dread, slept on their arms at night, and the presence of Titus was constantly necessary to encourage them in order to hold their own; for a retreat *en masse*, which the Romans were several times on the point of making, would have proved as disastrous to the army of Titus as it did to that of Cestius Gallus. The Hebrews' impetuosity, valor, swiftness and death-defying fury, combined with the natural shrewdness of the race, sharpened by danger and excitement, proved too much for the Romans, and it was only by their vast superiority in numbers and arms that they maintained their position. When a ram had been put in position opposite a tower in the north of the wall and the battering commenced, negotiations were opened with Titus by one upon the tower, whose name was Castor, which, it appears, were broken off by misunderstanding and the cowardice of Josephus, who was afraid to come near the wall; and so, after an interval of a few hours, the attack was continued.

11. The Contest About Bezetha.

The twelfth day of *Iyar* a breach had been battered into the wall of Bezetha, and the Romans proceeded to take possession of that part of the city with the promise, Josephus informs us, not to demolish it, but to protect the life and property of the citizens. The warriors, however, overawed the men of peace and drove the Romans again out of the city. Three days longer the Hebrews kept the Romans at bay before the walls of Bezetha, but on the fourth they were overpowered and forced back behind the walls of Acra. Bezetha was given up to the Romans after every inch of ground had been heroically contested on both sides.

12. Overtures of Peace.

Josephus does not inform us how many Romans had been slain before the walls of Jerusalem before Bezetha had been taken. Yet their losses must have been very heavy, for Titus made another attempt to get possession of the city by treaty. In the first place, he held a grand parade of his whole army at a spot where the whole maneuver could be seen from the walls and roofs of the city. He paid off the soldiers, all of whom appeared in full and dazzling armor, which the Hebrews in the city saw for four successive days. This was a terrifying spectacle for those who had before their eyes part of the city captured and the rest threatened by famine, and an enemy apparently invincible. Then Josephus was sent to persuade the defenders of the city to surrender, and to offer them the right hand of Cæsar for their security. But there were certainly not many in the city who placed any confidence in the words of Josephus, nor could they trust in Cæsar's word after they knew what had been done in Galilee, Samaria, Idumea and Perea, by Vespasian and his generals, who slaughtered thousands to whom sacred promises of security had been given. Nor could anything change the oath of the Zealots to fight for liberty or death, and their established principle to die as freemen is preferable to living as slaves. Non-combatant citizens, however, embraced this opportunity and left the city with more or less hidden treasures, and were permitted by Titus to seek other homes. The Zealots stopped this emigration by rigorous measures, although the famine was already upon them.

13. Barbarous Outrages.

There were many non-combatants in the city who would not leave because they surely believed God would not deliver the holy city and temple into the enemy's power; and others who could not leave with their wives and children and would not desert them. The scarcity of food compelled many, especially of the poorer class, to leave the city for the purpose of collecting food. Instantly, a cavalry camp was established at the junction of the Gihon and Kedron Creeks, to capture those who came out of the city. As many as five hundred were captured in one day, all of whom were scourged and crucified before the eyes of those upon the walls and roofs of the city. This was only one more of the barbarous outrages which will forever stain with infamy the Roman name, and more especially the names of Titus and Vespasian. The Zealots made use of that occurrence to prove that no Roman's promise was reliable, and that desertion from the city was to run into the jaws of inevitable death.

14. The Romans Once More Defeated.

Meanwhile, the construction of siege works was steadily continued by the enemy, and the Zealots lost none of their daring bravery. The young King of Cammagena came with a band of young warriors to assist the Romans. He thought it was easy for his warriors, who were trained in Macedonian tactics, to take the city, and tried his skill by an assault upon the wall. But he soon discovered that those upon the wall were his superiors in the fight, and seeing his men wounded and falling in large numbers, he was forced to beat a retreat. Nor had the Romans the courage to take any portion of the walls by storm. After fifteen days' hard work, the Fifth and Twelfth Legions had succeeded in raising two embankments opposite the wall connecting Fort Antonia with the eastern wall near the Fishpond, while the Tenth and Fifteenth Legions erected similar works near the Acra wall at the northeastern pond. Now the engines were mounted and all was ready for the attack. John, however, had constructed a mine from within to a point under the Roman works, filled it with all kinds of combustibles, and set it on fire. The embankments, men and engines fell down with a terrible crash, and in a few minutes all was enveloped in flames. So this scheme to take the Temple Mount proved disastrous to the Romans. Two days later, Simon made an attack on the other works of the enemy, and a most furious engagement was fought, which ended with the destruction of the Romans' works and engines, and a severe chastisement inflicted on them. They were very much discouraged by the furious bravery and alacrity of their enemies, and the sudden destruction of all the works raised with so much sacrifice and exertion.

15. A Wall to Isolate the City.

A council of war was convoked by Titus, in which his opinion prevailed, that the city could not be taken and its inhabitants could not be prevented from bringing provisions into it, as the area was too large to be blockaded, and the subterranean passages too many to be guarded. It was resolved that famine only could overcome the defenders of Jerusalem, and therefore, a wall to encompass the whole city was necessary. A hundred thousand or more of men went to work to erect the wall. The work progressed rapidly, as it was built at a distance from the city, not to be reached by any of the three hundred and thirty engines worked upon the wall. As the wall progressed, so did the famine in the city. The warriors became unable to undertake any more sallies. Persons died in large numbers from starvation, and the dead bodies were thrown over the wall. Gradually this also was neglected, the dead remained in the city and added to the many miseries, the stench and pestilence from the decaying bodies.

16. Terror Within and Slaughter Without.

When Titus saw that the crucifixion of deserters did him no good, he again permitted them to pass through his lines. A rumor was started that the Hebrew deserters leaving their homes swallowed gold and gems to get them out of the city, the Arabs and Syrians captured the deserters and ripped them open to seek treasures in their bowels. So hundreds, or perhaps thousands, lost their lives, till Titus prevented it and gave free passage to all deserters. No doubt large numbers made use of that privilege, although the Zealots treated the captured deserters or their remaining families with merciless rigor. One of the ex-highpriest's sons deserted, and this highpriest, Matthias b. Theophilus, was the very man who opened the gates of Jerusalem for Simon and his men. Yet this very Simon ordered the execution of Matthias b. Theophilus and his three remaining sons. Many rich men, Josephus maintains, were executed on this or that pretext to get hold of their wealth. Terror, anarchy, pestilence and famine, undoubtedly, drove many out of the city, although more of the non-combatants remained in the city than a prudent commander would have kept there. One wealthy woman ate the flesh of her own child which she had seen perish of starvation, and when the hungry warriors came to her house for food, she angrily threw the remains of her child before them, which shocked even the men used to bloodshed and death. It was said of another very wealthy woman, Martha, the wife of the slain highpriest, Joshua b. Gamala, that she picked barley grains from the dung of the horses in the valley to preserve her life. The most horrid scenes within the city passed unnoticed, as none wrote of them and few escaped to tell the tales of woe. The seventeenth day of *Tammuz*, however, was considered the most memorable, for on that day the daily sacrifices in the temple were stopped for ever. There was nothing left to be sacrificed, and there were no men to attend to the divine service; many of them were slain and the survivors were engaged in the defense of the temple. The defenders of the temple had consumed whatever there was in the inner court, wine, oil or flour; and John had sold most of the costly vessels and utensils to sustain himself.

17. A Useless Breach in the Wall.

Under all these miseries, however, none was permitted to speak of surrendering. The Romans had raised new embankments opposite the wall of Fort Antonia, and John with his men made another attempt to destroy them, but failed in accomplishing it. The heavy rains played against the wall and one night part of it fell down. But to the utter amazement of the Romans, the Zealots had erected a new wall right behind the one battered down. It was a severe disappointment, and Titus himself began to despair of success. Some courageous soldiers attempted to scale the wall, and were terribly chastised by the defenders above. Several other similar attempts were equally unsuccessful.

18. The Romans on the Temple Mount.

About the time when the daily sacrifice in the temple had been stopped, Titus began to undermine Fort Antonia, and made another attempt, with the aid of Josephus, to persuade the Zealots to surrender the city. He failed in this latter attempt, but succeeded in bringing a number of chosen men into the tower of Antonia who, under the command of Cerealis, made the daring attempt of surprising the guards of the temple. They were not found asleep, and a furious battle was fought from three to eleven in the morning. It was a drawn battle, says Josephus; still the Romans retired without any success. Meanwhile, however, a wide breach was made in the tower, and the legions marched up to the Temple Mount and began to throw up embankments against the temple.

19. THE TEMPLE CLOISTERS DESTROYED.

Next day an attempt was made by a body of the defenders of the temple to cut their way through the enemy on Mount Olives. A hard-fought battle ended with the retreat of the Hebrews back to the Temple Mount. The cloisters of the temple on the west and north were now the breastworks of the Hebrews. They filled them with combustibles and retreated into the first temple court (Court of Women). Many of the Romans with ladders mounted the cloisters to take possession of the position. When the roof was well crowded, the cloisters were fired and enveloped the Romans in a sheet of flames, in which many perished. The next day the Romans burnt down the eastern cloisters also.

20. THE DESTRUCTION OF THE TEMPLE.

On the eighth day of *Ab*, the embankments being finished, Titus gave orders to set on fire the four gates on the west side and to bring into action the heaviest rams against the outer buildings, as six days' battering with lighter rams had made no impression on the masonry, and digging under the northern gate had proved fruitless, the foundations being too deep and too broad. Simultaneously with this, a general attack was opened and became more furious and irresistible with every passing moment. The flames spread rapidly, and the warriors inside fought desperately for every inch of ground, till every spot of the temple court was covered with its slain champions and the corpses swam in blood. Titus and his immediate lieutenants succeeded in entering the main building from the east side, and inspected the *sanctum sanctorum*. Josephus maintains that Titus was inclined to save the building, and gave orders to the soldiers to put out the fire, but the Hebrews fought those soldiers also, and by their furious and incessant attacks so enraged the Romans that they became unmanageable and set on fire the main building also. However, the passage in Sulpicius Severus (*Chronicon* xxx. 11, 6), which it is supposed belongs to Tacitus, contradicts this statement of Josephus. It is maintained there that in the council of war, Titus defended his opinion that the temple should be demolished in order to extirpate the religion perpetuated in that structure (1). On the 10th day of *Ab*, the whole Temple Mount was one lake of fire, and the Hebrews, men, women and children to the number of ten thousand, perished in the flames; some by suicide, and most of them under the swords of the enemy. Except those who, by hunger and fatigue, were so exhausted that they could offer no resistance, the Hebrews made the most heroic defense to the very last moment. One band of Zealots cut their way through the Roman legions and reached the city. But the non-combatants, of whom no less than six thousand were in the inner cloisters, were all massacred in cold blood; every building on the temple mount was fired, every nook and corner was searched for plunder, so that many Romans, in search of prey, perished in the flames. So God and humanity were outraged by a horde of furious savages under the treacherous and insatiable Roman eagle; and yet Josephus has made the attempt to justify Titus, and to put the blame chiefly on the Zealots.

21. The Lamentation of the Hebrews.

Five hundred and eighty-six years (516 B. C. to 70 A. C.), the sublime structures graced Mount Moriah. It was the pride and center of all Israel, and the place, in the belief of all, where God's glory was visible on earth. As a building, it was the most renowned in the world; as a center of intelligence, it was the only place where the great doctrine of Monotheism and its sublime ethics were preserved and promulgated. Princes, kings and emperors, philosophers, and men of piety, had honored and ornamented it; millions of all nations and tongues had knelt in its courts and worshiped the Most High; every spot of it was holy by historical reminiscences and the sanctifying feelings of worshiping multitudes. There stood on Mount Moriah the victory of genius, the triumph of spirit, the glory of truth, the pride and center of Israel. And now it was enveloped in flames, its ground covered with the blood and bodies of its champions. The savage cries of the plundering and slaying hordes, the moans and shrieks of the dying women and children, mingling with the horrid lamentation resounding from all parts of the city, were terribly re-echoed from the mountains and valleys far and wide, as far as Mount Moriah could be seen. The flood of tears shed was, perhaps,

---

(1) See Jacob Bernay's *ueber die Chronik des Sulpicius Severus.*

as large as the flood of blood, and the sorrows of the living were more painful than those of the dying. So on the same day as the temple of Solomon was destroyed, from the ninth to the tenth day of *Ab*, the second temple also fell; and the people of Israel still fasts and mourns on the ninth day of *Ab*.

22. THE FALL OF ZION.

The bridge between the temple and Zion was broken off, and the garrison of the city asked of Titus the privilege of leaving with their wives and children for the wilderness. This did not suit the bloodthirsty son of Vespasian, and he refused; he demanded unconditional surrender, which meant death or life-long slavery. The Zealots refused to surrender. Some of the great men, and among them also the Izatus family of the royal blood of Adiabene, surrendered and were sent in chains to Rome. On the eleventh and twelfth days of *Ab*, Ophel and Acra were set on fire. The siege of Zion was continued to the twentieth day of *Ab*, when the west side wall was attacked. Many of the besieged fled, many were killed inside because they planned a surrender, and the others offered as stout a resistance as if pestilence and famine and fatigue had no influence on their bodies. Under miseries and horrors indescribable, Zion was defended to the eighteenth day of *Ellul*, when a breach was made in the wall and the Romans entered Zion. Now the carnage and plundering began, and fire finished the work of horrid destruction. Next day Titus commanded not to slay non-combatants, but it was after all who were too old, too young or too infirm to be used as slaves had been slain. The young men were sent into the Egyptian mines, although eleven thousand of those captives perished from want of food, most of them voluntarily preferring death to slavery. The most stately men were carried captives with Titus to be preserved for the triumph or the arena. Women, lads and men were sold to the slave traders and dragged into various countries. Some of the warriors escaped by subterranean passages, others failed in the same attempt, and among the latter were Simon b. Gorion and John of Gischala, both of whom were sent in chains to Rome. Simon was preserved for the triumph and was then slain, and John was condemned to imprisonment for life. The whole number of captives taken during the war was 97,000, and the number slain was 1,100.000. There were among them a very large proportion of Judaized Gentiles. One-tenth of the whole Hebrew people, and one-sixth, perhaps, of the inhabitants of Palestine perished in that war. With the numerous emigrants who had left the country during that period, there were, perhaps, no more than four millions of Hebrews left in all Palestine. And now Zion and Jerusalem were deserted, and, mostly in ruins, the surrounding towns and plantations were no more, and the Hebrew people bled from a thousand wounds. It was crushed, an object of hatred and scorn, and mourned hopelessly.

23. The Holy Vessels and Treasures.

Whatever was above ground on Mount Moriah, archives, treasures, precious vessels, spices and costly materials, was certainly consumed in the conflagration, with the exception, perhaps, of what the soldiers took as spoil. Some of the vessels and treasures hidden under ground were delivered to Titus by a priest called Jesus b. Thebuthus and Phineas, the treasurer, to ransom their lives. These trophies, described by Josephus (Wars iv., viii. 3 and vii., v. 5), among them also a Scroll of the Law, were carried in the triumph of Titus in Rome to the Temple of Jupiter Capitolinus. It is maintained in the Talmud (*Me'ilah* 17 *b*) that R. Eliezer b. Jose, some time after 138 A. C., saw there the curtain from the temple. Presentations of those vessels are still on the Titus Arch in Rome.

24. Other Barbarities of Titus.

When the army found no more corpses to strip and no more people to plunder and slay, says Josephus naively, Titus ordered the demolition of the entire city, except the western wall and three towers, left there the Tenth Legion, under command of Trentius Rufus, rewarded and lauded his soldiers, and then left for Caesarea, and then for Caesarea Philippi, where he enjoyed the pleasures of games and shows. The captives, to the number of twenty-five hundred, were thrown before wild beasts or forced to kill one another in wild combat. He next went to Berytus, where those games were repeated, and a still larger number of captives were sacrificed. That was Roman chivalry and the lauded generosity of Titus. If the ruins of Jerusalem and its temple, the blood of the massacred thousands of women, children and hoary heads did not give the lie to all who praised Roman civilization and the humanity of Vespasian and Titus, this outrageous slaughter of captives must certainly have done it. Humanity revolts at the mere recollection of the atrocious brutalism.

25. IN ANTIOCH AND ALEXANDRIA.

The fall of Jerusalem encouraged the enemies of the Hebrews in Alexandria and Antioch, and they asked Vespasian and Titus to ostracise the Hebrews of those cities. In Antioch a plot and false accusation against the Hebrew was enacted. But the new emperor and his son did not grant those petitions, and the rights of the Hebrews there remained as they had been. Vespasian and then Titus returned to Rome, and were honored there with a triumph, which Josephus described with all the servile adulation of a faithful slave.

26. HERODION, MACHERUS AND MASADA.

When Titus had left Palestine the surviving Hebrew warriors still held three fortified cities, viz.: Herodion, near Jerusalem, Macherus, on the southern line of Perea, and Masada, on the western shore of the Dead Sea. The first governor of Palestine appointed by Titus, Cerealis, did not take those places. His successor (71 A. C.), Lucilius Bassus, took Herodion, and after a desperate struggle also Macherus, which was held by Eleasar, while the citadel was commanded by Juda b. Jair, who had distinguished himself in Jerusalem. The most desperate and most skillful combat took place before Masada, conducted on the part of the Romans by Flavius Sylva, the successor of Bassus, and on the part of the Hebrews by Eleazar b. Jair. When the last hope of successful defense had vanished, the nine hundred inhabitants slew one another, and when, the next morning, the Romans entered the city, they found their corpses and but two old women alive. This was the last act of the drama. It closed with the death of the heroes of Masada, who would not violate their oath of freedom or death.

27. AFTER THE CATASTROPHE.

Many of the Zealots fled to Parthia, Arabia, Egypt and Cyrene, and continued to struggle against Rome. Nor did the Hebrews of Palestine consider themselves vanquished. They took up the mighty struggle again and again. At that moment, however, the war was over for the time being. Vespasian commanded that all the land of Judea, which included Idumea and Perea, should be sold to the highest bidders, who should hold it only as feudal land; a large portion thereof was given to Roman soldiers, to Josephus, and, perhaps, also to other favorites of the emperor; that no city should be built again in that country; and that the taxes paid to the temple of Jerusalem should henceforth be paid by the Hebrews to the Temple of Jupiter Capitolinus. Shortly after, the Onias Temple in Egypt was also closed for ever. Vespasian certainly believed that he had destroyed both the political and religious existence of the Hebrews. It was in his power to destroy temples, cities and armies, but not the spirit, which remained the invisible and invincible rock and center of the Hebrew people. That spirit of truth outlived the house of Flavius, the Roman Empire, and will outlive all dynasties and empires.

28. A RETROSPECT.

Whether Josephus was a traitor or a patriot will forever remain undecided, although the favors bestowed on him by Vespasian, the large estates given him by the emperor, and the home he enjoyed in the imperial palace, perhaps prove that he always served the interests of Rome at the expense of his people. But his entire party did so right from the beginning, and it can not be said that their motives were not patriotic. Like his party, Josephus also deceived the Zealots. The wrongs of which he was personally guilty were, that he did not lay down his command when the delegates brought him the order to that effect from the central authority in Jerusalem; that he remained with Titus in the dubious character of an informer or pacificator; and that he described the fall of Jerusalem and the temple more in a triumphant than in the mourning tone of a Hebrew patriot. Still, the man who afterward wrote the history of his people with so much research, skill and affection can hardly be branded as a traitor. The same may be said of Agrippa II. and his sister, Berenice. They adhered to the peace party from beginning to end, and remained in Rome the favorites also of the imperial house of Flavius. Titus would certainly have married Berenice, if the Roman grandees had not been so bitterly opposed to it, and he was finally forced to send her out of his palace and of Rome. The same is true of Rabbi Jochanan b. Saccai, his disciples, the Hillel Pharisees and the House of Hillel. All of them were opposed to the war, and left the Zealots to their own fate. It is evident that they commenced the reconstruction in Jamnia without molestation, hence the government must have favored them directly or indirectly; and it was there and then that the *Bath-kol* decided all disputed *halachoth* (with a few exceptions) in favor of the Hillelites,

so that the Shammaites and Zealots, whatever remained of
them, were excluded from the reconstruction of Judaism.
This was an effectual declaration that, like Josephus, Agrippa
and compatriots, the Hillelites did not sympathize with the
Shammaites and Zealots (2). Yet they could not justly be
called traitors, as they acted on inherited principles, viz.:
that the laws and religion of Israel were the main treasures
to be guarded and rescued; it matters not who stood at the
head of the political machinery. Therefore, it must forever
remain undecided which party was the main cause of the
great calamity. Had the peace party, with its far-seeing
statesmen and its predominance of the religious idea, prevailed, Jerusalem, the temple and the Hebrew commonwealth might have been preserved to rise again to importance. Had the peace party not weakened and obstructed
the Zealots and the war party, had the whole Hebrew people been a unit and armed earnestly for a war of independence after the defeat of Cestius Gallus, they might have
driven the Romans out of Asia, and history would have
taken quite another turn. At all events, none will dare
condemn those death-defying warriors who fought like lions
and died like demi-gods for an idea. Generation after generation suffered and submitted to the obnoxious foreign
yoke; when the wrongs had become insufferable, they rose
like men, fought like patriots, and died like Hebrews. Who
will dare condemn heroic champions of a sublime idea in
their graves? Our feelings are with the Zealots, who would
certainly not have committed the outrages chronicled by
Josephus, for they fought for an idea, had not the peace
party betrayed them from the beginning and the foreign invaders driven them to desperation. They were, perhaps,
wrong in principle, and laid too much stress on the political
idea; but they were great in the execution. great in fact.
Compare them to the fighting men of Cromwell, the American and French revolutions, and condemn them if you can.
We honor their memory. They closed the history of the
Hebrews' second commonwealth with immortal glory.

(2) The story narrated in the Talmud, that Vespasian wanted to
slay Gamliel, the son of Simon b. Gamliel, but R. Jochanan b. Saccai
saved him, is very uncertain, as is the death of Simon by the Romans. Had not the Hillel family enjoyed the favor of Vespasian and
Titus, how could that very Gamliel have become *Nassi* a few years
after the catastrophe? Or how did the family acquire the great
wealth for which it was distinguished? Gamliel's power and wealth
from and after 80 B. C., are noticed, *Berachoth* 27 *b*, *Yerushalmi* and
elsewhere.

CHAPTER XXVII.

The Inheritance.

1. RUINS AND RECOLLECTIONS.

Eighteen hundred years have rolled over that classical land since the fall of Jerusalem; and yet every one of its prominent spots has been retained in the memory of the civilized world. There are Hebron, Jerusalem and Jericho, Bethel, Bethlehem and Shechem, Samaria, Tiberias, Cæsarea and Ptolemais, all well known to us to-day; and there are the numerous ruins identified or unidentified, all testifying to the facts of history connected with the various spots, and animating the hearts of thousands with sentiments of admiration for a glorious past, never to be obliterated from the memory of man, especially of those whose ancestors were the actors in the grand drama. Why did the Hebrews, in eighteen centuries of wrongs and miseries, not give up their identity? Because truth preserves its own apostles; and because such recollections can never be forgotten. A great history is the Hebrews' indestructible inheritance.

2. THE COINS.

Other monuments which testify to the truth of history are the coins preserved in various Numismatic collections, described last by Dr. M. A. Levy (1). There are extant coins of Simon, the Asmonean, and of his descendants, viz.: John Hyrcan, Juda Aristobul, Alexander Jannai, Queen Salome and Antigonus; the coins between the reign of Queen Salome and that of her grandson are missing. Next came the coins of Herod I., his three sons, Archelaus, Antipas and Philip, and his grandsons, Agrippa I. and Herod of

---

1. *Geschichte der juedischen Muenzen*, etc., Leipzig, 1862.

Chalcis; also of Agrippa's son, Marcus Agrippa, King of Chalcis. No coins are extant of Agrippa II. From the period of the last war two kinds of coins are extant; the one bears the name of Eleasar, the priest, and the other of Simon, the prince, dated the first or second year of the liberation of Jerusalem. All effigies on these coins are either vessels of the temple, the staff of Aaron, the vine, palm, or dates in baskets; and all inscriptions are in Greek or ancient Hebrew letters, the whole alphabet of which has been recovered from these coins, except the *Teth, Samech* and *Pai*. All coins with the Hebrew square letters are counterfeits.

3. THE CULTURE.

The culture of the Hebrews was not extinguished with their national capital and sanctuary. The fugitives and the deported ones carried out to Parthia, Arabia, Asia Minor, to the Caucasus, as well as to Spain, the lower Danube and the Rhine, the rich culture of an ancient and unique civilization, distinguished not only in advanced agriculture and pomology, in the domestic arts of building, weaving, dyeing, forging implements and arms, in medical, juridical and political knowledge and experience: but also in the highest ideas of man concerning God, duty, and the destiny and dignity of man. Those fugitives and exiles carried new elements of culture to the nations among whom they came, and left their home, although vanquished and largely devastated, in a state of high culture, with many populous centers of industry and commerce, seats of learning and religion, like Jamnia, Tiberias, Sepphoris, Bethar, Usha, Lydda, Bene Berak. It was said of the people of Bethar, that they rejoiced over the fall of Jerusalem, so that Bethar might be the largest city in the country.

4. THE LAW.

The intellectual force of the Hebrews, especially from and after the period of the revolution, was most actively applied in the making of laws. That system of laws, which was afterward compiled and expounded in the collections called *Mishnah, Tosephta, Mechilta, Saphra, Siphri,* and to a large extent also in the two Talmuds of Jerusalem and Babylon, also called "The Oral Law" (תורה שבעל פה), had been produced and developed in the second commonwealth by legislative enactments, juridical decisions of officiating judges, and the opinions of learned lawyers (*Sopherim* and *Ta'na'im*). It was characteristic of the Hebrew people, and especially of the Pharisees, to establish law, to press every duty of man in the form of law, derived from or based upon the Law of Moses. That which is true or good must be done, and whatever must be done can not be left to the judgment of the individual; it must be expressed in the form of law, obligatory upon all. This was the leading idea which led to thorough organization and uniformity in society and the State; but on the other hand, it produced formalism, a paucity of free motives, and that anxiety, to do everything so and not otherwise, in that particular time, place and manner, which by a change of circumstances often proved destructive to the very object and purpose of the law. These national laws were preserved in the memory of the doctors and in "Private Scrolls" (מגלות סתרים). In these private scrolls, the laws and opinions were undoubtedly grouped about the Pentateuch passages, from which they were supposed to have been derived (מדרש הלכה), to which were added the general laws (הלכה פשוטה) as constructed by the doctors of law. These private scrolls naturally must have contained a vast number of private and conflicting opinions on subjects not referring to public law. In Jamnia, however, where the *Bath kol* abrogated the laws of the Shammaites, the majority rule (אחרי רבים להטות) was established, so that all laws, customs or observances had to be henceforth practiced according to the decision of the majority of the Sanhedrin. This deprived the private scrolls of their worth and authority, and they were gradually suppressed and lost, merged in the ancient rabbinical literature. This majority rule directed against prevailing sectarianism, and the disputes of the rabbis of the last eighty years, brought unity and uniformity to the surviving Hebrews; but it was, in many instances, hostile to free research and development. It made of the remaining Hebrews a compact congregation, and provided them with a portable Palestine, although it overruled private opinion and pressed the mind in the narrow forms of law. However, the public laws, inherited of the Hebrews' Second Commonwealth, are the lasting monuments of an advanced civilization. This is especially the case with the criminal law, which is far superior to the Roman law, and stands upon the height of humanitarian doctrine.

5. The Agada.

The Hebrew mind was not entirely ingulfed in the law or *halachah*. The Prophets and afterward also the

Hagiography, were read and expounded in the synagogues and academies; and in these books themselves is the beginning of the *Agada* or *Hagadah*. The term is derived from *Nagad*, and in the Hebrew *Hiphil* or Aramaic *Aphel* form signifies to narrate, to tell, to communicate. The noun which actually means narrative, that which is told, communicated or spoken, has been adopted to designate speeches or addresses, on passages of scriptures or events of history, to elucidate or illustrate religious and moral doctrines. It is the homily or sermon delivered in the synagogue or academy or also on particular occasions, of which, in most cases, only the text and chief points (ראשי פרקים) have been committed to writing. The *Meturgam*, who translated and expounded Scriptures for the audience, was also the preacher. The skillful orators were called מרד אגדתא, "Masters of the Agada." The books or scrolls in which the material was preserved were called ספרי אגדתא. "Books of the Agada," afterward plainly אגדתא or מדרש. All forms of poetry were resorted to for illustration and ornamentation, so that the *Agada* or *Midrash* gradually became a variegated flower garden of truth and fiction, sublime doctrines of religion and ethics, philosophy and science, framed in fantastical fabrics of fiction. In aftertimes the Agada was subjected to thirty-two hermeneutic rules by Rabbi Eleasar, son of Rabbi Jose, the Galilean; nevertheless, it always remained more or less a free exercise of ingenuity and wit, of religious, ethical or philosophical genius. The authors of ABOTH, ABOTH of Rabbi Nathan, and PIRKEI Rabbi Eliezer, convey the idea that the system and main material of the Palestinean Agada was a traditional inheritance from the Hebrews' Second Commonwealth. This is also evident by the numerous Agada productions of R. Jochanan b. Saccai, his disciples and colleagues, and such other teachers who lived and taught before and immediately after the fall of Jerusalem. Their sayings and illustrations are characteristic for strength and beauty, and bear the stamp of antiquity. If the best portion of the Palestinean Agada had not been inherited from the Second Commonwealth, it would not have been adopted so largely in the New Testament, not only in the Gospels, but also in the Epistles, and the system would not have so extensively influenced the fathers of the Church. Besides it is well known that the Hillelites and Shammaites also discussed some of the main Agada problems (2). No Agada books

(2) *Erubin* 13 b; *Hagigah* 12 a; *Rosh Hashanah* 16 b; end of *Aboth*, R. Nathan, and *Ibid.* end of Perek II.

from the second commonwealth are now extant, except those of the Apocrypha, Philo and the Alexandrian Hebrew poets. PIRKEI, Rabbi Eliezer, was re-written by Mar Samuel in the third century; ABOTH Rabbi Nathan was written at the end of the second century, and ABOTH itself somewhat later. The inherited material is scattered through the three PESIKTA books, also MECHILTA, SIPHRI and TOSEPHTA, RABBAH to Genesis, and other MIDRASHIM; and especially through the two Talmuds of Jerusalem and Babylon. The names added to respective passages are criteria that they did not originate later than the lifetime of that particular teacher; but this is no proof that any such passage was not much older than the teacher who quotes or expounds the tradition, or attempts to base it on a Scriptural passage. The main material of the AGADA, as well as the principal laws of the HALACHA, was inherited from the second commonwealth.

6. THE SECTS.

The Sadducees went under in the catastrophe. As a class or sect, no trace is left of them after the fall of Jerusalem. Here and there a Sadducee is mentioned in the Talmud in controversy with a rabbi, but the term is usually taken in place of MIN, sectarian, Jew-Christian, or dissenter. The Essenes, with the exception of their celebatic colonies west of the Dead Sea and further to the north, also went under in the catastrophe or were amalgamated with the Pharisees. The celebatic Essenes were non-combatants, would not even tolerate an armor among them, hated the cities and kept at a distance from them, ate no animal flesh, had no property, no families, hence had nothing to do with the war. Philo says there were altogether four thousand of them (Mangey's edition, Vol. II. p. 457-459). Plinius, the Elder, in his Natural History (L. v. Cap. 16 and 17), mentions these Essenes after the fall of Jerusalem. Polyhistor (xxxv. 7-12) and Porphyrius, in the third century, and Epiphanius, in the fourth, still mention them, but it is not clear that they still existed, or else Eusebius must have known it. In the Talmud frequent reference is made to such ascetic and peculiar saints, but they are never called Essenes. Hegesippus (Euseb. Eccles. Hist. iv. 22) mentions two more Jewish sects, viz.: the Homerobaptists, identified with the טובלי שחרית of the Talmud, who have not become known as a sect; and the Masbotheans, unknown in Jewish sources. The Zealots and the Shammaites disappeared after the catastrophe, at least in Palestine. Only here and there a Shammaite doctor is mentioned in the Talmud. The Hillel Pharisees and the Christians only escaped from the catastrophe to become, afterward, two antagonistic heirs of the same mother.

7. LITERATURE.

The closing passage of Ecclesiastes (xii. 9-14) was added to that book by the compilers of the third part of the Canon, a fit epilogue to the whole collection; hence it points to the days of Simon, the Asmonean prince. In that epilogue are mentioned many MESHALIM, poetical productions, DIBREI CHACHAMIM, philosophical productions, and BA'ALEI ASUPHOTH, compilers of books, or grammarians and critics, authenticating and correcting old books, in connection with a solemn warning against the making of many books. Therefore, it admits of no doubt that a vast number of books of that period have been lost, only a few of which have been preserved in Greek and other translations. This is also evident from the Antiquities of Josephus, who must have had access to books unknown now. Epiphanius also maintains that Ptolemy Philadelphus received from Jerusalem no less than seventy-two apocryphal books in addition to the Canon. It appears that no book of the Canon has been lost, because Josephus (*contra* Apion i. 8) speaks of twenty-two holy books, viz.: Five books of Moses, thirteen books of the Prophets, and four books of hymns and precepts. These books were: 1. Joshua; 2. Judges; 3. Samuel; 4. Kings; 5. Ruth; 6. Esther; 7. Chronicles; 8. Isaiah; 9. Jeremiah; 10. Ezekiel; 11. The Twelve Minor Prophets; 12. Daniel, and 13. Ezra and Nehemiah, only that he preferred the Apocryphal to the Canonical Ezra. The other four books were Psalms, Proverbs, Job, Ecclesiastes and Canticles and Lamentations, although it is not evident that he knew Canticles. The rabbis shortly after Josephus mentioned the same books of the Canon (*Baba Bathra* 14 *b*), only that they count five books of Moses, eight of Prophets, and nine books of Hagiography, viz.: Ruth, Psalms, Job, Proverbs, Ecclesiastes and Canticles and Lamentations, Daniel, Esther, Ezra and Nehemiah, Chronicles, being also twenty-two books. There can be no doubt that both sources refer to the same books. Therefore, it is certain that no canonical book has been lost, although passages of Prophets and Hagiography, not guarded with the same vigilance and zeal as the Pentateuch, may have been lost, changed or misplaced. The books lost were of the classes of the apocryphal and the profane literature. Among the books lost must be counted: 1. "The Chronicles of the Highpriests" (I. Maccabees xvi. 24), which were the official records of history, as were the Chronicles of the kings of Judah or of Israel in former days. 2. The five books of Jason of Cyrene, on the history of the Maccabees (II. Maccab. ii. 23). 3. The history of the Hebrews under the Ptolemys, of which the third book of the Maccabees is a fragment. 4. The MEGUILLATH TA'ANITH mentioned in the MISHNAH (*Ta'anith* ii. 8), a historical calendar, in which were narrated the national events distinguishing certain days of the year as national half holidays, when fasting or public mournings were not permitted; parts of this lost book are in the MEGUILLATH *Ta'anith*, written at a later date. 5. The Records of the Sanhedrin, kept by the two scribes of that body. 6. All the MEGUILLOTH YUCHSIN, the Genealogic Records, which were kept with particular care under the supervision of the Sanhedrin, not only for the priests, but also for laymen. 7. The history of Justus of Tiberias and other historians of that period (the former was extant in the Middle Ages), mentioned by Josephus (Life 65). 8. The Maccabean books of the Hillelites and Shammaites written during or previous to the last war, of which the extant *Meguillath Antiochus* appears to be a fragment. 9. The first work of Josephus, to be noticed below (3). 10. Lastly, we mention among the lost books also a Greek history of the Jews mentioned by Alexander Polyhistor, to which Josephus (Antiq. i., xv.) refers. He quotes the words of Polyhistor, thus: "CLEODEMUS, the prophet, who was also called MALCHUS, who wrote a history of the Jews, in agreement with the history of Moses, their legislator, relates," etc. This list of lost books in one department of knowledge shows what amount of poetical, philosophical and juridical literature must have been lost. We record now the literature preserved.

8. THE FIRST BOOK OF THE MACCABEES.

This book of sixteen chapters, added to the Septuagint, was originally Hebrew or Aramaic. Jerome reports that he saw the Hebrew original, and Eusebius preserved its title as SARBETH SARBANE EL, which was, perhaps, originally SHARBATH SAR BENAI EL, "The Descendants (4) of the

---

(3) Concerning the lost work of Josephus, see preface to "The Jewish War."

(4) See Fuerst in שרב II. and the Syriac SHRAIB.

Prince of the Lord's Children," referring to the sons of Mattathia, whose exploits the book describes. This book contains, after a brief review of Alexander's conquests and the division of his empire among his successors, the history of the Maccabean revolution to the demise of Simon, with all the chronological and geographical accounts. It is free of the miraculous element, impartial in praise and censure, brief and clear in style, and, according to Dr. Zunz (5), it may be placed next to the prophetical books of Samuel and Kings. Josephus and other historians have been led by First Maccabees, and modern critics have accepted it as the authentic source of that period of history. The original and the name of its author are lost, because it had not been accepted in the Canon, which had been closed before. It was written during the lifetime of John Hyrcan, as the end of the book shows, hence from the Daybooks of the Highpriests, the primary and official sources. Had the Canon not been closed before the book appeared, it would certainly have been added to it.

9. The Second Book of the Maccabees.

This book of fifteen chapters, added to the Septuagint, was originally Greek. It opens with an epistle addressed to the Hebrews of Egypt and to Aristobul, tutor of the king, by the people and Sanhedrin, concerning the *Hanukah* festival or Feast of Lights to be observed; in which interpolations are detectable. The main part of the book pretends (ii. 23) to be an abstract of the five books written by Jason of Cyrene, and narrates the history from the coming of Heliodorus to Jerusalem to the death of Nicanor. While this book contains a number of particulars explanatory or supplementary to the main facts in the First Maccabees, it is given so much to the miraculous and dwells so often on the supernatural, that its historical value is impaired. Jason of Cyrene wrote at a considerable distance from Palestine and from secondary reports, which he colored in the style of the Egyptian Hebrews with the miraculous and supernatural. Still Second Maccabees, as a supplement to the first, is of historical value.

10. The Third Book of the Maccabees.

This book of seven chapters, added to the Septuagint, is a fragment of a larger history of the Hebrews, and con-

---
(5) *Gottesdienstliche Vortraege*, p. 123.

tains the history of Ptolemy Philopator, his conduct and discomfiture in Jerusalem, his persecution of the Egyptian Hebrews, and their final rescue by a miracle. It begins and ends abruptly, and closes with a doxology. It contains history with the Egyptian colophon, or the stamp of Asia Minor.

11. The Fourth Book of the Maccabees (6).

This book, also called the Dominion of Reason, ascribed to Josephus, is no history. It contains some narratives from the Maccabean time, as the stories of the martyr Eleazar, of Hannah and her seven sons, taken from Second Maccabees. It is a Greek sermon, in the style of Philo's ethical discourses, to harmonize Scriptural and philosophical ideas. It is artistically finished in style and construction, written and delivered before the fall of Jerusalem, neither in Palestine nor by Josephus. The author's name and place are unknown. It is a monument of Hellenistic Hebrew philosophy, eloquence and theological research, and affords us a better knowledge of Jason of Cyrene, to whom it frequently refers. This book was reviewed last by Dr. J. Freudenthal (Breslau, 1869).

12. The Works of Josephus.

One of the most excellent legacies bequeathed to posterity by the men of the Hebrews' Second Commonwealth is the work of Flavius Josephus, consisting of four different books, viz.: 1. The Jewish War; 2. The Antiquities of the Jews; 3. The Life of Flavius Josephus; and 4. Flavius Josephus against Apion. Although all these books were written after the fall of Jerusalem, yet the writer and the material which he compiled eminently belong to the preceding period. The three books concerning the Jewish opinions about God and his essence, and about the laws, and the revision of his Jewish War, with a supplement to the year ninety-three, which he promised to produce (end of Antiquities), were not written or have not reached posterity. Josephus was an historian of a superior order. His information was vast and varied. His presentations of places, persons and occurrences are lucid, graphic, almost approaching the plastic. His details are illustrative of the main facts, which he always provides with topographical and chronological support. His style is not as compact as

---

(6) Translated in German, Leipzig, 1867.

that of Tacitus, nevertheless it is nervous and classical. His work is no mean proof of what the Hebrew mind then was in that particular department.

13. THE JEWISH WAR.

After Josephus had written, in the Hebrew or Aramaic language, a history of the Roman war upon Judea, and had sent it to the Hebrews of the East (this book was lost), he translated it into Greek, because, as he says (Wars, Sec. 1), quite a number of books had been written which, in his estimation, did not come up to the standard of truth. Those books have been lost and the statements of Josephus can be controlled only by his own confessions in his autobiography. Although he boasts (Life 5) that the Emperor Titus declared this the only authentic book on the war in Judea, and Agrippa confirmed it, it is, nevertheless, evident that he did flatter and lionize the Romans, and unjustly decry and defame the so-called robbers and Zealots. The Greek translation before us consists of seven books, each book is divided into chapters. and each chapter into paragraphs. It begins with the time of Antiochus Epiphanes, gives a brief account of events to the time of Herod and his included, furnishes a meager record of his successors, and begins a detailed history with Florus (Book II., xiv.), who was the immediate cause of the war. He closes his narratives with the year 73, and published this work in the year 75. The book was originally written while that war was fresh in his memory; he was under many obligations to Vespasian, Titus, Agrippa and others, and full of strong prejudices against the Zealots and those who denounced him as a traitor. He partly confessed this in his autobiography and by his promise to revise the Jewish War. He did atone for his misdeeds by his other books.

14. ANTIQUITIES OF THE JEWS.

This work consists of twenty books, each divided into chapters and these into paragraphs. It contains the history from the creation, according to the accounts of Moses, to the coming of Florus to Palestine, so that his "Wars" is the continuation of his "Antiquities." It appeared in the thirteenth year of Domitian, hence in the year 94 A. C., at the solicitation of Epaphroditus, a Roman doctor. It was written Greek and for Greeks, to prove the antiquity and expound the laws of the Hebrew people, not without a proselytizing tendency, as the struggle of Paganism and

Judaism was then at its height in Rome. As far as the Bible contains the history, Josephus transcribed it, with all the miracles, except in the Esther, Ezra and Nehemiah stories, where he was led by apocryphal sources, added thereto information from foreign sources, also spurious tales, as in the life of Moses, and was frequently led by the Septuagint rather than the Hebrew original, because he wrote for Greeks. From Nehemiah to Florus, his sources, besides the books of the Maccabees, are, for the most part, unknown, and many of those that were known are lost. He interpreted the laws of Moses by the practice and opinions of his own days, deviating in a number of cases from the accepted HALACHAH. He, like other classical writers, added speeches and prayers of his own composition, and exercised no criticism on his original sources. With all his philosophy he was superstitious, either in fact or pretension, in regard to omens, predictions, dreams and exorcism, if he did not cling to mysticism for the benefit of his Gentile readers. Still he was not only a faithful historian, but had evidently the intention to glorify his people in order to atone for the sins committed in his "Wars," and is more liberal in bestowing praise than censure. He did color facts but never disfigured them. In his "Antiquities" Josephus is a patriot of profound feelings, and a priest with whom the temple, its priests and rituals are by far most important. Like many historians, he neglects the life and doings of the people, and narrates the fate of its rulers, priests and soldiers. And yet the Hebrews have just cause to be proud of having found such a historian, whose words have been so well preserved and rendered in all languages of the civilized nations.

15. THE LIFE OF FLAVIUS JOSEPHUS.

This book consists of seventy-six paragraphs, and gives a full account of his life to that time. It bears no date, but its closing paragraph shows that it was written during the life of Domitian, who had made his land in Judea tax free, punished his accusers, who appear to have been quite numerous, and even the Empress Domitian is mentioned as having bestowed on him great favors. Josephus tells us that he married, the first time, by command of Vespasian, a captive Jewess, whom he divorced. She left him one son, Hyrcan. Then he married a Jewess of Crete, of whom he had two sons, Justus and Simonides Agrippa. This "Life," which is an appendix to his "Antiquities," was written as a sort of self-defense against the frequent accusations pre-

ferred against him as a traitor to both the Hebrews and the
Romans. He defends himself as well as the case would
admit, especially against Justus of Tiberias, and other historians, and forgets not to prove his attachment and fidelity
to Judaism as a man and a priest. He did considerably
modify his statements made in " Wars " twenty years before, but he did not tell the whole truth; nor did he refer
to his conduct at Jotapata.

16. Flavius Josephus against Apion.

If any proof were necessary that Josephus did not abandon Judaism and was not decapitated by Domitian, his
books against Apion prove both. Long after his " Life,"
about 100 A. C., he wrote those two wonderful books in defense of his people. They were taken together under the
above head. But the first book of thirty-five paragraphs
was written against those Greeks to whom he refers in the
" Antiquities " xx., and especially against Agatharchides,
Manetho, Cheremon and Lysimachus, who denied the high
antiquity of the Hebrews and misrepresented their history
and laws. The second book of forty-two paragraphs was
written in refutation of what the Alexandrian Apion, in the
time of Caligula, had written against the Hebrews. Remarkable in these books is the earnest and calm tone as
well as the overwhelming force of the argument. Most remarkable, however, in them is the eminent erudition of
Josephus in the classical literature. Quite a number of ancient authors have become known to posterity by the quotations of Josephus. The spirit of these two books shows
that the question, at that moment, excited the minds for
or against Judaism, and in the closing paragraphs of the
second book he appears most forcibly as the advocate of
Judaism among the Gentiles. His epilogue is written in a
spirit of firm conviction that the world must accept Judaism as the rock of salvation, and that vast multitudes, as
well as the philosophers of all ages, had embraced it already, admired the laws and institutions of Israel, observed
the Sabbath and the dietary laws, and sought to imitate
the concord and justice of Israel. It is maintained that
these books were written in Palestine, but none states precisely where and when. Anyhow, they must have been
written a number of years after his "Antiquities" and "Life,"
hence about 100 A. D. The influence on the Gentile mind
by the works of Josephus can hardly be overestimated.
They exercised none on the Hebrews. Neither he nor his

works are mentioned in Jewish sources. None before the author of JOSEPHON (7) in the Middle Ages, defended him. He was a traitor in the estimation of his cotemporaries, and in Rome he moved in the imperial circle too distant from his co-religionists to be forgiven. Still, whatever his conduct during the war and his misrepresentations in the history thereof may have been, he did atone for all of them by the works described. When and where he died has remained unknown.

17. PHILO JUDÆUS.

Philo of Alexandria (1–60 A. C.), the brother of the Alabarch Alexander, the great disciple of Moses and Plato, was an oak with its roots in Palestine and Greece, its trunk in Alexandria, its branches and foliage stretching far away into the regions of Judaism and Christianity. He was perfectly Hebrew in his feelings, hopes, faith and childlike obedience to the laws and customs of Israel; and perfectly Greek by education and association, culture and learning. He mastered with a wonderful energy all that Greece offered in letters, sciences and philosophy; and loved enthusiastically the intellectual treasures of Palestine. Like his master, Plato, to whose productions his were compared in beauty and depth, he was poetically philosophical; and like his other master, Moses, whose words he expounded, he was a model of ethical depth and metaphysical sublimity. Philo was the man in whom the diverging cultures of Palestine and Greece were harmoniously blended. In him, who, like King Solomon, was called YEDID-YAHH, "the beloved one of the Lord," the discursive and spontaneous reason, the philosopher's and prophet's functions were united in one human nature. To teach the great lesson of reason and faith harmonized was the object of his existence. It is the quintessence of all his writings. Besides the prominence of his family, his embassy to Caligula, and his two pilgrimages to Jerusalem, nothing is known of his life, which must have been that of a secluded reasoner, who occasionally appeared before a select congregation as a teacher and orator. So much the better his writings have become known to posterity.

18. THE WORKS OF PHILO.

The works ascribed to Philo have not been sufficiently studied to distinguish the authentic from the interpola-

---

(7) יוסיפון by pseudonymous Joseph ben Gorion, the priest, as quoted by RASHI, and others, in the twelfth century.

tions (8). The Therapeuts, described and lauded in one of Philo's books, have been taken by Eusebius to be Christian monks of the second century. Passages have undoubtedly been interpolated in other books of Philo by Christian writers. Some of his books, like two on the Covenant and four of the five books on " What befell the Jews under Caius," have been lost. Another number of his books are found now in the Armenian only, and have been published with a Latin translation by John Baptist Aucher, Venice, 1822 and 1826. The Greek books ascribed to Philo are the following: 1. On the Creation of the World; 2. The Allegories of the Law, three books, a hexaemeron; 3. The Cherubim and Flaming Sword; 4. The Sacrifices of Cain and Abel; 5. On the Principle that "The worse is made to serve the better;" 6. Of the Posterity of Cain; 7. Of the Giants; 8. On the Immutability of God; 9. On Agriculture; 10. The Plantation of Noah; 11. On Drunkenness; 12. On the words, "And Noah awoke;" 13. The Confusion of Tongues; 14. The Migration of Abraham; 15. Of him who shall inherit Divine Things; 16. On Assemblies for Learning; 17. On the Fugitives; 18. On the Change of Names; 19. On Dreams, two books; 20. On the Life of a Political Man, or on Joseph; 21. The Life of Moses; 22. On the Decalogue; 23. Circumcision; 24. On Monarchy, two book; 25. On the Rewards of the Priesthood; 26. On Animals Fit for Sacrifices; 27. On Sacrifices; 28. On Particular Laws; 29. On the Week; 30. The Sixth and Seventh Commandments; 31. The Eighth, Ninth and Tenth; 32. On Justice; 33. On the Election and Creation of the Prince; 34. Fortitude; 35. Humanity; 36. Penitence; 37. Rewards and Punishments; 38. Execrations; 39. Nobility; 40. Efforts after Virtue and Liberty; 41. The Contemplative Life (the Essenes); 42. The Incorruptibility of the World; to which must be added, 43. A Writing against Flaccus; 44. An Account of his Embassy to Rome; 45. On the World; and several fragments. These works have been printed, Paris, 1552, and again, 1640, Geneva, 1613, London (Dr. Mangey), 1742, in two vols. Leipzig (Richter), 1828-1830, in eight vols, and lastly by Tauchnitz, 1851, etc. The English translation, in four volumes, is in Bohn's Ecclesiastical Library. Fragments of German translations exist; a publication of the whole is now in process in Vienna, viz., translated by Dr. Friedlander. Writers on

---

(8) *Der juedische Alexandrismus eine Erfindung christlicher Lehrer*, etc., by Dr. Kirschbaum, Leipzig, 1841.

Philo are Dahl, Bryant, Gfroerer, Creuzer, Grossman, Wolff, Ritter, Beer, Daehne, Bernhard Ritter (9), and three hundred years ago, Azariah De Rossi, or *Min Ha'adomim* (10). The works of Philo may be divided into the Philosophical, Historical and Exegetical, the latter of which are most numerous, and form, in their connection, a philosophical-homiletic commentary to the Law of Moses.

19. The Hermeneutics of Philo.

In expounding the laws, Philo's hermeneutics differed not from that of the Palestinean sages, although he often differs from them in his conclusions (*halachah*), because he followed chiefly the text of the Septuagint, the practice of the law in Alexandria, which differed from that of Palestine, and in many cases he gives his own independent opinion, as did also Josephus. In other cases, the Palestinean *halachah* may not have been fixed when he wrote. In his ethical and philosophical expositions of Scriptures he, like many others, adopted the allegoric method where it was deemed necessary to harmonize Scriptures and philosophy, and, like Aristobul, he adopted the hermeneutic rules of the Stoics and of the *Agada* sages of Palestine (11). Neither the method nor the rules of interpretation were new. Yet the material produced by this apparatus was new in ethical depth and in harmonization of the intellectual treasures of Greece and Palestine. His *Agada* is the same as the Palestinean, only that it proved to the enlightened Gentiles how all that is good and true in Grecian wisdom is also contained in the great text-book of Monotheism, only that the latter also contained the wisdom of wisdoms, the theology of Moses and the prophets, of which the philosophers and poets had only a faint knowledge.

20. The Theology of Philo.

In order to understand Philo (or also Josephus) correctly, it must always be borne in mind that he spoke and wrote not for Hebrews; he did so for Judaizing Gentiles who knew and appreciated the Bible. Therefore, he made use of the

---

(9) *Philo und die Halacha*, etc., which enlarges on the subject treated on originally by

(10) *Me'or Enayim*, by Azariah, written (Hebrew) in Italy, 1571, a book of various sections and subjects.

(11) See Carl Siegfried's *Philo von Alexandrien als Ausleger des alten Testaments*.

Septuagint and not of the Hebrew text. In that form the
Bible was known to the Gentiles. Therefore, in his theology also, Philo accommodated himself to the philosophical theories and terms to which his hearers and readers were used. While he consistently teaches one incomprehensible God, who is above all human descriptions and conceptions, YEHOVAH, he called God in so far as he is manifested in the material universe and has become ELOHIM, the LOGOS, as did Plato and Zoroaster (by another word), the first born son of God; and in so far as God is manifested in human history as ADONAI, he hypostasized him as eternal Wisdom, Goodness, Love, Mercy, etc. So he did with all attributes and manifestations of Deity, to bring the ideas under Greek terms and to shape them for the Greek conception, without thinking for a moment on a division of the substance. Basing upon the loftiest conception of Deity, he expounded Scriptures by this fundamental truth, and developed therefrom the most sublime views about Providence, immortality of the soul and future reward, the final union of mankind, the government of man by the principle of justice, etc., the entire system of religion and ethics, which that one fundamental principle includes. Posterity misunderstood his hypostases, and took poetic-philosophical terms for essences; still none could dim the brilliancy of his ethics and profoundness of his love for man.

21. THE POETS.

Egypt, Asia Minor and other Grecian countries produced a number of poets who were either Hebrews or Judaizing Greeks. We add to this class after Aristobul, the writers of several Sibylline poems (12); Ezekielos, the dramatic poet, of whose drama, "The Exode," a fragment is extant (13); Philo, the Elder, an epic poet (14): Theodotus, who wrote the history of Jacob (Eusebius); Phokylides, a parapatetic reasoner and the author of Judaizing gnomical poems (15); and a number of others, who wrote in the Eastern Grecian dialect, with the intention to glorify the intellectual heroes, history, law and religion of Israel, in all popular forms of Grecian poetry. Whoever wishes to understand the origin of Christianity must take into careful consideration those Greco-Hebrew writers, and the dis-

---

(12) See Sibylline Books, published Amsterdam, 1689, and later in Copenhagen, 1821-1822.
(13) See *Franz Delitzsch's Zur Geschichte der juedischen Poesie*, p. 211.
(14) *Ludwig Philippson's Ezechiel und Philo*, Berlin, 1830.
(15) *Prof. Birnay's Ueber das Phokylides Gedicht.*

persion of Hebrews over Africa and Europe from and after Alexander the Great, and especially after Pompey's conquests in the East.

22. THE LITURGY.

The liturgy of the temple carried into the synagogues remained unchanged, as introduced by the Great Synod, and has remained the groundwork of the Hebrew prayer-book to this day. Its main elements were the SHEMA (Deut. vi. 4-9; xi. 13-21; to which was added Numbers xv. 37-41); the BERACHOTH "benedictions," two before and one after the SHEMA, which were much shorter than those in the common prayer-book (16), and the seven benedictions of the *Tephilah*, "daily prayer," changed afterward to eighteen and nineteen, the fourth of which commenced אתה חונן, "Thou bestowest knowledge upon man," etc., which was replaced on Sabbath and holidays by קדושת היום, "the sanctification of the day;" the reading of the Law and the benedictions before and after; the reading of Prophets and the sermon connected therewith, closed with the most ancient benediction, the KADDISH, from which was made the Christian prayer "Our Father, who art in Heaven," etc., אבינו שבשמים, which form is also preserved in the Talmud, and has been changed into אבינו מלכנו, "Our Father, our King," etc. The additional benediction for Sabbaths, holidays, new moons, New Year and Day of Atonement, have been preserved in later compositions. The *Berachah*, in the briefest form, to precede and succeed every enjoyment in life, contains the Hebrew's articles of faith in so concise a form that every one was bound to know them well. It was impressed upon all as a safeguard against paganism, vice and corruption. Its main words, like those of all ancient prayers, are taken from the Bible, and its object was to remind the Hebrew, at all times and places, that his God is with him, and Israel's law and covenant direct him.

The Psalms, SHIR, were the next element of the liturgy in temple and synagogue, as they are now. They were the texts for the grand choruses of the Levites, for pilgrims and domestic devotion. Besides the Canonical Psalms, there were the exotic Psalms of David, of which Atapasius counts over 3,000, and the Psalms of Solomon (17). Most

---

(16) Dr. Zunz, *Gottesdienstliche Vortraege der Juden*, Berlin, 1832, p. 369.

(17) *Der Psalter Salomo's von Ehuard Ephr. Geiger*; German by J. Wellhausen, in Pharis. and Sadduc., p. 138.

of them are products of the Grecian synagogue; perhaps of the great Basilika of Alexandria, which was the largest in the world. Among the Psalms of Solomon, some are in the Musivstyle, and appear to be of Palestinean origin. Christian phrases have been interpolated in numerous cases. The responses in the temple were almost exclusively from the Psalms, except the ברוך שם כבוד מלכותו לעולם ועד, which was a *Berachah*, and most likely read, "Praised be God and the glory of His kingdom, for ever and aye," which the people said in the temple as often as the tetragrammaton was pronounced.

The Confession, VIDUI, also of Biblical origin, was another element of public worship. Three confessions of the highpriest on the Day of Atonement are preserved in the Talmud (18), and have partly been adopted in the common liturgy.

The Prayer, TEPHILLAH, petition or supplication, was an element of the public service; but it was not written, as it was held that prayer must be spontaneous (19). Only in exceptional cases were such prayers written. Of these are preserved, the prayer of the highpriest on the Day of Atonement (*Yerushalmi*); the prayers for public fasts (MISHNAH, *Ta'anith* II.); also the prayer of Ishmael Fabi (*Berachoth* 7 *a*).

The Reading of the Law was another element of public service, the corresponding sections of each holiday at the holiday (MISHNAH, *Yoma* vii); one of the one hundred and seventy-five sections in which the Pentateuch was divided was read every Sabbath morning and evening, Monday and Thursday (at least ten verses thereof), except on four Sabbaths (ארבע פרשיות), between the Sabbath next to the month of *Adar* and that before Passover, when other sections were read (Meguillah iii. 4). On *Hanukah*, *Purim*, new moon, public fasts, and the meetings of the Commoners, sections of the Pentateuch were read. Men were called to read; the first opened with the benediction, and the last reader closed with another benediction. The entire groundwork of modern Jewish worship was established during the Second Commonwealth.

(18) YERUSHALMI, *Yoma* iii. 7; iv. 2; MISHNAH, do., do. This book of the *Mishnah*, treating on the temple service for the Day of Atonement, it is reported (*Yoma* 14 *b*), was written by Simon, the lord of Mizpah, hence before the destruction of the Temple.

(19) MISHNAH *Berachoth* iv. 4.

23. Other Literature.

The poets were silent; none did lament over the fall of Jerusalem and the destruction of the temple. The age was too rational and tragic for poetry. The Mashal, parable, fable, personification, or also hyperbole, was the most common form of poetry, many of which are preserved in the Talmuds and Gospels. The moral sentences, the song of the maidens in the vineyards on the fifteenth day of Ab and the Day of Atonement, and some more lyrical fragments are extant (20). Of the Christian literature, besides some epistles, it is the Revelation of John, which was written during the last war, and the Book of Henoch (21), which, about the same time, was written in Egypt. The former was written by an outspoken Jew-Christian, lamenting over the fate of Jerusalem and prophesying the destruction of Rome; while the latter was written by an Egyptian Messiahnist, with all the pessimism which the catastrophe of Jerusalem produced, and many of the mysterious superstitions which coursed among a certain class of mystics, and found their way into various rabbinical works, especially during the Middle Ages.

And so my task is done. I have written this history with the proud feeling that man is better than his history, in which the onward march of enlightenment and humanization is so often interrupted by barbarous multitudes. The triumph of progress can not be fully achieved before the civilization of the entire human family has become a fact. Had the Hebrews not been disturbed in their progress a thousand and more years ago, they would have solved all the great problems of civilization which are being solved now under all the difficulties imposed by the spirit of the Middle Ages. The world is not yet redeemed.

(20) Delitzsch, p. 193.
(21) *Das Buch Henoch*, by Dr. A. Dilimann, Leipzig, 1858; also Ad. Jellinek, *Beth Hamidrash*, II., p. xxx.

www.ingramcontent.com/pod-product-compliance
Lightning Source LLC
Chambersburg PA
CBHW032017220426
43664CB00006B/280